The Principal Navigations, Voyages, Traffiques and Discoveries of the English Nation — Volume 11

Richard Hakluyt

Alpha Editions

This edition published in 2024

ISBN 9789362517401

Design and Setting By
Alpha Editions
www.alphaedis.com
Email - info@alphaedis.com

As per information held with us this book is in Public Domain.
This book is a reproduction of an important historical work.
Alpha Editions uses the best technology to reproduce historical work
in the same manner it was first published to preserve its original nature.
Any marks or number seen are left intentionally to preserve.

Contents

OF THE ENGLISH NATION IN AFRICA.	- 1 -
LINUS.	- 205 -
APPENDIX	- 309 -
THE OMISSIONS OF CALES VOYAGE.	- 310 -
INDICES.	- 312 -

OF THE ENGLISH NATION IN AFRICA.

* * * * *

The voyage of Henrie Eatle of Derbie, after Duke of Hereford, and lastly Henry the fourth King of England, to Tunis in Barbarie, with an army of Englishmen mitten by Polidore Virgill. pag. 1389.

Franci interim per inducias nacti ocium, ac simul Genuensium precibus defatigati, bellum in Afros, qui omnem oram insulásque Italiae latiocinijs infestas reddebant, suscipiunt. Richardus quoque rex Angliæ rogatus auxilium, mittit Henricum comitem Derbiensem cum electa Anglicæ pubis manu ad id bellum faciendum. Igitur Franci Anglíque viribus et animis consociatis in Africam traijciunt, qui vbi littus attigere, eatenus à Barbaris descensione prohibiti sunt, quoad Anglorum sagittariorum virtute factum est, vt aditus pateret: in terram egressi recta Tunetam vrbem regiam petunt, ac obsident. Barbari timore affecti de pace ad eos legates mittunt, quam nostris dare placuit, vt soluta certa pecuniae summa ab omni deinceps Italiae, Galliaeque ora mamis abstinerent. Ita peractis rebus post paucos menses, quàm eo itum erat, domum repediatum est.

The same in English.

The French in the meane season hauing gotten some leasure by meanes of their truce, and being sollicited and vrged by the intreaties of the Genuois vndertooke to wage warre against the Moores, who robbed and spoyled all the coasts of Italy, and of the Ilandes adiacent. Likewise Richard the second, king of England, being sued vnto for ayde, sent Henry the Earle of Derbie with a choice armie of English souldiers vnto the same warfare. Wherefore the English and French, with forces and mindes vnited, sayled ouer into Africa, who when they approached vnto the shore were repelled by the Barbarians from landing, vntill such time as they had passage made them by the valour of the English archers. Thus hauing landed their forces, they foorthwith marched vnto the royall citie of Tunis, and besieged it. Whereat the Barbarians being dismayed, sent Ambassadours vnto our Christian Chieftaines to treat of peace, which our men graunted vnto them, vpon condition that they should pay a certaine summe of money, and that they should from thenceforth abstaine from piracies vpon all the coasts of Italy and France. And so hauing dispatched their businesse, within a fewe moneths after their departure they returned home.

This Historie is somewhat otherwise recorded by Froysard and Holenshed in manner following, pag 473.

In the thirteenth yeere of the reigne of King Richard the second, the Christians tooke in hand a iourney against the Saracens of Barbarie through sute of the Genouois, so that there went a great number of Lords, Knights, and Gentlemen of France and England, the Duke of Burbon being their Generall. Out of England there went Iohn de Beaufort bastarde sonne to the Duke of Lancaster (as Froysard hath noted) also Sir Iohn Russell, Sir Iohn Butler, Sir Iohn Harecourt and others. They set forwarde in the latter ende of the thirteenth yeere of the Kings reigne, and came to Genoa, where they remayned not verie long, but that the gallies and other vessels of the Genouois were ready to passe them ouer into Barbarie. And so about midsomer in the begining of the foureteenth yere of this kings reigne the whole army being embarked, sailed forth to the coast of Barbary, where neere to the city of Africa they landed: [Sidenote: The Chronicles of Genoa] at which instant the English archers (as the Chronicles of Genoa write) stood all the company in good stead with their long bowes, beating backe the enemies from the shore, which came downe to resist their landing. After they had got to land, they inuironed the city of Africa (called by the Moores Mahdia) with a strong siege: but at length, constrained with the intemperancy of the scalding ayre in that hot countrey, breeding in the army sundry diseases, they fell to a composition vpon certaine articles to be performed in the behalfe of the Saracens: and so 61 dayes after their arriuall there they tooke the seas againe, and returned home, as in the histories of France and Genoa is likewise expressed. Where, by Polidore Virgil it may seeme, that the lord Henry of Lancaster earle of Derbie should be generall of the English men, that (as before you heard) went into Barbary with the French men and Genouois.

* * * * *

The memorable victories in diuers parts of Italie of Iohn Hawkwood English man in the reigne of Richard the second, briefly recorded by M. Camden.

Ad alteram ripam fluuij Colne oppositus est Sibble Heningham, locus natalis, vt accepi, Ioannis Hawkwoodi (Itali Aucuthum corruptè vocant) quem illi tantopere ob virtutem militarem suspexerunt, vt Senatus Florentinus propter insignia merita equestri statua et tumuli honore in eximiæ fortitudinis, fideíque testimonium ornauit. Res eius gestas Itali pleno ore prædicant; Et Paulus Iouius in elogijs celebrat: sat mihi sit Iulij Feroldi tetrastichon adijcere.

> Hawkoode Angloram decus, et decus addite genti
>   Italicæ, Italico presidiúmque solo,
> Vt tumuli quondam Florentia, sic simulachri
>   Virtutem Ionius donat honore tuam.

William Thomas in his Historie of the common wealthes of Italy, maketh honorable mention of him twise, to wit, in the commonwealth of Florentia and Ferrara.

* * * * *

The Epitaph of the valiant Esquire M. Peter Read in the south Ile of Saint Peters Church in the citie of Norwich, which was knighted by Charles the fift at the winning of Tunis in the yeere of our Lord 1538.

Here vnder lieth the corpes of Peter Reade Esquire, who hath worthily serued, not onely his Prince and Countrey, but also the Emperour Charles the fift, both at his conquest of Barbarie, and at his siege at Tunis, and also in other places. Who had giuen him by the sayd Emperour for his valiant deedes the order of Barbary. Who dyed the 29 day of December, in the yeere of our Lord God 1566.

* * * * *

The voyage of Sir Thomas Chaloner to Alger with Charles the fift 1541, drawen out of his booke De Republica instauranda.

Thomas Chalonerus patria Londinensis, studio Cantabrigensis, educatione aulicus, religione pius, veréque Christianus fuit. Itaque cum iuuenilem ætatem, mentémque suam humanioribus studijs roborasset, Domino Henrico Kneuetto à potentissimo rege Henrico eius nominis octauo ad Carolum quintum imperatorem transmisso legato, vnà cum illo profectus est, tanquam familiaris amicus, vel eidem, à consilijs. Quo quidem tempore Carolo quinto nauali certamine à Genua et Corsica in Algyram in Africa contra Turcas classem soluente ac hostiliter proficiscente, ornatissimo illo Kneuetto legato regis, Thoma Chalonero, Henrico Knolleo, et Henrico Isamo, illustribus viris eundem in illa expeditione suapte sponte sequentibus, paritérque militantibus, mirifice vitam suam Chalonerus tutatus est. Nam triremi illa, in qua fuerat, vel scopulis allisa, vel grauissimis pro cellis conquassata, naufragus cum se diù natatu defendisset, deficientibus viribus, brachijs manibusque languidis ac quasi eneruatis, prehensa dentibus cum maxima difficultate rudenti, quæ ex altera triremi iam propinqua tum fuerat eiecta, non sine dentium aliquorum iactura sese tandem recuperauit, ac domum integer relapsus est.

The same in English.

Thomas Chaloner was by birth a Londiner, by studie a Cantabrigian, by education a Courtier, by religion a deuout and true Christian. Therefore after he had confirmed his youth and minde in the studies of good learning, when Sir Henry Kneuet was sent ambassadour from the mighty Prince Henry the 8. to the Emperour Charles the fift, he went with him as his familiar friend, or as one of his Councell. At which time the said Charles the 5. passing ouer from Genoa and Corsica to Alger in Africa in warlike sort, with a mighty army by sea, that honourable Kneuet the kings ambassadour, Thomas Chaloner, Henry Knolles, and Henry Isham, right worthy persons, of their owne accord accompanied him in that expedition, and serued him in that warre, wherin Thomas Chaloner escaped most wonderfully with his life. For the galley wherein he was, being either dashed against the rockes, or shaken with mighty stormes, and so cast away, after he had saued himselfe a long while by swimming, when his strength failed him, his armes and hands being faint and weary, with great difficulty laying hold with his teeth on a cable, which was cast out of the next gally, not without breaking and losse of certaine of his teeth, at length recouered himselfe, and returned home into his countrey in safety.

* * * * *

The woorthy enterprise of Iohn Foxe an Englishman in deliuering 266. Christians out of the captiuitie of the Turkes at Alexandria, the 3 of Ianuarie 1577.

Among our Merchants here in England, it is a common voiage to traffike into Spaine: whereunto a ship, being called The three halfe Moones, manned with 38. men, and well fensed with munitions, the better to encounter their enemies withall, and hauing wind and tide, set from Portsmouth, 1563. and bended her iourney toward Siuill a citie in Spaine, intending there to traffique with them. [Sidenote: Iohn Foxe taken 1563.] And felling neere the Streights, they perceiued themselues to be beset round with eight gallies of the Turkes, in such wise, that there was no way for them to flie or escape away, but that either they must yeeld or els be sunke. Which the owner perceiuing, manfully encouraged his company, exhorting them valiantly to shew their manhood, shewing them that God was their God, and not their enemies, requesting them also not to faint in seeing such a heape of their enemies ready to deuour them; putting them in mind also, that if it were Gods pleasure to giue them into their enemies hands, it was not they that ought to shew one displeasant looke or countenance there against; but to take it patiently, and not to prescribe a day and time for their deliuerance, as the citizens of Bethulia did, but to put themselues vnder his mercy. And againe, if it were his mind and good will to shew his mighty power by them, if their enemies were ten times so many, they were not able to stand in their hands; putting them likewise in mind of the old and ancient woorthinesse of their countreymen, who in the hardest extremities haue always most preuailed and gone away conquerors, yea, and where it hath bene almost impossible. Such (quoth he) hath bene the valiantnesse of our countreymen, and such hath bene the mightie power of our God.

With other like incouragements, exhorting them to behaue themselues manfully, they fell all on their knees making their prayers briefly vnto God: who being all risen vp againe perceiued their enemies by their signes and defiances bent to the spoyle, whose mercy was nothing els but crueltie, whereupon euery man tooke him to his weapon.

Then stood vp one Groue the master, being a comely man, with his sword and target, holding them vp in defiance agaynst his enemies. So likewise stood vp the Owner, the Masters mate, Boateswaine, Purser, and euery man well appointed. Nowe likewise sounded vp the drums, trumpets and flutes, which would haue encouraged any man, had he neuer so litle heart or courage in him.

Then taketh him to his charge Iohn Foxe the gunner in the disposing of his pieces in order to the best effect, and sending his bullets towards the Turkes, who likewise bestowed their pieces thrise as fast toward the Christians. But shortly they drew neere, so that the bowmen fel to their charge in sending forth their arrowes so thicke amongst the Gallies, and also in doubling their shot so sore vpon the gallies, that there was twise so many of the Turkes slaine, as the number of the Christians were in all. But the Turks discharged twise as fast against the Christians, and so long, that the ship was very sore stricken and bruised vnder water. Which the Turkes perceiuing, made the more haste to come aboord the Shippe: which ere they could doe, many a Turke bought it deerely with the losse of their liues. Yet was all in vaine, and boorded they were, where they found so hote a skirmish, that it had bene better they had not medled with the feast. For the Englishmen shewed themselues men in deed, in working manfully with their browne bils and halbardes: where the owner, master, boateswaine, and their company stoode to it so lustily, that the Turkes were halfe dismaied. [Sidenote: The valour and death of their Boatswaine.] But chiefly the boateswaine shewed himself valiant aboue the rest: for he fared amongst the Turkes like a wood Lion: for there was none of them that either could or durst stand in his face, till at the last there came a shot from the Turkes, which brake his whistle asunder, and smote him on the brest, so that he fell downe, bidding them farewell, and to be of good comfort, encouraging them likewise to winne praise by death, rather then to liue captiues in misery and shame. Which they hearing, in deed intended to haue done, as it appeared by their skirmish: but the prease and store of the Turkes was so great, that they were not able long to endure, but were so ouerpressed, that they could not wield their weapons: by reason whereof, they must needs be taken, which none of them intended to haue bene, but rather to haue died: except onely the masters mate, who shrunke from the skirmish, like a notable coward, esteeming neither the valure of his name, nor accounting of the present example of his fellowes, nor hauing respect to the miseries, whereunto he should be put. But in fine, so it was, that the Turks were victors, whereof they had no great cause to reioyce, or triumph. Then would it haue grieued any hard heart to see these Infidels so violently intreating the Christians, not hauing any respect of their manhood which they had tasted of, nor yet respecting their owne state, how they might haue met with such a bootie, as might haue giuen them the ouerthrow; but no remorse hereof, or any thing els doth bridle their fierce and tirannous dealing, but that the Christians must needs to the gallies, to serue in new offices: and they were no sooner in them, but their garments were pulled ouer their eares, and torne from their backes, and they set to the oares.

I will make no mention of their miseries, being now vnder their enemies raging stripes. I thinke there is no man wil iudge their fare good, or their bodies vnloden of stripes, and not pestered with too much heate, and also with too much cold: but I will goe to my purpose, which is, to shew the ende of those, being in meere miserie, which continually doe call on God with a steadfast hope that he will deliuer them, and with a sure faith that he can doe it.

Nigh to the citie of Alexandria, being a hauen towne, and vnder the dominion of the Turkes, there is a roade, being made very fensible with strong wals, whereinto the Turkes doe customably bring their gallies on shoare euery yeere, in the winter season, and there doe trimme them, and lay them vp against the spring time. In which road there is a prison, wherein the captiues and such prisoners as serue in the gallies, are put for all that time, vntill the seas be calme and passable for the gallies, euery prisoner being most grieuously laden with irons on their legges, to their great paine, and sore disabling of them to any labour taking. [Sidenote: The Englishmen carried prisoners vnto an Hauen nere Alexandria.] Into which prison were these Christians put, and fast warded all the Winter season. But ere it was long, the Master and the Owner, by meanes of friends, were redeemed: the rest abiding still by the miserie, while that they were all (through reason of their ill vsage and worse fare, miserably starued) sauing one Iohn Fox, who (as some men can abide harder and more miserie, then other some can, so can some likewise make more shift, and worke more deuises to helpe their state and liuing, then other some can doe) being somewhat skilfull in the craft of a Barbour, by reason thereof made great shift in helping his fare now and then with a good meale. Insomuch, til at the last, God sent him fauour in the sight of the keeper of the prison, so that he had leaue to goe in and out to the road, at his pleasure, paying a certaine stipend vnto the keeper, and wearing a locke about his leg: which libertie likewise, sixe more had vpon like sufferance: who by reason of their long imprisonment, not being feared or suspected to start aside, or that they would worke the Turkes any mischiefe, had libertie to go in and out at the sayd road, in such maner, as this Iohn Fox did, with irons on their legs, and to returne againe at night.

In the yeere of our Lord 1577. in the Winter season, the gallies happily comming to their accustomed harborow, and being discharged of all their mastes, sailes, and other such furnitures, as vnto gallies doe appertaine, and all the Masters and mariners of them being then nested in their owne homes: there remained in the prison of the said road two hundred threescore and eight Christian prisoners, who had bene taken by the Turks force, and were of sixteen sundry nations. Among which there were three Englishmen, whereof one was named Iohn Foxe of Woodbridge in Suffolke, the other William Wickney of Portsmouth, in the Countie of Southampton, and the third Robert Moore of Harwich in the Countie of Essex. Which Iohn Fox hauing bene thirteene or fourteene yeres vnder their gentle entreatance, and being too too weary thereof, minding his escape, weighed with himselfe by what meanes it might be brought to passe: and continually pondering with himself thereof, tooke a good heart vnto him, in hope that God would not be alwayes scourging his children, and neuer ceassed to pray him to further his pretended enterprise, if that it should redound to his glory.

Not farre from the road, and somewhat from thence, at one side of the Citie, there was a certaine victualling house, which one Peter Vnticaro had hired, paying also a certaine fee vnto the keeper of the road. This Peter Vnticaro was a Spaniard borne, and a Christian, and had bene prisoner about thirtie yeeres, and neuer practised any meanes to escape, but kept himselfe quiet without touch or suspect of any conspiracie: vntill that nowe this John Foxe vsing much thither, they brake one to another their mindes, concerning the restraint of their libertie and imprisonment. So that this Iohn Fox at length opening vnto this Vnticaro the deuise which he would faine put in practise, made priuie one more to this their intent. Which three debated of this matter at such times as they could compasse to meete together: insomuch, that at seuen weekes ende they had sufficiently concluded how the matter should be, if it pleased God to farther them thereto: who making fiue more priuie to this their deuise, whom they thought they might safely trust, determined in three nights after to accomplish their deliberate purpose. Whereupon the same Iohn Fox, and Peter Vnticaro, and the other sixe appointed to meete all together in the prison the next day, being the last day of December: where this Iohn Fox certified the rest of the prisoners, what their intent and deuise was, and how and when they minded to bring their purpose to passe: who thereunto perswaded them without much a doe to further their deuise. Which the same Iohn Fox seeing, deliuered vnto them a sort of files, which he had gathered together for this purpose, by the meanes of Peter Vnticaro, charging them that euery man should be readie discharged of his yrons by eight of the clocke on the the next day at night.

[Sidenote: Januarie.] On the next day at night, this said Iohn Fox, and his sixe other companions, being all come to the house of Peter Vnticaro, passing the time away in mirth for feare of suspect, till the night came on, so that it was time for them to put in practise their deuise, sent Peter Vnticaro to the master of the roade, in the name of one of the Masters of the citie, with whom this keeper was acquainted, and at whose request he also would come at the first: who desired him to take the paines to meete him there, promising him, that he would bring him backe againe. The keeper agreed to goe with him, willing the warders not to barre the gate, saying, that he would not stay long, but would come againe with all speede.

In the meane season, the other seuen had prouided them of such weapons, as they could get in that house: and Iohn Fox tooke him to an olde rustie sword blade, without either hilt or pomell, which he made to serue his turne, in bending the hand ende of the sword, in steed of a pomell, and the other had got such spits and glaiues as they found in the house.

The keeper now being come vnto the house, and perceiuing no light, nor hearing any noyse, straight way suspected the matter: and returning backward, Iohn Fox standing behind the corner of the house, stepped foorth vnto him: who perceiuing it to be Iohn Fox, saide, O Fox, what haue I deserued of thee, that thou shouldest seeke my death? Thou villaine (quoth Fox) hast bene a bloodsucker of many a Christians blood, and now thou shalt know what thou hast deserued at my handes: wherewith he lift vp his bright shining sword of tenne yeeres rust, and stroke him so maine a blowe, as therewithall his head claue a sunder, so that he fell starke dead to the ground. Whereupon Peter Vnticaro went in, and certified the rest how the case stood with the keeper: who came presently foorth, and some with their spits ranne him through, and the other with their glaiues hewed him in sunder, cut off his head, and mangled him so, that no man should discerne what he was.

Then marched they toward the roade, whereinto they entered softly, where were six warders, whom one of them asked, saying, who was there? quoth Fox and his company, all friendes. Which when they were all within, proued contrary: for, quoth Fox, my masters, here is not to euery man a man, wherefore looke you play your parts. Who so behaued themselues in deede, that they had dispatched these six quickly. Then Iohn Fox intending not to be barred of his enterprise, and minding to worke surely in that which he went about, barred the gate surely, and planted a Canon against it.

Then entred they into the Gailers lodge, where they found the keyes of the fortresse and prison by his bed side, and there had they all better weapons.

In this chamber was a chest, wherein was a rich treasure, and all in duckats, which this Peter Vnticaro, and two more, opening, staffed themselues so full as they could, betweene their shirts and their skinne: which Iohn Fox would not once touch, and sayde, that it was his and their libertie which he sought for, to the honour of his God, and not to make a marte of the wicked treasure of the Infidels. Yet did these words sinke nothing into their stomakes, they did it for a good intent: so did Saul saue the fattest Oxen, to offer vnto the Lord, and they to serue their owne turnes. But neither did Saul scape the wrath of God therefore, neither had these that thing which they desired so, and did thirst after. Such is Gods iustice. He that they put their trust in, to deliuer them from the tyrannous hands of their enemies, he (I say) could supply their want of necessaries.

Nowe these eight being armed with such weapons as they thought well of, thinking themselues sufficient champions to encounter a stronger enemie, and coming vnto the prison, Fox opened the gates and doores thereof, and called forth all the prisoners, whom he set, some to ramming vp the gate, some to the dressing vp of a certaine gallie, which was the best in all the roade, and was called the captaine of Alexandria, whereinto some caried mastes, sailes, oares, and other such furniture as doth belong vnto a gallie.

At the prison were certaine warders, whom Iohn Fox and his companie slewe: in the killing of whom, there were eight more of the Turkes, which percciued them, and got them to the toppe of the prison: vnto whom Iohn Fox, and his company, were faine to come by ladders, where they found a hot skirmish. For some of them were there slaine, some wounded, and some but scarred, and not hurt. As Iohn Fox was thrise shot through his apparell, and not hurt. Peter Vnticaro, and the other two, that had armed them with the duckats, were slaine, as not able to weild themselues, being so pestered with the weight and vneasie carying of the wicked and prophane treasure: and also diuerse Christians were aswell hurt about that skirmish, as Turkes slaine.

Amongst the Turkes was one thrust thorowe, who (let vs not say that it was ill fortune) fell off from the toppe of the prison wall, and made such a lowing, that the inhabitants thereabout (as here and there scattering stoode a house or two) came and dawed [Footnote: To awaken: here to bring back to his senses. I know of no other instance where it bears just this meaning. "The other side from whence the morning daws." (*Polyolbion* X.)] him, so that they vnderstood the case, how that the prisoners were paying their ransomes: wherewith they raised both Alexandria which lay on the west side of the roade, and a Castle which was at the Cities end, next to the roade, and also an other Fortresse which lay on the Northside of the roade: so that nowe they had no way to escape, but one, which by mans reason (the two holdes lying so vpon the mouth of the roade) might seeme impossible to be a way for them. So was the red sea impossible for the Israelites to passe through, the hils and rockes lay so on the one side, and their enemies compassed on the other. So was it impossible, that the wals of Iericho should fall downe, being neither vndermined, nor yet rammed at with engines, nor yet any mans wisedome, pollicie, or helpe set or put thereunto. Such impossibilities can our God make possible. He that helde the Lyons iawes from renting Daniel asunder, yea, or yet from once touching him to his hurt: can not he hold the roring cannons of this hellish force? He that kept the fiers rage in the hot burning Ouen, from the three children, that praised his name, can not he keepe the fiers flaming blastes from among his elect?

Now is the road fraught with lustie souldiers, laborers, and mariners, who are faine to stand to their tackling, in setting to euery man his hand, some to the carying in of victuals, some munitions, some oares, and some one thing, some another, but most are keeping their enemie from the wall of the road. But to be short, there was no time mispent, no man idle, nor any mans labour ill bestowed, or in vaine. So that in short time, this gally was ready trimmed vp. Whereinto euery man leaped in all haste, hoyssing vp the sayles lustily, yeelding themselues to his mercie and grace, in whose hands are both winde and weather.

Now is this gally on flote, and out of the safetie of the roade: now haue the two Castles full power vpon the gally, now is there no remedy but to sinke: how can it be auoided? The canons let flie from both sides, and the gally is euen in the middest, and betweene them both. What man can deuise to saue it? there is no man, but would thinke it must needes be sunke.

There was not one of them that feared the shotte, which went thundring round about their eares, nor yet were once scarred or touched, with fiue and forty shot, which came from the Castles. Here did God hold foorth his buckler, he shieldeth now this gally, and hath tried their faith to the vttermost. Now commeth his speciall helpe: yea, euen when man thinks them past all helpe then commeth he himselfe downe from heauen with his mightie power, then is his present remedie most readie prest. For they saile away, being not once touched with the glaunce of a shot, and are quickly out of the Turkish canons reach. Then might they see them comming downe by heapes to the water side, in companies like vnto swarmes of bees, making shew to come after them with gallies, in bustling themselues to dresse vp the gallies, which would be a swift peece of worke for them to doe, for that they had neither oares, mastes, sailes, gables, nor any thing else ready in any gally. But yet they are carrying them into them, some into one gally, and some into another, so that, being such a confusion amongst them, without any certaine guide, it were a thing impossible to ouertake them: beside that, there was no man that would take charge of a gally, the weather was so rough, and there was such an amasednes amongst them. And verely I thinke their God was amased thereat: it could not be but he must blush for shame, he can speake neuer a word for dulnes, much lease can he helpe them in such an extremitie. Well, howsoeuer it is, he is very much to blame, to suffer them to receiue such a gibe. But howsoeuer their God behaued himselfe, our God shewed himselfe a God indeede, and that he was the onely liuing God: for the seas were swift vnder his faithfull, which made the enemies agast to behold them, a skilfuller Pilot leades them, and their mariners bestirre them lustily: but the Turkes had neither mariners, Pilot, nor any skilfull Master, that was in a readinesse at this pinch.

When the Christians were safe out of the enemies coast, Iohn Fox called to them all, willing them to be thankfull vnto almighty God for their deliuerie, and most humbly to fall downe vpon their knees, beseeching him to aide them vnto their friends land, and not to bring them into an other daunger, sith hee had most mightily deliuered them from so great a thraldome and bondage.

Thus when euery man had made his petition, they fell straight way to their labour with the oares, in helping one another, when they were wearied, and with great labour striuing to come to some Christian land, as neere as they could gesse by the starres. But the windes were so diuers, one while driuing them this way, that they were now in a newe maze, thinking that God had forsaken them, and left them to a greater danger. And forasmuch as there were no victuals now left in the gally, it might haue beene a cause to them (if they had beene the Israelites) to haue murmured against their God: but they knew how that their God, who had deliuered them out of Ægypt, was such a louing and mercifull God, as that hee would not suffer them to be confounded, in whom he had wrought so great a wonder: but what calamitie soeuer they sustained, they knew it was but for their further triall, and also (in putting them in mind of their farther miserie) to cause them not to triumph and glory in themselues therefore. [Sidenote: Extremity of famine.] Hauing (I say) no victuals in the galley, it might seeme that one miserie continually fel vpon an others neck: but to be briefe, the famine grew to be so great, that in 28 dayes, wherein they were on the sea, there died eight persons, to the astonishment of all the rest.

So it fell out, that vpon the 29 day, after they set from Alexandria, they fell on the Isle of Candie, and landed at Gallipoli, where they were made much of by the Abbot and Monks there, who caused them to stay there, while they were well refreshed and eased. [Sidenote: John Fox his sword kept as a monument in Gallipoli.] They kept there the sworde, wherewith Iohn Fox had killed the keeper, esteeming it as a most precious iewell, and hung it vp for a monument.

When they thought good, hauing leaue to depart from thence, they sayled along the coast, till they arriued at Tarento, where they solde their gallie, and deuided it, euery man hauing a part thereof. The Turkes receiuing so shamefull a foile at their hand, pursued the Christians, and scoured the seas, where they could imagine that they had bent their course. And the Christians had departed from thence on the one day in the morning, and seuen gallies of the Turkes came thither that night, as it was certified by those who followed Fox, and his companie, fearing least they should haue bene met with. And then they came a foote to Naples, where they departed a sunder, euery man taking him to his next way home. From whence Iohn Fox tooke his iourney vnto Rome, where he was well entertayned of an Englishman, who presented his worthy deede vnto the Pope, who rewarded him liberally, and gaue him his letters vnto the king of Spaine, where he was very well entertained of him there, who for this his most worthy enterprise gaue him in fee twenty pence a day. From whence, being desirous to come into his owne countrie, he came thither at such time as he conueniently could, which was in the yeere of our Lorde God, 1579. Who being come into England, went vnto the Court, and shewed all his trauell vnto the Councell: who considering of the state of this man, in that hee had spent and lost a great part of his youth in thraldome and bondage, extended to him their liberalitie, to helpe to maintaine him now in age, to their right honour, and to the incouragement of all true hearted Christians.

* * * * *

The copie of the certificate for Iohn Fox, and his companie, made by the Prior, and the brethren of Gallipoli, where they first landed.

We the Prior, and Fathers of the Couent of the Amerciates, of the city of Gallipoli, of the order of Preachers doe testifie, that vpon the 29 of Ianuary last past, 1577, there came into the said citie a certaine gally from Alexandria, taken from the Turkes, with two hundreth fiftie and eight Christians, whereof was principal Master Iohn Fox, an Englishman, a gunner, and one of the chiefest that did accomplish that great worke, whereby so many Christians haue recouered their liberties. In token and remembrance whereof, vpon our earnest request to the same Iohn Fox, he hath left here an olde sworde, wherewith he slewe the keeper of the prison: which sword we doe as a monument and memoriall of so worthy a deede, hang vp in the chiefe place of our Couent house. And for because all things aforesaid, are such as we will testifie to be true, as they are orderly passed, and haue therefore good credite, that so much as is aboue expressed is true, and for the more faith thereof, we the Prior, and Fathers aforesaide, haue ratified and subscribed these presents. Geuen in Gallipoly, the third of Februarie 1577.

> I Frier Vincent Barba, Prior of the same place, confirme the premisses, as they are aboue written.
> I Frier Albert Damaro, of Gallipoly, Subprior, confirme as much.
> I Frier Anthony Celleler of Gallipoly, confirme as aforesaid.
> I Frier Bartlemew of Gallipoly, confirme as aboue said.
> I Frier Francis of Gallipoly, confirme as much.

* * * * *

The Bishop of Rome his letters in the behalfe of Iohn Fox.

Be it knowen vnto all men, to whom this writing shall come, that the bringer hereof Iohn Fox Englishman, a Gunner, after he had serued captiue in the Turkes gallies, by the space of foureteene yeeres, at length, thorough God his helpe, taking good opportunitie, the third of Ianuarie last past, slew the keeper of the prison, (whom he first stroke on the face) together with four and twentie other Turkes, by the assistance of his fellow prisoners: and with 266. Christians (of whose libertie he was the author) launched from Alexandria, and from thence arriued first at Gallipoly in Candie, and afterwardes at Tarento in Apulia: the written testimony and credite of which things, as also of others, the same Iohn Fox hath in publike tables from Naples.

Vpon Easter eue he came to Rome, and is now determined to take his iourney to the Spanish Court, hoping there to obtaine some reliefe toward his liuing: wherefore the poore distressed man humbly beseecheth, and we in his behalfe do in the bowels of Christ, desire you, that taking compassion of his former captiuitie, and present penurie, you doe not onely suffer him freely to passe throughout all your cities and townes, but also succour him with your charitable almes, the reward whereof you shall hereafter most assuredly receiue, which we hope you will afford to him, whom with tender affection of pitie wee commende vnto you. At Rome, the 20 of Aprill 1577.

> Thomas Grolos Englishman Bishop of Astraphen.
> Richard Silleum Prior Angliæ.
> Andreas Ludouicus Register to our Soueraigne Lord the Pope, which for the greater credit of the premises, haue set my seale to these
> presents. At Rome, the day and yeere aboue written.
> Mauricius Clement the gouernour and keeper of the English Hospitall in the citie.

* * * * *

The King of Spaine his letters to the Lieutenant, for the placing of Iohn Fox in the office of a Gunner.

To the illustrious Prince, Vespasian Gonsaga Colonna, our Lieutenant and Captaine Generall of our Realme of Valentia. Hauing consideration, that Iohn Fox Englishman hath serued vs, and was one of the most principall, which tooke away from the Turkes a certaine gallie, which they haue brought to Tarento, wherein were two hundred, fiftie, and eight Christian captiues: we licence him to practise, and giue him the office of a Gunner, and haue ordained, that he goe to our said Realme, there to serue in the said office in the Gallies, which by our commandement are lately made. And we doe commaund, that you cause to be payed to him eight ducats pay a moneth, for the time that he shall serue in the saide Gallies as a Gunner, or till we can otherwise prouide for him, the saide eight duckats monethly of the money which is already of our prouision, present and to come, and to haue regarde of those which come with him. From Escuriall the tenth of August, 1577.

 I the King,
  Iuan del Gado.

And vnder that a confirmation of the Councell.

* * * * *

The voyage made to Tripolis in Barbarie, in the yeere 1583. with a ship called the Iesus, wherein the aduentures and distresses of some Englishmen are truely reported, and other necessary circumstances obserued. Written by Thomas Sanders.

This voyage was set foorth by the right worshipfull sir Edward Osborne knight, chiefe merchant of all the Turkish company, and one master Richard Staper, the ship being of the burden of one hundred tunnes, called the Iesus, she was builded at Farmne a riuer by Portsmouth. The owners were master Thomas Thomson, Nicholas Carnaby, and Iohn Gilman. The master was one Aches Hellier of Black-wall, and his Mate was one Richard Morris of that place: their Pilot was one Anthonie Ierado a Frenchman, of the prouince of Marseils: the purser was one William Thomson our owners sonne: the merchants factors were Romane Sonnings a Frenchman, and Richard Skegs seruant vnto the said master Staper. The owners were bound vnto the marchants by charter partie therevpon, in one thousand markes, that the said ship by Gods permission should goe for Tripolis in Barbarie, that is to say, first from Portsmouth to Newhauen in Normandie, from thence to S. Lucar, otherwise called Saint Lucas, in Andeluzia, and from thence to Tripolie, which is in the East part of Africa, and so to returne vnto London. [Sidenote: Man doth purpose, and God doth dispose.] But here ought euery man to note and consider the workes of our God, that many times what man doth determine God doth disappoint. The said master hauing some occasion to goe to Farmne, tooke with him the Pilot and the Purser, and returning againe by meanes of a perrie of winde, the boat wherein they were, was drowned, with the said master, the purser, and all the company: onely the said Pilot by experience in swimming saued himselfe: these were the beginnings of our sorrowes. [Sidenote: A new master chosen.] After which the said masters mate would not proceed in that voiage, and the owner hearing of this misfortune, and the unwillingnesse of the masters mate, did send downe one Richard Deimond, and shipped him for master, who did chuse for his Mate one Andrew Dier, and so the said ship departed on her voiage accordingly: that is to say, about the 16. of October, in An. 1583. she made saile from Portsmouth, [Sidenote: The new master died.] and the 18 day then next following she arriued at Newhauen, where our saide last master Deimond by a surfeit died. The factors then appointed the said Andrew Dier, being then masters mate, to be their master for that voiage, who did chuse to be his Mates the two quarter masters of the same ship, to wit, Peter Austine, and Shillabey, and for Purser was shipped one Richard Burges. Afterward about the 8. day of Nouember we made saile forthward, and by force of weather we were driuen backe againe into Portesmouth, where we renued our victuals and other necessaries, and then the winde came faire. About the 29. day then next following we departed thence, and the first day of December by meanes of a contrarie winde, we were driuen to Plimmouth. The 18. day then next following, we made foorthward againe, and by force of weather we were driuen to Falmouth, where we remained vntill the first day of Ianuary: at which time the winde comming faire, we departed thence, and about the 20. day of the said moneth we arriued safely at S. Lucar. [Sidenote: The Iesus arriued in Tripolis.] And about the 9. day of March next following, we made saile from thence, and about the 18. day of the same moneth we came to Tripolis in Barbarie, where we were verie well intertained by the king of that countrey, and also of the commons. The commodities of that place are sweete oiles: the king there is a merchant, and the rather (willing to preferre himselfe before his commons) requested our said factors to traffique with him, and promised them that if they would take his oiles at his owne price, they should pay no maner of custome, and they tooke of him certaine tunnes of oile: and afterwarde perceiuing that they might haue farre better cheape notwithstanding the custome free, they desired the king to licence them to take the oiles at the pleasure of his commons, for that his price did exceede theirs: whereunto the king would not agree, but was rather contended to abate his price, insomuch that the factors bought all their oyles of the king custome free, and so laded the same aboord.

[Sidenote: Another ship of Bristow came to Tripolis.] In the meane time there came to that place one Miles Dickenson in a ship of Bristow, who together with our said Factors tooke a house to themselues there. Our

French Factor Romane Sonnings desired to buy a commodity in the market, and wanting money, desired the saide Miles Dickenson to lend him an hundred Chikinoes vntill he came to his lodging, which he did, and afterward the same Sonnings mette with Miles Dickenson in the streete, and deliuered him money bound vp in a napkin: saying, master Dickenson there is the money I borrowed of you, and so thanked him for the same: hee doubted nothing lesse then falshoode, which is seldome knowne among marchants, and specially being together in one house, and is the more detestable betweene Christians, they being in Turkie among the heathen. The said Dickenson did not tell the money presently, vntill he came to his lodging, and then finding nine Chikinoes lacking of his hundred, which was about three pounds, for that euery Chikino is woorth seuen shillings of English money, he came to the sayde Romane Sonnings and deliuered him his handkerchiefe, and asked him howe many Chikinoes hee had deliuered him! Sonnings answered, an hundred: Dickenson, said no: and so they protested and swore on both parts. But in the ende the said Romane Sonnings did sweare deepely with detestable othes and curses, and prayed God that he might shewe his workes on him, that other might take ensample thereby, and that he might be hanged like a dogge, and neuer come into England againe, if he did not deliuer vnto the sayde Dickenson an hundred Chikinoes. And here beholde a notable example of all blasphemers, curses and swearers, how God rewarded him accordingly: for many times it cometh to passe, that God sheweth his miracles vpon such monstrous blasphemers, to the ensample of others, as nowe hereafter you shall heare what befell to this Romane Sonnings.

There was a man in the said towne a pledge, whose name was Patrone Norado, who the yere before had done this Sonnings some pleasure there. The foresaid Patrone Norado was indebted vnto a Turke of that towne in the summe of foure hundred and fiftie crownes, for certain goods sent by him into Christendome in a ship of his owne, and by his owne brother, and himselfe remained in Tripolis as pledge vntill his said brothers returne: and, as the report went there, after his brothers arriual into Christendome, he came among lewde companie, and lost his brothers said ship and goods at dice, and neuer returned vnto him againe.

[Sidenote: A conspiracie practiced by the French Factor, to deceiue a Turkish marchant of 450 crowns.] The said Patrone Norado being voyde of all hope, and finding now opportunitie, consulted with the said Sonnings for to swimme a seaboorde the Islands, and the ship being then out of danger, should take him in (as after was confessed) and so to goe to Tolan in the prouince of Marseilis with this Patrone Norado, and there to take in his lading.

The shippe being readie the first day of May, and hauing her sayles all aboorde, our sayde Factors did take their leaue of the king, who very courteously bidde them farwell, and when they came aboorde, they commanded the Master and the companie hastily to get out the ship: the Master answered that it was vnpossible, for that the winde was contrary and ouer-blowed. And he required vs vpon forfeiture of our bandes, that we should doe our endeuour to get her foorth. Then went wee to warpe out the shippe, and presently the king sent a boate aboord of vs, with three men in her, commaunding the saide Sonnings to come a shoare: at whose coming, the king demaunded of him custome for the oyles: Sonnings answered him that his highnesse had promised to deliuer them custome free. But notwithstanding the king weighed not his said promise, and as an infidell that hath not the feare of God before his eyes, nor regarde of his worde, albeit he was a king, hee caused the sayde Sonnings to pay the custome to the vttermost penie. And afterwarde willed him to make haste away, saying, that the Ianizaries would haue the oyle ashoare againe.

These Ianizaries are souldiers there vnder the great Turke, and their power is aboue the Kings. And so the saide Factor departed from the king, and came to the waterside, and called for a boate to come aboorde, and he brought with him the foresaid Patrone Norado. [Sidenote: The beginning of their troubles, and occasion of all their miserie.] The companie inquisitiue to know what man that was, Sonnings answered, that he was his countrymen, a passenger: I pray God said the companie, that we come not into trouble by this man. Then said Sonnings angerly, what haue you to do with any matters of mine? if any thing chance otherwise then well, I must answer for all.

Now the Turke vnto whom this Patrone Norado was indebted, missing him (supposed him to be aboorde of our shippe) presently went vnto the King, and tolde him that hee thought that his pledge Patrone Norado was aboord of the English ship, whereupon the King presently sent a boat aboord of vs, with three men in her commanding the said Sonnings to come a shoare, and not speaking any thing as touching the man, he saide that he would come presently in his owne boate, but as soone as they were gone, he willed vs to warp foorth the ship, and saide that he would see the knaues hanged before he would goe a shoare. And when the king sawe that he came not a shoare, but still continued warping away the shippe, he straight commaunded the gunner of the bulwarke next vnto vs, to shoote three shootes without ball. Then we came all to the said Sonnings, and asked of him what the matter was that we were shot at, he said that it was the Ianizaries who would haue the oyle a shoare againe, and willed vs to make haste away, and after that he had discharged three shots without ball, he commaunded all the gunners in the towne to doe their indeuour to sinke vs, but the Turkish gunners could not once strike vs, wherefore the king sent presently to the Banio: (this Banio is the prison whereas all the captiues lay at night) and promised if that there were any that could either sinke vs, or else cause vs to come in againe, he should haue a hundred crownes, and his libertie. With that came foorth a Spaniard called Sebastian, which had bene an olde seruitor in Flanders, and he said, that vpon the performance of that promise, hee would vndertake either to sinke vs, or to cause vs to come in againe, and therto he would gage his life, and at the first shotte he split our rudders head in pieces, and the second shotte he shotte vs vnder the water, and the third shotte he shotte vs through our foremast with a Coluering shot, and thus he hauing rent both our rudder and maste, and shot vs vnder water, we were inforced to goe in againe.

This Sebastian for all his diligence herein, had neither his liberty, nor an hundred crownes, so promised by the said king, but after his seruice done was committed againe to prison, whereby may appeare the regard that the Turke or infidell hath of his worde, although he be able to performe it, yea more, though he be a king.

Then, our merchants seeing no remedie, they together with fiue of our companie went a shoare, and then they ceased shooting: they shot vnto vs in the whole, nine and thirtie shootes, without the hurt of any man.

And when our marchants came a shoare, the King commaunded presently that they with the rest of our companie that were with them, should be cheined foure and foure, to a hundred waight of yron, and when we came in with the ship, there came presently aboue an hundred Turks aboord of vs, and they searched vs, and stript our very clothes from our backes, and brake open our chests, and made a spoyle of all that we had: and the Christian caitifes likewise, that came a boord of vs made spoyle of our goods, and vsed vs as ill as the Turkes did. And our masters mate hauing a Geneua Bible in his hand, there came the kings chiefe gunner, and tooke it out from him, who shewed me of it, and I hauing the language, went presently to the kings treasurer, and tolde him of it, saying, that sith it was the will of God that we should fall into their handes, yet that they should grant us to vse our consciences to our owne discretion, as they suffered the Spaniards and other nations to vse theirs, and he graunted vs: then I told him that the maister gunner had taken away a Bible from one of our men: the Treasurer went presently and commaunded him to deliuer vp the Bible againe, which he did: and within a litle after he tooke it from the man againe, and I shewed the Treasurer of it, and presently he commaunded him to deliuer it againe: saying, thou villaine, wilt thou turne to Christianitie againe? for he was a Renegado, which is one that first was a Christian, and afterwards becommeth a Turke, and so he deliuered me the Bible the second time. And then I hauing it in my hand, the gunner came to me, and spake these wordes, saying, thou dogge, I wil haue the booke in despight of thee, and tooke it from me, saying: If thou tell the kings treasurer of it any more, by Mahomet I will be reuenged of thee. Notwithstanding I went the third time vnto the kings Treasurer, and tolde him of it, and he came with me, saying thus vnto the gunner: by the head of the great Turke, if thou take it from him againe, thou shalt haue an hundred bastonadoes. And foorthwith he deliuered me the booke, saying, he had not the value of a pin of the spoyle of the ship, which was the better for him, as hereafter you shall heare: for there was none, neither Christian nor Turke that tooke the value of a peniworth of our goods from vs, but perished both bodie and goods within seuenteene moneths following, as hereafter shall plainely appeare.

Then came the Guardian Basha, which is the keeper of the kings captiues, to fetch vs all a shoare, and then I remembring the miserable estate of poore distressed captiues, in the time of their bondage to those infidels, went to mine owne chest, and tooke out thereof a iarre of oyle, and filled a basket full of white Ruske to carie a shoare with me, but before I came to the Banio, the Turkish boyes had taken away almost all my bread, and the keeper saide, deliuer me the iarre of oyle, and when thou commest to the Banio thou shalt haue it againe, but I neuer had it of him any more.

But when I came to the Banio, and sawe our Marchants and all the rest of our company in chaines, and we all ready to receiue the same reward, what heart in the world is there so hard, but would haue pitied our cause, hearing or seeing the lamentable greeting there was betwixt vs: all this happened the first of May 1584.

[Sidenote: The Englishmen arraigned.] And the second day of the same moneth, the King with all his counsell sate in Judgment vpon vs. The first that were had forth to be arraigned, were the Factors, and the Masters, and the King asked them wherefore they came not a shoare when he sent for them. And Romaine Sonnings answered, that though he were king on shoare, and might commaunde there, so was hee as touching those that were vnder him: and therefore said, if any offence be, the fault is wholly in my selfe, and in no other. Then foorthwith the king gaue iudgement, that the saide Romaine Sonnings should be hanged ouer the Northeast bulwarke: from whence he conueyed the forenamed Patrone Norado, and then he called for our Master Andrew Dier, and vsed fewe wordes to him, and so condemned him to be hanged ouer the walles of the Westermost bulwarke.

Then fell our other Factor (named Richard Skegs) vpon his knees before the king, and said, I beseech your highnesse either to pardon our Master, or else suffer me to die for him, for he is ignorant of this cause. And then the people of that countrey fauouring the said Richard Skegs besought the king to pardon them both. So then the king spake these wordes: Beholde for thy sake, I pardon the Master. Then presently the Turkes shouted, and cried, saying: Away with the Master from the presence of the king. And then he came into the Banio whereas we were, and tolde vs what had happened, and we all reioyced at the good hap of master Skegs, that hee was saued, and our Master for his sake.

[Sidenote: Master Dier condemned to be hanged ouer a bulwarke.] But afterward our ioy was turned to double sorrow, for in the meane time the kings minde was altered: for that one of his counsell had aduised him, that vnlesse the Master died also, by the lawe they could not confiscate the ship nor goods, neither captive any of the men: whereupon the king sent for our Master againe, and gaue him another iudgement after his pardon for one cause, which was that hee should be hanged. Here all true Christians may see what trust a Christian man may put in an infidels promise, who being a King pardoned a man nowe, as you haue heard, and within an houre after hanged him for the same cause before a whole multitude: and also promised our Factors their oyles custome free, and at their going away made them pay the vttermost penie for the custome thereof.

[Sidenote: A Frenshman turned Turke, in hope of his life, and afterwards was hanged.] And when that Romaine Sonnings saw no remedy but that he should die, he protested to turne Turke, hoping thereby to haue saued his life. Then said the Turke, if thou wilt turne Turke, speake the words that thereunto belong: and he did so. Then saide they vnto him, Now thou shalt die in the faithe of a Turke, and so hee did, as the Turkes reported that were at his execution. And the forenamed Patrone Norado, whereas before he had libertie and did nothing he then was condemned slaue perpetuall, except there were paiment made of the foresaid summe of money.

Then the king condemned all vs, who were in number sixe and twentie, of the which, two were hanged (as you haue heard) and one died the first day wee came on shoare, by the visitation of Almightie God: and the other three and twentie he condemned slaues perpetually vnto the great Turke, and the ship and goods were confiscated to the vse of the great Turke: and then we all fell downe vpon our knees, giuing God thankes for this sorrowfull visitation, and giuing our selues wholy to the Almightie power of God, vnto whom all secrets are knowen, that he of his goodnesse would vouchsafe to looke vpon vs.

Here may all true Christian hearts see the wonderfull workes of God shewed vpon such infidels, blasphemers, whoremasters, and renegate Christians, and so you shall reade in the ende of this booke, of the like vpon the vnfaithfull king and all his children, and of as many as tooke any portion of the said goods.

[Sidenote: Euery fiue men allowed but two pence of bread a day.] But first to shewe our miserable bondage and slauerie, and vnto what small pittance and allowance wee were tied, for euery fiue men had allowance but fiue aspers of bread in a day, which is but two pence English: and our lodging was to lye on the bare boards, with a very simple cape to couer vs, wee were also forceably and most violently shauen, head and beard, and within three dayes after, I and six more of my fellowes, together with fourescore Italians and Spaniards were sent foorth in a Galeot to take a Greekish Carmosell, which came into Africa to steale Negroes, and went out of Tripolis vnto that place, which was two hundred and fourtie leagues thence, but wee were chained three and three to an oare, and wee rowed naked aboue the girdle, and the Boteswaine of the Galley walked abaft the maste, and his Mate afore the maste, and eche of them a bulls pissell dried in their handes, and when their diuelish choller rose, they would strike the Christians for no cause: and they allowed vs but halfe a pound of bread a man in a day without any other kinde of sustenance, water excepted. And when we came to the place whereas wee saw the Carmosell, we were not suffered to haue neither needle, bodkin, knife, or any other weapon about vs, nor at any other time in the night, vpon paine of one hundred bastonadoes: wee were then also cruelly manackled in such sort, that we could not put our handes the length of one foote asunder the one from the other, and euery night they searched our chaines three times, to see if they were fast riueted: Wee continued fight with the Carmosell three houres, and then wee tooke it, and lost but two of our men in that fight, but there were slaine of the Greekes fiue, and foureteene were cruelly hurt, and they that were sound, were presently made slaues and chained to the oares: and within fifteene dayes after we returned againe into Tripolis, and then wee were put to all maner of slauerie. [Sidenote: The Turkes builded a church.] I was put to hewe stones, and other to cary stones, and some to draw the Cart with earth, and some to make morter, and some to draw stones, (for at that time the Turkes builded a church:) And thus we were put to all kinde of slauerie that was to be done. And in the time of our being there, the Moores that are the husbandmen of the countrey rebelled against the king, because he would haue constrained them to pay greater tribute then heretofore they had done, so that the Souldiours of Tripolis marched foorth of the towne to haue ioyned battell against the Moores for their rebellion, and the King sent with them foure pieces of Ordinance, which were drawen by the captiues twenty miles into the Country after them, and at the sight thereof the Moores fled and then the Captaines returned backe againe. Then I and certaine Christians more were sent twelue miles into the countrey with a Cart to lode timber, and we returned againe the same day.

[Sidenote: The Christians sent 3. times a weeke 30 miles to fetch wood.] Nowe the king had 18. captiues, which three times a weeke went to fetch wood thirtie miles from the towne: and on a time he appointed me for one of the 18. and wee departed at eight of the clocke in the night, and vpon the way as wee rode vpon the camels, I demaunded of one of our company, who did direct vs the way? he sayd, that there was a Moore in our company which was our guide: and I demavnded of them how Tripolis and the wood bare one of the other? and hee said, East Northeast and West Southwest. And at midnight or neere thereabouts, as I was riding vpon my camel, I fell asleepe, and the guide and all the rest rode away from me, not thinking but I had bene among them. When I awoke, and finding my selfe alone durst not call nor hallow for feare least the wilde Moores should heare me, because they holde this opinion, that in killing a Christian they do God good seruice: and musing with my selfe what were best for me to do, if I should goe foorth, and the wilde Moores should hap to meete with mee, they would kill mee: and on the other side, if I should returne backe to Tripolis without any wood or company, I should be most miserably vsed: therefore of two euils, rather I had to goe foorth to the loosing of my life, then to turne backe and trust to their mercie, fearing to bee vsed as before I had seene others: for vnderstanding by some of my company before, howe Tripolis and the saide wood did lie one off another, by the North starre I went forth at aduenture, and as God would haue it, I came right to the place where they were, euen about an houre before day: there altogether wee rested and gaue our camels prouender, and assoone as the day appeared, we rode all into the wood: and I seeing no wood there, but a sticke here and a sticke there, about the bignesse of a mans arme growing in the sand, it caused mee to maruile how so many camels should be loden in that place. The wood was Iuniper, we needed no axe nor edge toole to cut it, but pluckt it vp by strength of hands rootes and all, which a man might easily do, and so gathered it together, a little at one place and so at another, and laded our camels, and came home about seuen of the clocke that night following: because I fell lame, and my camel was tired, I left my wood in the way.

[Sidenote: Eighteene captiues run away from Tripolis.] There was in Tripolis that time a Venetian, whose name was Benedetto Venetiano, and seuenteene captiues more of his company, which ranne away from Tripolis in a boate, and came in sight of an Island called Malta, which lieth fourtie leagues from Tripolis right North, and being within a mile of the shoare, and very faire weather, one of their company said, In dispetto de Dio adesso venio a pilliar terra, which is as much to say: In the despite of God I shall now fetch the shoare, [Sidenote: The iudgement of God vpon blasphemers.] and presently there arose a mighty storme, with thunder and raine and the wind at North, their boate being very small, so that they were inforced to beare vp roome, and to sheare right afore the winde ouer against the coast of Barbarie from whence they came, and rowing vp and downe the coast, their victuals being spent, the 21. day after their departure they were inforced through the want of food to come ashoare, thinking to haue stolne some sheepe: but the Moores of the country very craftily perceiuing their intent, gathered together a threescore horsemen, and hid themselues behinde a sandie hill, and when the Christians were come all a shoare, and past vp halfe a mile into the countrey, the Moores rode betwixt them and their boate, and some of them pursued the Christians, and so they were all taken and brought to Tripolis, from whence they had before escaped: and presently the king commaunded that the foresaide Benedetto with one more of his company should lose their eares, and the rest should be most cruelly beaten, which was presenly done. [Sidenote: The Greene Dragon.] This king had a sonne which was a ruler in an Island called Gerbi, whereunto arriued an English shippe called the Greene Dragon, of the which was Master one M. Blonket, who hauing a very vnhappy boy in that shippe, and vnderstanding that whosoeuer would turne Turke should be well enterteined of the kings sonne, this boy did runne a shoare, and voluntarily turned Turke. Shortly after the kings sonne came to Tripolis to visite his father, and seeing our company, hee greatly fancied Richard Burges our Purser, and Iames Smith: they were both yong men, therefore he was very desirous to haue them to turne Turkes, but they would not yeeld to his desire, saying: We are your fathers slaues, and as slaues wee will serue him. Then his father the king sent for them, and asked them if they would turne Turkes? And they saide: If it please your highnesse, Christians we were borne, and so we will remaine, beseeched the king that they might not bee inforced thereunto. [Sidenote: The Kings sonne had a captiue that was sonne to one of the Queenes Maiesties guard, that was forced to turne Turke.] The king had there before in his hosue a sonne of a yeoman of our Queenes guard, whom the kings sonne had inforced to turne Turke, his name was Iohn Nelson: him the king caused to be brought to these yong men, and thea said vnto them: Wil not you beare this your countreymen company, and be Turke as hee is? And they saide, that they would not yeeld thereunto during life. But it fell out, that within a moneth after, the kings sonne went home to Gerbi againe, being sixe score miles from Tripolis, and carried our two foresaid yong men with him, which were Richard Burges, and Iames Smith: and after their departure from vs, they sent vs a letter, signifying that there was no violence shewed vnto them as yet, but within three dayes after they were violently vsed, for that the kings sonne demaunded of them againe, if that they would turne Turke? Then answered Richard Burges, a Christian I am, and so I will remaine. Then the kings sonne very angerly said vnto him: By Mahomet thou shall presently be made Turke. Then called he for his men, and commaunded them to make him Turke, and they did so, and circumcised him, and would haue had him speake the wordes that thereunto belonged, but he answered them stoutly that he would not: and although they had put on him the habite of a Turke, yet sayd he, A Christian I was borne, and so I will remaine, though you force me to doe otherwise.

And then he called for the other, and commaunded him to be made Turke perforce also: but he was very strong, for it was so much as eight of the kings sonnes men could doe to holde him, so in the ende they circumcised him, and made him Turke. Now to passe ouer a little, and so to shewe the maner of our deliuerance out of that miserable captiuitie.

[Sidenote: The first motion for those Engmens deliuerie.] In May aforesaid, shortly after our apprehension, I wrote a letter into England vnto my father dwelling in Tauistoke in Deuonshire, signifying vnto him the whole estate of our calamities: and I wrote also to Constantinople, to the English Embassadour, both which letters were faithfully deliuered. But when my father had receiued my letter, and vnderstood the trueth of our mishap, and the occasion thereof, and what had happened to the offenders, he certified the right honourable the earle of Bedford thereof, who in short space acquainted her highnesse with the whole cause thereof, and her Maiestie like a most mercifull princesse tendering her Subiects, presently tooke order for our deliuerance. Whereupon the right worshipful sir Edward Osborne knight directed his letters with all speed to the English Embassadour in Constantinople, to procure our deliuery: and he obtained the great Turkes Commission, and sent it foorthwith to Tripolis, by one Master Edward Barton, together with a Iustice of the great Turkes, and one souldiour, and another Turke, and a Greeke which was his interpretour, which could speake besides Greeke, Turkish, Italian, Spanish and English. And when they came to Tripolis, they, were well interteined. And the first night they did lie in a Captaines house in the towne: all our company that were in Tripolis came that night for ioy to Master Barton and the other Commissioners to see them. Then master Barton said vnto vs, welcome my good countreymen, and louingly interteined vs, and at our departure from him, he gaue vs two shillings, and said, Serue God, for to morrow I hope you shall be as free as euer you were; We all gaue him thankes and so departed.

The next day in the morning very early, the King hauing intelligence of their comming, sent word to the keeper, that none of the Englishmen (meaning our company) should goe to worke. Then he sent for Master Barton and the other Commissioners, and demaunded of the saide Master Barton his message: the Iustice answered, that the great Turke his Souereigne had sent them vnto him, signifying that he was informed that a certaine English shippe, called the Iesus, was by him the saide king confiscated, about twelue months since, and nowe my saide Souereigne hath here sent his especiall commission by vs vnto you, for the deliuerance of the saide shippe and goods, and also the free libertie and deliuerance of the Englishmen of the same shippe, whom you haue taken and kept in captiuitie. [Sidenote: The Englishmen released.] And further the same Iustice saide, I am authorized by my said soueraigne the great Turke to see it done: And therefore I commaund you by vertue of this commission, presently to make restitution of the premisses or the value thereof: and so did the Justices deliuer vnto the King the great Turkes commission to the effect aforesaide, which commission the king with all obedience receiued: and after the perusing of the same, he foorthwith commanded all the English captiues to be brought before him, and then willed the keeper to strike off all our yrons, which done, the king said, You Englishmen, for that you did offend the lawes of this place, by the same lawes therefore some of your company were condemned to die as you knowe, and you to bee perpetuall captiues during your liues: notwithstanding; seeing it hath pleased my soueraigne lord the great Turke to pardon your said offences, and to giue you your freedome and libertie, beholde, here I make deliuery of you to this English Gentleman: so hee deliuered vs all that were there, being thirteene in number, to Master Barton, who required also those two yong men which the Kings sonne had taken with him. Then the king answered that it was against their lawe to deliuer them, for that they were turned Turkes: and touching the ship and goods, the king said, that he had solde her, but would make restitution of the value, and as much of the goods as came vnto his hands, and so the king arose and went to dinner, and commaunded a Iew to goe with Master Barton and the other commissioners, to shew them their lodging, which was a house prouided and appointed them by the said king. And because I had the Italian and Spanish tongues, by which their most trafique in that countrey is, Master Barton made me his Cater to buy his victuals for him and his company, and deliuered me money needfull for the same. Thus were wee set at libertie the 28. day of April, 1585.

[Sidenote: The plagues and punishments that happened to the King and his people.] Nowe to returne to the kings plagues and punishments, which Almighty God at his will and pleasure sendeth vpon men in the sight of the world, and likewise of the plagues that befell his children and others aforesaide. First when we were made bondmen, being the second day of May 1584. the king had 300. captiues, and before the moneth was expired, there died of them of the plague 150. [Sidenote: The king lost 150. camels taken by the wilde Moores.] And whereas they were 26. men of our company, of whom two were hanged, and one died the same day that wee were made bondslaues: that present moneth there died nine more of our company of the plague, and other two were forced to turne Turkes as before is rehearsed: and on the fourth day of June next following the king lost 150 camels, which were taken from him by the wilde Moores: and on the 28. day of the saide moneth of Iune, one Geffrey Maltese, a renegado of Malta, ranne away to his countrey, and stole a Brigandine which the king had builded for to take the Christians withall, and carried with him twelue Christians more which were the kings captiues. Afterward about the tenth day of Iuly next following, the king road foorth vpon the greatest and fairest mare that might be seene, as white as any swanne: hee had not ridden fourtie paces from his house, but on a sudden the same mare fell downe vnder him starke dead, and I with six more were commaunded to burie her, skinne, shoes and all, which we did. And about three moneths after our deliuerie, Master Barton, with all his residue of his company departed from Tripoli to Zante, in a vessell, called a Settea, of one Marcus Segoorus, who dwelt in Zante, and after our arriuall at Zante we remained fifteene dayes there aboorde our vessell, before wee could haue Platego, (that is, leaue to come a shoare) because the plague was in that place, from whence wee came: and about three dayes after we came a shoare, thither came another Settea of Marseils bound for Constantinople. [Sidenote: Two Englishmen shipped to Constantinople with M. Barton.] Then did Master Barton, and his company, with two more of our company, shippe themselues as passengers in the same Settea, and went to Constantinople. But the other nine of vs, that remained in Zante, about three monethes after, shipt our selues in a ship of the said Marcus Segoorus, which came to Zante, and was bound for England. [The souldiers of Tripolis kil the king.] In which three monethes, the souldiers of Tripolie killed the said king. And then the kings sonne, according to the custome there, went to Constantinople, to surrender vp all his fathers treasure, goods, captiues, and concubines, vnto the great Turke, and tooke with him our saide Purser Richard Burges, and Iames Smith, and also the other two Englishmen, which he the said kings sonne had inforced to become Turkes, as is aforesayd. And they the said Englishmen finding now some opportunitie, concluded with the Christian captiues which were going with them vnto Constantinople, being in number about one hundred and fiftie, to kill the kings sonne, and all the Turkes which were aboorde of the Galley, and priuily the saide Englishmen conueyed vnto the saide Christian captiues, weapons for that purposes. And when they came into the maine Sea, towards Constantinople (vpon the faithfull promise of the sayde Christian captiues) these foure Englishmen lept suddenly into the Crossia, that is, in the middest of the Galley, where the canon lieth, and with their swordes drawne, did fight against all the foresaid Turkes, and for want of helpe of the saide Christian captiues, who falsly brake their promises, the said Master Blonkets boy was killed, and the sayde Iames Smith, and our Pursser Richard Surges, and the other Englishman, were taken and bound into chaines, to be hanged at their arriual in Constantinople: and as the Lordes will was, about two dayes after, passing through the gulfe of Venice, at an Island called Cephalonia, they met with two of the duke of Venice his Gallies, [Marginal Note: Two Gallies of Venice tooke the King of Tripolie his galley, and killed the kings sonne, and all the Turkes in it, and released all the Christians being in number 150.] which tooke that Galley, and killed the kings sonne, and his mother, and all the Turkes that were there, in number 150. and they saued the Christian captiues, and would haue killed the two Englishmen because they were circumcised, and become Turkes, had not the other Christian captiues excused them, saying, that they were inforced to be Turkes, by the kings sonne, and shewed the Venetians also, how they did enterprise at sea to fight against all the Turks, and that their two fellowes were slaine in that fight. Then the Venetians saued them, and they, with all the residue of the said captiues, had their libertie, which were in number 150. or thereabouts, and the said Gallie, and all the Turkes treasure was confiscated to the vse of the state of Venice. And from thence our two Englishmen traueiled homeward by land, and in this meane time we had one more of our company, which died in Zante, and afterward the other eight shipped themselues at Zante, in a shippe of the said Marcus Segorus, which was bound for England: and before we departed thence, there arriued the Assension, and the George Bonauenture of London in Cephalonia, in a harbour there, called Arrogostoria, whose Marchants agreed with the Marchants of our shippe, and so laded all the marchandise of our shippe into the said ships of London, who tooke vs eight in as passengers, and so we came home, and within two moneths after our arriuall at London, our said Purser Richard Surges, and his fellow came home also: for the which we are bound to praise Almightie God, during our liues, and as duetie bindeth vs, to pray for the preseruation of our most gracious Queene, for the great care her Maiestie had ouer vs, her poore Subjects, in seeking and procuring of our deliuerance aforesaide: and also for her honourable priuie Counsell, and I especiall for the prosperitie and good estate of the house of the late deceased, the right honourable the Earle of Bedford, whose honour I must confesse, most diligently at the suite of my father now departed, traueiled herein: for the which I rest continually bounden to him, whose soule I doubt not, but is already in the heauens in ioy, with the Almightie, vnto which place he vouchsafe to bring vs all, that for our sinnes suffered most vile and shameful death vpon the Crosse, there to liue perpetually world without ende, Amen.

* * * * *

The Queenes letters to the Turke 1584. for the restitution of the shippe called the Iesus, and the English captiues detained in Tripolie in Barbarie, and for certaine other prisoners in Argier.

ELIZABETHA, Dei ter maxhni et vnici coeli terræque conditoris gratia, Angliæ, Franciæ, et Hiberniæ Regina, fidei Christianæ contra omnes omnium inter Christianos degentium, Christíque nomen falsò profitentium idololatrias, inuistissima et potentissima defensatrix: augustissimo, inuictissimôque principi, Zultan Murad Can, Musulmanici regni dominatori potentissimo, imperijque Orientis Monarchæ, supra omnes soli et supremo salutem, et multos cum summa rerum optimarum affluentia foelices et fortunatos annos.

Augustissime et potentissime Imperator, biennio iam peracto, ad Cæsaream vestram Maiestatem scripsimus, vt dilectus noster famulus Guilielmus Harebornus, vir ornatissimus pro legato nostro Constantinopoli, alijsque Musulmanici imperij ditionibus, sublimi vestra authoritate reciperetur: simul etiam Angli subditi nostri commercium et mercaturam, in omnibus illis prouincijs exerceant, non minùs liberè quàm Galli, Poloni, Veneti, Germani, cæteríque vestri confoederati, qui varias Orientis partes peragrant, operam nauantes, vt mutuis commercijs coniungatur Oriens, cum Occidente.

Quæ priuilegia, cum nostris subditis Anglis inuictissima vestra Maiestas literis et diplomate suo liberalissimè indulserit, facere non potuimus, quin quas maximas animus noster capere potest gratias, eo nomine ageremus: sperantes fore, vt hæc instituta commerciorum ratio maximas vtilitates, et commoda vtrinque, tam in imperij vestri ditiones, quàm regni nostri prouincias secum adferat.

Id vt planè fiat, cûm nuper subditi nostri nonnulli Tripoli in Barbaria et Argellæ ab eius loci incolis voluntatem vestram fortè nescientibus malè habiti fuerint, et immaniter diuexati, Cæsaream vestram Maiestatem beneuolè rogamus, vt per Legatum nostrum eorum causam cognoscas, et postremò earum prouinciarum proregibus ac præfectis imperes, vt nostri liberè in illis locis, sine vi aut iniuria deinceps versari, et negotia gerere possint.

Et nos omni opera vicissim studebimus ea omnia præstare, quæ Imperatoriæ vestræ Maiestati vllo pacto grata fore intelligemus: quam Deus vnicus mundi conditor optimus maximus diutissimè incolumem et florentem seruet. Datæ in palatio nostro Londini, quinto die Mensis Septembris: anno IESV CHRISTI Seruatoris nostri, 1584. Regni verò nostri vicessimo sexto.

The same in English.

Elizabeth, by the grace of the most high God, and onely maker of heauen and earth, of England, France and Ireland Queene, and of the Christian faith, against all the Idolaters and false professors of the Name of CHRIST dwelling among the Christians, most inuincible and puissant defender: to the most valiant and invincible Prince, Zultan Murad Can, the most mightie ruler of the kingdome of Musulman, and of the East Empire the onely and highest Monarch aboue all, health and many happy and fortunate yeres, with great aboundance of the best things.

Most noble and puissant Emperour, about two yeeres nowe passed, wee wrote vnto your Imperiall Maiestie, that our welbeloued seruant, William Hareborne, a man of great reputation and honour, might be receiued vnder your high authoritie, for our Ambassadour in Constantinople, and other places, vnder the obedience of your Empire of Musulman: And also that the Englishmen, being our Subiects, might exercise entercourse and marchandize in all those Prouinces, no lesse freely then the French, Polonians, Venetians, Germanes, and other your confederats, which traueile through diuers of the East parts: endeuouring that by mutuall trafique, the East may be ioyned and knit to the West.

Which priuileges, when as your most puissant Maiestie, by your letters and vnder your dispensation most liberally and fauourably granted to our Subiects of England, wee could no lesse doe, but in that respect giue you as great thankes, as our heart could conceiue, trusting that it wil come to passe, that this order of trafique, so well ordeined, will bring with it selfe most great profits and commodities to both sides, as well to the parties subiect to your Empire, as to the Prouinces of our kingdome. Which thing that it may be done in plaine and effectuall maner, whereas some of our Subiects of late at Tripolis in Barbarie, and at Argier, were by the inhabitants of those places (being perhaps ignorant of your pleasure) euill intreated and grieuously vexed, wee doe friendly and louingly desire your Imperial Maiestie, that you will vnderstand their causes by our Ambassadour, and afterward giue commaundement to the Lieutenants and Presidents of those Prouinces, that our people may henceforth freely, without any violence, or iniurie, traueile, and do their businesse in those places.

And we againe with all endeuour, shall studie to performe all those things, which we shall in any wise vnderstand to be acceptable to your Imperiall Maiestie, which God, the onely maker of the world, most best and most great, long keepe in health, and flourishing. Given in our pallaice at London, the fift day of the moneth of September, in the yeere of IESVS CHRIST our Saviour, 1534. And of our raigne, the 26.

* * * * *

The Turkes letter to the King of Tripolis in Barbarie, commanding the restitution of an English ship, called the Iesus, with the men, and goods, sent from Constantinople, by Mahomet Beg, a Iustice of the Great Turkes, and an English Gentleman, called Master Edward Barton. Anno 1584.

Honourable, and worthy Bassa Romadan Beglerbeg, most wise and prudent Iudge of the West Tripolis, wee wish the ende of all thy enterprises happie, and prosperous. By these our highnesse letters, wee certifie thee, that the right honourable, William Hareborne, Ambassadour in our most famous Porch, for the most excellent Queenes Maiestie of England, in person, and by letters hath certified our highnesse, that a certaine shippe, with all her furniture, and artillerie, worth two thousand duckets, arriuing in the port of Tripolis, and discharged of her lading and marchandize, paide our custome according to order, and againe, the marchants laded their shippe with oyle, which by constraint they were inforced to buy of you and hauing answered in like maner the custome for the same, determined to depart: a Frenchman assistant to the Marchant, vnknowen to the Englishmen, caried away with him another Frenchman indebted to a certaine Moore in foure hundred duckets, and by force caused the Englishmen, and shippe to depart: who neither suspecting fraude, nor deceite, hoised sailes. In the meane time, this man, whose debter the Frenchman had stollen away, went to the Bassa with the supplication, by whose meanes, and force of the Castle, the Englishmen were constrained to returne into the port, where the Frenchman, author of the euill, with the Master of the ship an Englishman, innocent of the crime were hanged, and sixe and twentie Englishmen, cast into prison, of whom through famine, thirst, and stinke of the prison, eleuen died, and the rest like to die. Further, it was signified to our Maiestie also, that the marchandise and other goods, with the shippe, were worth 7600. duckets: which things if they be so, this is our commandemeht, which was granted and giuen by our Maiestie, that the English shippe, and all the marchandize, and whatsoeuer else taken away bee wholy restored, and that the Englishmen be let goe free, and suffered to returne into their countrey. Wherefore when this our commaundement shall come vnto thee, wee straightly commaund, that the foresaid businesse be diligently looked vnto, and discharged. And if it be so, that a Frenchman, and no Englishman hath done this craft, and wickednesse vnknowen to the Englishmen, and as authour of the wickednesse is punished, and that the Englishmen committed nothing against the peace and league, or their articles: also if they payd custome according to order, it is against law, custome of Countreys, and their priuilege, to hinder or hurt them. Neither is it meete, their shippe, marchandise, and all their goods taken, should be withholden. We will therefore, that the English shippe, marchandize, and all other their goods, without exception, be restored to the Englishmen: also that the men bee let goe free, and if they will, let none hinder them, to returne peaceably into their Countrey: do not commit, that they another time complaine of this matter, and how this businesse is dispatched, certifie vs at our most famous porche.

Dated in the Citie of Constantinople, in the 992. yeere of Mahomet, and in the ende of the moneth of October; and in the yeere of IESVS 1584.

* * * * *

A letter of Master William Hareborne, the English Ambassadour, Ligier in Constantinople, to the Bassa Romadan, the Beglerbeg of Tripolis in Barbarie, for the restoring of an English shippe called the Iesus, with the goods, and men, detained as slaues, Anno 1585.

Molto magnifico Signor,

Noi ha stato significato per diuerse lettere di quanto ha passato circa diuina naue nostra chiamata Iesus, sopra il quale in agiuto di Ricciardo Skegs, vno de gli nostri mercanti di essa gia morto, veniua vn certo Francese per sopra cargo, chiamato Romano Sonings, il quale per non esser ben portato secondo che doueua, volendo importer seco vn altro Francese debitore a certi vostri sensa pagarcene, per giusticia era appicato col patron Inglese Andre Dier, che come simplice credendo al detto Francese, senza auedercene de la sua ria malitia non retornaua, quando da vostra magnifica Signoria gli era mandato. La morte del detto tristo Francese approuiamo como cosa benfatta. [Sidenote: Edoardo Barton et Mahumed Beg.] Ma al contrario, doue lei ha confiscato la detta naue e mercantia en essa, et fatto sciaui li marinari, como cosa molto contraria a li priuilegij dal Gran Signor quattro anni passati concessi, et da noi confirmati di parte de la Serenissima Magesta d'Ingilterra nostra patrona, e molto contraria a la liga del detto Gran Signor, il quale essendo dal sopra detto apieno informato, noi ha conceduto il suo regale mandamento di restitutione, la qual mandiamo a vostra magnifica Signoria col presente portator Edoardo Barton, nostro Secretario, et Mahumed Beg, droguemano di sua porta excelsa, con altre lettere del excellentissimo Vizir, et inuictissimo capitan di mar: chiedendo, tanto di parte del Gran Signor, quanto di sua Serenissima Magesta di V. S. M. che gli huomini, oglij, naue col fornimento, danare, et tutti altri beni qualconque, da lei et per vestro ordine da gli nostri tolti siano resi à questo mio Secretario liberamente senza empacho alcuno, como il Gran Signor da sua gratia noi ha conceduto, specialmente per esser detti oglij comprati per ordine di sua Serenissima Magestà, per prouisione della Corte sua. Il qual non facendo, protestiamo per questa nostra al incontra di esso tutti futuri danni che puono succedere per questa cagione, como authore di quelli, contrario à la Santa liga giurata de li duoi Rei, patroni nostri, como per li priuilegij, che lei mostrerà il nostra, consta: per obseruatione de gli quali noi stiamo di fermo en questa excelsa Porta. Et cosi responderete nel alro mondo al solo Iddio, et quà al Gran Signor questo massimo peccato commesso da lei al incontra di tanti poueracchi, che per questa crudeltà sono in parte morti, in parti retenuti da esso en duro cattiuerio. Al contrario, piacendo lei euitar questo incommodo et restarcene en gratia del Signor Iddio, et li nostri patroni, amicheuolmente, (como conuien à par vostro di mostrarsi prudente gouernatore, et fidel seruitor al patrono) ad impirete questa nostra guistissima domanda, per poter resultarui à grand honore et commodò per la tratta di marchantia, che faronno a laduenire li nostri in quella vostra prouincia. Li quali generalmente, tanto quelli, como tutti altri che nel mar riscontrarete, siano, secondo che manda il Grand Signor, de vostra Signoria magnifica amicheuolmente recolti et receunti: Et noi non mancharemo al debito di ottimo amico en qualconche occurenza vostra, piacendo lei amicitia nostra como desideramo. Il Signor Iddio lei conceda (adimpiendo questa nostra giusta rechiesta, per cauar noi di piu futura fatica in questo negocio, et lei di disgratia) ogni vera felicità, et supremo honore. Data in Palazzo nostro che fu da Rapamat appresso Pera di 15. di Genero 1585.

Il Ambassiatore de la Majesta Serenissima d'Ingilterra, amico de vostra Signoria magnifica, piacendo lei.

The same in English.

Right honourable Lord, it hath bene signified vnto vs by diuers letters, what hath fallen out, concerning a certaine shippe of ours, called the Iesus, into which, fore the helpe of Richard Skegs, one of our Marchants in the same, nowe deceased, there was admitted a certaine Frenchman called Romaine Sonnings, which for his ill behauiour, according to his deserts, seeking to cary away with him another Frenchman, which was indebted to certaine of your people, without paying his creditours, was hanged by sentence of iustice, together with Andrew Dier, the master of the said ship, who simply and without fraude, giuing credite to the said Frenchman, without any knowledge of his euil fact, did not returne when hee was commaunded, by your honourable Lordship. The death of the said lewde Frenchman we approue as a thing well done, but contrarywise, whereas your Lordship hath confiscated the said ship with the goods therein, and hath made slaues of the Mariners, as a thing altogether contrary to the priuileges of the Grand Signior, granted foure yeeres since, and confirmed by vs on the behalfe of the most excellent the Queenes Maiestie of England our Mystresse, and altogether contrary to the league of the saide Grand Signior, who being fully informed of the aforesaid cause, hath granted vnto vs his royall commandement of restitution, which we send vnto your honourable Lordship, by the present bearer Edward Barton our Secretaire, and Mahomet Beg, one of the Iustices of his stately Court, with other letters of the most excellent Admirall, and most valiant Captaine of the Sea, requiring your honourable Lordship, as well on the behalfe of the Grand Signior, as of the Queenes most excellent Maiestie, my Mystresse, that the men, oyles, shippe, furniture, money, and all other goods whatsoeuer, by your

Lordship, and your order taken from our men, be restored vnto this my Secretary freely, without delay, as the Grand Signior of his goodnesse hath graunted vnto vs, especially in regard that the same oyles were bought by the commaundement of our Queenes most excellent Maiestie, for the prouision of her Court. Which if you performe not, wee protest by these our leters against you, that you are the cause of all the inconueniences which may ensue vpon this occasion, as the authour thereof, contrary to the holy league sworne by both our Princes, as by the priuileges, which this our seruant will shewe you, may appeare. For the seeing of which league performed, wee remaine here as Ligier in this stately Court. And by this meanes you shall answere in another world vnto God alone, and in this world vnto the Grand Signior, for this hainous sinne committed by you against so many poore soules, which by this your cruelty are in part dead, and in part detained by you in most miserable captiuitie. Contrarywise, if it shall please you to auoyd this mischiefe, and to remaine in the fauour of Almighty God, and of our Princes, you shall friendly fulfill this our iust demaund (as it behooueth you to shew your selfe a prudent Gouernour, and faithfull seruant vnto your Lord) and the same may turne to your great honour, and profite, by the trade of marchandize, which our men in time to come, may vse in that gouernment of yours: which generally, as well those poore men, as all others, which you shall meete at the sea, ought to be according to the commandement of the Grand Signior, friendly entertained and receiued of your honourable Lordship, and we will not faile in the dueties of a speciall friend, whensoeuer you shall haue occasion to vse vs, as we desire. Almighty God grant vnto your Lordship (in the fulfilling of this our iust request, whereby wee may be deliuered from further trouble in this matter, and your selfe from further displeasure) all true felicitie, and increase of honour.

Giuen in our Pallace from Rapamat in Pera, the 15 of Ianuarie 1585.

* * * * *

The voyage passed by sea into Aegypt, by Iohn Euesham Gentleman. Anno 1586.

The 5 of December 1586 we departed from Grauesend in the Tiger of London, wherein was Master vnder God for the voyage Robert Rickman, and the 21. day at night we came to the Isle of Wight: departing from thence in the morning following we had a faire winde, so that on the 27 day wee came in sight of the rocke of Lisbone, and so sayling along we came in sight of the South Cape, the 29 of the same, and on the morrowe with a Westerly winde we entered the straights: and the second of Ianuary being as high as Cape de Gate, we departed from our fleete towards Argier. And the 4 day we arriued at the port of Argier aforesaid, where we staied till the first of March. [Sidenote: Tunis.] At which time we set saile towardes a place called Tunis, to the Eastward of Argier 100 leagues, where we arriued the 8 of the same. This Tunis is a small citie vp 12 miles from the sea, and at the port or rode where shipping doe ride, is a castle or fort called Goletta, sometimes in the handes of the Christians, but now of the Turkes; at which place we remained till the third of Aprill: at which time wee set saile towardes Alexandria, and hauing sometime faire windes, sometime contrary, we passed on the 12 day betweene Sicilia and Malta (where neere adioyning hath beene the fort and holde of the knights of the Rhodes) and so the 19 day we fell with the Isle of Candy, and from thence to Alexandria, where we arriued the 27 of April, and there continued till the 5 of October.

[Sidenote: The description of Alexandria.] The said citie of Alexandria is an old thing decayed or ruinated, hauing bene a faire and great citie neere two miles in length, being all vauted vnderneath for prouision of fresh water, which water commeth thither but once euery yeere, out of one of the foure riuers of paradise (as it is termed) called Nilus, which in September floweth neere eighteene foote vpright higher then his accustomed manner, and so the banke being cut, as it were a sluce, about thirty miles from Alexandria, at a towne called Rossetto, it doth so come to the saide Citie, with such aboundance, that barkes of twelue tunne doe come vpon the said water, which water doth fill all the vaults, cesternes, and wels in the said Citie, with very good water, and doth so continue good, till the next yeere following: for they haue there very litle raine or none at all, yet have they exceeding great dewes. Also they haue very good corne, and very plentifull; all the Countrey is very hot, especially in the monethes of August, September, and October. Also within the saide Citie there is a pillar of Marble, called by the Turkes, King Pharaoes needle, and it is foure square, euery square is twelue foote, and it is in height 90 foote. Also there is without the wals of the said Citie, about twentie score paces, another marble pillar, being round, called Pompey his pillar: this pillar standeth vpon a great square stone, euery square is fifteene foote, and the same stone is fifteene foote high, and the compasse of the pillar is 37 foote, and the height of it is 101 feete, which is a wonder to thinke how euer it was possible to set the said pillar vpon the said square stone. The port of the said Citie is strongly fortified with two strong Castles, and one other Castle within the citie, being all very well planted with munition: [Sidenote: Cayro.] and there is to the Eastward of this Citie, about three dayes iourney the citie of Grand Cayro, otherwise called Memphis: it hath in it by report of the registers bookes which we did see, to the number of 2400 Churches, and is wonderfully populous, and is one dayes iourney about the wals, which was iourneyed by one of our Mariners for triall thereof. Also neere to the saide citie there is a place called the Pyramides, being as I may well terme it, one of the nine wonders of the world: that is, seuen seuerall places of flint and marble stone, foure square, the wals thereof are seuen yards thicke in those places that we did see: the squarenes is in length about twentie score euery square, being built as it were a pointed diamond, broad at the foote, and small or narrow at the toppe: the heigth of them, to our judgement, doth surmount twise the heighth of Paules steeple: within the said Pyramides, no man doth know what there is, for that they haue no entrance but in the one of them, there is a hole where the wall is broken, and so we went in there, hauing torch light with vs, for that it hath no light to it, and within the same, is as it were a great hall, in the which there is a costly tombe, which tombe they say, was made for kinq Pharao in his life time, but he was not buried there, being drowned in the red sea: also there are certaine vauts or dungeons, which goe downe verie deepe vnder those Pyramides with faire staires, but no man dare venter to goe downe into them, by reason that they can cary no light with them, for the dampe of the earth doth put out the light: the red sea is but three dayes iourney from this place, and Ierusalem about seuen dayes iourney from thence: but to returne to Cayro. There is a Castle wherein is the house that Pharaoes wiues were kept in, and in the Pallace or Court thereof stande 55 marble pillars, in such order, as our Exchange standeth in London: the said pillars are in beigth 60 foote: and in compasse 14 foote: also in the said Citie is the castle were Joseph was in prison, where to this day they put in rich men, when the king would haue any summe of money of them: there are seuen gates to the sayd prison, and it goeth neere fiftie yardes downe right: also, the water that serueth this castle, commeth out of the foresaide riuer of Nilus, vpon a wall made with arches, fiue miles long, and it is twelue foote thicke. Also there are in old Cayro two Monasteries, the one called S. Georges, the other S. Maries: and in the Courts where the Churches be, was the house of king Pharao. In this Citie is great store of marchandize, especially pepper, and nutmegs, which come thither by land, out of the East India: and it is very plentifull of all maner of victuals, especially of bread, rootes, and hearbes: to the Eastwards of Cayro, there is a Well, fiue miles off called Matria, and as they say, when the Virgin Marie fled from Bethleem, and came into Ægypt, and being there, had neither water, nor any other thing to sustaine them, by the prouidence of God, an Angell came from heauen, and strake the ground with his wings, where presently issued out a fountaine of water: and the wall did open where the Israelites did hide themselues, which fountains or well is walled foure square till this day. [Sidenote: Carthage.] Also we were at an old Citie, all ruinated and destroyed, called in olde time, the great Citie of Carthage where Hannibal and Queene Dido dwelt: this Citie was but narrow, but was very long: for there was, and is yet to bee seene, one streete three mile long, to which Citie fresh water was brought vpon arches (as afore) aboue 25 miles, of which arches some are standing to this day. [Sidenote: Argier.] Also we were at diuers other places on the coast, as we came from Cayro, but of other antiquities we saw but few. The towne of Argier which was our first and last part, within the streights standeth vpon the side of an hill, close vpon the sea shore: it is very strong both by sea and land, and it is very well victualed with all manner of fruites bread and fish good store, and very cheape. It is inhabited with Turkes, Moores, and Iewes, and so are Alexandria and Cayro. In this towne are a great number of Christian captiues, whereof there are of Englishmen onely fifteene, from which port we set sayle towardes England, the seuenth of Ianuarie, Anno 1587, and the 30 day of the sayd moneth, we arriued at Dartmouth on the coast of England.

* * * * *

The second voyage of M. Laurence Aldersey, to the Cities of Alexandria, and
  Cayro in Aegypt. Anno 1586.

I Embarked my selfe at Bristoll, in the Hercules, a good ship of London, and set saile the 21 day of Februarie, about ten of the clocke in the morning, hauing a merry winde: but the 23 day, there arose a very great storme, and in the mids of it we descried a small boate of the burden of ten tunnes, with foure men in her, in very great danger, who called a maine for our helpe. Whereupon our Master made towards them, and tooke them into our ship, and let the boate, which was laden with timber, and appertained to Chepstow, to runne a drift. The same night about midnight arose another great storme, but the winde was large with vs, vntill the 27 of the same moneth, which grew then somewhat contrary: yet notwithstanding we held on our course, and the tenth day of March, we descried a saile about Cape Sprat, which is a little on this side the streight of Gibraltare, but we spake not with her. The next day we described twelue saile more, with whom we thought to haue spoken, to haue learned what they were, but they made very fast away, and we gaue them ouer.

Thursday the 16 of March, we had sight of the streights, and of the coast of Barbary. The 18 day we passed them, and sailed towards Patras. Vpon the 23 of March, we met with the Centurion of London which came from Genoa, by whom we sent letters to England, and the foure men also which we tooke in, vpon the coast of England, before-mentioned.

The 29th of March we came to Goleta a small Iland, and had sight of two shippes, which we iudged to be of England.

Tuesday the fourth of April, we were before Malta, and being there becalmed, our Maister caused the two ship boates to be had out, and they towed the ship, till we were out of sight of the Castle of Malta. The 9 day of April we came to Zante, and being before the towne, William Aldridge, seruant to Master Thomas Cordall of London, came aboord us, with whom our Master and twelue more of our company, thought to haue gone on shoare: but they could not be permitted: so we all came aboard againe, and went to Patras, where we arriued vpon good Friday, and lay there with good enterteinement at the English house, where was the Consull Master Grimes, Ralph Ashley, and Iohn Doddington, who very kindly went with vs, and shewed vs the pleasures of the towne.

They brought vs to the house of the Cady, who was made then to vnderstand of the 20 Turks that wee had aboard, which were to goe to Constantinople, being redeemed out of captiuitie, by sir Francis Drake in the West Indies, and brought with him into England, and by order of the Queenes Maiestie sent now into their Countrey. Whereupon the Cady commanded them to be brought before him, that he might see them: and when, he had talked with them, and vnderstood howe strangely they were deliuered, he marueiled much, and admired the Queenes Maistie of England, who being but a woman, is notwithstanding of such power and renowne amongst all the princes of Christendome, with many other honourable wordes of commending her Maiestie. So he tooke the names of those 20 Turkes, and recorded them in their great bookes, to remaine in perpetuall memory. After this, our foresaid countreyman brought mee to the Chappel of S. Andrew where his tombe or sepulchre is, and the boord vpon which he was beheaded, which boord is now so rotten, that if any man offer to cut it, it falleth to powder, yet I brought some of it away with me.

Vpon Tuesday in Easter weeke, wee set out towards Zante againe, and the 24. of April with much adoe, wee were all permitted to come on shoare, and I was caried to the English house in Zante, where I was very well entertained. The commodities of Zante are Currants and oyle: the situation of the Towne is vnder a very great hill, vpon which standeth a very strong Castle, which commaundeth the Towne. At Zante wee tooke in a Captaine and 16. souldiers, with other passengers. Wee departed from Zante vpon Tuesday the 15. of April, and the next day we ankered at a small Iland, called Striualia, which is desolate of people, sauing a fewe religious men, who entertained vs well, without taking any money: but of courtesie we bestowed somewhat vpon them for their maintenance, and then they gaue vs a couple of leane sheepe, which we caried aboord. The last day of Aprill, wee arriued at Candie, at a Castle, called Sowday, where wee set the Captaine, Souldiers, and Mariners ashoare, which wee tooke in at Zante, with all their carriage.

[Sidenote: The Islands of Milo, in olde time called Sporades.] The second day of May wee set saile againe, and the fourth day came to the Islands of Milo, where we ankered, and found the people there very courteous, and tooke in such necessaries as we wanted. The Islands are in my iudgement a hundred in number, and all within the compasse of a hundred miles.

The 11. day, the Chaus, which is the greatest man there in authoritie, for certaine offences done in a little Chappell by the water side, which they saide one of our shippe had done, and imputed it to mee, because I was seene goe into it three dayes before, came to vs, and made much a doe, so that we were faine to come out of our shippe armed: but by three pieces of golde the brabling was ended, and we came to our shippe. This day wee also set saile, and the next day passed by the Castle of Serpeto, which is an old ruinated thing, and standeth vnder a hils side.

The 13. day we passed by the Island of Paris, and the Island of the bankes of Helicon, and the Island called Ditter, where are many boares, and the women bee witches. The same day also wee passed by the Castle of Timo, standing vpon a very high mountaine, and neere vnto it is the Island of Diana.

The 15. of May, wee came to Sio, where I stayed thirtie and three dayes. In it is a very proper Towne, after the building of that Countrey, and the people are civil: and while we were here there came in sixe Gallies, which had bene at Alexandria, and one of them which was the Admiral, had a Prince of the Moores prisoner, whom they tooke about Alexandria, and they meant to present him to the Turke. The towne standeth in a valley, and a long the water side pleasantly. There are about 26. winde-mils about it, and the commodities of it are cotton wooll, cotton yarne, mastike, and some other drugs.

As we remained at Sio, there grew a great controuersie betweene the mariners of the Hercules, and the Greekes of the towne of Sio, about the bringing home of the Turkes, which the Greekes took in ill part, and the boyes cried out, Viue el Re Philippe: whereupon our men beate the boyes, and threwe stones, and so a broile beganne, and some of our men were hurt: but the Greekes were fetcht out of their houses, and manacled together with yrons, and threatned to the Gallies: about fortie of them were sent to the prison, and what became of them when we were gone, we know not, for we went thence within two dayes after, which was the 19. of Iune.

The 20. day wee passed by the Island of Singonina, an Island risen by the casting of stones in that place: the substance of the ground there is brimstone, and burneth sometimes so much that it bloweth vp the rockes.

The 24. of Iune wee came to Cyprus, and had sight in the way of the aforesaide sixe Gallies, that came from Alexandria, one whereof came vnto vs, and required a present for himselfe, and for two of the other Gallies, which we for quietnesse sake gaue them.

The 27. of Iune, wee came to Tripolie, where I stayed till the fift of Iuly, and then tooke passage in a smal barke called a Caramusalin, which was a passage boat, and was bound for Bichieri, thirteene miles on this side Alexandria, which boate was fraighted with Turkes, Moores, and Iewes.

The 20. day of Iuly, this barke which I passed in ranne vpon a rocke, and was in very great danger, so that we all began some to be ready to swimme, some to leape into the shippe boate, but it pleased God to set vs quickly off the rocke, and without much harme.

[Sidenote: The English house in Alexandria.] The 28. of Iuly I came to Bichieri, where I was well entertained of a Iewe which was the Customer there, giuing me Muskadine, and drinking water himselfe: hauing broken my fast with him, he prouided mee a Camell for my carriage, and a Mule for mee to ride vpon, and a Moore to runne by me to the City of Alexandria, who had charge to see mee safe in the English house, whether I came, but found no Englishmen there: but then my guide brought me aboord a ship of Alderman Martins, called the Tyger of London, where I was well receiued of the Master of the said ship, whose name was Thomas Rickman, and of all the company.

The said Master hauing made me good cheere, and made me also to drinke of the water of Nilus, hauing the keyes of the English house, went thither with me himselfe, and appointed mee a faire chamber, and left a man with me to prouide me all things that I needed, and euery day came himselfe to me, and caried me into the City, and shewed me the monuments thereof, which be these.

[Sidenote: The monuments of Alexandria.] Hee brought mee first to Pompey his pillar, which is a mighty thing of gray marble, and all of one stone, in height by estimation about 52. yards, and the compasse about sixe fadome.

The City hath three gates, one called the gate of Barbaria, the other of Merina, and the thirde of Rossetto.

He brought me to a stone in the streete of the Citie, whereupon S. Marke was beheaded: to the place where S. Katerine died, hauing there hid herselfe, because she would not marry: also to the Bath of S. Katerine.

I sawe there also Pharaos needle, which is a thing in height almost equall with Pompeys pillar, and is in compasse fiue fadome, and a halfe, and all of one stone.

I was brought also to a most braue and daintie Bath, where we washed our selues: the Bath being of marble, and of very curious workemanship.

The Citie standeth vpon great arches, or vawtes, like vnto Churches, with mightie pillars of marble, to holde vp the foundation: which arches are built to receiue the water of the riuer of Nilus, which is for the vse of the Citie. It hath three Castles, and an hundred Churches: but the part that is destroyed of it, is sixe time more then that part which standeth.

The last day of Iuly, I departed from Alexandria towards Cayro in a passage boate, wherein first I went to Rossetto, standing by the riuer side, hauing 13. or 14. great churches in it, their building there is of stone and bricke, but as for lodging, there is little, except we bring it with vs.

From Rosetto wee passed along the riuer of Nilus, which is so famous in the world, twise as broad as the Thames at London: on both sides grow date trees in great abundance. The people be rude, insomuch that a man cannot traueile without a Ianizary to conduct him.

[Sidenote: The Turkes Lent.] The time that I stayed in Ægypt, was the Turkes and Moores Lent, in all which time they burne lamps in their churches, as many as may hang in them: their Lent endureth 40. dayes, and they haue three Lents in the yere: during which time they neither eate nor drinke in the day time, but all the night they do nothing else.

Betwixt Rossetto and Cayro there are along the water side three hundred cities and townes, and the length of the way is not aboue three hundred miles.

To this famous Citie of Cayro I came the fift day of August, where I found M. William Alday, and William Cæsar, who intertained me in very good sort. M. Cæsar brought mee to see the Pyramides which are three in number, one whereof king Pharao made for his owne tombe, the tombe it selfe is almost in the top of it: the monuments bee high and in forme 4. square, and euery of the squares is as long as a man may shoote a rouing arrowe, and as high as a Church, I sawe also the ruines of the Citie of Memphis hard by those Pyramides.

The house of Ioseph is yet standing in Cayro, which is a sumptuous thing, hauing a place to walke in of 56. mighty pillars, all gilt with gold, but I saw it not, being then lame.

The 11. day of August the lande was cut at Cayro, to let in the water of the riuer of Nilus, which was done with great ioy and triumph.

The 12. of August I set from Cayro towards Alexandria againe, and came thither the 14. of August The 26. day there was kept a great feast of the Turkes and Moores, which lasted two dayes, and for a day they neuer ceased shooting off of great Ordinance.

[Sidenote: The English Consul at Argier.] From Alexandria I sailed to Argier, where I lay with M. Typton Consull of the English nation, who vsed me most kindly, and at his owne charge. Hee brought mee to the kings Court, and into the presence of the King, to see him, and the maners of the Court: the King doeth onely beare the name of a king, but the greatest gouernment is in the hands of the souldiers.

The king of Potanca is prisoner in Argier, who comming to Constantinople, to acknowledge a duety to the great Turke, was betrayed by his owne nephew, who wrote to the Turke, that he went onely as a spy, by that meanes to get his kingdome. I heard at Argier of seuen Gallies that were at that time cast away at a towne called Formentera: three of them were of Argier, the other foure were the Christians.

We found here 13. Englishmen, which were by force of weather put into the bay of Tunis, where they were very ill vsed by the Moores, who forced them to leaue their barke: whereupon they went to the Councell of Argier, to require a redresse and remedy for the iniurie. They were all belonging to the shippe called the Golden Noble of London, whereof Master Birde is owner. The Master was Stephen Haselwood, and the Captaine Edmond Bence.

The thirde day of December, the pinnesse called the Mooneshine of London, came to Argier with a prize, which they tooke vpon the coast of Spaine, laden with sugar, hides, and ginger: the pinnesse also belonging to the Golden Noble: and at Argier they made sale both of shippe and goods, where wee left them at our comming away, which was the seuenth day of Ianuarie, and the first day of February, I landed at Dartmouth, and the seuenth day came to London, with humble thankes to Almightie God, for my safe arriuall.

* * * * *

A letter of the English Ambassadour to M. Haruie Millers, appointing him Consull for the English nation in Alexandria, Cairo, and other places of Egypt.

Hauing to appoint our Consull in Cayro, Alexandria, Egypt, and other parts adiacent, for the safe protection of body and goods of her Maiesties subiects; being well perswaded of your sufficient abilitie; in her Maiesties name I doe elect and make choise of you, good friend Haruie Millers, to execute the same worshipfull office, as shall be required for her Maiesties better seruice, the commodity of her subiects, and my contentation: hauing and enioying for merit of your trauell in the premises the like remuneration incident to the rest of ours in such office in other parts of this Empire. Requiring you (all other affaires set aside) to repaire thither with expedition, and attend vpon this your charge, which the Almighty grant you well to accomplish. For the due execution whereof, wee heerewith send you the Grand Signiors Patent of priuilege with ours, and what els is needfull therefore, in so ample maner, as any other Consull whosoeuer doeth or may enioy the same. In ayd whereof, according to my bounden duety to her Maiesty our most gracious Mistresse, I will be ready alwayes to employ my selfe to the generall benefit of her Maiesties subiects, for your maintenance in all iust causes incident to the same. And thus eftsoones requiring and commanding you as aboue sayd, to performe my request, I bid you most heartily well to fare, and desire God to blesse you. From my mansion Rapamat night Pera this 25 of April 1583.

* * * * *

A letter to the right honourable William Hareborne her Majesties Ambassadour with the Grand Signior from Alger.

Right honorable, we haue receiued your honors letters dated in Constantinople the 5. of Nouember, and accordingly deliuered that inclosed to the king of this place, requiring of him, according as you did command vs in her Maiesties name, that he would vouchsafe to giue order to all his Captaines and Raies that none of them should meddle with our English shippes comming or going to or from these parts, for that they haue order not to passe by the Christian coast, but vpon the coast of Barbary, and shewing him of the charter giuen by the Grand Signior, requiring him in like case that for the better fulfilling of the amity, friendship and holy league betweene the Grand Signior and her Maiesty, he would giue us fiue or six safe-conducts for our ships, that meeting with any of his gallies or galliots, they might not meddle with them neither shoot at them: who made me answere he would neither giue me any safe conduct nor commission to his men of war not to meddle with them, for that he trusted to take some of them this yere, and made good account thereof. In like maner I spake to the chiefe of the Ianisers and the Leuents, who made me answere, the best hope they had this yere was to take some of them, and although they haue the Grand Signiors commandement we care not therefore: for we will by policy, or one meanes or other prouoke them to shoot some ordinance, which if they do but one piece, the peace is broken, and they be good prizes. And some of them say further, we care not for his safe-conduct, for if they shew it vs, we will conuey it away, we are sure the dogs cannot be beleeued against vs. The premisses considered, your honour is with all speed to procure the Grand Signior his fauorable letters directed to Hazan, the Cady, Captaines, Ianisers, and Leuents, and another like to Romadan Bassa, king of Tripolis, commanding them in no maner whatsoeuer to deale with our English ships bound into those parts or returning thence with their commodities, although they should shoot one at another: for when our ships shall meet them, for that, as your honor is aduertised, the gallies of Carthagena, Florence, Sicilia and Malta haue made a league to take all our ships comming in or going out of the Grand Signiors dominions, therefore if they meet with any of these gallies of Alger or Tripolis, thinking they be of them, and not knowing them a far off, they may shoot at them, which if therefore they should make them prizes, were against Gods lawes, the Grand Signior his league, all reason and conscience, considering that all the world doth know that Marchants ships laden with marchandise do not seeke to fight with men of warre, but contrariwise to defend themselues from them, when they would do them harme. Wherefore if your honour do not get out two letters of the Grand Signior as aforesayd, and send them hither with all speed by some one of your gentlemen accompanied with a chaus of the Court, or some other of the Grand Signiors servants, it is impossible that our English ships can escape freely from these or the Christians: for either they must of force go on the Christian coast, and so fall into their hands, or els on this coast, and fall into the kings of this towne, or Tripolis, their hands which if they should, will neuer be recouered. And if your honor cannot obtaine this thing, I beseech your honour in the behalfe of all the English marchants (who sent me hither to follow such order as your honour should giue me) to certifie her Maiesty, to the end that they may be commanded to leaue off traffique, and not to lose their goods, and her poore subiects the Mariners. And thus humbly taking my leaue, I desist from troubling your honor. From Algier the tenth of February 1583.

* * * * *

A letter of M. Harborne to Mustapha, challenging him for his dishonest dealing in translating of three of the Grand Signior his commandements.

Domine Mustapha, nescimus quid sibi velit, cum nobis mandata ad finem vtilem concessa perperàm reddas, quæ male scripta, plus damni, quàm vtilitatis adferant: quemadmodum constat ex tribus receptis mandatis, in quibus summum aut principale deest aut aufertur. In posterum noli ita nobiscum agere. Ita enim ludibrio erimus omnibus in nostrum et tuum dedecus. Cum nos multarum actionum spem Turcicè scriptarum in tua prudentia reponimus, ita prouidere debes, vt non eueniant huiusmodi mala. Quocirca deinceps cum mandatum aut scriptum aliquod accipias, verbum ad verbum conuertatur in Latinum sermonem, ne damnum insequatur. Nosti multos habere nos inimicos conatibus nostris inuidentes, quorum malitiæ vestræ est prudentiæ aduersari. Hi nostri, Secretarius et minimus interpres ex nostra parte dicent in tribus illis receptis mandatis errata. Vt deinceps similes errores non eueniant precamur. Ista emendes, et cætera Serenissimæ regiæ Maiestatis negocia, vti decet vestræ conditionis hominem, meliùs cures. Nam vnicuique suo officio strenuè est laborandum vt debito tramite omnia succedant: quod spero te facturum. Bene vale.

* * * * *

The Pasport in Italian granted to Thomas Shingleton Englishman, by the king of Algier. 1583.

Noi Assan Basha Vicere et lochotenente e capitan della iurisditione de Algier doniamo e concediamo libero saluo condutto a Thomas Shingleton mercadante, che possi con suo vassello e marinare de che natione se siano, e mercadantia di qual si voglia natione, andare et venire, e negotiari, e contrattare liberamente in questa citta de Algier et altri locha de la nostra iurisditione cosi di ponente comi di Leuante: et cosi anchora commandiamo al capitan di maare di Algier et d'altri lochi de nostra iurisditione, Rais de Vasselli et Capitani de Leuante, et altri capitani di vasselli tanto grossi como picholi, si comnanda a qual si voglia, che truando il sopradetto Thomas Shingleton Inglese nelli mari di Genua, Francia Napoli, Calabria, e Sardigna con suo vassello e mercantia, et homini de che nationi si siano, non gli debba molestare, ne piggliare, ne toccare cosa de nessuna manero tanto di denare, como di qual si voglia altra robba, sotto la pena e disgratia di perdir la vita et la robba: Et per quanto hauete a caro la gratia del Gran Signor nostro patrone Soltan Murates Ottomano, lo lasciarete andare per suo camino senza dargli nessuno impedimento. Dato in Algieri in nostro regio Palazzo, sigillato del nostro reggio sigillo, e fermato della gran ferma, et scritto del nostro reggio Secretario, il di 23 de Ienaro, 1583.

The same in English.

We Assan Bassha Viceroy and lieutenant, and captaine of the iurisdiction of Algier, giue and grant free safeconduct to Thomas Singleton marchant, that with his ship and mariners, of what nation soeuer they be, and with his marchandize of what countrey soeuer, he may go and come, and trade and traffique freely in this city of Algier, and other places of our iurisdiction, as well of the West as of the East. And in like sort we further command the captaine of the sea of Algier, and other places of our iurisdiction, the Reiz of vessels and captaines of the Leuant, and other captaines of vessels aswell great as small, whosoeuer they be, we do command them, that finding the forsayd Thomas Shingleton Englishman in the seas of Genua, France, Naples, Calabria, and Sardinia, with his ship and merchandize, and men of what nation soeuer they be, that they molest them not, neither take nor touch any kind of thing of theirs, neither money nor any other kind of goods, vnder paine and peril of loosing of their liues and goods: and as you make account of the fauour of the Grand Signor our lord Sultan Murates Hottoman, so see you let him passe on his way without any maner of impediment. Dated at Alger in our kingly palace, signed with our princely

Signet, and sealed with our great seale, and writen by our Secretarie of estate, the 23. of Ianuarie, 1583.

* * * * *

A letter written in Spanish by Sir Edward Osborne, to the king of Alger, the 20. of Iuly, 1584 in the behalfe of certeine English captiues there detained.

Muy alto y poderoso Rey,

Sea seruida vostra alteza. Como la muy alta y potentissima magestad del Gran Sennor tiene hecho articulos de priuilegios con la Serenissima Magestad de nuestra Reyna d'Inglatierra, para los vassalos della poder libremente yr y boluer, y tratar por mar y tierra en los dominios de su potentissima Magestad, Como a la clara paresce por los dichos articulos, de che embiamos el tractado al Senor Iuan Tipton nuestro commissario, para le muestrar a vostra Alteza. Contra el tenor de los quales articulos por dos galeras de su ciudad de Alger ha sido hechado al fondo en la mar vn des nuestros nauios que venia de Patras, que es en la Morea, cargado de corintes y otras mercaderias, que alla se compraron, y las mas de la gente del la matados y ahogados en la mar, y el resto est an detenidos por esclauos: cosa muy contraria a los dichos articulas y priuilegios. Que es occasion, que por esto supplicamos a vostra Alteza muy humilmente, que, pues que la potentissimo magestad del grand Sennor es seruida nos fauorescer por los dichos articulos, tambien sea seruida vostra Alteza assistimos en ellos, otorgandonos por vostra autoridad su auida y fauor, segun que esperamos, para que puedan estar libres, y boluer para aca aquellos pobres hombres ansi hechos esclauos, como dicho es. Y ansi mismo, que mande vostra Alteza dar orden a los capitanes, maestres y gente de las galeras, que nos dexen de aqui adelante hazer nuestro trafico con seys naos cada anno para Turquia a los dominios del Gran Sennor a paz y a saluo, por no cotrariar a los dichos nuestros priuilegios, Lleuando cada vna de nuestras dichas naos pot se conoscer vn saluo condutto de su alta et potentissima magestad. Y con esta vostra tan senallada merced y fauor que en esso reciberemos, quedaremos nosotros con grandissima obligation a vostra Alteza de seruir la por ello, segun que el dicho Sennor Iuan Tipton, a quien nos reportamos de todo lo demas, mejor informira vostra Alteza: Cuya serenissima persona y estado supplicamos y pidimos a Dios omnipotente prosperu y accrescente con toda felicitad y honra. Del la ciuidad de Londres a los veynte dias de Iulio del mil y quinientos y ocbenta y quatro annos.

Al seruitio de vuestra Alteza per y en hombre de todos los tratantes en Tutquia, lo el Mayor de Londres,

Edward Osborne.

The same in English.

Right high and mightie king,

May it please your highnesse to vnderstand, that the most high and most mightie maiestie of the Grand Signor hath confirmed certaine articles of priuileges with the most excellent maiestie of our Queene of England, that her subjects may freely go and come, and traffique by sea and land in the dominions of his most mighty maiesty, as appeareth more at large by the said articles, whereof we haue sent the copy vnto M. Iohn Tipton our Commissarie to shew the same vnto your highnes. [Sidenote: An English ship sunke by two gallies of Alger.] Against the tenor of which articles, one of our ships which came from Patras which is in Morea, laden with corants and other merchandizes which were bought in those parts, was sunke by 2. gallies of your citie of Alger, and the greatest number of the men thereof were slain and drowned in the sea, the residue being detained as slaues: An acte very contrary to the meaning of the aforesaid articles and priuileges: which is the occasion that by these presents we beseech your highnesse very humbly that since it hath pleased the most mightie maiestie of the Grand Signor to fauour vs with the sayd priuileges, it would please your Highnesse in like maner to assist vs in the same, graunting vs by your authoritie, your ayde and fauour, according as our hope is that these poore men so detained in captiuitie, as is aforesaid, may be set at libertie, and returne into their countrey. And likewise that your highnesse would send to giue order to the captaines, masters and people of your gallies, that from hencefoorth they would suffer vs to vse our traffique with six ships yerely into Turkie vnto the dominions of the Grand Signor in peace and safetie, that they do not withstand those our said priuileges, euery one of our foresaid ships carying with them a passeport of his most high and most mightie maiestie to be knowen by. And for that your so singular fauour and curtesie which in so doing we shall receiue, we on our part with all bounden duetie vnto your highnesse, will seeke to honour you in that behalfe, according as the sayd Master Iohn Tipton (to whom wee referre our selues touching all other circumstances) shall more at large informe your highnesse, whose most excellent person and estate, we pray and beseech Almighty God to prosper and increase with all felicitie and honour. From the Citie of London, the 20. of Iuly, 1584.

At the seruice of your highnesse, for and in the name of our whole company trading into Turkie, I Maior of London. Edward Osburne.

* * * * *

Notes concerning the trade of Alger.

The money that is coined in Alger is a piece of gold called Asiano, and Doublaes, and two Doublaes make an Asiano, but the Doubla is most vsed, for all things be sold by Doublaes, which Doubla is fiftie of their Aspers there.

The Asper there is not so good by halfe and more, as that in Constantinople; for the Chekin of gold of the Turkes made at Constantinople
is at Alger worth an 150 Aspers, and at Constantinople, it is but 66. Aspers.

The pistolet and roials of plate are most currant there.

The said pistolet goeth for 130. Aspers there: and the piece of 4 roials goeth for 40 Aspers, but oftentimes is sold for more, as men need them to carie vp into Turkie.

Their Asianos and Doublaes are pieces of course gold, worth here but 40. s. the ounce, so the same is currant in no place of Turkie out of the kingdom of Alger, neither the Aspers, for that they be lesse then others be, for they coine them in Alger.

The custome to the king is inward 10. per centum, to the Turke, to be paid of the commoditie it selfe, or as it shall be rated.

There is another custome to the Ermine, of one and an halfe per centum, which is to the Iustice of the Christians: the goods for this custome are rated as they are for the kings custome.

Hauing paid custome inwards, you pay none outwards for any commoditie that you doe lade, more then a reward to the gate keepers.

The waight there is called a Cantare for fine wares, as mettals refined, and spices &c. which is here 120. li. subtil.

Mettall not refined, as lead, iron, and such grosse wares, are sold by a great Cartare, which is halfe as big againe: so it is 180. li. subtil of ours here.

The measure of corne is by a measure called a Curtia, which is about 4. bushels of our measure, and corne is plentiful there and good cheape, except when there hapneth a very dry yeere.

The surest lodging for a Christian there is in a Iewes house: for if he haue any hurt, the Iew and his goods shall make it good, so the Iew taketh great care of the Christian and his goods that lieth in his house, for feare of punishment.

An Englishman called Thomas Williams, which is M. Iohn Tiptons man, lieth about trade of merchandize in the streete called The Soca of the Iewes.

* * * * *

Notes concerning the trade in Alexandria.

Alexandria in Egypt is a free port, and when a man commeth within the castles, presently the Ermyn sends aboord to haue one come and speake with him to know what goods are aboord: and then hee will set guards aboord the ship to see all the goods discharged. And then from the Ermin you goe to the Bye, [Marginal note: This is another officer.] onely for that he will inquire newes of you, and so from thence to the Consuls house where you lie. The Venetians haue a Consul themselues. But all other nations goe to the French nations Consul, who will giue you a chamber for your selues apart, if you will so haue it.

The customs inward of all commodities are ten in the hundred, and the custome is paid in wares also that you buy: for the same wares in barter you pay also ten in the hundred, at the lading of the wares. [Marginal note: Other smal customs you pay besides, which may be at two in the hundred: and for Consulage you pay two in the hundred.] But if you sell for mony, you pay no more custome but the ten aforesaid, and one and a halfe in the hundred, which is for the custome of the goods you lade for the sayd mony, for more custome you pay not. But for all the money you bring thither you pay nothing for the custome of the same. And if you sell your wares for mony, and with the same money buy wares, you pay but two in the hundred for the custome thereof. And if you steale any custome, if it be taken, you pay double custome for that you steale.

The weight of Alexandria is called Pois Forforeine, which is a kintal in that place, which maketh at Marseils 109. li. of Marseils waight, at 15 ounces the pound, which is 103. li. of 16. ounces to the li. There is another waight called Pois Gerrin, which is 150. li. of Marseils waight, by which are sold all things to eate: but spice is sold by the former waight.

From Alexandria to Cairo is three daies journey, but you must take a Ianissarie with you: and to go vp thither by water it is 8. dayes journey. Roials of Spaine are currant mony there, and are the best money you can cary. And 4. roials are worth 13. Medins, and 2. Medins, are 3. Aspers. Pistolets and crownes of France and Dollers will goe, but of all Roials are best.

Rice is not permitted to goe out of the land, but is kept for a victuall. But with a present to the Bye and Ermine some may passe.

All sortes of spices be garbled after the bargaine is made, and they be Moores which you deale withall, which be good people and not ill disposed. And after you be searched and haue leaue to passe, you must presently depart out of the port, and if you doe not, they will search you againe. And you must depart in the day, for in the night the castles will not suffer you to depart. The duetie to the Consul is 2 in the hundred, for his aide, and meate, and drinke and all. And the port of Alexandria is good when one is within it with good ankers and cables. Silver is better currant then gold in Alexandria, but both are good.

Commonly the Carauans come thither in October from Mecca to Cairo, and from thence to Alexandria, where the merchants be that buy the spices, and therefore the spices are brought most to Alexandria, where each Christian nation remaineth at the Consuls houses. Yet oftentimes the Christians go vp to Cairo to buy drugs and other commodities there, as they see cause. And the commodities there vendible are all sorts of kersies, but the most part blewes, and of clothes all colours except mingled colours and blacks. Pepper is usually sold for 24. ducats the quintal, Ginger for 14. ducats. You most take canuas to make bags to put your commoditie in from Alexandria, for there is none. There is also fine flaxe, and good store of Buffe hides.

* * * * *

A letter of the English ambassador to M. Edward Barton.

Master Barton I send you 3. commandements in Turkish, with a copy thereof in English, to the ende our ships might not come in danger of breach of league, if they should shoote at the gallies of those of Algier, Tunis, and Tripolis in the West: which after you haue shewed the Bassas, receiue againe into your hands, and see them registred, and then deliuer one of them to our friend M. Tipton, and the like you are to do with the priuilege which you cary with you, and see them iointly registered in the Cadies booke, deliuering the copy of the said priuilege sealed by the Cadi, also to the sayd our friend M. Tipton, taking a note of his hand for the receipt thereof, and for deliuerie at all times to vs or our assignes. And require them in her maiesties and the grand Signors name, that they will haue our ships passing too and fro vnder licence and safeconduct for recommended in friendly maner. Touching your proceedings in Tripolis with Romadan, as I haue not receiued any aduise thereof, since your departure, so must I leaue you to God and my former direction. The ship patronised of Hassan Rayes, which you wrote to be ours, prooued to be a Catalonian. As for ours, by report of that Hassan and other Iewes in his ship, it was affirmed to be sold to the Malteses, which with the rest you are to receiue there. And hauing ended these affaires and registred our priuilege, and these three commandements, in Tripolis, Tunis, and Alger, I pray you make speedy returne, and for that which may be recouered, make ouer the same either to Richard Rowed for Patrasso in Morea, or otherwise hither to Iohn Bate in the surest maner you may, if the registring of that your priuilege and these commandements will not suffer you in person to returne with the same. From my mansion Rapamat in Pera this 24. of Iune 1584.

* * * * *

The commaundement obtained of the Grand Signior by her Maiesties ambassador

M. Wil. Hareborne, for the quiet passing of her subiects to and from his dominions, sent in An. 1584 to the Viceroyes of Algier, Tunis, and Tripolis in Barbary.

To our Beglerbeg of Algier.

We certifie thee by this our commandement, that the right honorable Will. Hareborne ambassador to the Queenes maiestie of England hath signified vnto vs, that the ships of that countrey in their comming and returning to and from our Empire, on the one part of the Seas haue the Spaniards, Florentines, Sicilians, and Malteses, on the other part our countreis committed to your charge: which abouesaid Christians will not quietly suffer their egresse and regresse, into, and out of our dominions, but doe take and make the men captiues, and forfeit the shippes and goods, as the last yeere the Maltese did one, which they tooke at Gerbi, and to that end do continually lie in wait for them to their destruction, whereupon they are constrained to stand to their defence at any such time as they might meet with them. Wherefore considering by this means they must stand vpon their guard, when they shall see any gallie afarre off, whereby if meeting with any of your gallies and not knowing them, in their defence they do shoot at them, and yet after when they doe certainly know them, do not shoote any more, but require to passe peaceably on their voiage, which you would deny, saying, the peace is broken because you haue shot at vs, and so make prize of them contrary to our priuileges, and against reason: for the preuenting of which inconuenience the said ambassadour hath required this our commaundement. We therefore command thee, that vpon sight hereof thou doe not permit any such matter in any sort whatsoeuer, but suffer the sayd Englishmen to passe in peace according to the tenour of our commandement giuen, without any disturbance or let by any meanes vpon the way, although that meeting with thy gallies, and not knowing them afarre off, they taking them for enemies should shoote at them, yet shall you not suffer them to hurt them therefore, but quietly to passe. Wherefore looke thou that they may haue right, according to our priuilege giuen them, and finding any that absenteth himself, and wil not obey this our commandement, presently certify vs to our porch, that we may giue order for his punishment, and with reverence giue faithfull credite to this our commandement, which hauing read, thou shalt againe returne it vnto them that present it. From our palace in Constantinople, the 1. of Iune 1584.

* * * * *

A letter of the honorable M. Wil. Hareborne her maiesties ambass. with the grand Signior to M. Tipton, appointing him Consul of the English in Algier, Tunis, and Tripolis of Barbarie.

Master Tipton, I haue receiued among others, yours of the 10. of Nouember 1584. by Soliman Sorda, certifying the receipt of mine of the 24. of Iune 1584. with the 3. commandements, which not being registred, let it now be done. Where you write the force of the priuilege to be broken by our ships in shooting, and therefore be lawfully taken, you are deceiued, for of those taken in then, hath the grand Signior now deliuered vs free, Wil. Moore, and Rob. Rawlings, and further promised the rest in like case, wheresoeuer they be, and that hereafter no violence shalbe shewed, considering ours be merchants ships which go peaceably in their voiage, and were ignorant of the orders of Algier, neither knew afar off, whether they were friends or the Christians gallies in league with vs, of whom they most doubted, who not suffring our ships to come into these parts, wil make prize of the goods and captiue the men, so as they are not to let them come nigh them: and since ours haue not done contrary to the articles of the same priuilege, wherein is no order for Algier prescribed vs, as both by the originall now sent vs, and also by the copy now sent you from London you may perceiue, they according to right are as abouesaid to be set free, and their goods restored, which if it be not there accomplished as the grand Signior hath now commanded, and most faithfully promised, neither yet in case of their denial, those offenders punished here, and our injuries redressed, we are to demand our Congie, and command our merchants her maiesties subiects, to end their traffike here, which in our countrey commodities is prooued and found by the great Signior to be so beneficial to his countries as we are assured so well thereof, as also for the honor which his ancestors neuer had of friendship with so mighty a prince as is her maiesty, he wil not but maintaine the faith promised her, and the intercourse in due force. And where you say that the grand Signor his letters, in the behalf of the French, were no more accepted there, then of a mean man, nor tooke no place, that is not material to vs, our letters are after another sort much more effectuall. For our case and theirs be found far different, in that they be not onely now out of fauour with him, but also the commodities which they bring hither, as sugar, paper, bracelets, ropes of bast, almonds, &c., all which may be here wel spared, and we contrarily so wel esteemed, as he neuer denied vs any thing since our comming demanded, which neither their ambassador, nor the Venetian could haue here, and therefore we rest perswaded, knowing the wisdom of the Beglebeg, who is aduised by his friends from hence, of this our credite with his master, he wil so respect his commandements, as to accomplish the tenor thereof according to our desire. And where you say that the Ianizers rule all there, I know right wel that if things be not done as the grand Signior commandeth, his lieutenant must answer it. And therefore I am fully perswaded if he doe what he may they dare not resist him, for if they should, those rebels should not be vnpunished of the grand Signior. And though they speake their pleasures among themselues there, yet they be not so brutish, but they wel consider that their master the grand Signior may not be gainsaid or mocked of any. For vpon his word dependeth the life or death euen of the chiefest, as I haue seene since my comming hither. So whatsoeuer these Ianizaries say, they will be better aduised in their deedes then to withstand their Viceroy, if he himselfe wil vse his lawfull power, which if hee doe not, hee cannot purge himselfe here of their euill proceedings against the grand Signiors friends: for the feet may not rule the bodie, but contrarywise, the head, the feete, and all the rest of the members. And for that neither for feare, affection or otherwise you omit as a faithfull true subiect to her maiestie to do your dutie, I do by my warrant going herewith charge you, and in her maiesties name, to the vttermost to vse your good and faithfull endeuour, as becommeth a true subiect, and in all things that may concerne her maiesties good seuice, assisting the Chaus with the rest of our messengers in counsel, trauel, and what els shall be thought requisite for your good discharge of your duetie. And to the end you may boldly proceed herein as also for the good opinion sir Edward Osborne and the company haue of you, and I no lesse perswaded of youre wisedome, vpright dealing, and good experience in those parts, do send you herewith the grand Signiors and our patents for exercising the office of Consul there, in Tripolis and Tunis: by virtue of which authoritie you may without feare proceed as the office doeth chalenge in defence of our priuilege, to redresse all iniuries offred our nation. Which if you cannot get reformed there of the Beglerbies vpon your complaint, I thereof aduertised, shal doe it here, and to the vttermost maintaine you in al rightful causes whatsoeuer, doubt you not. And hereafter according to your aduise, I wil and doe giue our ships order not to fight with any gallies of Alger, but to hoise out their skiffe and go aboord to shew them their safeconduct, and to present the captain with a garment, and you there in such like case are to take order that they do not forceably take any thing from them. [Sidenote: The Inuentorie of our ships and goods sunke and taken by the gallies of Alger.] Nothing doubting but the Viceroy (whose friendship in her maiesties behalfe I desire) will not onely performe the same your iust request, and according to right, restore to libertie our men since the priuilege taken, but also cause those that tooke and sunke our ships to answere the value, which I haue set down truly, and rather with the least in the Inuentorie translated into Turkish, whereof the inclosed is the copy in English, which I send to the end you may be the better informed of my demand by this our Chaus Mahomet, with whom in all things you are to conferre of matters expedient, for the honor of her maiesties countrey, and the commoditie, and libertie of poore captiues, which if the Viceroy do wel consider, according to his wisdome, as the grand Signior doeth thereof, he shal wel perceiue it not onely a great honour to his master as aforesaid, to continue this amitie with her maiestie, but chiefly to the whole estate of his kingdom exceeding profitable, which by this means shall be abundantly serued with the chiefest commodities they want, with many other things of more importance to the grand Signior his contentation, not herein to be mentioned. For I know the Viceroies experienced wisdom can wel consider thereof, in such sort as he wil not deny to accomplish his masters commandement, and our earnest request in so small a matter as this we require, whereof I expect no refusall: for thereby he shall increase his honor with the grand Signior, be in credite with her maiestie, be void of trouble which hereafter by future suite against him may happen, and his gallies free of such doubtful issue as doeth chance, fighting with our ships. Which, as it is well knowen to all the world, haue so great hearts as neuer cowardly to yeeld to their enemies. And that therefore in that respect (after the prouerbe, like esteeme of their like) they are the more of such a valiant prince as is their Viceroy and his couragious souldiers to be in all friendship cherished and better esteemed. If the captaine Bassa had bene returned from Capha, I would in like maner haue procured his letters, which for that he is not, I doubt nothing but that the grand Signiors will suffise. Thus commending your selfe and these proceedings to the almighty his merciful direction, I bid you most heartily wel to fare. From my mansion Rapamat nigh Pera, this 30. of March, 1585.

* * * * *

Series vel registrum valoris nauium, bonorum, et hominum per triremes Argerienses ereptorum, vna cum captiuorum hominum nominibus, Beglerbego
Argeriensi Hassano.

1 Salomon de Plimmouth habuit 36. homines, onerata cum sale, onere trecentorum doliorum, valore Florenorum 5600.

2 Elizabetha de Garnesey cum decem hominibus Anglis, reliquis Britonibus, valore Florenorum 2000.

3 Maria Martin de London onere centum et triginta doliorum, rectore Thoma More cum triginta quinque hominibus, reuertens de Patrasso cum mandato Cæsareo, valore Florenorum 1400.

4 Elizabeth Stokes de London, rectore Dauid Fillie de London, Patrassum veniens cum mandato Cæsareo: huius præcipuus valor erat in talleris

numeratis, quos habuit Richardus Gibben, qui adduxit etiam Serenissimæ Reginæ: maiestatis literas Cæsari et oratori. Valor reliquus in mercibus vna cum superiori in talleris, effecit Florenorum 21500.

5 Nicolaus de London, rectore Thoma Forster, onerata cum vuis siccis, valore Florenorum 4800.

In tempore Romadan Beglerbegi Argiræ spoliatæ et ereptæ naues, merces, et
 homines.

1 Iudith de London, rectore Iacobo Beare, cum hominibus 24. valore Florenorum 3100.

2 Iesus de London, rectore Andræa Dier, cum 21. hominibus. Valorem huius et 14. homines, reliquis mortuis, reddidit Romadan Bassa Tripolitanus Secretario legati, Edwardo Barten, valore Florenorum 9000.

Nomina hominum mancipatorum et viuentium tunc temporis, quando Cæsar illustrissimus, et dominus Orator Chauseum Mahumetem miserunt Algiram.

1 Ante foedus initum in naue Peter de Bristow. Iohn Winter, Robert Barton.

2 In naue Swallow de London. Rich. Crawford, Anthony Eluers, Wil. Rainolds.

Post foedus initum in naue Britona. Iames Yoong.

1 In naue Rabnet de Hampton. Thomas Lisney.

1 In naue Salomon. Iohn Tracie, Wil. Griffith, Wil. Cocke.

1 In naue Elizabeth. Iohn Woodward, Giles Naper, Leonard Iames, Oliuer Dallimore, and Richard Maunsell.

2 In naue Maria Martin. Thomas Moore, Wil. White, Wil. Palmer, Nich. Long,
Peter March, Rich. Haslewood, Wil. Dewly, Wil. Cowel, Iohn Franke, Henry
Parker, Iohn Cauendish, Moises Robinson, Iames Sotherich, Henry Howel, Nich. Smith, Henry Ragster, Rich. Dauison, Rich. Palmer.

3 In naue Elizabeth Stokes. Dauid Fillie, Walter Street, Laurence Wilkins, Morgan Dauis, Iohn Quinte, Ambrose Harison, Iohn Peterson, Tristram Vois, Roger Ribbe.

4 In naue Nicholas, Thomas Forster rector nauis et eius nautæ.

* * * * *

To Assan Aga, Eunuch and Treasurer to Hassan Bassa king of Alger, which Assan Aga was the sonne of Fran. Rowlie of Bristow merchant, taken in the
Swalow.

I receiued your letters of Will. Hamor gentleman my seruant very thankfully, aswel for the feruant faith that by his report I heare you haue in our lord Iesus Christ, by whose onely merits and bloodshedding, you together with vs and all other good Christians so truly beleeuing, shalbe saued, as also for your faithfull obedience like a true subiect to her Maiestie, naturally louing your countrey and countreymen, declared in your fauourable furtherance of the said Wil. Hamore, procuring their redemption. Of which your good and vertuous actions, as I reioice to vnderstand, so wil I impart the same to your singuler commendation, both to our mistresse her Maiestie, and her most honorable counsellors the nobilitie of England, to whom assure your selfe the report shalbe very welcome. And now this second time I am inforced by duetie to God and her maiesty, as also by the smal regard your master had of the Grand Signors former commandements, to complaine vnto him, though not so vehemently as I had occasion by his most vnworthy answer. But I hope, and the rather by your means, he will not contrary this second commandement, threatning him, not obseruing the same, losse of office and life. The due execution whereof by your vertuous and careful industry procured, wil manifest to all the world, especially to her maiesty, and me her ambassador, your true Christian mind and English heart, intentiuely bent to Gods honor, and the libertie of the poore men, for which I trust you be ordained another Ioseph, to folow his example in true pietie, in such sort that notwithstanding your body be subiect to Turkish thraldom, yet your vertuous mind free from those vices, next vnder God addict to the good seruice of your liege Lady and soueraigne princes, her most excellent maiesty, wil continually seeke by all good meanes to manifest the same in this and the like faithful seruice to your singuler commendation, wherby both my selfe and others in that place hauing found you in all good offices faithfully affectionated, may in like case performe the like towards you, when and where you may haue occasion to vse me: which as I for my part do assuredly promise, and wil no lesse faithfully performe: so accordingly I expect herein, and hereafter the like of you, whom most heartily saluted I commend to the diuine tuition and holy direction. From my house Rapamar, this 28. of June 1586.

Your louing and good friend her Maiesties Ambassador with the Grand Signor,

Wil. Hareborne.

* * * * *

The originall of the first voyage for traffique into the kingdom of Marocco in Barbarie, begun in the yeere 1551. with a tall ship called the Lion of London, whereof went as captaine Master Thomas Windam, as appeareth by this extract of a letter of Iames Aldaie, to the worshipfull master Michael Locke, which Aldaie professeth himselfe to haue bene the first inuentor of this trade.

Worshipful Sir, hauing lately bene acquainted with your intent to prosecute the olde intermitted discouerie for Catai, if therein with my knowledge, trauell or industrie I may doe you seruice, I am readie to doe it and therein to aduenture my life to the vttermost point. Trueth it is, that I haue bene by some men (not my friends) euill spoken of at London, saying that although I be a man of knowledge in the Arte of Nauigation and Cosmographie, and that I haue bene the inuentor of some voyages that be now growen to great effect; yet say they maliciously and without iust cause, that I haue not bene willing at any season to proceed in those voyages that I haue taken in hand, taking example especially of two voyages. The one was when I was master in the great Barke Aucher of the Leuant, in which voyage I went not, but the causes they did not know of my let from the same, nor of the other. But first the very trueth is, that I was from the same voyage letted by the Princes letters, which my Master Sebastian Gabota had obtained for that purpose, to my great griefe. And as touching the second voyage which I inuented for the trade of Barbarie, the liuing God knoweth that I say most true, that when the great sweate was, (whereon the chiefe of those with whom I ioyned in that voyage died, that is to say, Sir Iohn Lutterell, Iohn Fletcher, Henry Ostrich and others) I my selfe was also taken with the same sweate in London, and after it, whether with euill diet in keeping, or how I know not, I was cast into such an extreame feuer, as I was neither able to ride nor goe: and the shippe being at Portesmouth, Thomas Windam had her away from thence, before I was able to stand vpon my legges, by whom I lost at that instant fourescore pound. Besides I was appointed by them that died (if they had liued) to haue had the whole gouernment both of shippe and goods, because I was to them the sole inuenter of that trade.

In the first voyage to Barbary there were two Moores, being noblemen, whereof one was of the Kings blood, conuayed by the said Master Thomas Windham into their Countrey out of England,

Yours humble at your commandement,

Iames Alday.

* * * * *

The second voyage to Barbary in the yeere 1552. Set foorth by the right worshipfull Sir Iohn Yorke, Sir William Gerard, Sir Thomas Wroth, Master Frances Lambert, Master Cole and others; Written by the relation of Master Iames Thomas then Page to Master Thomas Windham chiefe Captaine of this voyage.

The shippes that went on this voyage were three, whereof two were of the Riuer of Thames, That is to say, the Lyon of London, whereof Master Thomas Windham was Captaine and part owner, of about an hundred and fiftie tonnes: The other was the Buttolfe about fourescore tunnes, and a Portugall Carauel bought of certaine Portugals in Newport in Wales, and fraightened for this voyage, of summe sixtie tunnes. The number of men in the Fleete were an hundred and twentie. The Master of the Lyon was one Iohn Kerry of Mynhed in Somersetshire, his Mate was Dauid Landman. The chiefe Captaine of this small Fleete was Master Thomas Windham a Norffolke gentlemen borne, but dwelling at Marshfield-parke in Somerset shire. This Fleete departed out of King-rode neere Bristoll about the beginning of May 1552. being on a Munday in the morning: and the Munday fortnight next ensuing in the euening came to an ancker at their first port in the roade of Zafia, or Asafi on the coast of Barbarie, standing in 32. degrees of latitude, and there put on land part of our Marchandise to be conueied by land to the citie of Marocco: which being done, and hauing refreshed our selues with victuals and water, we went to the second port called Santa Cruz, where we discharged the rest of our goods, being good quantitie of linnen and woollen cloth, corall, amber, Iet, and diuers other things well accepted of the Moores. In which road we found a French ship, which not knowing whether it were warre or peace betweene England and France, drewe her selfe as neere vnder the towne wals as she could possible, crauing aide of the towne for her defence, if need were, which in deed seeing vs draw neere, shot at vs a piece from the wals, which came ouer the Lion our Admirall, between the maine mast and her foremast. [Sidenote: The English were at Santa Cruz the yere before being 1551.] Whereupon we comming to an anker, presently came a pinnes aboord vs to know what we were, who vnderstanding that we had bene there the yere before, and came with the good leaue of their king in marchant wise, were fully satisfied, and gaue vs good leaue to bring our goods peaceably on shore, where the Viceroy, whose name was Sibill Manache, within short time after came to visite vs, and vsed vs with all curtesie. But by diuers occasions we spent here very neere three moneths before we could get in our lading, which was Sugar, Dates, Almonds, and Malassos or sugar Syrrope. And for all our being here in the heate of the Sommer, yet none of our company perished by sicknesse. Our ships being laden, we drew into the Sea for a Westerne wind for England. But being at sea, a great leake fell vpon the Lion, so that we were driuen to Lancerota, and Forteuentura, where, betweene the two Ilands, we came to a road, whence wee put on land out of our sayd ship 70. chests of Sugar vpon Lancerota, with some dozen or sixteene of our company, where the inhabitants supposing we had made a wrongfull prize of our carauell, suddenly came with force vpon our people, among whom I my selfe was one, tooke vs prisoners, and spoiled the sugars: which thing being perceiued from our ships, they manned out three boates, thinking to rescue vs, and draue the Spaniards to flight, whereof they slew eighteene, and tooke their gouernour of the Iland prisoner, who was a very aged gentleman about 70 yeeres of age. But chasing the enemies so farre, for our recouerie, as pouder and arrowes wanted, the Spaniardes perceiuing this, returned, and in our mens retire they slew sixe of them. Then a Parle grew, in the which it was agreed, that we the prisoners should be by them restored, and they receiue their olde gouernour, giuing vs a testimonie vnder his and their hands, what damages wee had there receiued, the which damages were here restored, and made good by the king of Spaine his marchants vpon our returne into England. After wee had searched and mended our leake, being returned aboord, we came vnder saile, and as wee were going to the sea on the one side of the Iland, the Cacafuego and other ships of the king of Portugals Armada entered at the other, and came to anker in the road from whence we were but newly departed, and shot off their great ordinance in our hearing. And here by the way it is to bee vnderstood that the Portugals were much offended with this our new trade into Barbarie, and both in our voiage the yeere before, as also in this they gaue out in England by their marchants, that if they tooke vs in those partes, they would vse vs as their mortall enemies, with great threates and menaces. But by God and good prouidence wee escaped their hands. From this Iland shaping our coast for England, we were seuen or eight weekes before we could reach the coast of England. The first port wee entered into was the hauen of Plimmouth, from whence within short time wee came into the Thames, and landed our marchandise at London, about the ende of the moneth of October, 1552.

* * * * *

A voiage made out of England vnto Guinea and Benin in Affrike, at the charges of certaine marchants Aduenturers of the Citie of London, in the yeere of our Lord 1553.

I was desired by certaine of my friends to make some mention of this Voiage, that some memorie thereof might remaine to our posteritie, if either iniquitie of time consuming all things, or ignorance creeping in by barbarousness and contempt of knowledge should hereafter bury in obliuion so woorthie attempts, so much the greatlier to bee esteemed, as before neuer enterprised by Englishmen, or at the least so frequented, as at this present they are, and may bee, to the great commoditie of our marchants, if the same be not hindered by the ambition of such, as for the conquering of fortie or fiftie miles here and there, and erecting of certaine fortresses, thinke to be Lordes of half the world, enuying that other should enioy the commodities, which they themselues cannot wholly possesse. And although such as haue bene at charges in the discouering and conquering of such landes ought by good reason to haue certaine priuileges, preheminences, and tributes for the same, yet (to speake vnder correction) it may seeme somewhat rigorous, and agaynst good reason and conscience, or rather agaynst the charitie that ought to be among Christian men, that such as inuade the dominions of other should not permit other friendly to vse the trade of marchandise in places neerer, or seldome frequented of them, whereby their trade is not hindered in such places, where they themselues haue at their owne election appointed the Martes of their traffike. But forasmuch as at this present it is not my intent to accuse or defend, approoue or improoue, I will cease to speake any further hereof, and proceed to the description of the first voyage, as briefly and faithfully as I was aduertised of the same, by the information of such credible persons, as made diligent inquisition to know the trueth thereof, as much as shall be requisite, omitting to speake of many particular things, not greatly necessarie to be knowen: which neuerthelesse, with also the exact course of the navigation, shall be more fully declared in the second voiage. And if herein fauour or friendship shall perhaps cause some to thinke that some haue bene sharply touched, let them lay apart fauour and friendship, and giue place to trueth, that honest men may receiue prayse for well doing, and lewd persons reproch, as the iust stipend of their euill desertes, whereby other may be deterred to doe the like, and vertuous men encouraged to proceed in honest attempts.

But that these voyages may be more plainly vnderstood of all men, I haue thought good for this purpose, before I intreat hereof, to make a briefe description of Africa, being that great part of the world, on whose West side beginneth the coast of Guinea at Cabo Verde, about twelue degrees in latitude, on this side the Equinoctiall line, and two degrees in longitude from the measuring line, so running from the North to the South, and by East in some places, within 5, 4, and 3 degrees and a halfe vnto the Equinoctiall, and so foorth in maner directly East and by North, for the space of 36 degrees or thereabout, in longitude from the West to the East, as shall more plainly appeare in the description of the second voyage.

A briefe description of Afrike gathered by Richard Eden.

In Africa the lesse are these kingdoms: the kingdom of Tunis and Constantina, which is at this day under Tunis, and also the region of Bugia, Tripoli, and Ezzah. This part of Afrike is very barren by reason of the great deserts, as the deserts of Numidia and Barca. The principall ports of the kingdome of Tunis are these: Goletta, Bizerta, Potofarnia, Bona, and Stora. The chiefe cities of Tunis are Constantina and Bona, with diuers other. Vnder this kingdom are many Ilands, as Zerbi, Lampadola, Pantalarea, Limoso, Beit, Gamelaro, and Malta, where at this present is the great master of the Rhodes. Vnder the South of this kingdom are the great deserts of Lybia. All the nations in this Africa the lesse are of the sect of Mahomet, and a rusticall people, liuing scattred in villages. The best of this part of Afrike is Barbaria lying on the coast of the sea Mediterraneum.

Mauritania (now called Barbaria) is diuided into two parts, as Mauritania Tingitana, and Cæsariensis. Mauritania Tingitania is now called the kingdom of Fes, and the kingdom of Marocco. The principall citie of Fes is called Fessa: and the chiefe citie of Marocco is named Marocco.

Mauritania Cæsariensis is at this day called the kingdom of Tremisen, with also the citie called Tremisen or Telensin. This region is full of deserts, and reacheth to the Sea Mediterraneum, to the citie of Oram, with the port of Mersalquiber. The kingdom of Fes reacheth vnto the Ocean Sea, from the West to the citie of Argilla: and the port of the sayd kingdom is called Sala.

The kingdom of Marocco is also extended aboue the Ocean Sea, vnto the citie of Azamor and Azafi, which are vpon the Ocean Sea, toward the West of the sayd kingdom. Nere Mauritania Tingitana (that is to say, by the two kingdoms of Fes, and Marocco) are in the Sea, the Ilands of Canarie, called in old time, The fortunate Ilands. Toward the south of this region is the kingdom of Guinea, with Senega, Ialofo, Gambra, and many other regions of the Blacke Moores, called Aethiopians or Negros all which are watered with the riuer Negro, called in old time Niger. In the sayd regions are no cities, but onely certaine lowe cottages made of boughes of trees, plastered with chalke, and couered with strawe. In these regions are also very great deserts.

The kingdom of Marocco hath vnder it these seuen kingdoms: Hea, Sus, Guzula, the territorie of Marrocca, Duccala, Hazchora, and Tedle. The kingdom of Fes hath as many: as Fes, Temesne, Azgar, Elabath, Errif, Garet, and Elcair. The kingdom of Tremisen hath these regions: Tremisen, Tenez, and Elgazair, all which are Machometists. But all the regions of Guinea are pure Gentiles, and idolatrous, without profession of any religion, or other knowledge of God, then by the law of nature.

Africa the great is one of the three parts of the world, knowen in old time, and seuered from Asia, on the East by the riuer Nilus, on the West from Europe by the pillars of Hercules. The hither part is now called Barbarie, and the people Moores. The inner part is called Lybia and Aethiopia. Afrike the lesse is in this wise bounded: On the West it hath Numidia; On the East

Cyrenaica: On the North, the sea called Mediterraneum. In this countrey was the noble city of Carthage.

In the East side of Afrike beneath the red sea, dwelleth the great and mighty Emperour and Christian king Prester Iohn, well knowen to the Portugales in their voyages to Calicut. His dominions reach very farre on euery side: and hath vnder him many other Kings both christian and heathen that pay him tribute. This mightie prince is called Dauid the Emperour of Aethiopia. Some write that the king of Portugall sendeth him yeerely eight ships laden with marchandize. His kingdom confineth with the red Sea, and reacheth far into Afrike toward Aegypt and Barbarie. Southward it confineth with the Sea toward the Cape de Bona Speranza: and on the other side with the sea of sand, called Mare de Sabione, a very dangerous sea lying between the great citie of Alcair, or Cairo in Aegypt, and the country of Aethiopia: In the which way are many vnhabitable deserts, continuing for the space of fiue dayes iourney. And they affirme, that if the sayd Christian Emperour were not hindered by those deserts (in the which is great lacke of victuals, and especially of water) he would or now haue inuaded the kingdom of Egypt, and the citie of Alcair. The chiefe city of Ethiopia, where this great emperor is resident, is called Amacaiz, being a faire citie, whose inhabitants are of the colour of an Oliue. There are also many other cities, as the city of Saua vpon the riuer of Nilus, where the Emperour is accustomed to remaine in the Sommer season. There is likewise a great city named Barbaregaf, and Ascon, from whence it is said that the Queene of Saba came to Hierusalem to heare the wisedom of Salomon. This citie is but litle, yet very faire, and one of the chiefe cities in Ethiope. In this prouince are many exceeding high mountains, vpon the which is said to be the earthly paradise: and some say that there are the trees of the Sunne and Moone, whereof the antiquitie maketh mention: yet that none can passe thither by reason of great deserts of an hundred daies iourney. Also beyond these mountains is the Cape of Bona Speranza. And to haue said thus much of Afrike it may suffice.

The first voiage to Guinea and Benin.

In the yeere of our Lord 1553. the twelfth day of August, sailed from Portsmouth two goodly ships, the Primerose and the Lion, with a pinnas called the Moone, being all well furnished aswell with men of the lustiest sort, to the number of seuen score, as also with ordinance and victuals requisite to such a voiage: hauing also two captaines, the one a stranger called Anthonie Anes Pinteado, a Portugall, borne in a towne named The Port of Portugall, a wise, discreet, and sober man, who for his cunning in sailing, being as well an expert Pilot as a politike captaine, was sometime in great fauour with the king of Portugall, and to whom the coasts of Brasile and Guinea were committed to be kept from the Frenchmen, to whom he was a terrour on the Sea in those parts, and was furthermore a gentleman of the king his masters house. But as fortune in maner neuer fauoureth but flattereth, neuer promiseth but deceiueth, neuer raiseth but casteth downe againe: and as great wealth and fauour haue alwaies companions, emulation and enuie, he was after many aduersities and quarels made against him, inforced to come into England: where in this golden voyage he was euil matched with an vnequal companion, and vnlike match of most sundry qualities and conditions, with vertues few or none adorned. Thus departed these noble ships vnder saile on their voyage: But first captaine Windam putting forth of his ship at Portsmouth a kinsman of one of the head marchants, and shewing herein a muster of the tragicall partes hee had conceiued in his braine, and with such small beginnings nourished so monstrous a birth, that more happy, yea and blessed was that yong man being left behind, then if he had bene taken with them, as some do wish he had done the like by theirs. Thus sailed they on their voyage, vntill they came to the Iland of Madera, where they tooke in certaine wines for the store of their ships, and paid for them as they agreed of the price. At these Ilands they met with a great Galion of the king of Portugall, full of men and ordinance: yet such as could not haue preuailed if it had attempted to withstand or resist our ships, for the which cause it was set foorth, not onely to let and interrupt these our shippes of their purposed voiage, but al other that should attempt the like: yet chiefly to frustrate our voiage. For the king of Portugall was sinisterly informed, that our ships were armed to his castle of Mina in those parties, whereas nothing lesse was ment.

After that our ships departed from the Iland of Madera forward on their voiage, began this worthy captaine Pinteados sorow, as a man tormented with the company of a terrible Hydra, who hitherto flattred with him, and made him a faire countenance and shew of loue. Then did he take vpon him to command all alone, setting nought both by captain Pinteado, and the rest of the marchants factors, sometimes with opprobrious words, and sometimes with threatnings most shamfully abusing them, taking from Pinteado the seruice of the boies and certain mariners that were assigned him by the order and direction of the worshipful merchants, and leauing him as a common mariner, which is the greatest despite and grief that can be to a Portugale or Spaniard, to be diminished of their honor, which they esteem aboue all riches. Thus sailing forward on their voiage, they came to the Ilands of Canarie, continuing their course from thence vntil they arriued at the Iland of S. Nicholas, where they victualled themselues with fresh meat, of the flesh of wild goats, whereof is great plenty in that Iland, and in maner of nothing els. From hence following on their course and tarying here and there at the desert Ilands in the way, because they would not come too timely to the countrey of Guinea for the heat, and tarying somewhat too long (for what can be well ministred in a common wealth, where inequalitie with tyrannie wil rule alone) they came at the length to the first land of the country of Guinea, where they fel with the great riuer of Sesto, where they might for their marchandizes haue laden their ships with the graines of that countrey, which is a very hote fruit, and much like vnto a fig as it groweth on the tree. For as the figs are full of small seeds, so is the said fruit full of graines, which are loose within the cod, hauing in the mids thereof a hole on euery side. This kind of spice is much vsed in cold countries, and may there be sold for great aduantage, for exchange of other wares. But our men, by the perswasion or rather inforcement of this tragicall captaine, not regarding and setting light by that commoditie, in comparison of the fine gold they thirsted, sailed an hundred leagues further, vntil they came to the golden land: where not attempting to come neere the castle pertaining to the king of Portugall, which was within the riuer of Mina, they made sale of their ware only on this side and beyond it, for the gold of that country, to the quantitie of an hundred and fiftie pounds weight, there being in case that they might haue dispatched all their ware for gold, if the vntame braine of Windam had, or could haue given eare to the counsell and experience of Pinteado. For when that Windam not satisfied with the gold which he had, and more might haue had if he had taried about the Mina, commanding the said Pinteado (for so he tooke vpon him) to lead the ships to Benin, being vnder the Equinoctial line, and an hundred and fifty leagues beyond the Mina, where he looked to haue their ships laden with pepper: and being counselled of the said Pinteado, considering the late time of the yeere, for that time to go no further, but to make sale of their wares such as they had for gold, wherby they might haue bene great gainers: Windam not assenting hereunto, fell into a sudden rage, reuiling the sayd Pinteado, calling him Iew, with other opprobrious words, saying, This whoreson Iew hath promised to bring vs to such places as are not, or as he cannot bring vs vnto: but if he do not, I will cut off his eares and naile them to the maste. Pinteado gaue the foresaid counsell to go no further for the safegard of the men and their liues, which they should put in danger if they came too late, for the Rossia which is their Winter, not for cold, but for smothering heate, with close and cloudie aire and storming weather, of such putrifying qualitie, that it rotted the coates of their backs: or els for comming to soone for the scorching heat of the sunne, which caused them to linger in the way. [Sidenote: The king of Benin his court.] But of force and not of will brought he the ships before the riuer of Benin, where riding at an Anker, they sent their pinnas vp into the riuer 50 or 60 leagues, from whence certaine of the marchants with captaine Pinteado, Francisco, a Portugale, Nicholas Lambert gentleman, and other marchants were conducted to the court where the king remained, ten leagues from the riuer side, whither when they came, they were brought with a great company to the presence of the king, who being a blacke Moore (although not so blacke as the rest) sate in a great huge hall, long and wide, the wals made of earth without windowes, the roofe of thin boords, open in sundry places, like vnto louers to let in the aire.

And here to speake of the great reuerence they giue to their king, it is such, that if we would giue as much to our Sauior Christ, we should remooue from our heads many plagues which we daily deserue for our contempt and impietie.

So it is therefore, that when his noble men are in his presence, they neuer looke him in the face, but sit cowring, as we vpon our knees, so they vpon their buttocks, with their elbowes vpon their knees, and their hands before their faces, not looking vp vntil the king command them. And when they are comming toward the king, as far as they do see him, they do shew such reuerence, sitting on the ground with their faces couered as before. Likewise when they depart from him, they turn not their backs toward him, but goe creeping backward with like reuerence.

[Sidenote: The communication between the king of Benin and our men.] And now to speake somewhat of the communication that was between the king and our men, you shall first vnderstand that he himselfe could speake the Portugall tongue, which he had learned of a child. Therefore after he had commanded our men to stand vp, and demanded of them the cause of their comming into that countrey, they answered by Pinteado, that they were marchants trauelling into those parties for the commodities of his countrey, for exchange of wares which they had brought from their countries, being such as should be no lesse commodious for him and his people. The king then hauing of old lying in a certaine store house 30 or 40 kintals of Pepper (euery kintall being an hundred weight) willed them to looke vpon the same, and againe to bring him a sight of such marchandizes as they had brought with them. [Sidenote: The kings gentlenes towards our men.] And thereupon sent with the captaine and the marchants certaine of his men to conduct them to the waters side, with other to bring the ware from the pinnas to the court. Who when they were returned and the wares seen, the king grew to this ende with the merchants to prouide in 30 dayes the lading of al their ships with pepper. And in case their merchandizes would not extend to the value of so much pepper, he promised to credite them to their next returne, and thereupon sent the country round about to gather pepper, causing the same to be brought to the court: So that within the space of 30 dayes they had gathered fourescore tunne of pepper.

In the meane season our men partly hauing no rule of themselues, but eating without measure of the fruits of the countrey, and drinking the wine of the Palme trees that droppeth in the night from the cut of the branches of the same, and in such extreme heate running continually into the water, and vsed before to such sudden and vehement alterations (then the which nothing is more dangerous) were thereby brought into swellings and agues: insomuch that the later time of the yeere comming on, caused them to die sometimes three and sometimes 4 or 5 in a day. Then Windam perceiuing the time of the 30 daies to be expired, and his men dying so fast, sent to the court in post to Captaine Pinteado, and the rest to come away and to tary no longer. But Pinteado with the rest, wrote backe to him againe, certifying him of the great quantity of pepper they had alreadie gathered, and looked daily for much more: desiring him furthermore to remember the great praise and name they should win, if they came home prosperously, and what shame of the contrary. With which answere Windam not satisfied, and many of their men dying dayly, willed and commaunded them againe either to come away forthwith, or els threatened to leaue them behinde. When Pinteado heard this answere, thinking to perswade him with reason, hee tooke his way from the court toward the ships, being conducted thither with men by the kings commandement.

[Sidenote: The Death of Windham.] In the meane season Windam all raging, brake vp Pinteados Cabin, brake open his chestes, spoiled such prouision of cold stilled waters and suckets as he had prouided for his health, and left him nothing, neither of his instruments to saile by, nor yet of his apparell: and in the meane time falling sicke, himselfe died also. Whose death Pinteado comming aboord, lamented as much as if he had bene the deerest friend he had in the world. [Sidenote: Pinteado euill vsed of the mariners.] But certaine of the mariners and other officers did spit in his face, some calling him Iewe, saying that he had brought them thither to kill them: and some drawing their swords at him, making a shew to slay him. Then he perceiuing that they would needs away, desired them to tarry that he might fetch the rest of the marchants that were left at the court, but they would not grant this request. Then desired he them to giue him the ship-boate, with as much of an old saile as might serue for the same, promising them therwith to bring Nicholas Lambert and the rest into England, but all was in vaine. [Sidenote: This Lambert was a Londiner borne, whose father had bin Lord Maior of London.] Then wrote he a letter to the court to the marchants, informing them of all the matter, and promising them if God would lend him life to returne with all haste to fetch them. And thus was Pinteado kept ashipboord against his will, thrust among the boyes of the ship, not vsed like a man, nor yet like an honest boy, but glad to find fauour at the cookes hand. Then departed they, leauing one of their ships behind them, which they sunke for lacke of men to cary her. [Sidenote: The death of Pinteado.] After this, within 6 or 7 dayes sayling, dyed also Pinteado for uery pensiuenesse and thought that stroke him to the heart. A man worthy to serue any prince, and most vilely vsed. And of seuenscore men came home to Plimmouth scarcely forty, and of them many died. [Sidenote: Pinteado first perswaded our men to the voiage of Guinea.] And that no man should suspect these words which I haue saide in commendation of Pinteado, to be spoken vpon fauour otherwise then trueth, I haue thought good to adde hereunto the copie of the letters which the king of Portugall and the infant his brother wrote vnto him to reconcile him, at such time as vpon the king his masters displeasure (and not for any other crime or offence, as may appeare by the said letters) he was only for pouertie inforced to come into England, where he first perswaded our marchants to attempt the said voyages to Guinea. But as the king of Portugall too late repented him that he had so punished Pinteado, vpon malicious informations of such as enuied the mans good fortune: euen so may it hereby appeare that in some cases euen Lions themselues may either be hindered by the contempt, or aided by the helpe of the poore mise, according vnto the fable of Esope.

* * * * *

The copie of Anthonie Anes Pinteado his letters patents, whereby the king of Portugall made him knight of his house, after all his troubles and imprisonment, which, by wrong information made to the king, he had susteined of long time, being at the last deliuered, his cause knowen and manifested to the king by a gray Friar the kings Confessor.

[Sidenote: Seven hundred reis are ten shillings. Alcayre is halfe a bushell.] I the king doe giue you to vnderstand lord Francis Desseaso, one of my counsell and ouerseer of my house, that in consideration of the good seruice which Anthony Anes Pinteado, the sonne of Iohn Anes, dwelling in the towne called the Port, hath done vnto me, my will and pleasure is, to make him knight of my house, allowing to him in Pension seuen hundred reis monethly, and euery day one alcayre of barly, as long as he keepeth a horse, and to be paid according to the ordinance of my house. Prouiding alwaies that he shall receiue but one marriage gift. And this also in such condition, that the time which is accepted in our ordinance, forbidding such men to marry for getting such children as might succeede them in this allowance, which is 6 yeres after the making of this patent, shalbe first expired before he do marry. I therfore command you to cause this to be entred in the booke called the Matricula of our houshold, vnder the title of knights. And when it is so entred, let the clarke of the Matricula, for the certeintie therof, write on the backside of this Aluala, or patent, the number of the leafe wherein this our grant is entred. Which done, let him returne this writing vnto the said Anthonie Anes Pinteado for his warrant.

I Diego Henriques haue written this in Almarin the two and twentie day of September, in the yeere of our Lord 1551. And this beneuolence the king gaue vnto Anthonie Anes Pinteado, the fiue and twentie day of Iuly this present yeere.

Rey.

The Secretaries declaration written vnder the kings grant.

Your Maiestie hath vouchsafed, in respect and consideration of the good seruice of Anthonie Anes Pinteado, dwelling in the port, and sonne of Iohn Anes, to make him knight of your house, with ordinarie allowance, of seuen hundred reis pension by the moneth, and one alcaire of barley by the day, as long as he keepeth a horse: and to be paide according to the ordinance of your house, with condition that hee shall haue but one marriage gift: and that not within the space of sixe yeres after the making of these letters Patents. The Secretaries note. Entred in the booke of the Matricula. Fol. 683.

Francisco de Siquera.

The copie of the letter of Don Lewes the infant, and brother to the king of Portugall, sent into England to Anthonie Anes Pinteado.

Anthony Anes Pinteado, I the infant brother to the king, haue me heartily commended vnto you. Peter Gonsalues is gone to seeke you, desiring to bring you home againe into your countrey. And for that purpose he hath with him a safe conduct for you, granted by the king, that therby you may freely and without all feare come home. And although the weather be foule and stormie, yet faile not to come: for in the time that his Maiestie hath giuen you, you may doe many things to your contentation and gratifying the king, whereof I would be right glad: and to bring the same to passe, I will do all that lieth in me for your profite. But forasmuch as Peter Gonsalues will make further declaration hereof vnto you, I say no more at this present. Written in Lisbone, the eight day of December. Anno 1552.

The infant Don Lewes.

All these foresaid writings I saw vnder seale, in the house of my friend Nicholas Liese, with whom Pinteado left them, at his vnfortunate departing to Guinea. But, notwithstanding all these friendly letters and faire promises, Pinteado durst not attempt to goe home, neither to keepe companie with the Portugals his countrey men, without the presence of other: forasmuch as he had secrete admonitions that they intended to slay him, if time and place might haue serued their wicked intent.

* * * * *

The second voyage to Guinea set out by Sir George Barne, Sir Iohn Yorke, Thomas Lok, Anthonie Hickman and Edward Castelin, in the yere 1554.

The
Captaine whereof was M. Iohn Lok.

As in the first voiage I haue declared rather the order of the history, then the course of the nauigation, whereof at that time I could haue no perfect information: so in the description of this second voyage, my chiefe intent hath beene to shew the course of the same, according to the obseruation and ordinarie custome of the mariners, and as I receiued it at the handes of an expert Pilot, being one of the chiefe in this voyage, who also with his owne handes wrote a briefe declaration of the same, as he found and tried all things, not by coniecture, but by the art of sayling, and instruments perteining to the mariners facultie. Not therefore assuming to my selfe the commendations due vnto other, neither so bold as in any part to change or otherwise dispose the order of this voyage so well obserued by art and experience, I haue thought good to set forth the same, in such sort and phrase of speech as is commonly vsed among them, and as I receiued it of the said Pilot, as I haue said. Take it therefore as followeth.

[Sidenote: Robert Gainsh was master of the Iohn Euangelist.] In the yeere of our Lord 1554 the eleuenth day of October, we departed the riuer of Thames with three goodly ships, the one called the Trinitie, a ship of the burden of seuenscore tunne, the other called the Bartholomew, a ship of the burden of ninetie, the third was the Iohn Euangelist, a ship of seuen score tunne. With the sayd ships and two pinnesses (wherof the one was drowned on the coast of England) we went forward on our voyage, and stayed at Douer fourteene dayes. We staied also at Rie three or foure dayes. Moreouer last of all we touched at Dartmouth.

The first day of Nouember at nine of the clocke at night, departing from the coast of England, we set off the Start, bearing Southwest all that night in the sea, and the next day all day, and the next night after, vntill the third day of the said moneth about noone, making our way good, did runne threescore leagues.

The 17. day in the morning we had sight of the Ile of Madera, which doth rise to him that commeth in the Northnortheast part vpright land in the west part of it, and very high: and to the Southsoutheast a low long land, and a long point, with a saddle thorow the middest of it, standing in two and thirtie degrees: and in the West part, many springs of water running downe from the mountaine, and many white fieldes like vnto corne fields, and some white houses to the Southeast part of it: and the toppe of the mountaine sheweth very ragged, if you may see it, and in the Northeast part there is a bight or bay as though it were a harborow: Also in the said part, there is a rocke a little distance from the shoare, and ouer the sayd bight you shall see a great gappe in the mountaine.

The 19 day at twelue of the clocke we had sight of the isle of Palmes and Teneriffa and the Canaries. The Ile of Palme riseth round, and lieth Southeast and Northwest, and the Northwest part is lowest. In the South is a round hill ouer the head land, and another round hill aboue that in the land. There are between the Southeast part of the Ile of Madera and the Northwest part of the Ile of Palme seuen and fifty leagues. This Isle of Palme lieth in eight and twenty degrees. And our course from Madera to the Ile of Palme was South and South and by West, so that we had sight of Teneriffa and of the Canaries. The Southeast part of the Ile of the Palme, and the Northnortheast of Teneriffa lie Southeast and Northwest, and betweene them are 20 leagues. Teneriffa and the great Canary called Gran Canaria, and the West part of Forteuentura stande in seuen and twenty degrees and a halfe. Gomera is a faire Island but very ragged, and lieth Westsouthwest off Teneriffa. And whosouer wil come betweene them two Ilands must come South and by East, and in the South part of Gomera is a towne and a good rode in the said part of the Iland: and it standeth in seuen and twentie degrees and three terces. Teneriffa is an high land, with a great high pike like a sugar loafe, and vpon the said pike is snow throughout all the whole yeere. And by reason of that pike it may be knowen aboue all other Ilands, and there we were becalmed the twentieth day of Nouember, from sixe of the clocke in the morning, vntill foure of the clocke at afternoone.

The two and twentieth day of Nouember, vnder the Tropike of Cancer the Sunne goeth downe West and by South. Vpon the coast of Barbarie fiue and twentie leagues by North Cape blanke, at three leagues off the maine, there are fifteene fadomes and good shelly ground, and sande among and no streames, and two small Ilands standing in two and twentie degrees and a terce.

From Gomera to Cape de las Barbas is an hundred leagues, and our course was South and by East. The said Cape standeth in two and twentie and a halfe: and all that coast is flatte, sixteene or seuenteene fadome deepe. Seuen or eight leagues off from the riuer del Oro or Cape de las Barbas, there vse many Spaniardes and Portugals to trade for fishing, during the moneth of Nouember: and all that coast is very low lands. Also we went from Cape de las Barbas Southsouthwest, and Southwest and by South, till we brought our selues in twentie degrees and a halfe, reckoning our selues seuen leagues off: and there were the least sholes of Cape Blanke.

Then we went South vntil we brought our selues in 13 degrees, reckoning our selues fiue and twentie leagues off. And in 15 degrees we did reare the Crossiers, and we might haue reared them sooner if we had looked for them. They are not right a crosse in the moneth of Nouember, by reason that the nights are short there. Neuertheless we had the sight of them the 29 day of the said moneth at night.

The first of December, being in 13 degrees we set our course South and by East, vntill the fourth day of December at 12 of the clocke the same day. Then we were in nine degrees and a terce, rekoning our selues 30 leagues of the sholes of the riuer called Rio Grande, being Westsouthwest off them, the which sholes be 30 leagues long.

The fourth of December we beganne to set our course Southeast, we being in sixe degrees and a halfe.

The ninth day of December we set our course Eastsoutheast: the fourteenth day of the sayde moneth we set our course East, we being in fiue degrees and a halfe, reckoning our selues thirty and sixe leagues from the coast of Guinea.

The nineteenth of the said moneth we set our course East and by North, reckoning our selues seuenteene leagues distant from Cape Mensurado, the said Cape being Eastnortheast of vs, and the riuer of Sesto being East.

The one and twentieth day of the said moneth, we fell with Cape Mensurado to the Southeast, about two leagues off. This Cape may be easily knowen, by reason yet the rising of it is like a Porpose-head. Also toward the Southeast there are three trees, whereof the Eastermost tree is the highest, and the middlemost is like a hie stacke, and the Southermost like vnto a gibet: and vpon the maine are foure or fiue high hilles rising one after another like round hommocks or hillocks. And the Southeast of the three trees, brandiernwise: and all the coast along is white sand. The said Cape standeth within a litle in six degrees.

The two and twentieth of December we came to the riuer of Sesto, and remained there vntill the nine and twentieth day of the said moneth. Here we thought it best to send before vs the pinnesse to the riuer Dulce, called Rio Dulce, that they might haue the beginning of the market before the comming of the Iohn Euangelist.

At the riuer of Sesto we had a tunne of graines. This riuer standeth in sixe degrees, lacking a terce. From the riuer of Sesto to Rio Dulce are fiue and twentie leagues. Rio Dulce standeth in fiue degrees and a halfe. The river of Sesto is easie to be knowen, by reason there is a ledge of rockes on the Southeast part of the Rode. And at the entring into the hauen are fiue or sixe trees that beare no leaues. The is a good harborow, but very narow at the entrance into the riuer. There is also a rocke in the hauens mouth right as you enter. And all that coast betweene Cape de Monte, and cape de las Palmas, lieth Southeast and by East, Northwest and by West, being three leagues off the shore. And you shal haue in some places rocks two leagues off: and that, betweene the riuer of Sesto and cape de las Palmas.

Betweene the riuer of Sesto and the riuer Dulce are fiue and twentie leagues: and the high land that is betweene them both, is called Cakeado, being eight leagues from the riuer of Sesto. And to the Southeastwarde of it is a place called Shawgro, and another called Shyawe or Shauo, where you may get fresh water. Off this Shyawe lieth a ledge of rockes: and to the Southeastwarde lieth a hedland called Croke. Betweene Cakeado and Croke are nine or ten leagues. To the Southeastward off, is a harborow called S. Vincent: Right ouer against S. Vincent is a rocke vnder the water two leagues and a halfe off the shore. To the Southeastward of that rocke you shal see an island about three or foure leagues off: this island is not past a league off the shore. To the Eastsoutheast of the island, is a rocke that lieth aboue the water, and by that rocke goeth in the riuer Dulce, which you shall know by the said riuer and rocke. The Northwest side of the hauen is flat sand, and the Southeast side thereof is like an Island, and a bare plot without any trees, and so is it not in any other place.

In the Rode you shall ride in thirteene or foureteene fadomes, good oaze and sand, being the markes of the Rode to bring the Island and the Northeast land together, and here we ankered the last of December.

The third day of Ianuarie, we came from the riuer Dulce.

Note that Cape de las Palmas is a faire high land, but some low places thereof by the water side looke like red cliffes with white strakes like hie wayes, a cable length a piece, and this is the East part of the cape. This cape is the Southermost land in all the coast of Guinea, and standeth in foure degrees and a terce.

The coast from Cape de las Palmas to Cape Trepointes, or de Tres Puntas, is faire and cleare without rocke or other danger.

Twentie and fiue leagues from Cape de las Palmas, the land is higher then in any place, vntill we come to Cape Trepointes: And about ten leagues before you come to Cape Trepointes, the land riseth still higher and higher, vntill you come to Cape Trepointes. Also before you come to the said Cape, after other 5 leagues to the Northwest part of it, there is certaine broken ground, with two great rockes, and within them in the bight of a bay, is a castle called Arra, perteining to the king of Portugall. You shall know it by the said rockes that lie off it: for there is none such from Cape de las Palmas to Cape Trepointes. This coast lieth East and by North, West and by South. From Cape de las Palmas to the said castle is fourescore and fifteene leagues. And the coast lieth from the said castle to the Westermost point of Trepoyntes, Southeast and by South, Northwest and by North.

Also the Westermost point of Trepoyntes is a low lande, lying halfe a mile out in the sea: and vpon the innermost necke, to the land-ward, is a tuft of trees, and there we arriued the eleuenth day of Ianuary.

The 12 day of Ianuary we came to a towne called Samma or Samua, being 8 leagues from Cape Trepointes toward Eastnortheast. Betweene Cape Trepointes and the towne of Samua is a great ledge of rockes a great way out in the sea. [Sidenote: The pledge was sir Iohn Yorke his Nephew.] We continued foure dayes at that Towne, and the Captaine thereof would needs haue a pledge a shore. But when they receiued the pledge, they kept him still, and would trafficke no more, but shot off their ordinance at vs. They haue two or three pieces of ordinance and no more.

The sixteenth day of the said month we made reckoning to come to a place called Cape Corea, where captaine Don Iohn dwelleth, whose men entertained vs friendly. This Cape Corea is foure leagues Eastwarde of the castle of Mina, otherwise called La mina, or Castello de mina, where we arriued the 18 day of the month. [Sidenote: The castle of Mina perteining to the king of Portugall.] Here we made sale of all our cloth, sauing two or three packes.

The 26 day of the same moneth we weighed anker, and departed from thence to the Trinitie, which was seuen leagues Eastward of vs, where she solde her wares. Then they of the Trinitie willed vs to go Eastward of that eight or nine leagues, to sell part of their wares, in a place called Perecow, and another place named Perecow Grande, being the Eastermost place of both these, which you shal know by a great round hill neere vnto it, named Monte Rodondo, lying Westward from it, and by the water side are many high palme trees. From hence did we set forth homeward the thirteenth day of February, and plied vp alongst till we came within seuen or eight leagues to Cape Trepointes. About eight of the clocke the 15 day at afternoone, wee did cast about to seaward: and beware of the currants, for they will deceiue you sore. Whosoeuer shall come from the coast of Mina homeward, let him be sure to make his way good West, vntill he reckon himselfe as farre as Cape de las Palmas, where the currant setteth alwayes to the Eastward. And within twentie leagues Eastward of Cape de las Palmas is a riuer called De los Potos, where you may haue fresh water and balast enough, and plenty of iuory or Elephants teeth. This riuer standeth in foure degrees, and almost two terces. [Sidenote: Cabo de las Palmas.] And when you reckon your selfe as farre shot as Cape de las Palmas, being in a degree, or a degree and a halfe, you may go West, and West by North, vntill you come in three degrees: and then you may go Westnorthwest, and Northwest and by West, vntill you come in fiue degrees, and then Northwest. And in sixe degrees, we met Northerly windes, and great ruffling of tides. And as we could iudge, the currants went to the

Northnorthwest. Furthermore betweene Cape de Monte, and Cape Verde, go great currants, which deceiue many men.

The 22 day of Aprill, we were in 8 degrees and two terces: and so we ran to the Northwest, hauing the winde at Northeast and Eastnortheast, and sometimes at East, vntill we were at 18 degrees and a terce, which was on May day. And so from 18 and two terces, we had the winde at East and Eastnortheast, and sometimes at Eastsoutheast: and then we reckoned the Island of Cape verde Eastsoutheast of vs, we iudging our selues to be 48 leagues off. And in 20 and 21 degrees, we had the winde more Easterly to the Southward then before. And so we ran to the Northwest and Northnorthwest, and sometimes North and by West and North, until we came into 31 degrees, where we reckoned our selues a hundred and fourescore leagues Southwest and by South of the Island de los Flores, and there wee met with the winde at Southsoutheast, and set our course Northeast.

In 23 degrees we had the winde at the South and Southwest, and then we set our course Northnortheast, and so we ran to 40 degrees, and then we set our course Northeast, the winde being at the Southwest, and hauing the Ile de Flores East of us, and 17 leagues off.

In the 41 degrees we met with the winde at Northeast, and so we ran Northwestward, then we met with the winde Westnorthwest, and at the West within 6 leagues, running toward the Northwest, and then we cast about, and lay Northeast, vntill we came in 42 degrees, where we set our course Eastnortheast, iudging the Ile of Coruo South and by West of vs, and sixe and thirty leagues distant from vs.

A remembrance, that the 21st day of May we communed with Iohn Rafe, and he thought it best to goe Northeast, and iudged himselfe 25 leagues Eastward to the Isle de Flores, and in 39 degrees and a halfe.

Note, that on the fourth day of September, vnder nine degrees, we lost the sight of the North starre.

Note also, that in 45 degrees, the compasse is varied 8 degrees to the West.

Item, in 40 degrees the compasse did varie 15 degrees in the whole.

Item, in 30 degrees and a halfe, the compasse is varied 5 degrees to the West.

Be it also in memory that two or three daies before we came to Cape de 3 puntas, the pinnesse went alongst the shore, thinking to sell some of our wares, and so we came to anker three or foure leagues West and by South of the Cape de 3 puntas, where we left the Trinitie.

Then our pinnesse came aboord with all our men, the pinnesse also tooke in more wares. They told me moreouer that they would goe to a place where the Primrose was, and had receiued much gold at the first voyage to these parties, and tolde me furthermore that it was a good place: but I fearing a brigantine that was then vpon the coast, did wey and follow them, and left the Trinitie about foure leagues off from vs, and there we rode against that towne foure dayes: so that Martine by his owne desire, and assent of some of the Commissioners that were in the pinnesse, went a shoare to the towne, and there Iohn Berin went to trafique from vs, being three miles off trafiquing at an other towne. The towne is called Samma or Samua, for Samma and Sammaterra, are the names of the two first townes, where we did trafique for gold, to the Northeast of Cape de 3 puntas.

Hitherto continueth the course of the voyage, as it was described by the sayde Pilot. Nowe therefore I will speake somewhat of the countrey and people, and of such things as are brought from thence.

They brought from thence at the last voyage foure hundred pound weight and odde of gold, of two and twentie carrats and one graine in finenesse: also sixe and thirtie buts of graines, and about two hundred and fiftie Elephants teeth of all quantities. Of these I saw and measured, some of nine spans in length, as they were crooked. Some of them were as bigge as a mans thigh aboue the knee, and weyed about fourescore and ten pound weight a peece. They say that some one hath bin seene of an hundred and fiue and twentie pound weight. Other there were which they call the teeth of calues, of one or two or three yeeres, whereof some were a foot and a halfe, some two foot, and some 3 or more, according to the age of the beast. These great teeth or tusks grow in the vpper iaw downeward, and not in the nether iaw vpward, wherein the Painters and Arras workers are deceiued. At this last voyage was brought from Guinea the head of an Elephant, of such huge bignesse, that onely the bones or cranew thereof, beside the nether iaw and great tusks, weighed about two hundred weight, and was as much as I could well lift from the ground: insomuch that considering also herewith the weight of two such great teeth, the nether iaw with the lesse teeth, the tongue, the great hanging eares, the bigge and long snout or troonke, with all the flesh, braines, and skinne, with all other parts belonging to the whole head, in my iudgement it could weigh litle lesse then fiue hundred weight. [Sidenote: Sir Andrew Iudde. The contemplation of Gods works.] This head diuers haue seene in the house of the worthy marchant sir Andrew Iudde, where also I saw it, and beheld it, not only with my bodily eyes, but much more with the eye of my mind and spirit, considering by the worke, the cunning and wisedome of the workemaister: without which consideration, the sight of such strange and wonderfull things may rather seeme curiosities, then profitable contemplations.

[Sidenote: The decription and properties of the Elephant.] The Elephant (which some call an Oliphant) is the biggest of all foure footed beasts, his forelegs are longer then his hinder, he hath ancles in the lower part of his hinder legges, and fiue toes on his feete vndiuided, his snout or tronke is so long, and in such forme, that it is to him in the stead of a hand: for he neither eateth nor drinketh but by bringing his tronke to his mouth, therewith he helpeth vp his Master or keeper, therewith he ouerthroweth trees. Beside his two great tusks, he hath on euery side of his mouth foure teeth, wherewith he eateth and grindeth his meate: either of these teeth are almost a span in length, as they grow along in the iaw, and are about two inches in height, and almost as much in thicknesse. The tuskes of the male are greater then of the female: his tongue is very litle, and so farre in his mouth, that it cannot be seene: of all beastes they are most gentle and tractable, for by many sundry wayes they are taught, and doe vnderstand: insomuch that they learne to doe due honor to a king, and are quick sense and sharpenesse of wit. When the male hath once seasoned the female, he neuer after toucheth her. The male Elephant liueth two hundreth yeeres, or at the least one hundred and twentie: the female almost as long, but the floure of their age is but threescore yeres, as some write. They cannot suffer winter or cold: they loue riuers, and will often go into them vp to the snout, wherewith they blow and snuffe, and play in the water: but swimme they cannot, for the weight of their bodies. Plinie and Soline write, that they vse none adulterie. If they happen to meete with a man in wildernesse being out of the way, gently they wil go before him, and bring him into the plaine way. Ioyned in battel, they haue no small respect vnto them that be wounded: for they bring them that are hurt or weary into the middle of the army to be defended: they are made tame by drinking the iuise of barley. [Sidenote: Debate between the Elephant and the Dragon.] They haue continual warre against Dragons, which desire their blood, because it is very cold: and therefore the Dragon lying awaite as the Elephant passeth by, windeth his taile (being of exceeding length) about the hinder legs of the Elephant, and so staying him, thrusteth his head into his tronke and exhausteth his breath, or else biteth him in the eare, whereunto he cannot reach with his tronke, and when the Elephant waxeth faint, he falleth downe on the serpent, being now full of blood, and with the poise of his body breaketh him: so that his owne blood with the blood of the Elephant runneth out of him mingled together, which being colde, is congealed into that substance which the Apothecaries call Sanguis Draconis, (that is) Dragons blood, otherwise called Cinnabaris, although there be an other kinde of Cinnabaris, commonly called Cinoper or Vermilion, which the Painters vse in certaine colours.

[Sidenote: Three kinds of Elephants.] They are also of three kinds, as of the Marshes, the plaines, and the mountaines, no lesse differing in conditions.

Philostratus writeth, that as much as the Elephant of Libya in bignes passeth the horse of Nysea, so much doe the Elephants of India exceed them of Libya: for the Elephants of India, some haue bene seene of the height of nine cubits: the other do so greatly feare these, that they dare not abide the sight of them. Of the Indian Elephants onely the males haue tuskes, but of them of Ethiopia and Libya both kindes are tusked: they are of diuers heights, as of twelue, thirteene, and fourteene dodrants, euery dodrant being a measure of nine inches. Some write that an Elephant is bigger then three wilde Oxen or Buffes. They of India are black, or of the colour of a mouse, but they of Ethiope or Guinea are browne: the hide or skinne of them all is very hard, and without haire or bristles: their eares are two dodrants broad, and their eyes very litle. Our men saw one drinking at a riuer in Guinea, as they sailed into the land.

Of other properties and conditions of the Elephant, as of their marueilous docilitie, of their fight and vse in the warres, of their generation and chastitie, when they were first seene in the Theatres and triumphes of the Romanes, how they are taken and tamed, and when they cast their tusks, with the vse of the same in medicine, who so desireth to know, let him reade Plinie, in the eight booke of his naturall history. He also writeth in his twelft booke, that in olde time they made many goodly workes of iuory or Elephants teeth: as tables, tressels, postes of houses, railes, lattesses for windowes, images of their gods, and diuers other things of iuory, both coloured, and vncoloured, and intermixt with sundry kindes of precious woods, as at this day are made certaine chaires, lutes, and virginals. They had such plenty thereof in olde time, that (as far as I remember) Iosephus writeth, that one of the gates of Hierusalem was called Porta Eburnea, (that is) the Iuory gate. The whitenesse thereof was so much esteemed, that it was thought to represent the natural fairenesse of mans skinne: insomuch that such as went about to set foorth (or rather corrupt) naturall beautie with colours and painting, were reproued by this prouerbe, Ebur atramento candefacere, that is, To make iuory white with inke. The Poets also describing the faire necks of beautifull virgins, call them Eburnea colla, that is, Iuory necks. And to haue said thus much of Elephants and Iuory, it may suffice.

[Sidenote: The people of Africa.] Now therefore I will speake somewhat of the people and their maners, and maner of liuing, with an other briefe description of Africa also. It is to be vnderstood, that the people which now inhabite the regions of the coast of Guinea, and the midle parts of Africa, as Libya the inner, and Nubia, with diuers other great and large regions about the same, were in old time called Æthiopes and Nigritæ, which we now call Moores, Moorens, or Negroes, a people of beastly liuing, without a God, lawe, religion, or common wealth, and so scorched and vexed with the heat of the sunne, that in many places they curse it when it riseth. Of the regions and people about the inner Libya (called Libya interior) Gemma Phrysius writeth thus.

Libya interior is very large and desolate, in the which are many horrible wildernesses and mountaines, replenished with diuers kinds of wilde and monstrous beastes and serpents. First from Muritania or Barbary toward the South is Getulia, a rough and sauage region, whose inhabitants are wilde and wandering people. After these follow the people called Melanogetuli and Pharusij, which wander in the wildernesse, carrying with them great gourdes of water. [Sidenote: Æthiopes, Nigritæ. The riuer Nigritis or Senega.] The Ethiopians called Nigritæ occupy a great part of Africa, and are extended to the West Ocean. Southward also they reach to the riuer Nigritis, whose nature agreeth with the riuer of Nilus, forasmuch as it is increased and diminished at the same time, and bringeth forth the like beasts as the Crocodile. By reason whereof, I thinke this to be the same riuer which the Portugals called Senega: For this riuer is also of the same nature. It is furthermore marueilous and very strange that is said of this river: And this is, that on the one side thereof, the inhabitants are of high stature and black, and on the other side, of browne or tawne colour, and low stature, which thing also our men confirme to be true.

[Sindenote: People of Libya.] There are also other people of Libya called Garamantes, whose women are common: for they contract no matrimonie; neither haue respect to chastitie. After these are the nations of the people called Pyrei, Sathiodaphnitæ, Odrangi, Mimaces, Lynxamatæ, Dolopes, Aganginæ, Leuci Ethiopes, Xilicei Ethiopei, Calcei Ethiopes, and Nubi. These haue the same situation in Ptolome that they now giue to the kingdome of Nubia. Here are certaine Christians vnder the dominion of the great Emperour of Æthiopia, called Prester Iohn. From these toward the West is a great nation of people called Aphricerones, whose region (as faire as may be gathered by coniecture) is the same that is now called Regnum Orguene, confining vpon the East parts of Guinea. From hence Westward, and somewhat toward the North, are the kingdoms of Gambra and Budomel, not farre from the riuer of Senega. And from hence toward the inland regions, and along by the sea coast, are the regions of Ginoia or Guinea, which we commonly call Ginnee. [Sidenote: The Portugals Nauigation to Brasile.] On the Westside of these regions toward the Ocean, is the cape or point called Cabo verde, or Caput viride, (that is) the greene cape, to the which the Portugals first direct their course when they saile to America, or the land of Brasile. Then departing from hence, they turne to the right hand toward the quarter of the winde called Garbino, which is betweene the West and the South. But to speake somewhat more of Æthiopia: although there are many nations of people so named, yet is

Æthiopia chiefly diuided into two parts, whereof the one is called Aethiopia vnder Aegypt, a great and rich region. To this perteineth the Island Meroe, imbraced round about with the stremes of the riuer Nilus. In this Island women reigned in old time. Iosephus writeth, that it was sometime called Sabea: and that the Queene of Saba came from thence to Ierusalem, to heare the wisedom of Salomon. [Sidenote: Prester Iohn Emperour of Aethiopia.] From hence toward the East reigneth the said Christian Emperour Prester Iohn, whom some cal Papa Iohannes, and other say that he is called Pean Iuan (that is) great Iohn, whose Empire reacheth far beyond Nilus, and is extended to the coasts of the Red sea and Indian sea. The middle of the region is almost in 66. degrees of longitude, and 12. degrees of latitude. [Sidenote: People of the Eastside of Africa.] About this region inhabite the people called Clodi, Risophagi, Bobylonij, Axiuntæ, Molili, and Molibæ. After these is the region called Troglodytica, whose inhabitants dwel in caues and dennes: for these are their houses, and the flesh of serpents their meat, as writeth Plinie, and Diodorus Siculus. They haue no speach, but rather a grinning and chattering. There are also people without heads, called Blemines, hauing their eyes and mouth in their breast. Likewise Strucophagi, and naked Ganphasantes: Satyrs also, which haue nothing of men but onely shape. Moreouer Oripei, great hunters. Mennones also and the region of Smyrmophora, which bringeth foorth myrrhe. After these is the region of Azania, in the which many Elephants are found. A great part of the other regions of Africke that are beyond the Aequinoctiall line, are now ascribed to the kingdome of Melinde, whose inhabitants are accustomed to trafique with the nations of Arabia, and their king is ioyned in friendship with the king of Portugal, and payeth tribute to Prester Iohn.

The other Ethiope, called Æthiopia interior (that is) the inner Ethiope, is not yet knowne for the greatnesse thereof, but onely by the sea coastes: yet is it described in this manner. First from the Aequinoctiall toward the South, is a great region of Aethiopians, which bringeth forth white Elephants, Tygers, and the beastes called Rhinocerotes. Also a region that bringeth foorth plenty of cynamome, lying betweene the branches of Nilus. Also the kingdome of Habech or Habasi, a region of Christian men, lying both on this side and beyond Nilus. Here are also the Aethiopians, called Ichthiopagi (that is) such as liue onely by fish, and were sometimes subdued by the warres of great Alexander. Furthermore the Aethiopians called Rhapsij, and Anthropophagi, that are accustomed to eat mans flesh, inhabite the regions neere vnto the mountains called Montes Lunæ (that is) the mountaines of the Moone. Gazati is vnder the Tropike of Capricorne. After this followeth the front of Afrike, the Cape of Buena Speranza, or Caput Bonæ Spei, that is, the Cape of good hope, by the which they passe that saile from Lisbon to Calicut. But by what names the Capes and gulfes are called, forasmuch as the same are in euery globe and card, it were here superfluous to rehearse them.

Some write that Africa was so named by the Grecians, because it is without colde. For the Greeke letter Alpha or A signifies priuation, voyd, or without: and Phrice signifies colde. For in deed although in the stead of Winter they haue a cloudy and tempestuous season, yet is it not colde, but rather smothering hote, with hote showres of raine also, and somewhere such scorching windes, that what by one meanes and other, they seeme at certaine times to liue as it were in fornaces, and in maner already halfe way in Purgatorie or hell. Gemma Phrisius writeth, that in certaine parts of Africa, as in Atlas the greater, the aire in the night season is seene shining, with many strange fires and flames rising in maner as high as the Moone: and that in the element are sometime heard as it were the sound of pipes, trumpets and drummes: which noises may perhaps be caused by the vehement and sundry motions of such firie exhalations in the aire, as we see the like in many experiences wrought by fire, aire and winde. [Sidenote: The middle region of the aire is cold.] The hollowness also, and diuers reflexions and breaking of the cloudes may be great causes hereof, beside the vehement colde of the middle region of the aire, whereby the said fiery exhalations, ascending thither, are suddenly stricken backe with great force: for euen common and dayly experience teacheth vs, by the whissing of a burning torch, what noise fire maketh in the aire, and much more where it striueth when it is inclosed with aire, as appeareth in gunnes, and as the like is seene in onely aire inclosed, as in Organ pipes, and such other instruments that go by winde. [Sidenote: The strife of Elements. Winde.] For winde (as say the Philosophers) is none other then aire vehemently moued, as we see in a paire of bellowes, and such other.

[Sidenote: The heate of the Moone.] Some of our men of good credite that were in this last voiage to Guinea, affirme earnestly that in the night season they felt a sensible heat to come from the beames of the moone. [Sidenote: The nature of the starres.] The which thing, although it be strange and insensible to vs that inhabite cold regions, yet doeth it stand with good reason that it may so be, forasmuch as the nature of starres and planets (as writeth Plinie) consisteth of fire, and conteineth in it a spirit of fire, which cannot be without heat.

And, that the Moone giueth heate vpon the earth the Prophet Dauid seemeth to confirme in his 121. Psalme, where speaking of such men as are defended from euil by Gods protection, hee saith thus: Per diem Sol non exuret te, nec Luna per noctem. That is to say, In the day the Sunne shall not burne thee, nor the Moone by night.

They say furthermore, that in certaine places of the sea they saw certaine streames of water, which they call spouts, falling out of the aire into the sea, and that some of these are as bigge as the great pillars of Churches: insomuch that sometimes they fall into shippes, and put them in great danger of drowning. Some faine that these should be the Cataracts of heauen, which were all opened at Noes floud. But I thinke them rather to be such fluxions and eruptions as Aristotle in his booke de Mundo saith, to chance in the sea. For speaking of such strange things as are seene often times in the sea, he writeth thus. Oftentimes also euen in the sea are seene euaporations of fire, and such eruptions and breaking foorth of springs, that the mouthes of riuers are opened. Whirlepooles, and fluxions are caused of such other vehement motions, not only in the middest of the sea, but also in creeks and streights. At certaine times also, a great quantity of water is suddenly lifted vp and carried about with the Moone, &c. By which wordes of Aristotle it doth appeare that such waters be lifted vp in one place at one time, and suddenly fall downe in an other place at another time. [Sidenote: A strange thing.] And hereunto perhaps perteineth it that Richard Chancellor told me that he heard Sebastian Cabot report, that (as farre as I remember) either about the coasts of Brasile or Rio de Plata, his shippe or pinnesse was suddenly lifted from the sea, and cast vpon land, I wot not howe farre. [Sidenote: The power of nature.] The which thing, and such other like wonderfull and strange workes of nature while I consider, and call to remembrance the narrownesse of mans vnderstanding and knowledge, in comparison of her mightie power, I can but cease to maruell and confesse with Plinie, that nothing is to her impossible, the least part of whose power is not yet knowen to men. Many things more our men saw and considered in this voyage, woorthy to be noted, whereof I haue thought good to put some in memory, that the reader may aswell take pleasure in the variety of things, as knowledge of the historie. Among other things, therefore touching the maners and nature of the people, this may seeme strange, that their princes and noble men vse to pounce and rase their skinnes with pretie knots in diuers formes, as it were branched damaske, thinking that to be a decent ornament. [Sidenote: Fine iewels. A bracelet.] And albeit they goe in maner all naked, yet are many of them, and especially their women, in maner laden with collars, bracelets, hoopes, and chaines, either of gold, copper, or iuory. I my selfe haue one of their brassets of Iuory, weighing two pound and sixe ounces of Troy weight, which make eight and thirtie ounces: this one of their women did weare vpon her arme. It is made of one whole piece of the biggest part of the tooth, turned and somewhat carued, with a hole in the midst, wherein they put their handes to wear it on their arme. Some haue on euery arme one, and as many on their legges, wherewith some of them are so galled, that although they are in maner made lame thereby, yet will they by no meanes leaue them off. Some weare also on their legges great shackles of bright copper, which they thinke to bee no lesse comely. They weare also collars, bracelets, garlands, and girdles, of certain blew stones like beads. Likewise some of their women weare on their bare armes certaine foresleeues made of the plates of beaten golde. On their fingers also they weare rings, made of golden wires, with a knot or wreath, like vnto that which children make in a ring of a rush. Among other things of golde that our men bought of them for exchange of their wares, were certaine dog-chaines and collers.

They are very wary people in their bargaining, and will not lose one sparke of golde of any value. They vse weights and measures, and are very circumspect in occupying the same. They that shall haue to doe with them, must vse them gently: for they will not trafique or bring in any wares if they be euill vsed. At the first voyage that our men had into these parties, it so chanced, that at their departure from the first place where they did trafick, one of them either stole a muske Cat, or tooke her away by force, not mistrusting that that should haue hindered their bargaining in another place whither they intended to goe. But for all the haste they coulde make with full sailes, the fame of their misusage so preuented them, that the people of that place also, offended thereby, would bring in no wares: insomuch that they were inforced either to restore the Cat, or pay for her at their price before they could trafique there.

Their houses are made of foure postes or trees, and couered with boughes.

Their common feeding is of roots, and such fishes as they take, whereof they haue great plenty.

There are also such flying fishes as are seene in the sea of the West Indies. Our men salted of their fishes, hoping to prouide store thereof: but they would take no salt, and must therefore be eaten forthwith as some say. Howbeit other affirme, that if they be salted immediately after they be taken, they wil last vncorrupted ten or twelue dayes. But this is more strange, that part of such flesh as they caried with them out of England, which putrified there, became sweete againe at their returne to the clime of temperate regions.

They vse also a strange making of bread, in this maner. They grinde betweene two stones with their handes as much corne as they thinke may suffice their family, and when they haue thus brought it to floure, they put thereto a certaine quantitie of water, and make thereof very thinne dough, which they sticke vpon some post of their houses, where it is baked by the heate of the Sunne: so that when the master of the house or any of his family will eate thereof, they take it downe and eate it.

They haue very faire wheate, the eare whereof is two handfuls in length, and as bigge as a great Bulrush, and almost foure inches about where it is biggest. The stemme or straw seemeth to be almost as bigge as the litle finger of a mans hand, or litle lesse. The graines of this wheate are as big as our peason, round also, and very white, and somewhat shining, like pearles that haue lost their colour. Almost all the substance of them turneth into floure, and maketh little bran or none. I told in one eare two hundred and threescore graines. The eare is inclosed in three blades longer than it selfe, and of two inches broad a piece. And by this fruitfulnes the Sunne seemeth partly to recompence such griefes and molestations as they otherwise receiue by the feruent heate thereof. It is doubtlesse a worthy contemplation to consider the contrary effects of the sunne: or rather the contrary passions of such things as receiue the influence of his beames, either to their hurt or benefit. Their drinke is either water, or the iuise that droppeth from the cut branches of the barren Date trees, called Palmitos. For either they hang great gourdes at the said branches euery euening, and let them so hang all night, or else they set them on the ground vnder the trees, that the droppes may fall therein. They say that this kinde of drinke is in taste much like vnto whey, but somewhat sweeter, and more pleasant. They cut the branches euery euening, because they are seared vp in the day by the heate of the Sunne. They haue also great beanes as bigge as chestnuts, and very hard, with a shell in the stead of a huske.

Many things more might be saide of the maners of the people, and of the wonders and monstrous things that are engendered in Africke. But it shall suffice to haue saide this much of such things as our men partly sawe, and partly brought with them.

And whereas before speaking of the fruit of graines, I described the same to haue holes by the side (as in deede it hath, as it is brought hither) yet was I afterward enfourmed, that those holes were made to put stringes or twigges through the fruite, thereby to hang them vp to dry at the Sunne. They grew not past a foote and a halfe, or two foote from the ground, and are as red as blood when they are gathered. The graines themselues are called of the Phisicions Grana Paradisi.

[Sidenote: Shels that cleaue to ships.] At their comming home the keeles of their shippes were marueilously ouergrowne with certaine shelles of two inches length and more, as thicke as they could stand, and of such bignesse that a man might put his thumbe in the mouthes of them. They certainely affirme that in these there groweth a certaine slimie substance, which at the length slipping out of the shell and falling in the sea, becommeth those foules which we call Barnacles. The like shelles haue bene seene in ships returning from Iseland, but these shels were not past halfe an inch in length. Of the other that came from Guinea, I sawe the Primerose lying in the docke, and in maner couered with the said shels, which in my iudgement should greatly hinder her sayling. Their ships were also in many places eaten with the wormes called Bromas or Bissas, whereof mention is made in the Decades. These creepe betweene the plankes, which they eate through in many places.

[Sidenote: A secret.] Among other things that chanced to them in this voyage, this is worthy to be noted, that whereas they sailed thither in seuen weekes, they could returne in no lesse space then twentie weekes. The cause whereof they say to be this: That about the coast of Cabo Verde the winde is euer at the East, by reason whereof they were enforced to saile farre out of their course into the maine Ocean, to finde the winde at the West to bring them home. [Sidenote: The death of our men.] There died of our men at this last voyage about twentie and four, whereof many died at their returne into the clime of the colde regions, as betweene the Islands of Azores and England. [Sidenote: Fiue blacke Moores brought into England. Colde may be better abiden then heate.] They brought with them certaine black slaues, whereof some were tall and strong men, and could wel agree with our meates and drinkes. The colde and moyst aire doth somewhat offend them. Yet doubtlesse men that are borne in hot Regions may better abide colde, then men that are borne in colde Regions may abide heate, forasmuch as vehement heate resolueth the radicall moysture of mens bodies, as colde constraineth and preserueth the same.

This is also to be considered as a secret worke of nature, that throughout all Africke, vnder the Æquinoctial line, and neere about the same on both sides, the regions are extreeme hote, and the people very blacke. Whereas contrarily such regions of the West Indies as are vnder the same line are very temperate, and the people neither blacke, nor with curlde and short wooll on their heads, as they of Afrike haue, but of the colour of an Oliue, with long and blacke heare on their heads: the cause of which variety is declared in diuers places in the Decades.

It is also worthy to be noted that some of them that were at this voyage told me: That is, that they ouertooke the course of the Sunne, so that they had it North from them at noone, the 14. day of March. And to haue said thus much of these voyages, it may suffice.

* * * * *

The first voyage made by Master William Towrson Marchant of London, to the
  coast of Guinea, with two Ships, in the yeere 1555.

Vpon Munday the thirtieth day of September wee departed from the Isle of Wight, out of the hauen of Neuport with two good shippes, the one called

the Hart, the other the Hinde, both of London, and the Masters of them were
Iohn Ralph, and William Carter, for a voyage to bee made vnto the Riuer de Sestos in Guinea, and to other hauens thereabout.

It fell out by the varietie of windes, that it was the fourteenth day of October before wee coulde fetch Dartmouth: and being there arriued wee continued in that roade six dayes, and the 20. of October we warpt out of the hauen, and set saile, directing our course towards the Southwest, and the next morning we were runne by estimation thirty leagues.

The first of Nouember we found our selues to be in 31. degrees of latitude by the reckoning of our Master. This day we ranne about 40. leagues also.

The second day we ranne 36. leagues.

The third day we had sight of Porto Santo, which is a small Island lying in the sea, about three leagues long, and a league and a halfe broad, and is possessed by Portugals. It riseth as we came from the Northnorthwest like two small hilles neere together. The East end of the same Island is a high land like a saddle with a valley, which makes it to beare that forme. The West ende of it is lower with certaine small round hillocks. This Island lieth in thirty and three degrees. The same day at 11. of the clocke we raysed the Isle of Madera, which lieth 12. leagues from Porto Santo, towards the Southwest: that Island is a faire Island and fruitfull, and is inhabited by Portugals, it riseth afarre off like a great whole land and high. By three of the clocke this day at after noone we were thwart of Porto Santo, and we set our course Southwest, to leaue the Isle of Madera to the Eastward, as we did Porto Santo. These two Islands were the first land that we saw since wee left the coast of England. About three of the clocke after midnight wee were thwart of Madera, within three leagues of the West ende of it, and by meanes of the high hilles there, we were becalmed: We suppose we ranne this day and night 30. leagues.

The fourth day we lay becalmed vnder theIsle of Madera, vntill one of the clocke at afternoone, and then, the winde comming into the East, wee went our course, and ranne that day fifteene leagues.

The 5. day we ranne 15. leagues more.

The 6. day in the morning we raysed the Isle of Tenerif, otherwise called the Pike, because it is a very high Island, with a pike vpon the top like a loafe of suger. The same night we raised the Isle of Palma, which is a high land also, and to the Westward of the Isle of Tenerif.

The 7. day we perceiued the Isle of Gomera, which is an Island standing betwixt Tenerif and Palma, about 12. leagues Eastward from Palma, and 8.

leagues Westward from Tenerif: and for feare of being becalmed with the Isle of Tenerif, we left both it, and Gomera to the Eastward of vs, and went betwixt Palma and Gomera. We ranne this day and night 30. leagues.

Note that these Islands be 60. leagues from Madera, and that there are 3 Islands more to the Westward of Tenerif, named the Grand Canaria, Forte-ventura, and Lancerot, of which Island we came not in sight: they being inhabited by Spaniards.

This day also we had sight of the Isle of Ferro, which is to the Southwards 13. leagues from the other Islands, and is possessed by Spaniards. All this day and night by reason of the winde we could not double the point of the Isle of Ferro, except we would haue gone to the Westward of it, which had bene much out of our course: therefore we kept about, and ranne backe fiue houres Eastnortheast to the ende we might double it vpon the next boord, the winde continuing Southeast, which hath not bene often seene vpon that coast by any traueilers: for the winde continueth there for the most part Northeast, and East Northeast: so vpon the other boord by the next morning we were in a maner with the Island, and had roome ynough to double the same.

The 8. day we kept our course as neere the winde as wee could, because that our due course to fetch the coast of Barbary was Southeast and by East, but by the scant winde we could not goe our due course, but went as neere it as we could, and ranne this day and night 25. leagues.

The 9. day we ranne 30. leagues, the 10. 25. leagues, the 12. 24.

The 12. day we saw a saile vnder our Lee, which was as we thought a fishermen, so that wee went roome to haue spoken with him, but within one houre there fell such a fogge, that wee could not see the shippe nor one of vs the other: we shot off diuers pieces to the Hinde, but she heard them not: at afternoone she shot off a piece which wee heard, and made her answere with another: and within one halfe houre after the fogge brake vp, and we were within 4. leagues of the shoare vpon the coast of Barbary, and wee sounded and had 14. fadom water. The Barke also came roome with vs and their ankered by reason of the contrary winde. When we fell with the land, we could not iudge iustly what part of the land it was, because the most part of that coast is lowe land, and no part to be iudged of it but the fore part of the shoare, which is white like chalke or sand, and very deepe vnto the hard shoare: there immediatly we began to fish, and found great store of a kinde of fish which the Portugals commonly fish for vpon that coast, which they cal Pergosses, the Frenchmen call them Saders, and our men salt-water breames. Before the clearing vp of the fogge, the shippe which we followed shaped such a course that we could see her no more, by reason of our shooting off to finde the Hinde againe. This part of the coast of Barbary, by our Pilots reckoning, is about 16. leagues to the Eastwards of the riuer del Oro.

The 13. day in the afternoone wee spyed a saile comming towards vs, which wee iudged to be the saile that wee sawe the day before, and as soone as we spied him, wee caused the Hinde to way her ancre and to goe towardes him, and manned out our Skiffe in like case to lay him aboorde, or to discerne what hee was, and wee our selues within halfe an houre after wayed also: but after the saile had espied vs, hee kept about, and turned backe againe, and shortly after there fell such another fogge, that wee coulde not see him: which fogges continued all that night, so that wee were constrained to leaue the chase. This afternoone the winde came about, and wee went our course Southwest and by West, to goe cleare off the coast, wee ranne that night sixteene leagues.

The foureteenth day in the morning was verie foggie: but about twelue a clocke wee espied a Caruell of 60. tunne which was fishing, and we sent our Skiffe to him with fiue men, and all without any weapon sauing their Oares. [Sidenote: A Caruell taken.] The Caruell for haste let slippe her ancre, and set saile; and they seeing that, fearing that they should not fetch her, would tarry for no weapons, and in the ende ouertooke the Caruel, and made her to strike saile, and brought her away, although they had fourteene or fifteene men aboord, and euery man his weapon, but they had not the hearts to resist our men. After they were come to vs, they let fall their ancre, for wee had cast ancre because the winde was not good: I caused then the Skiffe to come for mee, and I went aboorde of them to see that no harme should bee done to them, nor to take any thing but that which they might spare vs for our money. [Sidenote: Great store of fish vpon the coast of Barbary.] So wee tooke of them 3. Tapnets of figges, two small pots of oyle, two pipes of water, foure hogsheads of saltfish which they had taken vpon the coast, and certaine fresh fish which they did not esteeme, because there is such store vpon that coast, that in an houre and sometime lesse, a man may take as much fish as will serue twentie men a day. For these things, and for some wine which wee dranke aboord of them, and three or foure great Cannes which they sent aboord of our shippes, I payed them twentie and seuen Pistoles, which was twise as much as they willingly would haue taken: and so let them goe to their ancre and cable which they had let slippe, and got it againe by our helpe. After this wee set saile, but the winde caused vs to ancre againe about twelue leagues off the riuer del Oro, as the Portugals tolde vs. There were fiue Caruels more in this place, but when they sawe vs, they made all away for feare of vs.

The 15. day we ridde still because of the winde.

[Sidenote: The Tropike of Cancer in 23. and a halfe.] The 16. day we set saile and ranne our course 40. leagues. This day, by the reckoning of our Pilots, we were right vnder the Tropike of Cancer. The 17. we ranne 25. leagues within sight for the most part of the coast of Barbary.

The 18. day wee ranne thirtie leagues, and at twelue of the clocke by the reckoning of our Pilots we were thwart of Cape Blanke.

The 22. day our Pilots reckoned vs to be thwart Cape Verde.

[Sidenote: The coast of Guinea.] The 12. day of December we had sight of land of Guinea, which as soone as we saw we halled into the land Northeast, and about 12. of the clocke at night we were neere the shoare within lesse then 2. leagues: and then we kept about and sounded, and found 18. fadom water. Afterwards we saw a light towards the shoare, which we thought to haue bene a ship, and thereby iudged it to be the riuer de Sestos, which light as soone as we espied, we came to an anker and armed our tops, and made all things ready to fight, because we doubted that it might be some Portugal or French man: this night we remained at an anker, but in the morning we saw no man, only we espied 4. rockes about 2. English miles from vs, one great rocke, and the 3. other smal ones, which when we sawe, we supposed that the light came from the shore, and so wayed, and set saile East Southeast along the shoare, because the Master did not well know the place, but thought that we were not so farre to the East as the riuer de Sestos.

This land all along is a low land, and full of very high trees all along the shoare, so that it is not possible to know the place that a man doth fall withall, except it be by the latitude. In these 24. houres I thinke we ran 16. leagues, for all the night we had a great gale as we were vnder saile, and had withall store of thunder and lightnings.

The 13. day for the most part we ran East Southeast all along the shoare, within two leagues alwayes of the same, and found the land all as at the first, ful of woods and great rocks hard aboord the shoare, and the billow beating so sore, that the seas brake vpon the shoare as white as snow, and the water mounted so high that a man might easily discerne it 4. leagues off, in such wise that no boate could land there. Thus we ran vntil 12. of the clocke, and then they tooke the Sunne and after iudged themselues to be 24. leagues past the riuer de Sestos to the Eastwards, by reason whereof we halled into the shoare within two English miles, and there ancred and found fifteene fadom water, and all off from the shoare the sea so smooth, that we might wel haue rid by an Hawser. All that after-noone we trimmed our boate and made her a saile, to the ende that she might go along by the shoare to seeke some place to water in: for wee could not goe back againe to the riuer de Sestos, because the winde blowes alwayes contrary, and the Currant runneth alwayes to the Eastwards, which was also against vs.

The 14. day we set saile and went back againe along the coast, and sent our boats hard aboord the shoare to seeke a watering place, which they found about 12. of the clock, and we being farre into the sea, met with diuers boats of the Countrey, small, long and narrow, and in euery boate one man and no more: we gaue them bread which they did eat, and were very glad of it. About 4. of the clocke our boats came to vs with fresh water: and this night we ankered against a Riuer.

The 15. day we wayed and set saile to goe neere the shoare, and with our leade wee sounded all the way, and found sometimes rockes, and sometimes faire ground, and at the shallowest found 7. fadoms alwayes at the least. So in fine we found 7. fadom and a halfe within an English mile of the shoare, and there we ankered in a maner before the mouth of the Riuer, and then wee sent our boats into the Riuer for water, which went about a mile within the Riuer, where they had very good water. [Sidenote: Riuer S. Vincent.] This Riuer lieth by estimation 8. leagues beyond the Riuer de Sestos, and is called in the Carde Riuer S. Vincent, but it is so hard to finde, that a boat being within halfe a mile of it shall not be able to discerne that it is a Riuer: by reason that directly before the mouth of it there lyeth a ledge of rockes, which is much broader then the Riuer, so that a boate must runne in along the shoare a good way betwixt the rockes and the shoare before it come to the mouth of the Riuer, and being within it, it is a great Riuer and diuers other Riuers fall into it: The going into it is somewhat ill, because that at the entring the seas doe goe somewhat high, but being once within it, it is as calme as the Thames.

[Sidenote: Cloth made of the barke of trees.] There are neere to the sea vpon this Riuer diuers inhabitants, which are mighty bigge men and go al naked except some thing before their priuie parts, which is like a clout about a quarter of a yard long made of the barke of trees, and yet it is like a cloth: for the barke is of that nature, that it will spin small after the maner of linnen. [Sidenote: The Negroes race their skinnes.] Some of them also weare the like vpon their heades being painted with diuers colours, but the most part of them go bare headed, and their heads are clipped and shorne of diuers sorts, and the most part of them haue their skin of their bodies raced with diuers workes, in maner of a leather Ierkin. The men and women goe so alike, that one cannot know a man from a woman but by their breastes, which in the most part be very foule and long, hanging downe like the vdder of a goate.

The same morning we went into the Riuer with our Skiffe, and caried certaine basons, manels, &c. [Sidenote: Graines of Guinea.] And there we tooke that day one hogs-head and 100 li. waight of Graines, and two Elephants teeth at a reasonable good reckoning. We solde them both basons, and Manellios, and Margarits, but they desired most to haue basons: For the most part of our basons wee had by estimation about 30. li. for a piece, and for an Elephants tooth of 30. li. waight, we gaue them 6.

The 16. day in the morning we went into the riuer with our Skiffe, and tooke some of euery sort of our marchandize with vs, and shewed it to the Negroes, but they esteemed it not, but made light of it, and also of the basons, Manellios and Margarits, which yesterday they did buy: howbeit for the basons they would haue giuen vs some graines, but to no purpose, so that this day wee tooke not by estimation aboue one hundreth pound waight of Graines, by meanes of their Captaine, who would suffer no man to sell any thing but through his hands, and at his price: he was so subtile, that for a bason hee would not giue 15. pound waight of Graines, and sometimes would offer vs smal dishfuls whereas before wee had baskets full, and when he saw that wee would not take them in contentment, the Captaine departed, and caused all the rest of the boates to depart, thinking belike that wee would haue followed them, and haue giuen them their owne askings. [Sidenote: The description of their townes and houses.] But after that we perceiued their fetch, wee wayed our Grapnel and went away, and then wee went on land into a small Towne to see the fashions of the Countrey, and there came a threescore of them about vs, and at the first they were afraid of vs, but in the end perceiuing that wee did no hurt, they would come to vs and take vs by the hand and be familiar with vs, and then we went into their Townes, which were like to twentie small houels, all couered ouer with great leaues and baggage, and all the sides open, and a scaffolde vnder the house about a yarde high, where they worke many pretie things of the barkes of trees, and there they lye also. In some of their houses they worke yron and make faire dartes, and diuers other things to worke their boates, and other things withall, and the women worke as well as the men. But when wee were there diuers of the women to shew vs pleasure danced and sung after their maner, full ill to our eares. Their song was thus:

Sakere, sakere, ho, ho. Sakere, sakore, ho, ho.

And with these words they leape and dance, and clap their hands. Beastes we could see none that they had, but two goates, small dogges, and small hennes: other beastes we saw none. After that we had well marked all things we departed and went aboord our ships: which thing the Captaine of the other towne perceiuing, sent two of his seruants in a boat with a basket of Graines, and made vs signes that if when wee had slept wee would come againe into their riuer, wee should haue store of Graines, and so shewed vs his Graines and departed.

The 17. day in the morning because we thought that the Negroes would haue done something because the Captaine sent for vs, I required the Master to goe on shoare, and sent the rest of our Marchants with him, and taried aboord my selfe by reason that the last day he esteemed our things so litle: so when the Master and the rest came into the riuer, the captaine with diuers others came to them, and brought Graines with them, and after that he saw that I was not there, he made signes to know where I was, and they made signes to him againe that I was in the ships: [Sidenote: Diago the name of a Captaine.] and then hee made signes to know who was Captaine by name of Diago, for so they call their Captaine, and they pointed to the master of the ship: then he began to shew his Graines, but he held them so vnreasonably, that there was no profit to be made of them: which things the Master perceiuing, and seeing that they had no store of Graines, came away, and tooke not aboue 50. pound waight of Graines. Then he went a shoare to the litle Towne where we were the day before, and one of them plucked a Gourd, wherewith the Negroes were offended, and came many of them to our men with their darts and great targets, and made signes to them to depart: which our men did, hauing but one bow and two or three swords, and went aboord the boate and came away from them: and assoone as they were come aboord we wayed and set saile, but the winde was off the Sea, so that we could not get out cleare of certaine rocks, and therefore we came to an ancre againe.

[Sidenote: The latitude of S. Vincent riuer is 4. degrees and a halfe.] This riuer is called Riuer S. Vincent, standing in 4. degrees and a halfe, and ebbeth and floweth there every 12. houres, but not much water when it ebbeth the most: while wee were there, it ebbeth one fadome and a halfe water.

[Sidenote: Leaues of exceeding length.] This countrey as farre as we could perceiue is altogether woody, and al strange trees, whereof wee knewe none, and they were of many sorts, with great leaues like great dockes, which bee higher then any man is able to reach the top of them.

[Sidenote: Long pease stalkes.] There are certaine peason by the Sea side, which grow vpon great and very long stalkes, one of the stalkes I measured and found it 27. paces long, and they grow vpon the sand like to trees, and that so neere the Sea, that sometimes the Sea floweth into the woods as we might perceiue by the water markes.

[Sidenote: Long womens breasts.] The trees and all things in this place grow continually greene. Diuers of the women haue such exceeding long breasts, that some of them wil lay the same vpon the ground and lie downe by them, but all the women haue not such breasts.

At this place all the day the winde bloweth off the Sea, and all the night off the land, but wee found it to differ sometimes, which our Master marueiled at.

This night at 9. of the clocke the winde came vp at the East, which ordinarily about that time was wont to come out of the North Northwest off the shoare: yet we wayed and halled off South with that winde all night into the Sea, but the next morning we halled in againe to the lande, and tooke in 6. Tunnes of water for our ship, and I thinke the Hinde tooke in as much.

I could not perceiue that here was any gold, or any other good thing: for the people be so wilde and idle, that they giue themselues to seeke out nothing: if they would take paines they might gather great store of graines, but in this place I could not perceiue two Tunne.

There are many foules in the Countrey, but the people will not take the paines to take them.

I obsetued some of their words of speach, which I thought good here to set downe.

> Bezow, bezow, Is their salutation.
> Manegete afoye, Graines ynough.
> Crocow, afoye, Hennes ynough.
> Zeramme, afoye, Haue ynough.
> Begge sacke Giue me a knife.
> Begge come, Giue me bread
> Borke, Holde your peace.
> Coutrecke. Ye lye.
> Veede, Put foorth, or emptie.
> Brekeke, Rowe.
> Diago, Their Captaine, and some
>   call him Dabo.

These and other wordes they speake very thicke, and oftentimes recite one word three times together, and at the last time longer then at the two first.

The 18. day towards night, as we were sailing along the coast, we met with certaine boats in the sea, and the men shewed vs that there was a riuer thwart of vs, where there were Graines to be sold, but we thought it not good to tary there, least the other ships should get before vs. This riuer hath lying before it three great rockes, and 5. small rocks, one great tree, and a little tree right by the riuer, which in height exceeded all the rest: we halled this night along the coast 16. leagues.

The 19. day as we coasted the shoare, about twelue of the clocke there came out to vs 3. boates to tell vs that they had graines, and brought some with them for a shew, but we could not tary there. We proceeded along the coast, and ancred by the shore all the night, and ran this day 10. leagues.

The 20. day the Hinde hauing ankered by vs amongst rockes, and foule gronnd, lost a small anker. At noone, as we passed along the coast, there came forth a Negro to vs, making signes, that if we would goe a shoare, wee should haue Graines, and where wee ankered at night, there came another to vs, and brought Graines, and shewed vs them, and made signes that wee should tary, and made a fire vpon the land in the night, meaning thereby to tell vs where we should land, and so they did in diuers other places vpon the coast, where they saw vs to anker. [Sidenote: The tides and nature of the shore.] In al the places where we haue ancred, since we came from our watring place, we haue found the tide alwayes running to the Westwards, and all along the coast many rockes hard aboord the shoare, and many of them a league off the shoare or more, we ran this day 12. leagues.

The 21 day, although we ranne all day with a good gale of winde, yet the tides came so sore out of the coast, that we were not able to runne aboue sixe leagues: and this day there came some Negroes to vs, as there had done other times.

The 22. wee ranne all day and night to double a point, called Das Palmas, and ranne sixteene leagues.

The 23. day about 3. of the clocke we were thwart of the point, and before we came to the Westermost part of it, we saw a great ledge of rocks, which lie West from the Cape about 3. leagues and a league or more from the land. Shortly after we had sight of the Eastermost part of the Cape, which lieth 4. leagues from the Westermost part, and vpon the very corner thereof lie two greene places, as it were closes, and to the Westwards of the Cape the land parted from the Cape, as it were a Bay, whereby it may well be knowen. Foure leagues more beyonde that there lieth a head-land in the sea, and about two leagues beyond the head-land there goeth in a great Bay, as it were a riuer, before which place we ankered all that night, which wee did, least in the night wee should ouerrunne a riuer where the last yeere they had all their Elephants teeth. [Sidenote: That was the yeere 1554.]

This Cape Das palmas lieth vnder foure degrees and a halfe, and betwixt the said Cape, and the riuer de Sestos is the greatest store of Graines to be had, and being past the said Cape there is no great store else where.

Where we ankered this night, we found that the tide, which before ran alwayes to the Westward, from this Cape runneth all to the Eastward: this day we ranne some 16. leagues.

The 24. day running our course, about eight of the clock there came forth to vs certaine boats, which brought with them small egges, which were soft without shels, and they made vs signes, that there was within the land fresh water, and Goates: and the Master thinking that it was the riuer which we sought, cast ancker and sent the boate on shoare, with one that knew the riuer, and comming neere the shoare, hee perceiued that it was not the riuer, and so came backe againe, and went along the shoare, with their oares and saile, and wee weyed and ranne along the shoare also: and being thirteene leagues beyond the Cape, the Master perceiued a place which he iudged to be the riuer, when wee were in deede two miles shot past it: yet the boate came from the shoare, and they that were in her saide, that there was no riuer: notwithstanding wee came to an ancker, and the Master and I tooke fiue men with vs in the boat, and when hee came neere the shoare, hee perceiued that it was the same riuer which hee did seeke: so we rowed in, and found the entrance very ill, by reason that the sea goeth so high: and being entred, diuers boats came to vs, and shewed vs that they had Elephants teeth, and they brought vs one of about eight pound, and a little one of a pound, which we bought: then they brought certaine teeth to the riuer side, making signes, that if the next day we would come againe, they would sell vs them: so we gaue vnto two Captaines, to either of them a manillio, and so we departed, and came aboord, and sent out the other boate to another place, where certaine boats that came into the sea, made vs signes that there was fresh water: and being come thither, they found a towne, but no riuer, yet the people brought them fresh water, and shewed them an Elephants tooth, making signes that the next day they would sel them teeth, and so they came aboord.

This riuer lieth by the Carde thirteene leagues from the Cape Das palmas, and there lieth to the Westwards of the same a rocke about a league in the sea, and the riuer it selfe hath a point of lande comming out into the Sea, whereupon grow fiue trees, which may well bee discerned two or three leagues off, comming from the Westward, but the riuer cannot bee perceiued vntill such time as a man be hard by it, and then a man may perceiue a litle Towne on ech side the riuer, and to ech Towne there belongeth a Captaine. The riuer is but small, but the water is good and fresh.

Two miles beyond the riuer, where the other towne is, there lieth another point into the Sea, which is greene like a close, and not aboue sixe trees vpon it, which growe one of them from the other, whereby the coast may well be knowen: for along all the coast that we haue hitherto sailed by, I haue not seene so much bare land.

In this place, and three or foure leagues to the Westward of it, al along the shoare, there grow many Palme trees, whereof they make their wine de Palma. These trees may easily be knowen almost two leagues off, for they be very high and white bodied, and streight, and be biggest in the midst: they haue no boughes, but onely a round bush in the top of them: and at the top of the same trees they boare a hoale, and there they hang a bottell, and the iuyce of the tree runneth out of the said hole into the bottle, and that is their wine.

From the Cape das Palmas, to the Cape Tres puntas, there are 100. leagues: and to the port where we purpose to make sales of our cloth beyond the Cape Tres puntas, 40. leagues.

Note, that betwixt the riuer De Sestos, and the Cape Das palmas, is the place where all the graines be gathered.

The language of the people of this place, as far as I could perceiue, differeth not much from the language of those which dwel where we watred before: but the people of this place be more gentle in nature then the other, and goodlier men: their building and apparel is all one with the others.

Their desire in this place was most of all to haue Manillios and Margarites: as for the rest of our things, they did litle esteeme them.

[Sidenote: Their maner of swearing by the water of the Sea.] About nine of the clocke there came boates to vs foorth, from both of the places aforsaid, and brought with them certaine teeth, and after they had caused me to sweare by the water of the Sea that I would not hurt them, they came aboord our ship three or foure of them, and we gaue them to eate of all such things as we had, and they did eate and drinke of all things, as well as we our selues. Afterwards we bought all their teeth, which were in number 14. and of those 14. there were 10. small: afterwards they departed, making vs signes that the next day we should come to their Townes.

[Sidenote: Two townes.] The 26. day because we would not trifle long at this place I required the Master to goe vnto one of the townes, and to take two of our marchants with him, and I my selfe went to the other, and tooke one with me, because these two townes stand three miles asunder. To these places we caried somewhat of euery kind of marchandize that we had: and hee had at the one Towne, nine teeth, which were but small, and at the other towne where I was, I had eleuen, which were also not bigge, and we left aboord with the Master certaine Manillios, wherewith he bought 12. teeth aboord the ship, in our absence: and hauing bought these of them, wee perceiued that they had no more teeth: so in that place where I was one brought to me a small goat, which I bought, and to the Master at the other place they brought fiue small hennes, which he bought also, and after that we saw there was nothing else to be had, we departed, and by one of the clocke we met aboord, and then wayed, and went East our course 18. leagues still within sight of land.

The 28. the wind varied, and we ranne into the sea, and the winde comming againe off the sea, wee fell with the land againe, and the first of the land which we raised shewed as a great red cliffe round, but not very high, and to the Eastward of that another smaller red cliffe, and right aboue that into the land a round hammoke and greene, which we tooke to be trees. We ranne in these 24. houres, not aboue foure leagues.

The 29. day comming neere to the shoare, we perceiued the red cliffe aforesaide to haue right vpon the top of it a great heape of trees, and all to the Westwards of it ful of red cliffes as farre as we could see, and all along the shoare, as well vpon the cliffes, as otherwise, full of wood: within a mile of the said great cliffe there is a riuer to the Eastwards, and no cliffes that we could see, except one small cliffe, which is hard by it. We ran this day and night 12. leagues.

The windes that wee had in this place by the reports of the people and of those that haue bene there, haue not bene vsuall, but in the night, at North off the lande, and in the day South off the Sea, and most commonly Northwest, and Southwest.

The 31. day we went our course by the shoare Northwards: this land is al along a low shoare, and full of wood, as all the coast is for the most part, and no rockes. This morning came out many boates which went a fishing, which bee greater boates then those which we sawe before, so that in some of them there sate 5. men, but the fashion of the boats is all one. In the afternoone about three of the clocke wee had sight of a Towne by the sea side, which our Pilots iudged to be 25. leagues to the Westwards of the Cape Tres puntas.

The third of Ianuary in the morning we fell with the Cape Tres puntas, and in the night passed, as our Pilots saide, by one of the Portugals castles, which is 8. leagues to the Westwards of the Cape: vpon the first sight of the Cape wee discerned it a very high land, and all growen ouer with trees, and comming neere to it, we perceiued two head lands, as it were two Bayes betwixt them, which opened right to the Westward, and the vttermost of them is the Easterne Cape, there we perceiued the middle Cape, and the Eastermost Cape: the middle Cape standeth not aboue a league from the West Cape, although the Card sheweth them to be 3. leagues one from the other: and that middle Cape hath right before the point of it a small rocke so neere to it, that it cannot be discerned from the Cape, except a man be neere to the shoare, and upon the same Cape standeth a great heape of trees, and when a man is thwart the same Cape to the Eastward, there riseth hard by it a round greene hommoke, which commeth out of the maine.

The thirde Cape is about a league beyond the middle Cape, and is a high land like to the other Capes, and betwixt the middle, and the thirde commeth out a little head or point of a land out of the maine, and diuers rocks hard aboord the shoare.

Before we came to the Capes, being about 8. leagues off them, wee had the land Southeast, and by East, and being past the Capes, the land runneth in againe East Northeast.

About two leagues beyond the farthest Cape there is a lowe glade about two miles long, and then the land riseth high againe, and diuers head lands rise one beyond another, and diuers rockes lie at the point of the first headland. The middest of these Capes is the neerest to the Southwards, I meane, further into the sea than any of the other, so that being to the Eastward of it, it may be discerned farre off, and being so to the Eastward it riseth with two small rockes.

This day we ankered for feare of ouershooting a towne called S. Iohns. Wee ran this day not aboue 8. leagues. In the afternoone this day there came a boate of the countrey from the shoare, with fiue men in her, and went along by vs, as we thought, to discerne our flagges, but they would not come neere vs, and when they had well looked vpon vs, they departed.

The fourth day in the morning, sailing by the coast, we espied a ledge of rockes by the shoare, and to the Westwards of them two great grene hils ioyning together, so that betweene them it was hollow like a saddle: and within the said rockes the Master thought the aforenamed Towne had stoode, and therefore we manned our boates, and tooke with vs cloth, and other marchandize, and rowed ashoare, but going along by the coast, we sawe that there was no towne, therefore wee went aboord againe.

From these two hils aforesaid, about two leagues to the Eastward, lie out into the Sea almost two miles a ledge of rockes, and beyond that a great Bay, which runneth into the North Northwestward, and the land in this place lieth North Northeast along the shoare: but the vttermost point of land in that place that we could see, lay Northeast, and by East from vs.

After that we were with a small gale of winde runne past that vttermost head-land, we sawe a great red cliffe, which the Master againe iudged to be the towne of S. Iohns, and then wee tooke our boate with marchandize, and went thither, and when we came thither, we perceiued that there was a towne vpon the toppe of the hill, and so wee went toward it, and when we were hard by it, the people of the towne came together a great sort of them, and waued vs to come in, with a peece of cloth, and so we went into a very faire Bay, which lieth to the Eastward of the cliffe, whereupon the towne standeth, and being within the cliffe, wee let fall our grapnell, and after that we had taried there a good space, they sent a boate aboord of vs, to shewe vs that they had golde, and they shewed us a peece about halfe a crowne weight, and required to know our measure, and our weight, that they might shewe their Captaine thereof: and wee gaue them a measure of two elles, and a waight of two Angels to shew vnto him, which they tooke, and went on shoare, and shewed it vnto their Captaine, and then they brought vs a measure of two elles, one quarter and a halfe, and one Crusado-weight of gold, making vs signes that so much they would giue for the like measure, and lesse they would not haue. After this, we taried there about an houre, and when we sawe that they would doe no otherwise, and withall vnderstood, that all the best places were before vs, wee departed to our shippes and wayed, and ranne along the shoare, and went before with our boate, and hauing sailed about a league, we came to a point where there lay foorth a ledge of rockes, like to the others before spoken of, and being past that people, the Master spied a place which hee saide plainely was the towne of Don Iohn: and the night was come vpon vs, so that we could not well discerne it, but we ankered as neere vnto the place as we could.

[Sidenote: The towne of Don Iohn.] The fift day in the morning we perceiued it to be the same towne in deede, and we manned our boates and went thither, and because that the last yeere the Portugals at that place tooke away a man from them, and after shot at them with great bases, and did beate them from the place, we let fall our grapnel almost a base shot off the shoare, and there we lay about two houres, and no boats came to vs. Then certaine of our men with the Hindes boate went into the Bay which lieth to the Eastward of the towne, and within that Bay they found a goodly fresh riuer, and afterwards they came and waued to vs also to come in, because they perceiued the Negroes to come downe to that place, which we did: and immediately the Negroes came to vs, and made vs signes that they had golde, but none of them would come aboord our boates, neither could we perceiue any boates that they had to come withall, so that we iudged that the Portugals had spoiled their boates, because we saw halfe of their towne destroyed.

Wee hauing stayed there a good space, and seeing that they would not come to vs, thrust our boates heads a shoare, being both well appointed, and then the Captaine of the Towne came downe being a graue man: and he came with his dart in his hand, and sixe tall men after him, euery one with his dart and his target, and their darts were all of yron, faire and sharpe, and there came another after them which caried the Captaines stoole: wee saluted him, and put off our caps, and bowed our selues, and hee like one that thought well of himselfe, did not mooue his cap, nor scant bowed his body, and sate him downe very solemnly, vpon his stoole: but all his men put off their caps to vs, and bowed downe themselues.

He was clothed from the loines down with a cloth of that Countrey making, wrapped about him, and made fast about his loynes with a girdle, and his cap of a certaine cloth of the Countrey also, and bare legged, and bare footed, and all bare aboue the loynes, except his head.

His seruants, some of them had cloth about their loines, and some nothing but a cloth betwixt their legges, and made fast before, and behinde to their girdles, and cappes of their owne making, some like a basket, and some like a great wide purse of beasts skinnes.

[Sidenote: Their weapons.] All their cloth, cordes, girdles, fishing lines, and all such like things which they haue, they make of the bark of certaine trees, and thereof they can worke things very pretily, and yron worke they can make very fine, of all such things as they doe occupy, as darts, fishhookes, hooking yrons, yron heads, and great daggers, some of them as long as a woodknife, which be on both sides exceeding sharpe, and bended after the maner of Turkie blades, and the most part of them haue hanging at their left side one of those great daggers.

Their targets bee made of such pils as their cloth is made of, and very closely wrought, and they bee in forme foure square, and very great, and somewhat longer then they bee broad, so that kneeling downe, they make their targets to couer their whole body. Their bowes be short, and of a pretie strength, as much as a man is able to draw with one of his fingers, and the string is of the barke of a tree, made flat, and about a quarter of an inch broad: as for their arrowes, I haue not as yet seene any of them, for they had wrapped them vp close, and because I was busie I could not stand about it, to haue them open them. Their golde also they worke very well.

When the Captaine was set, I sent him two elles of cloth, and two basons, and gaue them vnto him, and hee sent againe for a waight of the same measure, and I sent him a weight of two Angels, which he would not take, nether would hee suffer the towne to buy any thing, but the basons of brasse: so that wee solde that day 74. basons vnto the men of the towne, for about half an Angel weight, one with another, and nine white basons, which we solde for a quarter of an Angell a peece, or thereabouts.

We shewed them all our other things which we had, but they did not esteeme them.

About two of the clocke, the Captaine who did depart in the morning from vs, came againe, and brought with him to present mee withall, a henne, and two great rootes, which I receiued, and after made me signes that the countrey would come to his towne that night, and bring great store of gold, which in deed about 4. of the clocke they did: for there came about 100. men vnder 3. Captaines, well appointed with their darts and bowes, and when they came to vs, euery man sticked downe his dart vpon the shoare, and the Captaines had stooles brought them, and they sate downe, and sent a young man aboord of vs, which brought a measure with him of an ell, and one fourth part, and one sixteenth part, and he would haue that foure times for a waight of one Angell and twelue graines: I offered him two elles, as I had done before for two Angels weight, which he esteemed nothing, but still stucke at his foure measures aforesaide: yet in the ende, when it grew very late, and I made him signes, that I would depart, he came to foure elles for the weight abouesaid, and otherwise he would not deale, and so we departed. This day we tooke for basons sixe ounces and a halfe and one eight part.

The sixt day in the morning we manned our boates and the skiffe well, for feare of the Portugals which the last yeere had taken away a man from the other ships, and went on shoare, and landed, because they had no boates to come to vs, and so the young man which was with vs the night before was sent aboord, who seemed to haue dealt and bargained before with the Portugals for he could speake a litle Portuguise, and was perfect in weights and measures: at his comming be offered vs, as he had done before, one Angell, and twelue graines for four elles, and more he would not giue, and made signes, that if we would not take that, we should depart, which we did: but before we did indeede depart, I offered him of some rotten cloth three elles for his waight of an Angell and twelue graines, which he would not take, and then we departed making signes to him that we would go away, as indeede we would haue done, rather then haue giuen that measure, although the cloth was ill, seeing we were so neere to the places, which we iudged to be better for sale. Then we went aboord our ships which lay about a league off, and came backe againe to the shoare for sand and balaste: and then the Captaine perceiuing that the boats had brought no marchandize but came onely for water and sand, and seeing that we would depart, came vnto them, making signes againe to know whether would we not giue the foure elles, and they made signes againe, that we would giue them but three, and when they sawe that the boates were ready to depart, they came vnto them and gaue them the weight of our Angell and twelue graines, which we required before and made signes, that if we would come againe, they would take three elles. So when the boates came aboord, we layde wares in them both, and for the speedier dispatch I and Iohn Sauill went in one boat, and the Maister Iohn Makeworth, and Richard Curligin, in the other, and went on shoare, and that night I tooke for my part fiftie and two ounces, and in the other boate they tooke eight ounces and a quarter, all by one weight and measure, and so being very late, we departed and went aboord, and took in all this day three pound.

The seuenth day we went a shoare againe, and that day I tooke in our boate three pound 19 ounces, so that we dispatched almost all the cloth that we caried with us before noone, and then many of the people were departed and those that remained had litle golde, yet they made vs signes to fetch them some latten basons which I would not because I purposed not to trifle out the time, but goe thence with speede to Don Iohns towne. But Iohn Sauill and Iohn Makeworth were desirous to goe againe: and I, loth to hinder them of any profite, consented, but went not my selfe: so they tooke eighteene ounces of gold and came away, seeing that the people at a certaine crie made, were departed.

While they were at the shoare, there came a young fellow which could speake a little Portuguise, with three more with him, and to him I solde 39 basons and two small white sawcers, for three ounces, &c., which was the best reckoning that we did make of any basons: and in the forenoone when I was at the shoare, the Master solde fiue basons vnto the same fellow, for halfe an ounce of golde.

[Sidenote: 60. Portugales in the castle of Mina.] This fellow, as farre as we could perceiue, had bene taken into the Castle by the Portugales, and was gotten away from them, for he tolde vs that the Portugales were bad men, and that they made them slaues if they could take them, and would put yrons vpon their legges, and besides he tolde vs, that as many Frenchmen or Englishmen, as they could take (for he could name these two very well) they would hang them: he tolde vs further, that there were 60 men in the castle, and that euery yeere there came thither two shippes, one great, and one small caruell, and further, that Don Iohn had warres with the Portugals, which gaue mee the better courage to goe to his towne, which lieth not foure leagues from the Castle, wherehence our men were beaten the last yeere.

[Sidenote: The English in anno 1544 tooke away 5 Negroes.] This fellowe came aboord our shippe without much feare, and assoone as he came, he demaunded, why we had not brought againe their men, which the last yeere we tooke away, and could tell vs that there were fiue taken away by Englishmen: we made him answere, that they were in England well vsed, and were there kept till they could speake the language, and then they should be brought againe to be a helpe to Englishmen in this Countrey: and then he spake no more of that matter:

Our boates being come aboord, we wayed and set saile and a litle after spied, a great fire vpon the shoare, and by the light of the fire we might discerne a white thing, which they tooke to be the Castle, and for feare of ouersbooting the towne of Don Iohn we there ankered two leagues off the shoare, for it is hard to fetch vp a towne here, if a ship ouershoot it. This day we tooke seuen pound, and fiue ounces of gold.

This towne lieth in a great Bay, which is very deepe.

The people in this place desired most to haue basons and cloth. They would buy some of them also many trifles, as kniues, horsetailes, hornes: and some of our men going a shoare, sold a cap, a dagger, a hat, &c.

They shewed vs a certain course cloth, which I thinke to be made in France, for it was course wooll, and a small threed, and as thicke as wosted, and striped with stripes of greene, white, yellow &c. Diuers of the people did weare about their neckes great beades of glasse of diuerse colours. Here also I learned some of their language, [Marginal note: This language seemeth partly to be corrupt.] as followeth:

> Mattea, mattea, Is their salutation.
> Dassee, dassee, I thanke you.
> Sheke, Golde.
> Cowrte, Cut.
> Cracca, Kniues.
> Bassina, Basons.
> Foco, foco, Cloth.
> Molta, Much, or great store.

[Sidenote: Sight of the casle of Mina.] The eight day in the morning we had sight of the Castle, but by reason of a miste that then fell we could not haue the perfect sight of it, till we were almost at the towne of Don Iohn, and then it cleared vp, and we saw it and a white house, as it were a Chappell, vpon the hill about it, and then we halled into the shoare, within two English miles of Don Iohns towne, and there ankered in seuen fadome water. Here, as in many other places before, we perceiued that the currant went with the winde.

The land here is in some places low and in some high, and full of wood altogether.

[Sidenote: Don Iohns towne described.] The towne of Don Iohn is but litle, of about twentie houses, and the most part of the towne is walled in with a wall of a mans height, made with reede or sedge, or some such thing. Here we staied two or three houres after we had ankered, to see if any man would come vnto vs: and seeing that none did come, we manned our boates and put in marchandize, and went and ankered with our boates neere to the shoare: then they sent out a man to vs who made vs signes that that was the towne of Don Iohn, and that he himselfe was in the Countrey, and would be at home at the going downe of the Sunne, and when he had done, he required a reward, as the most part of them will doe which come first aboord, and I gaue him one ell of cloth and he departed, and that night we heard no more of him.

The ninth day in the morning we went againe with our boates to the shoare, and there came foorth a boate to vs, who made signes that Don Iohn was not come home, but would be at home this day: and to that place also came another boate from the other towne a mile from this, which is called Don Deuis, and brought with him gold to shew vs, making signes that we should come thither. I then left in this place Iohn Sauill, and Iohn Makeworth, and tooke the Hinde, and went to the other towne and there ankered, and tooke cloth and went to shore with the boate, and by and by the boates came to vs and brought a measure of foure yards long and a halfe, and shewed vs a weight of an angell and twelue graines, which they would giue for so much, and not otherwise: so I staied and made no bargaine. And all this day the barke lay at Don Iohns towne, and did nothing, hauing answere that he was not come home.

The tenth day we went againe to the shoare, and there came out a boat with good store of gold, and hauing driuen the matter off a long time, and hauing brought the measure to a nayle lesse then three elles, and their weight to an angell and twentie graines, and could not bring them to more, I did conclude with them and solde, and within one quarter of an houre I tooke one pound and a quarter of an ounce of golde: and then they made me signes to tary, till they had parted their cloth vpon the shoare as their manner is, and they would come againe, and so they went away, and layde the cloth all abroad vpon the sande peece by peece, and by and by one came running downe from the towne to them, and spake vnto them, and foorthwith euery man made as much haste as he could away, and went into the woods to hide his golde and his cloth: we mistrusted some knauery, and being waued by them to come a shoare, yet we would not, but went aboorde the Hinde, and perceiued vpon the hill 30 men whom we iudged to be Portugals: and they went vp to the toppe of the hill and there mustered and shewed themselues, hauing a flagge with them. Then I being desirous to knowe what the Hart did, tooke the Hindes boate and went towards her, and when I came neere to them they shot off two pieces of ordinance which I marueiled at: I made as much haste as I could to her, and met her boate and skiffe comming from the shoare in all haste, and we met aboord together. [Sidenote: The Portugales of the castle of Mina inuaded our men.] They shewed me that they had beene a shoare all that day, and had giuen to the two sonnes of Don Iohn, to either of them three yardes and a halfe of doth, and three basons betwixt them, and had deliuered him 3 yards of cloth more and the weight of an angell and 12 graines, and being on land did tarie for his answere, and in the meane time the Portugals came running from the hill vpon them, whereof the Negroes a litle before had giuen them warning, and bad them to go away, but they perceiued it not. The sonne of Don Iohn conspired with the Portugales against them, so that they were almost vpon them, but yet they recouered their boate and set off from the shoare, and the Portugales shot their calieuers at them, but hurt no man, and then the shippe perceiuing it, shot off the two peeces aforesayde among them. Hereupon we layde bases in both the boates, and in the Skiffe and manned them well, and went a shoare againe, but because of the winde we could not land, but lay off in the sea about ten score and shot at them, but the hill succoured them, and they from the rockes and from the hilles shot at vs with their halfe hakes, and the Negroes more for feare then for loue stoode by them to helpe them, and when we saw that the Negroes were in such subiction vnto them that they durst not sell vs any thing for feare of them we went aboord, and that night the winde kept at the East, so that we could not with our ship fetch the Hinde, but I tooke the boate in the night and went aboord the barke to see what was there to be done, and in the morning we perceiued the towne to be in like case layde with Portugales, so we wayed and went along the coast. [Sidenote: The towne of Don Iohn de Viso.] This towne of Iohn de Viso standeth vpon an hill like the towne of Don Iohn, but it hath beene burned, so that there are not passing sixe houses in it: the most part of the golde that comes thither comes out of the countrey, and no doubt if the people durst for feare of the Portugals bring forth their gold, there would be had good store: but they dare not sell any thing, their subiection is so great to the Portugales. The 11 day running by the shoare we had sight of a litle towne foure leagues from the last towne that we came from, and about halfe a league from that, of another towne vpon a hill, and halfe a league from that also of another great towne vpon the shoare: whither we went to set what could there be done: if we could doe nothing, then to returne to the other towne, because we thought that the Portugales would leaue the towne vpon our departure. Along from the castle vnto this place are very high hilles which may be seene aboue all other hilles, but they are full of wood, and great red cliffes by the sea side. The boates of these places are somewhat large and bigge, for one of them will carie twelue men, but their forme is alike with the former boates of the coast. There are about these townes few riuers: their language differeth not from the language vsed at Don Iohns towne: but euery one can speake three or foure words of Portuguise, which they vsed altogether to vs.

We sawe this night about 5 of the clocke 22 boates running along the shoare to the Westward, whereupon we suspected some knauery intended against vs. The 12 day therefore we set sayle and went further along the coast, and descried more townes wherein were greater houses then in the other townes, and the people came out of the townes to looke vpon vs, but we could see no boates. Two mile beyond the Eastermost towne are blacke rocks, which blacke rockes continue to the vttermost cape of the land, which is about a league off, and then the land runnes in Eastnortheast, and a sandy shoare againe: vpon these blacke rockes came downe certaine Negroes, which waued vs with a white flagge, but we perceiuing the principall place to be neere, would not stay, but bare still along the shoare: and as soone as we had opened the point of the land, we raysed another headland about a league off the point, which had a rocke lying off it into the sea, and that they thought to be the place which we sought. When we came thwart the place they knew it, and we put wares into our boate, and the ship being within halfe a mile of the place ankered in fiue fadome water and faire ground. We went on shoare with our boate, and ankered about ten of the clocke in the forenoone: we saw many boates lying vpon the shoare, and diuers came by vs, but none of them would come neere vs, being as we iudged afraid of vs: [Sidenote: Foure men taken away by the English.] because that foure men were taken perforce the last yeere from this place, so that no man came to vs, whereupon we went aboord againe, and thought here to haue made no saile: yet towardes night a great sort came downe to the water side, and waued vs on shoare with a white flagge, and afterwarde their Captaine came downe and many men with him, and sate him downe by the shoare vnder a tree: which when I perceiued, I tooke things with me to giue him: at last he sent a boat to call to vs, which would not come neere vs, but made vs signes to come againe the next day: but in fine, I got them to come aboord in offering them things to giue to their captaine, which were two elles of cloth, one latten bason, one white bason, a bottle, a great piece of beefe, and sixe bisket cakes, which they receiued making vs signes to come againe the next day, saying, that their Captain was Grand Capitane as appeared by those that attended vpon him with their darts and targets, and other weapons.

This towne is very great and stands vpon a hill among trees, so that it cannot well be seene except a man be neere it: to the Eastward of it vpon the hill hard by the towne stand 2. high trees, which is a good marke to knowe the towne. And vnder the towne lieth another hill lower then it, whereupon the sea beates: and that end next the sea is all great blacke rockes, and beyonde the towne in a bay lieth another small towne.

The 13 day in the morning we tooke our boate and went to shoare, and stayed till ten a clocke and no man came to vs: we went about therefore to returne aboord, and when the Negroes saw that, they came running downe with a flagge to waue vs againe, so we ankered againe, and then one shewed vs that the Captaine would come downe by and by: we sawe a saile in the meane time passe by vs but it was small, and we regarded it not. [Sidenote: The like they doe in the countrey of Prette Ianni.] Being on shore we made a tilt with our oares and sayle, and then there came a boate to vs with fiue men in her, who brought vs againe our bottle, and brought me a hen, making signes by the sunne, that within two houres the marchants of the countrey would come downe and buy all that we had: so I gaue them sixe Manillios to carry to their Captaine, and they made signes to haue a pledge of vs, and they would leaue vs another man: and we willing to do so, put one of our men in their boate, but they would not giue vs one of theirs, so we tooke our man againe, and there tarried for the marchants: and shortly after one came downe arrayed like their Captaine with a great traine after him, who saluted us friendly, and one of the chiefest of them went and sate downe vnder a tree, where the last yere the Captaine was wont to sit: and at last we perceiued a great many of them to stand at the ende of a hollow way, and behinde them the Portugales had planted a base, who suddenly shotte at vs but ouershot vs, and yet we were in a manner hard by them, and they shot at vs againe before we could ship our oares to get away but did no hurt. Then the Negroes came to the rocks hard by vs, and disharged calieuers at vs, and againe the Portugales shot off their base twise more, and then our ship shot at them, but the rockes and hilles defended them.

[Sidenote: Master Robert Gainshes voyage to Guinea in anno 1554.] Then we went aboord to goe from this place, seeing the Negroes bent against vs, because that the last yeere M. Gainsh did take away the Captaines sonne and three others from this place with their golde, and all that they had about them: [Sidenote: The English were offered to build a towne in Guine.] which was the cause that they became friends with the Portugales, whom before they hated, as did appeare the last yeere by the courteous intertainement which the Trinitie had there, when the Captaine came aboord the shippe, and brought them to his towne, and offered them ground to build a Castle in, and there they had good sales.

The 14 day we wayed and plyed backe againe to seeke the Hinde, which in the morning we met, and so we turned both back to the Eastwardes to see what we could doe at that place where the Trinitie did sell her eight frises the last yeere. The Hinde had taken eighteene ounces and a halfe more of golde of other Negroes, the day after that we left them. This day about one of the clocke we espied certaine boates vpon the sand and men by them and went to them with marchandizes, and tooke three ounces of gold for 18 fuffs of cloth, euery fuffe three yards and a halfe after one angell and 12 graines the fuffe, and then they made me signes that the next day I should haue golde enough: so the Master took the Hinde with Iohn Sauill and Iohn Makeworth, and went to seeke the place aforesaid, and I with Richard Pakeman remained in this place to see what we could do the next day: and when the Negroes perceiued our ship to go away, they feared that the other would follow, and so sent forth 2 boats to vs with 4 men in them, requiring vs to tary and to giue them one man for a pledge, and 2 of them should tary with vs for him, so Edward M. Morleis seruant seeing these men so earnest therein offered himselfe to be pledge, and we let him goe for two of them, one whereof had his waights and scales, and a chaine of golde aboute his necke, and another about his arme. They did eate of such things as we had and were well contented. In the night the Negroes kept a light vpon the shoare thwart of vs, and about one of the clocke we heard and saw the light of a base which shot off twise at the said light, and by and by discharged two calieuers, which in the end we perceiued to be the Portugals brigandine which followed vs from place to place, to giue warning to the people of the countrey, that they should not deale with vs.

The 15 day in the morning the Captaine came downe with 100 men with him, and brought his wife, and many others brought their wiues also, because their towne was 8 miles vp in the countrey, and they determined to lie by the sea side till they had brought what they would. When he was come he sent our man aboord, and required to haue two men pledges, and he himselfe would come aboord, and I sent him two, of whom he tooke but one, and so came aboord vs, he and his wife with diuers of his friends, and brought me a goate and two great rootes, and I gaue him againe a latten bason, a white bason, 6 manillios, and a bottell of Malmesie, and to his wife a small casket. After this we began to make our measure and weight: and he had a weight of his owne which held one angell and 14 graines, and required a measure of 4 elles and a halfe. In fine we concluded the 8 part for one angell and 20 graines, and before we had done, they tooke mine owne weight and measure.

The 16 day I tooke 8 li. 1 ounce of gold: and since the departure of the Hinde I heard not of her, but when our pledge went into the countrey the first night, he said he saw her cast anker aboue fiue leagues from this place. The 17 day I sold about 17 pieces of cloth, and tooke 4 li. 4 ounces and a halfe of gold. The 18 day the captaine desired to haue some of our wine, and offered halfe a ducket of gold for a bottell: but I gaue it him freely, and made him and his traine drinke besides. And this day also I tooke 5 li. 5 ounces of gold. The 19 day we sold about 18 clothes, and tooke 4 li. 4 ounces and one quarter of golde.

The 20 day tooke 3 li. sixe ounces and a quarter of golde. The 21 we tooke 8 li. 7. ounces and a quarter. The 22. 3. li. 8. ounces and a quarter. And this night about 4 of the clocke the Captaine who had layen all this while vpon the shoare, went away with all the rest of the people with him.

The 23 day we were waued a shoare by other Negroes, and sold them cloth, caskets, kniues, and a dosen of bels, and tooke 1 li. 10 ounces of gold. The 24 likewise we sold bels, sheetes, and thimbles, and tooke two li. one ounce and a quarter of gold. The 25 day we sold 7 dosen of smal bels and other things, and then perceiuing their gold to be done, we wayed and set sayle and went to leeward to seeke the Hinde, and about 5 of the clocke at night we had sight of her, and bare with her, and understood that shee had made some sales. The 26 day wee receiued out of the Hinde 48 li. 3 ounces and one eight part of golde, which they had taken in the time that we were from them. And this day vpon the request of a Negro that came vnto vs from a captaine, we went to shoare with our marchandize, and tooke 7 li. and one ounce of gold. At this place they required no gages of vs, but at night they sent a man aboord vs, which lay with vs all night, because we might knowe that they would also come to vs the next day. The 27 day in both our shippes we tooke 8. li. one ounce, three quarters and halfe a quarter of golde. The 28 we made sales for the companie, and tooke one pound and half an ounce of gold. The 29 day in the morning we heard two calieuers shot off vpon the shore, which we iudged to be either by the Portugales or by the Negroes of the Portugales: we manned our boates and armed our selues and went to shoare, but coulde finde nothing: for they were gone. The 30 day we made more sales for the companie and for the Masters.

The 31 we sent our boate to shoare to take in sand for balast, and there our men met the Negroes, with whom they had made sale the day before a fishing which did helpe them to fill sand, and hauing no gold, sold fish to our men for their handkerchiefs and nightkerchiefes.

The 1 day of February we wayed and went to another place, and tooke 1 li. 9. ounces 3 quarters of gold. The 2 day we made more sales: but hauing viewed our victuals we determined to tarie no long time vpon the coast, because the most part of our drinke was spent, and that which remained grew sowre. [Sidenote: They returne for England.] The 3 and 4 dayes we made some sales, though not great, and finding the wind this 4. day to come off the shoare, we set saile and ranne along the shoare to the Westwards: vpon this coast we found by experience that ordinarily about 2 of the clocke in the night the winde comes off the shoare at Northnortheast, and so continueth vntil eight of the clocke in the morning: and all the rest of the day and night it comes out of Southwest: and as for the tide or currant vpon this shoare, it goeth continually with the winde. The 5 day we continued sayling and thought to haue met with some English ships, but found none.

The sixt day we went our course Southwest to fetch vnder the line, and ranne by estimation 24 leagues.

The 13 day wee thought our selues by our reckoning to be cleare off the Cape das Palmas, and ranne 12 leagues.

The 22 day we were thwart of the Cape de Monte, which is to the Westward of the Riuer de Sestos, about 30 leagues.

The first day of March in a Ternado we lost the Hinde, whereupon we set vp a light and shot off a piece but could not heare of her, so that then we strooke our saile and taried for her, and in the morning had sight of her againe three leagues a sterne off vs.

Vpon the 22 day we found our selues to be in the height of Cape Verde, which stands in 14 degrees and a halfe.

From this day till the 29 day we continued our course, and then we found our selues to be in 22 degrees. This day one of our men called William King, who had bene long sicke, died in his sleepe, his apparel was distributed to those that lackt it, and his money was kept for his friends to be deliuered them at his comming home.

The 30 day we found our selues to be vnder the Tropike.

The 31 day we went our course, and made way 18 leagues.

From the first day of Aprill to the 20 we went our course, and then found our selues to bee in the height of the Asores.

The seuenth day of May we fell with the South part of Ireland, and going on shoare with our boate had fresh drinke, and two sheepe of the countrey people, which were wilde Kernes, and we gaue them golde for them, and bought further such other victuals as we had neede of, and thought would serue vs till we arriued in England.

The 14. day with the afternoone tide we went into the Port of Bristoll called Hungrode, and there ankered in safetie and gaue thankes to God for our safe arriuall.

* * * * *

The second voyage made by Maister William Towrson to the coast of Guinea, and the Castle of Mina, in the yeere 1556. with the Tiger of London, a ship of 120 tunnes, the Hart of London of 60 tunnes, and a Pinnesse of sixteene tunnes.

The fourteenth day of September, the yeere abouesayd, we departed from Harwich, and directed our course for the Isle of Sillie, to meete there with the Hart and Pinnesse, which were rigged and victualed at Bristoll, but arriuing there the eight and twientieth day we found them not, and therefore after long lying at Hull to tarrie for them, but not espying them, we turned backe to Plimmouth the 12 day of October, and being there, the Hart and the Pinnesse came to vs, so that the 15 of Nouember we all departed together from Plimmouth at one of the clocke in the after noone, and the 28 day we had sight of the Isle of Porto Santo, and the next day in the morning of Madera.

The third day of December we fell with the Ile of Palma, and the 9 we were thwart of Cape Blanke, and found there certaine Carauels fishing for Pargoes.

The 19 we found our selues in the height of Sierra Leona, and all this day we ranne thwart of certaine Currants, which did set to the West Southwestward so fast as if it had bene the ouerfall of a sand, making a great noyse like vnto a streame or tide-gate when the water is shoale: and to prooue whither we could finde ground in this place, we sounded and had 150 fadome, and no ground, and so departed.

The 30 of December we fell with the coast of Guinea, and had first sight of it about 4 leagues off. The best marke that we could take of the place to knowe it was three hilles, which lay Northeast and by East from vs: betwixt the Northermost two hilles there are two high and great trees standing in sight as it were a sailes breadth one from another, and a litle more to the Northwestwards are certaine hommocks. Hauing sayled somewhat into the shoare wee tooke our selues to be shotte somewhat past the riuer de Sestos, so that we kept about to fetch it. And a litle after we had sight of three sayles of shippes and two pinnesses which were in the weather of vs, and hauing sight of them we made our selues readie to meete them, and halled off our ships to fetch the winde as neere as we could: and hauing sayled about an houre or two, they also went about, and went as we went to make themselues readie, and when we had them in chase, they went away from vs: but when they had made themselues readie, they kept about againe, and came with vs verie finely appointed with their streamers, and pendants and ensignes, and noyse of trumpets very brauely: so when we met, they had the weather of vs, and we being determined to fight, if they had bene Portugals, waued them to come vnder our Lee, which they denied stoutly: then we demaunded of them whence they were, and they sayd of France, we told them againe that we were of London in England. They asked of vs what Portugals wee had seene, we answered, none but Fishermen: then they told vs that there were certaine Portugall ships gone to the Mina to defend it, and that they met with another at the riuer de Sestos, which was a ship of two hundred which they had burned, and had saued none but the master and two or three Negroes, and certaine others which were sore burned which they left a shoare there. Then they desired to come aboord of vs with their boates to talke with vs, and wee gaue them leaue. Then the captaine of the Admirall and diuers others came aboord very friendly, desiring vs to keepe them company because of the Portugals, and to goe to the Mina with them: wee told them that we had not watered, and that we were but now fallen with the coast, and they shewed vs that we were fiftie leagues past the riuer de Sestos: notwithstanding there was water enough to be had, and they would helpe vs to water with their owne boates because they would haue our companie. And told vs further, that they had bene sixe weekes vpon the coast, and had gotten but three tunnes of graines amongst them all: and when wee had heard them, we made our reckoning that although the Mina were cleare, yet if they did goe before vs, they would marre our market; and if it were not cleare, then if the Portugals were there and did take them, they would vnderstand that we were behind, and so would waite for vs. [Sidenote: They admit certaine Frenchmen into their companie.] And further we made account that if we went with them we should doe as well as they, if the coast were cleare: if it were not cleare, then by them we were assured to be the stronger. Therefore hauing considered thus much of their gentle offers, we tolde them that the next day wee would conferre more largely of the matter. Whereupon they desired me to come the next day to dinner to them, and to bring the masters of our ships with me, and such merchants as I thought good, promising to giue vs water out of their owne ships if we would take it, or els to tarie with vs and helpe vs to water with their own boats and pinnasses.

The 31 day in the morning the Admirall sent his boat aboord for me, and I tooke our masters and certaine of our marchants and went to him, who had prouided a notable banquet for vs, and intreated vs very friendly, desiring vs still to keepe his company, promising that what victuals were in his ships, or other things that might doe vs pleasure vntill the end, we should haue the one halfe of it, offering vs if we would to furle his Flags, and to bee at our commaundement in all things.

In the ende we agreed to come to an anker, and to send our boat on shore with the Admirals boat, and one of his pinnasses, and an Almaine which they had brought out of France, to seeke water, as for our pinnasse she came to an anker to seaward of vs all, and would not come at vs. All this night the boats continued on shore.

The first day of Ianuary our boats came to vs againe and had found no riuer. Whereupon we weighed and set saile, and ankred againe at another riuer.

The 2 day we went into the riuer and bargained, and tooke 5 small Elephants teeth.

The 3 day we tooke 5 more.

[Sidenote: An assault vpon elephants.] The fourth day the French Admirall and wee tooke fifteene small teeth. This day wee tooke thirtie men with vs and went to seeke Elephants, our men being all well armed with harquebusses, pikes, long bowes, crossebowes, partizans, long swordes, and swordes and bucklers: wee found two Elephants which wee stroke diuers times with harquebusses and long bowes, but they went away from vs and hurt one of our men. The fift day we set saile and ranne along the coast.

The 6 day we fell with the riuer de S. Andre, at which place the land is somewhat high to the Westward of the riuer, and a faire Baie also to the Westward of it: but to the Eastward of it it is lowe land.

The 7 day we went into the Riuer and found no village, but certaine wild Negros not accustomed to trade. It is a very great riuer and 7 fadome water in some places at the entring. Here we filled water, and after set saile.

The 8 day we sailed along the shore and came to the red cliffes, and went forward in sailing the 9 day also.

The 10 day we came together to confer with captaine Blundel Admiral of the French ships, Ierom Baudet his vice admiral, and Iohn de Orleans master of a ship of 70 tunne, and with their marchants, and agreed that when God should send vs to any place where wee might make sale, that we should be of one accord and not one of vs hurt the market of the other, but certaine of our boates to make the price for all the rest, and then one boate to make sale for euery shippe. This night our boats going to the shore met with certaine Negros, who said that they had gold, and therefore we here cast anker.

The 11 day all the day we tooke but one halfe angel weight of 4 graines, which we tooke by hand, for the people of this place had no weight: the Negros called this place Allow.

The 12 day we ran along the coast and found but one towne, but no boates would come out to vs, and therefore we went our course.

The 13 day I tooke my boat and went along the shore, and passed by diuers small townes, and was waued to come on shore at 3 places, but the sea went so high vpon the shore, that it was not possible for vs to land, neither could they come to vs if they had had boats, as I could see none but at one place, where there was one that would haue come vnto vs, but the Land-wash went so sore that it ouerthrew his boat, and one of the men was drowned, which the people lamented, and cried so sore, that we might easily heare them, and they got his body out of the sea, and caried it amongst them to their towne.

[Sidenote: The castle of Mina.] The 14 day we came within Saker-shot of the castle, and straightway they set forth an Almade to descry vs, and when they perceiued that we were no Portugals, they ranne within the towne againe: for there is a great towne by the Castle which is called by the Negros Dondou. Without this there lie two great rockes like Ilands, and the castle standeth vpon a point which sheweth almost like an Iland. Before we came at this castle, we found the land for fiue or six leagues to be high land, and about seuen leagues before we came to the castle, lowe land, vntil we came at the castle, and then wee found the land high againe. This castle standeth about fiue leagues to the East of Cape de Tres puntas. Here I tooke the boate with our Negros and ranne alongst the shore till I came to the Cape and found two small townes, but no boates at them, neither any traffique to be had. At these places our Negros did vnderstand them well, and one of them went ashore at all the places and was well receiued of them. This night we ankred at the Cape de Tres puntas.

The 15 day I tooke our boat and went along the shore, and about 3 leagues beyond the Eastermost part of the Cape we found a faire Bay where we ran in, and found a smal towne and certaine boates which belonged to the same towne, but the Negros in a long time would not come to vs, but at the last by the perswasion of our owne Negros, one boat came to vs, and with him we sent George our Negro a shore, and after he had talked with them, they came aboard our boates without feare, and I gaue to their captaine a bason, and two strings of Margarets, and they shewed vs about 5 duckats weight of gold, but they required so much for it that wee would not take it, because the Frenchman and we had agreed to make price of our goods all in one boat, and the price being made then euery man to sell in his owne boat, and no man to giue more then the price which should be set by vs al. This place is called Bulle, and here the Negros were very glad of our Negros, and shewed them all the friendship they could, when they had told them that they were the men that were taken away being now againe brought by vs.

The Negros here shewed vs that a moneth since there were 3 ships that fought together, and the two shippes put the other to flight: and before that at the castle of Mina there were 4 ships of the Portugals which met with one Frenchman, which Frenchman caused them all to flee, which shippe we tooke to be the Roebarge: for the Frenchmen of our company iudged her to be thereabout that time with her pinnasse also. And further, that after her went a shippe of twelue score named the Shaudet all alone, and after her a ship of fourescore, and both for the Mina. And there were two others also which they left, one at Cape Verde called the Leuriere of Diepe, and another at the riuer De Sestos, besides these 3 which all this time be in our company, whose names be these:

The Espoier of Hableneff which is the Admirall, whose captaine is Denis Blundell.

The Leuriere of Roan Viceadmirall, whose master is Ierome Baudet.

The other is of Hunfleur whose master is called Iohn de Orleans.

The sixteenth day I went along the shore with two pinasses of the Frenchmen, and found a Baie and a fresh riuer, and after that went to a towne called Hanta, twelue leagues beyond the Cape. At this towne our Negros were well knowen, and the men of the towne wept for ioy when they saw them, and demanded of them where Anthonie and Binne had bene: and they told them that they had bene at London in England, and should bee brought home the next voyage. So after this, our Negros came aboord with other Negros which brought a weight with them, which was so small that wee could not giue them the halfe of that which they demaunded for it.

The Negros here told vs that there were fiue Portugall shippes at the Castle, and one pinnasse, and that the Portugals did much harme to their Countrey, and that they liued in feare of them, and we told them againe, that we would defend them from the Portugals whereof they were very glad.

The 17 day we went a shoare and the Frenchmen with vs, but did no great good, the Negros were so vnreasonable, we sold 80. Manellios for one ounce of gold.

[Sidenote: The Negros brought home by our men.] Then wee departed and went to Shamma, and went into the riuer with fiue boates well appointed with men and ordinance, and with our noises of trumpets and drummes, for we thought here to haue found some Portugals but there were none: so wee sent our Negros on shoare, and after them went diuers of vs, and were very well receiued, and the people were very glad of our Negros, specially one of their brothers wiues, and one of their aunts, which receiued them with much ioy, and so did all the rest of the people, as if they had bene their naturall brethren: we comforted the captaine and told him that hee should not feare the Portugals, for wee would defend him from them: whereupon we caused our boats to shoote off their bases and harquebusses, and caused our men to come on shore with their long bowes, and they shot before the captaine, which he, with all the rest of the people, wondred much at, specially to see them shoot so farre as they did, and assaied to draw their bowes but could not. When it grew to be late, we departed to our ships, for we looked euery houre for the Portugals. And here the Negros shewed vs that there was an English ship at the Mina, which had brought one of the Negros againe, which Robert Gaynsh tooke away.

The 18 day we went into the riuer with no lesse strength then before, and concluded with the Negros to giue them for euery Fuffe two yardes and three nailes of Cloth, and to take for it one angel-duckat: so that we tooke in all 70 Duckats, whereof the Frenchmen had fortie, and wee thirtie.

The nineteenth day wee went a shore euery man for himselfe, and tooke a good quantitie of gold, and I for my part tooke foure pound and two ounces and a halfe of gold, and our Hartes boate tooke one and twentie ounces. At night the Negros shewed vs that the next day the Portugals would be with vs by land or by Sea: and when we were ready to depart, we heard diuers harquebusses shoote off in the woods by vs which wee knew to bee Portugals, which durst come no neerer to vs, but shot off in the woods to see if they could feare vs and so make vs to leaue our traffique.

The 20 day we manned our fiue boats, and also a great boat of the Frenchmens with our men and the Admirals, 12 of them in their murrians and corsets, and the rest all well appoynted, with foure trumpets, a drumme and a Fife, and the boate all hanged with streamers of Silke and pendants very faire, and went into the riuer and traffiqued, our man of warre lying off and on in the riuer to waft vs, but we heard no more of the Portugals. This day the Negros told vs that there were certain ships come into Hanta, which towne is about two leagues to the Westward of this place.

This 21 day we manned our boats againe and went to a place a league from this to the Westwards, and there found many Negros with another Captaine, and sold at the same rate that wee had done with the others.

The 22 day we went ashore againe and traffiqued in like sort quietly, and I tooke 4 pound and six ounces of gold.

The 23 day about night the Negros with their captaine came to vs and told vs that the king of Portugals ships were departed from the Castle, meaning the next day to plie to the windward to come to vs, giuing vs warning to take heed to our selues: we told them againe that wee were very glad of their comming, and would be ready at all times to meet them, and to assure them that wee were glad of it, wee sounded our trumpets, and shot off certaine bases whereof the Negros were very glad, and requested vs that if the Portugals sought to hinder our traffique, to shew them all the extremitie that we could, promising vs that if they came by land, they would aduertise vs thereof.

The 24 we went a shore with our trumpets and drummes, and traffiqued, and I bade the captaine of the towne to dinner.

[Sidenote: Fiue sailes of Portingals descried.] The 25 day we being a shore, our ships had descried fiue sailes of the king of Portugals, and our ships shot off ordinance to call vs away, and we threw euery man his caske ashore for water, and went to our ships, and by that time we had weighed and giuen order one to another what to do, it was night, so that that night nothing was done. We set saile and lay close all night to get the wind if we could: we were neere some of them, and one shot off a piece which wee iudged to be the Admirall of the Portugals, to cause the rest to come and speake with him: so all this night we made our selues ready for fight.

The 26 we came in with the shore and had sight of the Portugals where they rid at anker, and we bare with them, and we gaue all our men white scarffes, to the ende that the Frenchmen might know one the other if we came to boording: but the night came vpon vs that we could not fetch them, but we ankered within demie-Culuering shot of them.

[Sidenote: The fight with the Portugals.] The 27 day we weighed and so did the Portugals, and about eleuen of the clocke wee had the wind of them, and then we went roome with them, which when they pereeiued, they kept about to the shore againe, and wee after them, and when they were so neere the shore that they could not well runne any further on that boord, they kept about againe, and lay to the Seaward, and then we kept about with them, and were a head of them, and tooke in our topsailes and taried for them: and the first that came vp was a small barke which sailed so well that she cared not for any of vs, and caried good ordinance: and as soone as she came vp, she shot at vs, and ouershot vs, and then she shot at the Admirall of the Frenchmen, and shot him through in two or three places, and went forth a head of vs, because we were in our fighting sailes: then came vp another carauell vnder our Lee in like case which shot at vs and at the Frenchman, and hurt two of his men and shot him through the maine maste. And after them came vp the Admirall vnder our Lee also, but he was not able to doe vs so much harme as the small shippes, because he caried ordinance higher then they, neither were we able to make a good shot at any of them, because our shippe was so weake in the side, that she laid all her ordinance in the Sea: [Sidenote: The French forsake our men.] wherefore we thought to lay the great ship aboord, and as soone as the French Admirall went roome with him, be fell a sterne and could not fetch him, and after he fell asterne of two carauels more and could fetch none of them, but fell to Leeward of them all: and when he was to Leeward, he kept about to the shoreward, and left vs, and then we put out our topsailes and gaue them chase, and both the other Frenchmen kept the wind, and would not come neere vs, and our owne ship was a sterne so that she could not come to vs: and after we had folowed them about two houres to the seaward, they kept about againe towards the shore, thinking to pay vs as they went along by, and to haue the wind of the French Admirall which before ran in towards the shore, and we kept about with them, and kept still the wind of them thinking that our Viceadmiral and the other would haue folowed vs as wee willed them to do: but after that the Portugall was past by them, and euery one had shot at vs and our Viceadmirall, both our Viceadmirall and the two Frenchmen, and our owne pinnasse left vs in the laps, and ran to seaward, and we ran still along, and kept the wind of them to succour the French Admirall, who was vnder all of their Lees, and when they met with him, euery one went roome with him, and gaue him the broad side, and after they cast about againe, and durst not boord him, because they sawe vs in the weather of them, or els without doubt they had taken or sunke them, for three of them which were the smallest went so fast that it was not possible for a ship to boord them, and caried such ordinance that if they had had the weather of vs, they would haue troubled 3 of the best ships that we had, and as for their Admirall and Viceadmirall they were both notablie appointed.

When the Frenchman was cleare of them, hee laie as neere the winde as hee could, and wee followed them still towardes the shore, and there the Admirall ranne to Sea after the rest, and left vs all alone: and when the Portugals perceiued that we were alone, and gaue them chase, they kept about with vs and we with them, to keepe the wind of them, and we ranne still within base shot of them, but they shot not at vs, because we had the weather of them, and sawe that they could do vs no hurt: and thus we folowed one another vntil night, and in the night we lost them, but as for all the rest of our ships, they packed on all the sailes that they could and ranne to sea, and as they themselues confesse, they praied for vs, but as for helpe at their hands we could haue none.

The 28 day we met with our Viceadmirall, our pinnasse, and two of the Frenchmen, and the third was fled which was a ship of fourscore tunne, and belonged to Roan: and when I had the sight of the rest of our ships, I tooke our skiffe and went to them to know why they lost vs in such a case, and Iohn Kire made me answere that his ship would neither reare nor steere, and as for the pinnasse, Iohn Dauis made me answere that she would doe nothing, and that he could cary her no further, for her rudder was broken, so that the Hart was glad to towe her. Then I went to the French Admirall, and found himselfe to be a man of good stomacke, but the one halfe of his men were sicke and dead: and then I talked with the smaller Frenchman, and hee made me answere that he could doe nothing, saying, that his ship would beare no saile, and had 16 of his men dead and sicke, so he made vs plaine answere that he was able to doe nothing. After this the Frenchman durst not anker for feare of the Portugales.

The 29 day the master of the pinnasse came to vs and sayd that they were not able to keepe her any longer, and then wee viewed her and seeing there was no remedie, her rudder with all the iron worke being broken both aloft and belowe, wee agreed to breake her vp and to put the men into the Hart. So wee tooke out of her foure bases, one anker, and certaine fire wood, and set her on fire, and afterwards ran along the coast.

The thirtie day we went in to the shore, and spake with certaine Negros, who told vs that some French shippes had bene there, but wee could not bargaine with them they were so vnreasonable.

The 31 day I went to shore but did not traffike.

The 1 day of Februarie we weighed, seeing we could not bring the Negros to any reason, and came to another place which standeth vpon an hill.

The third day I went to a towne foure leagues from vs, and shot off two pieces, and the Captaine came to vs, and I sent Thomas Rippen a land who knew the Captaine, and assoone as he came on shore, the Captaine knew him and diuers of the Negros who then began to aske for mee, and hauing told the Captaine that I was in the boate, hee made no longer tarying but by and by caused two boates to be put to the Sea, and came to me himselfe, and when he sawe me, he cryed to me before hee came to the boat and seemed to be the gladdest man aliue, and so did all the companie that knew mee, and I gaue him a reward as the maner of the Countrey is, and caused the Frenchman to giue another, promising the next day to giue him wine: and that night because it was late, he would not talke of any price but left me a pledge, and tooke another of me and so departed.

The 4 day going on shore, I found that the ships of France which had bin there, had done much hurt to our markets but yet I tooke fiue ounces and a halfe of gold.

The fift day I tooke eight ounces and one eight part of gold: but I saw that the Negros perceiued the difference in Cloth betwixt ours and that which the Frenchmen had, which was better, and broader then ours: and then I told captaine Blundel that I would goe to the Leeward, because I perceiued that being there where his Cloth was sold, I should do no good, whereof hee was sorie.

The 6 day there came an almade and Negros aboord me, requesting me to come to their towne for they had much gold and many marchants: and so I went and found their old Captaine gone, and another in his place: but this night wee did no good, because the marchants were not come downe: so he required a pledge which I let him haue, and tooke another of him.

The 7 day George our Negro came to vs, who had followed vs at the least 30 leagues in a small boat, and when he came, the Negros and we soone concluded of price. I tooke this day fiue pound and one ounce, and 3 quarters of gold. This Negro we had left at Shamma at the time of the fight, who said that he saw the fight being on shore, and that when we were gone from the Portugals, the Portugals came into their riuer, and told them that the Englishmen had slaine two Portugals with a piece, which was in deed out of our ship, and they required harbour there, but the captaine of Shamma would not suffer them.

The 8 day we tooke nineteene pound three ounces and a halfe.

The 9 day we tooke two pound six ounces and a halfe.

The 10 day three pound.

[Sidenote: The Frenchmen bridled by the English.] The 11 day came to vs Ierome Bawdet the Viceadmiral of the Frenchmen and his pinnasse, and he shewed vs that where we left them there was no good to be done, and sayd he would goe to the Eastward, but we told him hee should not: and thereupon commaunded him to goe to his company which he was appointed to bee with, which hee refused to doe vntill wee had shot three or foure pieces at their pinnasse, and when the ship sawe that, she kept about, and ranne to Seaward, and durst come no neerer to vs, so the pinnasse went after her. We tooke this day one pound fiue ounces.

The 12 day there came one of the Frenchmens pinnasses to vs laden with cloth, and would haue made sale, but I would not suffer him, and therefore tooke him and sent him aboord of our ship, and caused him to ride there all day. We tooke fiue pound six ounces and a halfe.

The 14 day we tooke of some Negros 4 ounces of gold.

The 16 we came to another towne.

The 17 day I went a shore and vnderstood that 3 of the Portugall ships were at the Castle, and the other two at Shamma. The captaine of this towne was gone to the principall towne, to speake with their king, and would returne shortly as they told me, and so he did, and brought me a weight and measure, and I sent a man to see that principall towne, and their king. The Portugall ships rid so neere vs, that within 3 houres they might be with vs, yet were all contented to tary for sales.

The 18 day certaine of the kings seruants came to vs, and we tooke one pound two ounces, and one eight part of gold.

The 10 day we tooke fiue pound one ounce.

The 20 day one pound and foure ounces.

The 21 I tooke foure pound and one ounce, and the Negroes enquired for fine cloth, and I opened two pieces which were not fine enough, as they sayd, but seeing that we had no other, they bought of them. At night I prouided a gift, or present, and sent one marchant and a mariner with it to the king, to certifie him of our want of victuals, by reason whereof we could not stay long: for in deed we searched our ship, and the most part of our beere was leaked out of all our barrels.

The 22 day we tooke three ounces and a halfe.

[Sidenote: The offer of the king to the English to build a Fort.] The 23 our men came from the king Abaan, and told vs, that he had receiued them very friendly, but he had litle gold, but promised, if we would tary, to send into all his countrey for gold for vs, and he willed our men at their comming home to speake to our king to send men and prouision into his countrey, to build a castle, and to bring Tailors with them, to make them apparell, and good wares, and they should be sure to sell them: but for that present the Frenchmen had filled them full of cloth.

This towne standeth about foure leagues vp in the land, and is by the estimation of our men, as big in circuit as London, but the building is like to the rest of the countrey. They haue about this Towne great store of the wheate of the Countrey, and they iudge, that on one side of the towne there were one thousand rikes of Wheate, and another sorte of Corne which is called Mill, which is much vsed in Spaine.

[Sidenote: A pretie deuise to descrie the enemie.] About this towne they keepe good watch euery night, and haue to warne the watchmen certaine cordes made fast ouer their wayes which lead into the town, and certaine bels vpon them, so that if any man touch the cordes, the bels ring, and then the watchmen runne foorth of their watch houses to see what they be: and if they be enemies, if they passe the cord, they haue prouision with certaine nets hanged ouer the wayes, where they must passe, to let fall vpon them, and so take them, and otherwise then by the wayes it is not possible to enter the towne, by reason of the thickets and bushes which are about the same, and the towne is also walled round about with long cords, and bound together with sedge and certaine barkes of tree.

[Sidenote: The kings friendly entertainment of our men.] When our men came to the towne, it was about fiue of the clock in the morning, for there they trauell alwayes in the night by reason of the heate of the day: and about nine of the clocke, the king sent for them, for there may no man come to him before he be sent for, and then they would haue carried their present with them: but the Negros told them, that they must bee three times brought before him, before they might offer their gift: and when they came to him, he talked with them, and receiued them very friendly and kept them about half an hour, and then they departed, and after that sent for them againe three times, and last of all, they brought him their present, which he receiued thankfully, and then caused a pot of wine of Palme to be brought foorth, and made them drinke: and before they drinke, both here and in all the Countrey, they vse certaine ceremonies.

[Sidenote: Their ceremonies in drinking.] First, they bring foorth their pot of drinke, and then they make a hole in the ground, and put some of the drinke into it, and they cast the earth vpon it, which they digged forth before, and then they set the pot vpon the same, then they take a little thing made of a goord, and with that they take out of the same drinke, and put it vpon the ground in three places, and in diuers places they haue certaine bunches of the pils of Palme trees set in the ground before them, and there they put in some drinke, doing great reuerence in all places to the same Palme trees.

All these ceremonies first done, the king tooke a cup of gold, and they put him in wine, and hee dranke of it, and when he dranke, the people cried all with one voice, Abaan, Abaan, with certaine other words, like as they cry commonly in Flanders, vpon the Twelfe night, The kinning [sic—KTH] drinks: and when he had drunke, then they gaue drinke to euery one, and that done, the king licensed them to depart, and euery one that departeth from him boweth 3 times towards him, and waueth with both hands together, as they bow, and then do depart. The king hath commonly sitting by him 8 or 10 ancient men with gray beards.

This day we tooke one pound and 10 ounces of gold.

The 24 day we tooke 3 pound and 7 ounces.

The 25 we tooke 3 ounces and 3 quarters.

The 26 day we tooke 2 pound and 10 ounces.

The 27 two pound and fiue ounces.

The 28 foure pound, and then seeing that there was no more gold to be had, we weighed and went foorth.

The first day of March we came to a towne called Mowre, but we found no boats nor people there: but being ready to depart, there came two Almades to vs from another towne, of whom we tooke two ounces and a halfe of gold: and they tolde vs that the Negros that dwelled at Mowre were gone to dwell at Lagoua.

The second day we came thwart of the castle, and about two leagues off, and there saw all the fiue Portugall ships at anker, and this day by night we fetched Shamma.

[Sidenote: Ships of Portugall.] The third day we had sight of one tall ship, of about two hundred tunnes in the weather of vs, and within lesse then two leagues of our ships, and then we saw two more a sterne of her, the one a ship of fiue hundred or more, and the other a pinnesse: and these were a new fleet at that present arriued out of Portugall. Whereupon we wayed, and made shift to double out of the land, and then the winde comming to the South-southwest, the Hart going roome with them fell three leagues to the leewards of vs. These Portugals gaue vs the chase from nine of the clocke in the morning, till fiue at night, but did no good against vs. At last, we perceiuing the Admirall to be farre a sterne of his company, because his maine topmast was spent, determined to cast about againe with them, because we were sure to weather them, and the winde being as it was, it was our best course: but the Hart was so farre to the leeward, that we could not doe it, except we would lose her company, so that we tooke in some of our sailes, and went roome with him: which when he perceiued, he looffed to, and was able to lie as neere as he did before. At night, when we came to him, he would not speake to vs: then we asked of his company why he went so roome; and they made excuse that they were able to beare no saile by, for feare of bearing their foretopmast ouer boord: but this was a simple excuse.

The fourth day, being put from our watring place we began to seethe our meat in salt water, and to rebate our allowance of drinke, to make it indure the longer: and so concluded to set our course thence, for our owne countrey.

The 12 of March I found my selfe thwart of Cape das Palmas.

The 16 day we fell with the land, which we iudged to be the Cape Mensurado, about which place is very much high land.

The 18 day we lost sight of the Hart, and I thinke the willfull Master ran in with the shore of purpose to lose vs, being offended that I tolde him of his owne folly.

[Sidenote: Two small Ilands by Sierra Leona. Note.] The 27 day we fell in sight of two small Islands, which lie by our reckoning sixe leagues off the headland of Sierra Leona: and before we came in sight of the same Ilands, we made our reckoning to be forty or thirty leagues at the least off them. Therefore all they that saile this way are to regard the currents which set Northnorthwest, or els they may be much deceiued.

The 14 of April we met with two great ships of Portugall, which although they were in the weather of vs, yet came not roome with vs, whereby we iudged that they were bound for Calicut.

The 18 day we were in the heigth of Cape verde.

The 24 we were directly vnder the tropike of Cancer.

The first day of May Henry Wilson our Steward died: and the next day died Iohn Vnderwood.

[Sidenote: A French brauado.] The 23 we had sight of a shippe in the weather of vs, which was a Frenchman of 90 tunne, who came with vs as stoutly and as desperately as might be, and comming neere vs perceiued that we had bene vpon a long voyage, and iudging vs to be weake, as in deed we were, came neerer vs, and thought to haue layed vs aboord, and there stept vp some of his men in armour, and commanded vs to strike saile: whereupon we sent them some of our stuffe, crossebarres, and chaineshot, and arrowes, so thicke, that it made the vpper worke of their shippe flit about their eares, and then we spoiled him with all his men, and toare his shippe miserably with our great ordinance, and then he began to fall a sterne of vs, and to packe on his sailes, and get away: and we seeing that, gaue him foure or fiue good pieces more for his farewell; and thus we were rid of this French man, who did vs no harme at all. We had aboord vs a French man a Trumpeter, who being sicke, and lying in his bed, tooke his trumpet notwithstanding, and sounded till he could sound no more, and so died.

The 28 we conferred together, and agreed to go into Seuerne, and so to Bristoll, but the same night we had sight of the Lizard, and by reason of the winde, we were not able to double the lands end to go into Seuerne, but were forced to beare in with the Lizard.

The 29 day, about nine of the clocke in the morning, we arriued safely in Plimmouth, and praised God for our good arriuall.

* * * * *

The third and last voyage of M. William Towrson to the coast of Guinie, and the Castle de Mina, in the yeere 1577.

The thirtieth day of Ianuary, the yeere abouesayd, we departed out of the sound of Plimmouth, with three ships, and a pinnesse, whereof the names are these:

1 The Minion Admirall of the fleet.

2 The Christopher Viceadmirall.

3 The Tyger.

4 A pinnesse called the Vnicorne: being all bound for the Canaries, and from thence, by the grace of God, to the coast of Guinie.

The next day, being the last of this moneth, [Marginal note: It is to be vnderstood, that at this time there was warre betwixt England and France.] we met with two hulks of Dantzick, the one called the Rose, a ship of foure hundred tunnes, and the other called the Vnicorne, of an hundred and fifty tunnes, the Master of the Rose was called Nicholas Masse, and the Master of the Vnicorne Melchior White, both laden at Bourdeaux, and for the most part with wines. When we came to them, we caused them to hoise foorth their boats, and to come and speake with vs, and we examined euery one of them apart, what French mens goods they had in their shippes, and they said they had none: but by the contrarieties of their tales, and by the suspicion which we gathered of their false chartar-parties, we perceiued that they had French mens goods in them: we therefore caused one of them to fetch vp his bils of lading, and because he denied that he had any, we sent certaine with him, who caused him to goe to the place where he had hid them, and by the differences of his billes of lading, and his talke, we gathered, as before, that they had Frenchmens goods. Whereupon we examined them straightly, and first the Purser of the Vnicorne, which was the smaller shippe, confessed that they had two and thirty tunnes and a hogs-head of a French mans. Then we examined the Master in like case, and he acknowledged the same to be true. Then we examined also the Master of the great ship, and he confessed that he had an hundred and eight and twenty tunnes of the same French mans, and more they would not confesse, but sayd that all the rest was laden by Peter Lewgues of Hamburg, to be deliuered to one Henry Summer of Camphire, notwithstanding all their letters were directed to Hamburg, and written in Dutch without, and within in French.

When they had confessed that they had thus much French mens goods within their shippes, we conferred together what was best to be done with them. William Cretton and Edward Selman were of the opinion, that it should be good either to carry them into Spaine, and there to make sale of the goods, or els into Ireland, or to returne backe againe into England with them, if the winde would permit it. But I, waying what charge we had of our Masters, first by mouth, and afterwards by writing, that for no such matter we should in any case prolong the time, for feare of losing the voyage, and considering that the time of the yeere was very farre spent, and the money that we should make of the wines not very much, in respect of the commodity which we hoped for by the voyage, perswaded them that to goe into Ireland, the winde being Easterly as it was, might be an occasion that we should be locked in there with that winde, and so lose our voyage: and to cary them into Spaine, seeing they sailed so ill, that hauing all their sailes abroad, we kept them company onely with our foresailes, and without any toppe sailes abroad, so that in euery two dayes sailing they would haue hindered vs more then one; and besides that (the winde being Easterly) we should not be able to seaze the coast with them: besides all this the losse of time when we came thither was to be considered, whereupon I thought it not good to carry them any further.

And as for carying them into England, although the winde had bene good, as it was not, considering what charge we had of our Masters, to shift vs out of the way for feare of a stay by reason of the warres, I held it not in any wise conuenient.

But notwithstanding all this, certeine of our company not being herewith satisfied went to our Master to know his opinion therein, who made them a plaine answere, that to cary them into any place, it was not the best way nor the profit of their Masters. And he tolde them further, that if the time were prolonged, one moneth longer before they passed the Cape, but a few men would go the voyage. [Sidenote: The French mens goods seazed in the time of the warre vpon the losse of Cales.] All these things considered, we all paused, and determined at the last, that euery man should take out of the hulks so much as he could well bestow for necessaries, and the next morning to conclude what should be further done with them. So we tooke out of them for vs foureteene tunnes and a halfe of wine, and one tunne we put into the pinnesse.

More we tooke out one hogshead of Aquauitæ.
  Sixe cakes of rozzen.
  A small halser for ties: and certeine chestnuts.

The Christopher tooke out,
  Ten tunnes of wine, and one hogshead.
  A quantity of Aquauitæ.
  Shall-lines.
  Chesnuts.
  Sixe double bases with their chambers.

And then men broke vp the hulks chests, and tooke out their compasses, and running glasses, the sounding leade and line, and candles: and cast some of their beefe ouer board, and spoiled them so much, that of very pity we gaue them a compasse, a running glasse, a leade and a line, certaine bread and candles, but what apparel of theirs we could finde in their ship, we gaue them againe, and some money also of that which William Crompton tooke for the ransome of a poore Frenchman, who being then Pilot downe the Riuer of Bordeux, they were not able to set him a shore againe, by reason of the foule weather.

The Tyger also tooke out of the smaller hulke sixe or seuen tunnes of wine, one hogshead of Aquauitæ, and certeine rozzen, and two bases he tooke out of the great hulke.

The first day of February in the morning we all came together againe sauing W. Crompton who sent vs word mat he was contented to agree to that order which we should take.

Now Edward Selman was of this opinion, that it was not best to let the ships depart, but put men into them to cary them into England, which thing neither we nor our Master would agree vnto, because we thought it not good to vnman our ships going outward, considering how dangerous the time was: so that in fine we agreed to let them depart, and giue them the rest of the wine which they had in their ships of the Frenchmens for the fraight of that which we had taken, and for their ordinance, rozzen, aquauitæ, chesnuts, and other things which the company had taken from them. So we receiued a bill of their handes, that they confessed how much Frenchmens goods they had, and then we let them depart.

The 10 day we reckoned our selues to be 25 leagues from the Grand Canarie, and this day about nine of the clocke our pinnesse brake her rudder, so that we were forced to towe her at the sterne of the Minion, which we were able to doe, and yet kept company with the rest of our ships. About eleuen of the clocke this day we had sight of the Grand Canarie.

The 11 day when we came to the Iland we perceiued that it was the Ile of Tenerif, and then indeed wee had sight of the Grand Canarie, which lieth 12 leagues to the Eastwards of Tenerif: and because the road of Tenerif is foule ground, and nothing was there to be gotten for the helping of our pinnesse, hauing the winde long, we agreed to go with the Grand Canarie.

The 12 day we came into the roade of the towne of Canarie, which lieth one league from the same towne. And after we had shot off diuers pieces of ordinance to salute the towne and the castle, the gouernour and captiues of the Iland sent to vs which were the captaines of the ships, requiring vs to come a shoare.

[Sidenote: Two English Marchants Legiers in the Grand Canary.] And when we came to them they receiued vs very friendly, offering vs their owne Iennets to ride to the towne, and what other friendship they could shew vs: and we went to the towne with two English Marchants which lay there, and remained in their house that day. The second day following we came aboord to deliuer our marchandise, and to get our pinnesse mended.

The 14 day came into the road the Spanish fleet which was bound to the Emperours Indies, which were in number nineteene saile, whereof sixe were ships of foure hundred and fiue hundred a piece, the rest were of two hundred, an hundred and fifty, and of an hundred. When they were come to an ancre they saluted vs with ordinance, and so we did them in like case. And afterwards the Admirall (who was a knight) sent his pinnesse to desire me to come to him; and when I came to him he receiued me friendly, and was desirous to heare somewhat of the state of England and Flanders. And after he had me a banquet, I departed; and I being gone vnto the boat, hee caused one of his gentlemen to desire Francisco the Portugall, which was my interpreter, to require me to furle my flagge, declaring that hee was Generall of the Emperours fleet. Which thing (being come aboord) Francisco shewed me: and because I refused to furle it, and kept it foorth still, certaine of the souldiers in the ships shot diuers harquebush shot about the ship, and ouer the flagge: and at the same time there came certeine gentlemen aboord our ship to see her: to whom I sayd, that if they would not cause those their men to leaue shooting, I would shoot the best ordinance I had thorow their sides. And when they perceuied that I was offended, they departed, and caused their men of warre and souldiers to shoot no more, and afterwards they came to me againe, and tolde me that they punished their men. That done, I shewed them the ship, and made them such cheere as I could, which they receiued very thankfully: and the day following they sent for mee to dine with them, and sent me word that their General was very sory that any man should require me to furle my flagge, and that it was without his consent: and therefore he requested me not to thinke any vngentlenesse to be in him, promising that no man of his should misdemeane himselfe.

The 17 day we set saile in the road of Grand Canarie, and proceeded on our voyage.

The 20 in the morning we had sight of the coast of Barbarie, and running along the shore we had sight of Rio del Oro, which lieth almost vnder the tropike of Cancer.

The 21 day we found our selues to be in 20 degrees and a halfe, which is the heigth of Cape Blank.

The 25 we had sight of the land in the bay to the Northward of Cape Verde.

[Sidenote: Cape verde. Foure Ilands.] The 26 I tooke Francisco and Francis Castelin with me, and went into the pinnesse, and so went to the Tyger which was neerer the shore then the other ships, and went aboord her, and with her and the other ships we ranne West and by South, and West southwest, vntill about foure of the clocke, at which time we were hard aboord the Cape, and then we ran in Southwest, and beyond the Cape about foure leagues we found a faire Iland, and besides that two or three Ilands, which were of very high rocks being full of diuers sorts of sea foule, and of pigeons, with other sorts of land-foules, and so many, that the whole Iland was couered with the dung thereof, and seemed so white as if the whole Iland had bene of chalke; and within those Ilands was a very faire bay, and hard aboord the rocks eighteene fadom water, and faire ground. [Sidenote: A great trade of the Frenchmen at Cape verde.] And when we perceiued the bay, and vnderstanding that the Frenchmen had a great trade there, which we were desirous to know, we came to an ancre with the Tyger. And after that the Minion and the Christopher ancred in like case: then we caused the pinnesse to runne beyond another Cape of land, to see if there were any place to trade in there.

It being neere night I took our cocke and the Tygers skiffe, and went to the Iland, where we got certaine foules like vnto Gannards: and then I came aboord againe and tooke two of the Gannards which we had taken, and caried them to the captaine of the Christopher, and when I had talked with him I found him not willing to tary there, neither was I desirous to spend any long time there, but onely to attempt what was to be done. The Master of the Christopher told me he would not tary, being not bound for that place.

[Sidenote: A faire Iland where the French trade.] The 27 the Captaine of the Tyger and Edward Selman came to me, and Iohn Makeworth from the Christopher, and then we agreed to take the pinnessse, and to come along the shore, because that where we rid no Negros came to vs, and the night before our pinnesse brought vs word that there was a very faire Iland. And when I came beyond the point I found it so, and withall a goodly bay, and we saw vpon the maine certaine Negros which waued vs on shore, and then we came to an ancre with the pinnesse, and went a shore with our cocke, and they shewed vs where their trade was, and that they had Elephants teeth, muske, and hides, and offered vs to fetch downe their Captaine, if we would send a man with them, and they would leaue a pledge for him: then we asked him when any ship had bene there; and some of them sayd not in eight monethes, others, in sixe moneths, and others in foure and that they were Frenchmen.

Then we perceuing, the Christopher not willing to tary, departed from them, and set saile with the pinnesse and went aboord the Tyger.

The 10 day of March we fell with the coast of Guinea, fiue leagues to the Eastward of Cape de Monte, beside a riuer called Rio das Palmas.

The 11 we went to the shore, and found one man that could speake some Portuguise, who tolde vs that there were three French ships passed by; one of them two monethes past, and the other one moneth past. At this place I receiued nineteene Elephants teeth, and two ounces and halfe a quarter of golde.

The 12 we set saile to go to the riuer de Sestos.

The 13 at night we fell with the same riuer.

The 14 day we sent in our boats to take water, and rommaged our shippes, and deliuered such wares to the Christopher and Tyger, as they had need of.

The 15 we came together, and agreed to send the Tyger to another riuer to take in her water, and to see what she could do for graines.

After that we tooke marchandise with vs, and went into the riuer, and there we found a Negro which was borne in Lisbone, left there by a ship of Portugal which was burned the last yere at this riuer in fighting with three Frenchmen: and he told vs further, that two moneths past there were three Frenchmen at this place; and six weeks past there were two French ships at the riuer: and fifteene dayes past there was one. All which ships were gone towards the Mina. This day we tooke but few graines.

The 19 day considering that the Frenchman were gone before vs, and that by reason of the vnholesome aires of this place foureteene of our men in the Minion were fallen sicke, we determined to depart, and with all speed to go to the Mina.

The 21. wee came to the riuer de Potos, where some of our boats went in for water, and I went in with our cocke, and tooke 12 small Elephants teeth.

The 23. day, after we had taken as many teeth as we could get, about nine of the clocke we set saile to go towards the Mina.

The 31 we came to Hanta, and made sale of certaine Manillios.

[Sidenote: They descrie fiue saile of the Portugals.] The first Aprill we had sight of fiue saile of Portugals, whereupon we set saile and went off to sea to get the winde of them, which wee should haue had if the winde had kept his ordinary course, which is all the day at the Southwest, and Westsouthwest: but this day with a flaw it kept all the day at the East, and Eastsoutheast, so that the Portugals had the winde of vs, and came roome with the Tyger and vs untill night, and brought themselues all saue one, which sailed not so well as the rest, within shot of vs: then it fell calme, and the winde came vp to the Southwest, howbeit it was neere night, and the Christopher, by meanes of her boat, was about foure leagues to the leewards of vs. We tacked and ranne into the weather of the Admirall, and three more of his company, and when we were neere him we spake to him, but he would not answere. [Sidenote: The fight.] Then we cast about and lay in the weather of him; and casting about he shot at vs, and then wee shot at him, and shot him foure or fiue times thorow. They shot diuers times thorow our sailes, but hurt no man. The Tyger and the pinnesse, because it was night, kept out their sailes, and would not meddle with them. After we had thus fought together 2 houres or more, and would not lay him aboord because it was night, we left shooting one at the other, and kept still the weather of them. Then the Tyger and the pinnesse kept about and came to vs, and afterwards being neere the shore, we three kept about and lay to the sea, and shot off a piece to giue warning to the Christopher.

This night about 12 of the clocke, being very litle winde, and the Master of the Tyger asleepe, by the ill worke of his men the ship fel aboord of vs, and with her sheare-hooks cut our maine-saile, and her boat being betwixt vs was broken and suncke, with certaine marchandise in her, and the ships wales were broken with her outleger: yet in the ende we cleared her without any more hurt, but she was in hazzard to be broken downe to the water.

The second day we had sight of the Christopher, and were neere vnto her, so that I tooke our boat and went to her. And when I came thither, they shewed me, that after the Portugals had left vs, they went all roome with him, and about twelue a clocke at night met him, and shot at him, and hee at them, and they shot him thorow the sailes in diuers places, and did no other great hurt. And when we had vnderstood that they had bene with him as well as with vs, we agreed altogether to seeke them (if wee might finde them) and keepe a weather our places of traffique.

The third day we ran all day to the Southwestwards to seeke the Portugals, but could haue no sight of them, and halled into the shore.

The fourth day, when we had sight of land, we found that the current had set vs thirty leagues to the Eastwards of our reckoning, which we woondered at: for the first land we made was Lagua. Then I caused our boat to be manned, and the Christophers also, and went to the shore and tooke our Negro with vs. And on shore we learned that there were foure French ships vpon the coast: one at Perinnen, which is six leagues to the Westward of Laguoa: another at Weamba, which is foure leagues to the Eastward of Laguoa; a third at Perecow, which is foure leagues to the Eastward of Weamba: and the fourth at Egrand, which is foure leagues to the Eastward of Perecow.

When we had intelligence of these newes we agreed to go to the Eastwards with the Frenchmen to put them from their traffique, and shot off two or three pieces in our boats to cause the ships to way: and hauing bene about one houre vnder saile, we had sight of one of the French men vnder saile, halling off from Weamba to whome we gaue chase, and agreed in the night for feare of ouershooting them, that the Minion should first come to ancre, and after that about three houres, the Tyger and the Christopher to beare along all night.

The 5. day we found three of the French ships at ancre: one called La foye de Honfleur, a ship of 220 tunnes, another called the Ventereuse or small Roebarge of Honfleur, of 100 tunnes, both appertaining to Shawdet of

Honfleur, the third was called the Mulet de Batuille a ship of 120 tunnes, and this ship belonged to certaine Marchants of Roan.

[Sidenote: the English boord the Frenchmen.] When we came to them, we determined to lay the Admiral aboord, the Christopher the Viceadmirall, and the Tyger the smallest: but when we came nere them they wayed, and the Christopher being the headmost and the weathermost man, went roome with the Admirall: the Roebarge went so fast that wee could not fetch her. The first that we came to was the Mullet, and her wee layed aboord, and our men entred and tooke her, which ship was the richest except the Admirall: for the Admirall had taken about 80 pound of golde, and Roeberge had taken but 22 pound: and all this we learned of the Frenchmen, who knew it very well: for they were all in consort together, and had bene vpon the coast of Mina two moneths and odde dayes: howbeit the Roebarge had bene there before them with another ship of Diepe, and a carauel, which had beaten all the coast, and were departed one moneth before our arriuing there, and they three had taken about 700 pound of golde.

Assoone as we had layed the ship aboord, and left certaine men in her to keepe her, we set saile and gaue chase to the other two ships, and chased them all day and night, and the next day vntill three a clocke in the afternoone, but we could not fetch them: and therefore seeing that we brought our selues very farre to leeward of our place, we left the chase, and kept about againe to go with the shore.

The 7 day I sent for the captaine, marchants and Masters of the other ships, and when they came we weighed the golde which we had from the Frenchmen, which weighed fifty pound and fiue ounces of golde: this done we agreed to put men out of euery ship into the prise to keepe her.

The 12 day we came to the further place of the Mina called Egrand, and being come to an ancre, discharged all the marchants goods out of the prise, and would haue sold the ship with the victuals to the Frenchmen, but because she was leake they would not take her, but desired vs to saue their liues in taking them into our owne ships: then we agreed to take out the victuals and sinke the ship, and diuide the men among our ships.

The 15 at night we made an end of discharging the prise, and diuided all the Frenchmen except foure which were sicke and not able to helpe themselues; which foure both the Christopher and the Tyger refused to take, leauing them in their ship alone in the night, so that about midnight I was forced to fetch them into our ship.

The 15 of April, moouing our company for the voyage to Benin, the most part of them all refused it.

The 16, seeing the vnwillingnesse of the company to goe thither, we determined to spend as much time vpon the coast as we could, to the end we might make our voyage, and agreed to leaue the Minion here at Egrand, the Tyger to go to Pericow which is foure leagues off, and the Christopher to goe to Weamba, which is ten leagues to the weatherward of this place: and if any of them both should haue sight of more sailes then they thought good to meddle withall to come roome with their fellowes; to wit, first the Christopher to come with the Tyger, and then both they to come with vs.

We remained in this place called Egrand, vntill the last day of April, in which time many of our men fell sicke: and sixe of them died. And here we could haue no traffique with the Negros but three or foure dayes in the weeke, and all the rest of the weeke they would not come at vs.

The 3 of May not hauing the pinnesse sent vs with cloth from the other ships, as they promised, we solde French cloth, and gaue but three yards thereof to euery fuffe.

The 5 day the Negros departed, and told vs they would come to vs againe within foure dayes, which we determined there to tary, although we had diuers of our men sicke.

The 8 day, all our cloth in the Minion being sold, I called the company together, to know whether they would tary the sale of the cloth taken in the prise at this place or no: they answered, that in respect of the death of some of their men, and the present sicknesse of twentie more, they would not tary, but repaire to the other ships, of whom they had heard nothing since the 27 of April: and yet they had our pinnesse with them, onely to cary newes from one to another.

The 9 day we determined to depart hence to our fellowes, to see what they had done, and to attempt what was to be done at the towne of Don Iohn.

The 10 day in the morning we sat saile to seeke the Christopher and the Tyger.

The ll day the Captaine of the Christopher came to vs, and told vs that they could finde small doings at the places where they had bene.

The 12 William Crompton and I in our small pinnesse went to the Tyger and the Christopher at Perenine.

The 13 we sent away the Tyger to Egrand, because we found nothing to doe at Perenine, worth the tarying for.

The 14 our great pinnesse came to vs, and presently we put cloth into her, and sent her backe to Weamba, where she had bene before, and had taken there ten pound of golde.

The 15 the Minion came to vs, and the next day we went a shore with our boats, and tooke but one ounce of golde.

The 19 day hauing set saile we came to an ancre before Mowre, and there we tarried two dayes, but tooke not an ounce of golde.

The 21 we came to an ancre before Don Iohns towne.

[Sidenote: the great towne of Don Iohn.] The 22 we manned our boats and went to shore, but the Negros would not come at vs; then the Captaine of the Christopher and I tooke a skiffe and eight men with vs, and went and talked with the Negros, and they sayd that they would send a man to the great towne, where Don Iohn himselfe lay, to aduertise him of our comming.

The 23 we went ashore againe, and the Negros tolde vs that this day the marchants of Don Iohn would come downe: so we tarried there vntill night, and no man would come to vs: but diuers of the Negros made vs signes to depart.

The 24 the Captaine of the Christopher tooke his boat and went to Mowre, and when he came thither, certaine Negros came to him to know the price of his wares, but in the end there came an Almade, which he iudged came from the castle, and caused all the Negros to depart from him: and when he saw they would come no more to him, he went ashore and tooke certaine men with him, and then the Negros cast stones at them, and would not suffer them to come vp to their towne. And when they saw that, they tooke certaine of the Almades, and put them to the sea, and afterwards departed. The same morning I went a shore at Don Iohns towne, and tooke a white flag with me, but none of the Negros could come to me, which caused vs to iudge that the Portugals were in the towne. After this, our boat came to vs well manned, and I sent one man vp to the towne with a white flag in his hand, but when he was come thither, all the Negros went away and would not speake with him. Then I sent one alone into the woods after them, but they in no case would come to vs. When we saw that, we tooke twelue goats and fourteene hennes, which we found in the towne, and went aboord without doing any farther hurt to the towne: and when I came aboord, I found our pinnesse come from Cormatin, which had taken there two pound and fiue ounces of golde. Then after much ado with the froward Mariners, we went thitherwards with our ship, and the Christopher went to Mowre.

[Sidenote: A fight with the Negros.] The 25 day the Master of the Christopher sent his boat to the shore for balast, and the Negros would haue beaten the company from the shore, whereupon the company resisted them, and slew and hurt diuers of them, and hauing put them to flight, burned their towne, and brake all their boats.

The 26 day our pinnesse came to vs from Cormatin, and had taken two pound and eleuen ounces of golde: and Iohn Shirife tolde vs that the Negros of that place were very desirous to haue a ship come back againe to their towne.

The 27 we wayed and went to Cormatin.

The 28 the Christopher came to vs from Mowre and traffiqued there two dayes.

The second day of Iune the Tyger came to vs from Egrand, and the pinnesse from Weamba, and they two had taken about fifty pound of golde since they departed from vs.

The 4 day we departed from Cormatin to plie vp to Shamma, being not able to tary any longer vpon the coast for lacke of victuals, and specially of drinke.

The 7 day we had sight of fiue of the king of Portugals ships which came to an ancre besides the castle.

The 8 day George and Binny came to vs, and brought with them two pound of golde.

The 10 day in the morning I tooke our small pinnesse, and the Captaine of the Christopher with me, and manned her well, and went to the castle to view the Portugals ships, and there we found one ship of about 300 tunne, and foure carauels: when we had well viewed them, we returned backe againe to our ships which we found seuen leagues at sea.

The 11 day in the morning we found our selues wel shot toward Shamma, and the Tyger with vs, but the Minion and the pinnesse had not wayed that night, so that we were out of sight of them: and hauing brought our selues in the weather of the Portugals ships, we came to an ancre to tary for the Minion, or els we might haue fetched Shamma. At night the Minion and the pinnesse came vp to vs, but could not fetch so farre to the weatherward as we, and therefore they ancred about a league a weather The castle, and we waied in the Christopher, and went roome with her.

The 12 day the Tyger came roome with vs, and she and the Christopher finding themselues to stand in great need of victuals, would haue gone with the Portugals ships to haue fetched some of them forth: but our master and company would in no case consent to goe with them, for feare of hanging when we came home: and the other two ships being fully minded to haue gone, and fearing that their owne company would accuse them, durst not go to them.

After this, by reason of the want of victuals in the pinnesse, which could receiue no victuals from the other shippes, but from vs onely, we tooke out all our men, and put twelue Frenchmen into her, and gaue them victuals to bring them to Shamma.

The 19 day the Tyger and Minion arrived at Shamma, and the Christopher within two leagues off them, but could not fetch the winde by reason of the scantnesse of the winde, which hath bene so scant, that in fifteene dayes we haue plied to the windewards but twelue leagues, which before we did in one day and a night.

The 20 day I tooke our pinnesse, and went to the towne of Shamma to speake with the captaine, and he tolde me that there was no golde there to be had, nor as much as a hen to be bought, and all by reason of the accord which he had made with the Portugals, and I seeing that departed peaceably from him.

The 21 I put such things as we had into our small pinnesse, and tooke one marchant of our ship, and another of the Tyger, and sent her to Hanta, to attempt, if she could doe any thing there. That night they could doe nothing but were promised to haue golde the next day.

The next day (which was the 22) being come, we sent our pinnesse to Hanta againe, but there neither the captaine nor the Negros durst traffike with vs, but intised vs from place to place, and all to no purpose.

This day we put away our pinnesse, with fiue and twenty Frenchmen in her, and gaue them such victuals as we could spare, putting fifteene of them to the ransome of sixe crownes a man.

The 23 of Iune our pinnesse came to vs from Hanta, and tolde vs that the Negros had dealt very ill with them, and would not traffike with them to any purpose.

[Sidenote: Shamma burnt by the English.] The 24 we tooke our boat and pinnesse and manned them well, and went to the towne of Shamma, and because the Captaine thereof was become subiect to the Portugals we burned the towne, and our men seeking the spoile of such trifles as were there found a Portugals chest, wherein was some of his apparell, and his weights, and one letter sent to him from the castle, whereby we gathered that the Portugall had bene there of a long time.

The 25 day, about three of the clocke at afternoone, we set saile, and put into the sea, for our returne to England.

The last day of this moneth we fell with the shore againe, and made our reckoning to be eighteene leagues to the weatherward of the place where we set off. When we came to make the land, we found our selues to be eighteene leagues to the leeward of the place, where we set off, which came to passe, by reason of the extreme currant that runneth to the Eastward: when we perceiued our selues so abused, we agreed to cast about againe, and to lie as neere the winde as we could, to fetch the line.

The seuenth of Iuly we had sight of the Ile of S. Thome, ana thought to haue sought the road to haue arriued there: but the next morning the wind came about, and we kept our course.

The ninth, the winde varying, we kept about againe, and fell with the Iland of S. Thome, and seeking the road, were becalmed neere the Iland, and with the currant were put neere the shore, but could haue no ground to ancre: so that we were forced to hoise out our pinnesse, and the other ships their skiffs to towe from the Iland, which did litle good, but in the ende the winde put vs three leagues off the shore.

The tenth day the Christopher and the Tyger cast about, whereby we iudged them to haue agreed together, to goe seeke some ships in the road, and to leaue vs: our men were not willing to goe after them, for feare of running in with the Iland againe, and of putting our selues into the same danger that we were in the night before: but we shot off a piece, and put out two lights, and they answered vs with lights againe: whereupon we kept our course, and thought that they had followed vs, but in the morning we could not see them, so that they left vs willingly, and we determined to follow them no more. But the eleuenth day we altered our opinion and course, and consented to cast about againe for the Iland, to seeke our ships; and about foure of the clocke in the afternoone we met with them.

The 13 we fell againe with the Iland of S. Thome; and the same night we found our selues directly vnder the line.

[Sidenote: The description of the Ile of S. Thome.] This Iland is a very high Iland, and being vpon the West side of it, you shall see a very high pike, which is very small, and streight, as it were the steeple of a church, which pike lieth directly vnder the line, and at the same South end of the Iland to the Westward thereof lieth a small Iland, about a mile from the great Iland.

The third of August we departed from the Ile of S. Thome, and met the winde at the Southwest.

The 12 day we were in the height of Cape Verde.

The 22 day we fell with one of the Iles of Cape verde, called the Ile of Salt, and being informed by a Scotish man that we tooke among the Frenchmen vpon the coast, that there were fresh victuals to be had, we came to an ancre there.

The 23 day in the morning we manned our skiffe, and went a shore, and found no houses, but we saw foure men, which kept themselues alwayes farre from vs, as for cattell we could finde none, but great store of goats, and they were so wilde, that we could not take aboue three or foure of them: but there we had good store of fish, and vpon a small Iland which lay by the same we had great store of sea-birds.

At night the Christopher brake her cradle, and lost an ancre, so that she could tary no longer, so we all wayed, and set saile. Vpon the same Iland we left the Scotish man, which was the occasion of our going aland at that place, but how he was left we could not tell: but, as we iudged, the people of the Iland found him sleeping, and so caried him away; for at night I went my selfe to the Iland to seeke him, but could hear nothing of him.

[Sidenote: The great inconuenience by late staying vpon the coast of Guinie.] The 24 day the Master of the Tyger came aboord vs, and tolde vs that his men were so weake, and the shippe so leake, that he was not able to keepe her aboue the water, and therefore requested vs to go backe againe to the Iland, that we might discharge her, and giue her vp: but we intreated him to take paine with her awhile, and we put a French Carpenter into her, to see if he could finde the leake. This day we tooke a view of all our men, both those that were hole, and the sicke also, and we found that in all the three ships, were not aboue thirty sound men.

The 25 we had sight of the Ile of S. Nicholas, and the day following of the other Iles, S. Lucia, S. Vincent, and S. Anthony; which four Iles lie the one from the other Northwest, and by West, Souteast and by East.

The 26 we came againe with the Iland of S. Anthony, and could not double the Cape. This day Philip Iones, the Master of the Christopher, came aboord vs, who had beene aboord the Tyger, and tolde vs that they were not able to keepe the Tyger, because she was leake, and the Master very weake, and sayd further, he had agreed with the Master and the company, that if the next day we could double the Iland, we should runne to the leeward of it, and there discharge her: but if we could not double it, then to put in betwixt the Iland of S. Vincent and S. Anthony, to see if we could discharge her.

The third day of September I went aboord the Tyger, with the Master and Marchants with me, to view the shippe and men: and we found the shippe very leake, and onely six labouring men in her, whereof one was the Master gunner: so that we seeing that they were not able to keepe the ship, agreed to take in the men, and of the goods what we could saue, and then to put the ship away.

The fift day we went to discharge the Tyger.

The eight day, hauing taken out the artillery, goods, victuals, and gold of the Tyger, we gaue her vp 25 degrees by North the line.

The 27 we had sight of two of the Iles of the Azores, S. Mary, and S. Michael.

The fourth of October we found ourselues to be 41 degrees and a halfe from the line.

The sixt day the Christopher came to vs, and willed vs to put with the Cape, for they also were so weake, that they were not able to keepe the sea, and we being weake also, agreed to go for Vigo, being a place which many English men frequent.

The 10 day the Christopher went roome with the Cape, but we having a mery wind for England, and fearing the danger of the enemies, which ordinarily lie about the Cape: besides, not knowing the state of our countrey and Spaine, and although it were peace, yet there was little hope of friendship at their hands, considering the voyage that we had made, and we also being so weake, that by force and violence we could come by nothing, and doubting also that the king of Portugall knowing of our being there, might worke some way with the Counsell of Spaine to trouble vs: and further, considering that if we did put in with any harbor, we should not be able to come out againe, till we sent for more men into England, which would be a great charge, and losse of time, and meanes of many dangers. All these things pondred, we agreed to shoot off two pieces of ordinance, to warne the Christopher, and then we went our course for England: she hearing our pieces followed vs, and we carried a light for her, but the next day in the morning it was thicke, and we could not see her in the afternoone neither, so that we suspected that either she was gone with Spaine, or els that she should put foorth more sailes then we in the night, and was shot a head of vs, so that then we put forth our top-sailes, and went our course with England.

At the time when the Christopher left vs, we were within 120 leagues of England, and 45 leagues Northwest and by West from Cape Finister: and at the same time in our ships we had not aboue six Mariners and six Marchants in health, which was but a weake company for such a ship to seeke a forren harbour.

The 16 day about sixe of the clocke at night, we met with a great storme at the West-south-west, and West, and our men being weake, and not able to handle our sailes, we lost the same night our maine saile, foresaile, and spreetsaile, and were forced to lie a hulling, vntill the eighteenth day, and then we made ready an olde course of a foresaile, and put it to the yard, and therewith finding our selues far shot into the sleeue, we bare with our owne coast; but that foresaile continued not aboue two houres, before it was blowen from the yard with a freat, and then we were forced to lie a hull againe, vntil the nineteenth day of October in the morning, and then we put an olde bonnet to our foreyard, which, by the good blessing and prouidence of God, brought vs to the Ile of Wight, where we arriued the 20 of October in the afternoone.

* * * * *

The commodities and wares that are most desired in Guinie, betwixt Sierra Liona and the furthest place of the Mine.

Manils of brasse, and some of loade.

Basons of diuers sorts, but the most lattin.

Pots of course tinne, of a quart and more.

Some wedges of yron.

Margarites, and certaine other sleight beads.

Some blew Corall.

Some horse tailes.

Linnen cloth principally.

Basons of Flanders.

Some red cloth of low price, and some kersie.

Kettles of Dutch-land with brasen handles.

Some great brasse basons graued, such as in Flanders they set vpon their cupboords.

Some great basons of pewter, and ewers grauen.

Some lauers, such as be for water.

Great kniues of a low price.

Sleight Flanders-caskets.

Chests of Roan of a lowe price, or any other chests.

Great pinnes.

Course French couerings.

Packing sheets good store.

Swords, daggers, frise mantels, and gownes, clokes, hats, red caps, Spanish blankets, axe heads, hammers, short pieces of yron, sleight belles, gloues of a lowe price, leather bags, and what other trifles you will.

* * * * *

Certaine Articles deliuered to M. Iohn Lok, by Sir William Gerard Knight,
  M. William Winter, M. Beniamin Gonson, M. Anthony Hickman, and M. Edward
  Castelin the 8 of September 1561, touching a voyage to Guinea.

A remembrance for you M. Lok at your comming to the coast of Guinie.

First, when God shal send you thither, to procure, as you passe alongst the coast, to understand what riuers, hauens, or harboroughs there be; and to make your selfe a plat thereof, setting those places which you shall thinke materiall in your sayd plat, with their true eleuations.

Also you shall learne what commodities doe belong to the places where you shall touch, and what may be good for them.

It is thought good, that hauing a fort vpon the coast of Mina in the king of Habaans country, [Marginal note: The English marchants intend to fortifie in Ghinea, in the king of Habaans country.] it would serue to great purpose: wherfore you are especially sent to consider where the fort might be best placed, and vpon what ground: wherein are to be noted these things following.

1. That the ground so serue, that it ioyne to the sea on the one part, so as shippes and boats may come to lade and vnlade.

2. What molde of earth the ground is of.

3. What timber or wood may be had, and how it will be caried.

4. What prouision of victuals may be had in the countrey: and what kinde of our victuals will best serue to continue.

5. The place must be naturally strong, or such as may be made strong with a small charge, and afterwards kept with a few men.

6. How water may be prouided, if there be none to be had in the ground where the fort shall stand, or neere to it.

7. What helpe is to be had from the people of the country, either for the building of it, or for the defence thereof.

To mooue the king of Haban a farre off, for the making of a fort, and to note how he will like it; but vse your communication so, that although there might fall out good cause for the doing of it, yet he do not vnderstand your meaning.

Search the countrey so farre as you may, both alongst the coast, and into the land.

To learne what became of the marchants that were left at Benin.

The matters which shall be of importance to be noted we nothing doubt that you will omit, wherefore we referre the order of these affaires to your discretion.

Also we pray you as occasion shall serue that you ayd and helpe our factours, both with your counsell and otherwise; and thus God send you safely to returne.

William Gerrard, William Winter, Beniamin Gonson, Anthony Hickman, Edward
Castelin.

* * * * *

A letter of M. Iohn Lok to the worshipfull company of Marchants aduenturers for Guinie, written 1561, shewing reasons for his not proceeding in a voyage then intended to the foresayd countrey.

Worshipfull sirs; since the arriuall of M. Pet and Buttoll Monioy (as I vnderstand) for the voyage it is concluded that the Minion shall proceed on her voyage, if within 20 dayes she may be repaired of those hurts she hath receiued by the last storme: or in the moneth of Ianuary also, if the wind wil serue therfore. Wherefore for that your worships shall not be ignorant of my determined purpose in the same, with the reasons that haue perswaded me thereunto; I haue thought good to aduertise you thereof, trusting that your worships will weigh them, as I vprightly and plainly meane them. And not for any feare or discouragement that I haue of my selfe by the raging of the stormes of the sea, for that (I thanke the Lord) these haue not beene the first that I haue abiden, neither trust I they shalbe the last. First the state of the ship, in which, though I thinke not but M. Pet can do more for her strengthening than I can conceiue, yet for all that, it will neither mend her conditions, nor yet make her so stanch that any cabin in her shalbe stanch for men to lie drie in: the which sore, what a weakening it will be to the poore men after their labour, that they neither can haue a shift of apparell drie, nor yet a drie place to rest in, I referre to your discretion. For though that at Harwich she was both bound and caulked as much as might be, both within and without, yet for all that she left not, afore this flaw, in other weathers, being stressed, to open those seames, and become in the state she was before; I meane, in wetting her men: notwithstanding her new worke. And my iudgement, with that litle experience I haue had, leadeth me to thinke that the ship whose water works and footings be spent and rotten cannot be but leake for men. Next, the vnseasonable time of the yeere which is now present. And how onely by meanes of the vnseasonable times in the returne from the voyage home, many thereby haue decayed, to the great misery and calamity of the rest, and also to the great slander of the voyage, (which I much respect) the last and other voyage haue declared. And what it is to make the voyage in vnseasonable time, that hath the second voyage also declared. Wherefore weying and foreseeing this (as I may wel terme it) calamity and vneuitable danger of men, and that by men she must be brought home againe (except that God will shew an extraordinary miracle) I purpose not nor dare I venture with a safe conscience to tempt God herein. Againe, forsomuch as she is alone, and hath so little helpe of boat or pinnesse in her trade, and also for her watering, where a long time of force must be spent, my going, to the accomplishment of your expectations, will be to small effect for this time, because I shall want both vessell and men to accomplish it. And I would not gladly so spend my time and trauell, to my great charges and paine, and after, for not falling out accordingly, to lose both pot and water, as the prouerbe is. As for the Primrose, if she be there, her trade will be ended or euer we come there, so that she of force, by want of prouision, must returne: yea, though we should carry with vs a supply for her, yet is the meeting of her doubtfull, and though we met her, yet will the men not tarry, as no reason is they should: howbeit my opinion of her is that she is put into Ireland. The Flowerdeluce was in Milford. Thus for that your worships might vnderstand the whole cause why I doe not proceed, I haue troubled you at this time with this my long Letter. And, as God is my Iudge, not for feare of the Portugals, which there we shall meet (and yet alone without ayde) as here is a shippe which was in Lisbon, whose men say that there are in a readinesse (onely to meet vs) foure great ships, of the which one is accounted 700 tunnes, and other pinnesses: yet not for feare of them, nor raging of the seas (whose rage God is aboue to rule) but onely for the premisses: the sequell whereof must by reason turne to a great misery to the men; the which I for my part (though it might turne me to as much gaine as the whole commeth to) yet would I not be so tormented, as the sight thereof would be a corsiue to my heart, and the more, because foreseeing the same, I should be so leud, as yeelding, to haue runne into the danger thereof, and therefore I haue absolutely determined with my selfe not to goe this voyage. Howbeit if in a seasonable time of the yeere I had but one ship sufficient, though much lesse by the halfe, I would not refuse (as triall being made thereof should appeare) or if I had ability of my selfe to venture so much, it should well be seene. And this I speake to giue you to vnderstand that I refuse not this for feare: If you purpose to proceed heerein, send some one whom you please; to whom I will not onely deliuer the articles which I haue receiued, but also will giue some particular notes which I haue noted in the affaires which you haue committed vnto mee, with the best helpe and counsell I can. Thus the liuing God keepe your worships all. Bristoll this 11 of December 1561.

Your worships to comand to his power.

Iohn Lok.

* * * * *

The relation of one William Rutter to M. Anthony Hickman his master touching a voyage set out to Guinea in the yeere 1562, by Sir William Gerard, Sir William Chester, M. Thomas Lodge, the sayd Anthony Hickman, and Edward Castelin, which voyage is also written in verse by Robert Baker.

Worshipfull sir, my duty remembered, this shalbe to declare vnto you the discourse of this our voyage, since our departure out of England from Dartmouth; at which time I gaue you to vnderstand of our departure, which was the 25 of February 1562. Then hauing a prosperous winde we departed from thence, and sailed on our voyage vntill we arriued at Cauo verde the 20 of March, making no abode there, but sailed along the coast to our first appointed port Rio de Sestos, at which port we arriued the third of Aprill in the morning, hauing the sight of a Frenchman, who assoone as he perceiued vs, set saile and made to the sea: in the meane time we came to an anker in the rode: and after that he had espied our flag, perceiuing vs to be Englishman, he bare with the shore, and hailed our ships with his ordinance, at which time we the merchants of both the ships were in the riuer in traffike, and had vnderstanding of the Negroes that he had bene there three dayes before our comming: so we concluded together, that if he sent his pinnesse to traffike, we would not suffer him, vntill we had taken further order with their captaine and marchants. In the afternoone the pinnesse came into the riuer, whose men we willed to make no traffike vntill we had talked further with their captaine, whom we willed that night to come aboord our admirall: which was done. At which sayd time M. Burton and Iohn Munt went aboord the Minion where the Frenchmen were, and there concluded that they should tary by vs eight dayes, and suffer vs quietly to traffike, wherewith they were not well pleased. Wherevpon the next morning they departed from vs, sailing alongst the coast to the Eastward towards Potis, which he did to hinder our traffike that way: wherefore the marchants of the Minion and we concluded (forasmuch as at that present we vnderstood that were no sailes past alongst) that we should go before, to the end we might not be hindered of our traffike by the Frenchmen; which thing we did: and at our comming thither we found the Frenchmen in traffike to the West of Potis, by whom we passed, and arriued at Rio de Potis the 12 of April, where we remained in traffike vntill the 15 of the sayd moneth, and then departed from thence along the coast toward Sant Andre, where we appointed by agreement to tary for the Minion; and the 17 at night we came to the riuer of S. Andre, in which very day the Minion came vnto vs, telling vs that they met at cauo das Palmas a great ship and a caruell of the king of Portugals bound to the Mina, who gaue chase vnto them, and shot freely at them, and the Minion in her defence returned her the like: but God be praised the Minion had no hurt for that time. In the end we concluded to hasten towards cauo de tres puntus to haue put them from the castle, if by any meanes wee might; and when wee were come to the Cape, we lay a hull one night and two dayes, and doubting they had bene past, the Minion went neere the shore, and sent her merchants to a place called Anta, where beforetime we had traffike, and the next morning very early being the 21 of the sayd moneth, we againe had sight of the ship and the caruell a good way to sea-boord of vs. Then we presently set saile, and bare with the formost of them, hoping to haue got betweene the castle and them, but we came short of our purpose, which was no small griefe vnto vs all; and when they had gotten the castle to friend, they shot at vs freely, and we at them, and the castle at vs; but we profited litle. In the afternoone we set saile and came to the town of Don Iuan called Equi, where the 22 in the morning we went a shoare to traffike, but the Negros would not vntill they had newes from Don Luis, for at that time Don Iuan was dead, and the 23 came Don Luis his sonne and Pacheco minding to traffike with vs, at which said day came two gallies rowing along the shoare from the castle, minding to keepe vs from our traffike. The 24 we set saile and chased the galies to the castle againe. The Negroes being glad of that required vs to goe to Mowre, which is some 3 leagues behind, and thither would they come for that they stood in feare of the Portugals, and there we remained for the marchants that came out of the countrey which were come with their gold, but Anthonio don Luis his sonne, and Pacheco were aboord the Minion. And the 25 in the morning came the two galies from the castle againe vnto vs, the weather being very calme, they shot at vs and hit vs 3 times, and shortly after the wind came from the shore, at which instant we descried the ship, and the caruell comming toward vs, then we weighed and set saile, and bare as neere vnto them as we could: but it was night or euer wee met with them, and the night being very darke we lost them. The next day plying to the shore, at night we agreed to go with Cormantin, but the next morning being the 28 we were but a litle distant from the great ship and the 2 galies, hauing no wind at all, and the carauell hard aboord the shore. Then being calme, came the 2 galies rowing to the sterne of the Minion, and fought with her the most part of the forenoone: [Sidenote: Much hurt done in the Minion with firing a barrel of gunpouder.] and in the fight a mischance hapned in the Minions steward-roome by means of a barrell of pouder that tooke fire, wherewith were hurt the master gunner, the steward, and most part of the gunners: which the galies perceiuing, began to be more fierce vpon them, and with one shot cut halfe her foremast in twaine, that without present remedie shee was not able to beare saile, and presently vpon this the great ship sent her boat to the galies, who suddenly departed from vs. And after their departure we went aboord the Minion to counsell what were best to be done, at which time they were sore discomfited. Whereupon we deuised what was best to be done: and because wee knew that the Negros neither would nor durst traffike so long as the galies were on the coast it was therefore agreed that we should prepare our selues to depart to Rio de Sestos, and so we departed that day. [Sidenote: They returne.] The 14 of May in the rooming we fell with the land, and when wee came to it, we doubted what place it was, and sent our boates on land to know the trueth, and we found it to be Rio de Barbos, which is to be Eastward of sant Andre, and there remained in getting of water until the 21, where we lost the day before 5 of our men by meanes of overthrowing our black pinnasse. The 22 we departed from thence to Rio de Sesto, where we arriued the 2 of Iune, and the 4 wee departed from Rio de Sesto, and arriued (God bee thanked) the 6 of August within sight of the Stert in the West part of England, our men being very sicke and weake. We haue not at this present aboue 20 sound men that are able to labour, and we haue of our men 21 dead, and many more very sore hurt and sicke. Master Burton hath bene sicke this 6 weekes, and at this present (God strengthen him) is so weake that I feare he will hardly escape. Herein inclosed your worship shall receiue a briefe of all the goods sold by vs, and also what commodities we haue receiued for the same. Thus I leaue to trouble your worship, reseruing all things als to our generall meeting, and to the bringer hereof. From aboord the Primerose the 6 of August 1563.

Your obedient seruant

William Rutter.

There are brought home this voiage An. 1363. Elephants teeth 166 weighing 1758 pounds. Graines 22 buts full.

* * * * *

A meeting at Sir William Gerards house the 11 of Iuly 1564. for the setting foorth of a voyage to Guinea, with the Minion of the Queens, the Iohn Baptist of London, and the Merline of M. Gonson.

At this meeting were these chiefe aduenturers, Sir William Gerrard, sir William Chester, sir Thomas Lodge, Anthonie Hickman, and Edward Castelin. Where it was agreed that Francis Ashbie should be sent to Deptford to M. Gonson for his letters to Peter Pet to goe about the rigging of the Minion vpon the Queenes maiesties charges, and so the said Francis to repaire with the same letters to Gillingham with money to supplie our charge there.

Also that euery one of the fiue partners shall foorthwith call vpon their partners to supply towards this new rigging and victualling, 29 li. 10s. 6d. for euery 100. li. value.

Also that euery one of the fiue partners shall foorthwith bring in 50 li. towards the furniture of the premisses.

Likewise it is agreed that if M. Gonson giue his consent that the Merline shall be brought about from Bristoll to Hampton, that a letter be drawen whereunto his hand shall be, before order be giuen for the same.

* * * * *

The successe of this Voiage in part appeareth by certaine briefe relations extracted out of the second voyage of Sir Iohn Hawkins to the West Indies, made in the sayd yeere 1564, which I thought good to set downe for want of further instructions, which hitherto I could not by any meanes come by, albeit I haue vsed all possible indeuour for the obtaining of the same: Take them therefore in the meane season as foloweth.

Master Iohn Hawkins, with the Iesus of Lubeck a ship of 700. tonnes, and the Salomon, a ship of 7 score, the Tiger a barke of 50, and the Swalow 30 tonnes, being all well furnished with men to the number of one hundred threescore and ten, as also with ordinance and victuall requisite for such a voiage, departed out of Plimmouth the 18 day of October in the yeere of our Lord 1564. with a prosperous winde: at which departing, in cutting the foresaile, a marueilous misfortune happened to one of the officers in the ship, who by the pullie of the sheat was slaine out of hand, being a sorowfull beginning to them all. And after their setting out 10 leagues to the Sea, hee met the same day with the Minion a ship of the Queens Maiesties, whereof was captaine Dauid Carlet, and also her consort the Iohn Baptist of London being bound to Guinea likewise, who hailed one the other after the custome of the sea, with certaine pieces of ordinance for ioy of their meeting: which done, the Minion departed from him to seeke her other consort the Merline of London, which was a stone out of sight, leauing in M. Hawkins companie the Iohn Baptist her other consort.

Thus sailing forwards on their way with a prosperous wind until the 21 of the same moneth, at that time a great storme arose, the wind being at Northeast about 9 of the clocke at night, and continued so 23 houres together, in which storme M. Hawkins lost the company of the Iohn Baptist aforesaid, and of his pinnasse called the Swallow, the other 3 ships being sore beaten with the storme. The 23 day the Swalow, to his no small reioicing, came to him againe in the night 10 leagues to the Northward of Cape Finister, hauing put roomer and not being able to double the Cape, in that there rose a contrary wind at Southwest. The 25 the wind continuing contrary, he put into a place in Galicia called Ferol, where he remained 5 daies and appointed all the masters of his ships an order for the keeping of good company.

[Sidenote: The firing and sinking of the Merline bound for Guinea.] The 26 day the Minion came in also where he was, for the reioycing whereof he gaue them certaine pieces of ordinance after the curtesie of the Sea for their welcome, but the Minions men had no mirth because of their consort the Merline, whom at their departure from M. Hawkins vpon the coast of England, they went to seeke, and hauing met with her, kept company two dayes together, and at last by misfortune of fire (through the negligence of one of the gunners) the pouder in the gunners roome was set on fire, which with the first blast stroke out her poope, and therewithall lost 3 men, besides many sore burned (which escaped by the Brigandine being at her sterne) and immediatly to the great losse of the owners, and most horrible sight of the beholders, she sunke before their eies. The 30 day of the moneth M. Hawkins with his consorts and company of the Minion hauing now both the Brigandines at her sterne, weighed anker, and set saile on their voiage hauing a prosperous wind thereunto. The 4 of Nouember they had sight of the Iland of Madera, and the 6 day of Teneriffa, which they thought to haue bene the Canarie, in that they supposed themselues to haue bene to the Eastward of Teneriffa but were not: but the Minion beyng 3 or 4 leagues a head of vs kept on her course to Teneriffa, hauing better sight thereof then the other had, and by that means they parted company.

The foresaid Sir Iohn Hawkins passing on his voiage by Cauo Verde and Sierra Leona, and afterward crossing ouer the maine Ocean comming to the towne of Burboroata vpon the coast of Terra firma in the West Indies, had further information of the euill successe of this Guinean voyage, as in the same hereafter is verbatim mentioned.

The 29 of April, we being at anker without the road, a French ship called the green Dragon of Newhauen, whereof was captaine one Bon Temps came in, who saluted vs after the maner of the sea, with certaine pieces of ordinance, and we resaluted him with the like againe: with whom hauing communication, he declared that hee had bene at the Mina in Guinea, and was beaten off by the Portugals gallies, and enforced to come thither to make sale of such wares as he had: and further that the like was hapned vnto the Minion: also that captaine Dauid Carlet, and a marchant, with a dozen mariners were betraied by the Negros at their first arriuall thither, remaining prisoners with the Portugals, besides other misaduentures of the losse of their men hapned through the great lacke of fresh water, with great doubts of bringing home the ships: which was most sorrowfull for vs to vnderstand.

* * * * *

The voyage of M. George Fenner to Guinie, and the Islands of Cape Verde, in the yeere of 1566. with three ships, to wit the Admirall called the Castle of Comfort, the May Flower, and the George, and a pinnasse also:

Written by Walter Wren.

The 10 day of December, in the yeere abouesayd, we departed from Plimmouth, and the 12 day we were thwart of Vshant.

The 15 day in the morning being Sunday, wee had sight of Cape Finister, and the same night we lost the company of our Admiral, wherefore we sayled along the coast of Portugall, hoping that our Admiral had bene before vs.

The 18 day we met with a French ship of whom wee made inquirie for our Admirall, but he could not tell vs newes of him: so we followed our course to the Ilands of the Canaries.

The 25 day in the morning we fell with a small Iland called Porto Santo, and within 3 houres wee had sight of another Iland called Madera which is 6 leagues from Porto Santo.

The said 25 day being the day of the Natiuitie, we hoised out our boat, and fet Master Edward Fenner captaine of the May Flower aboord vs, being in the George, with the master whose name was Robert Cortise and others of the sayd shippe, and feasted them with such cheere as God had sent vs.

The 28 day we fel with an Iland called Tenerif, which is 27 leagues from the said Iland, and on the East side thereof we came to an anker in 40 fadome water, within a base shot of the shore, in a little Baie wherein were 3 or 4 small houses: which Baie and houses were distant from a litle towne called Santa Cruz, a league or thereabout, and as we rode in the said Baie, we might see an Iland called The grand Canarie, which was 6 or 7 leagues from vs.

The 29 day the May Flower for that she could not fet into ye road where we were at an anker, by reason the wind was off the shore, and because she bare more roomer from the land then we did, in the morning came bearing in with the towne of Santa Cruz, thinking to come to an anker in the road against the towne, and before she came within the reach of any of their ordinance, they shot at her foure pieces which caused her to come roome with vs, and came at last to an anker by vs. And about one of the clocke in the afternoone, the forenamed captaine of the May Flower wrote a letter a shoare, directing it to the head officer of the towne of Santa Cruz, to the intent to vnderstand the pretense of the shooting off the said ordinance.

The letter being written, Robert Courtise master of the May Flower, and Walter Wren were appointed to deliuer the same a land at 3 or 4 houses to bee conueid to the foresayd towne, and so went with six men in the boate, and rowed to the shore as neere as they might, for setting the boate on ground, for the sea went cruelly at the shore.

The people stood in number 30 persons with such armour as they had: the foresayd Wren called to them in Spanish, declaring to them that they had a letter which they would very gladly haue conueid vnto the towne, shewing that they would traffique with them as marchants, desiring their helpe for the conuenience of the same letter. With that one of the Spaniards willed vs to come on land, and we should be welcome, but doubting the worst, the said Walter answered them that they would not come on land, vntill they had answere of their letter which they had brought.

Whereupon one of the Spaniards vnraied himselfe, and lept into the water, and swam to the boat, whom we receiued. And he saluted vs, and demaunded what our request was: we made him answere, that by misfortune we lost the companie of our Admirall, and being bound to this Iland to traffique for wines and other things necessary for vs, do here mind to stay vntill he come.

Concerning our letter he made vs answere, that he would with all diligence cary it, and deliuer it according to the direction, and so the said Walter knit the letter in a bladder, and deliuered it unto him, and also gaue him foure roials of Spanish money for his paines: and promising that we should haue answere of it, he tooke his leaue and swamme againe on shore, where the people stood ready to receiue him. And after that they had talked with him, and vnderstood our meaning, some of them threw vp their hats, and the other put them off holding them in their hands, and made vs very curteous signes, alwaies desiring that the boat would come a land, but we resaluting them rowed backe againe aboord.

The 30 day the Gouernors brother of Santa Cruz came aboord the May Flower with sixe or seuen Spaniards with him, who concluded with the

Captaine that we might come a shoare and traffique with them, but that day we did not, for we had sufficient pledge of theirs for our assurance. Our Captaine entertained them well, and at their departure gaue them foure pieces of ordinance for a farewell, and bestowed vpon them two cheeses with other things.

The said Gouernors brother promised our Captaine that hee should haue sufficient pledges the morrow following, which was not done, whereupon wee grew suspicious, and went not that day a shore.

The first day of Ianuary our captaine sent Nicholas Day and Iohn Sumpter a shore, who were very well entertained with as many of our company as went after them.

In the said Iland is a maruellous high hill called the Pike, which is a far off more like a cloud in the aire, then any other thing: the hill is round and somewhat small at the top, it hath not bene knowen that euer any man could goe vp to the top thereof. And although it stand in 28 degrees which is as hote in Ianuary, as it is in England at Midsommer, yet is the top of the said hil Winter and Sommer seldome without snow.

In this Iland about two leagues from the said Santa Cruz is a citie called Anagona.

The third day wee departed about the Westerne point of the Iland, about 12 or 14 leagues from Santa Cruz, into a Baie which is right agaynst the house of one Petro de Souses, in which Baie we came to an anker the 5 day, where we heard that our Admirall had bene there at an anker 7 dayes before vs, and was gone thence to an Iland called Gomera, whereupon we set saile presently to seeke him.

The 6 day we came to an anker against the towne of Gomera, where we found our Admirall, which was very ioyfull of our comming, and we also of his sight.

In the sayd road we found Edward Cooke, in a tall ship, and a shippe of the Coppersmiths of London, which the Portugals had trecherously surprised in the Baie of Santa Cruz, vpon the coast of Barbarie, which ship we left there all spoiled.

Our General and merchants bought in the said towne for our provision, 14 buts of wine, which cost 15 duckats a but, which were offred vs at Santa Cruz in Tenerif for 8, 9, and 10 duckats.

The 9 day we departed from this road to another Baie, about 3 leagues off and there tooke in fresh water: and so the 10 day we set saile towards Cape Blanke, which is on the coast of Guinea.

The 12 day we fell into a Baie to the Eastward of Cape Pargos, which is 35 leagues from Cape Blanke. But hauing no knowledge of that coast, we went with Cape Blanke, and at the fall of the land we sounded and had 16 fadome water two leagues from the shore. The land is very lowe and white sand. [Sidenote: A good caueat.] Vpon the fall of the sayd coast beware how you borow in 12 or 10 fadome, for within 2 or 3 casts of the lead you may be on ground.

The 17 day we set saile from Cape Blanke, directing our course South and by East and South among, and so fell into a Baie to the Eastward of Cape Verde, about 16 leagues, and about six leagues from the shore. The sayd land seemed vnto vs as if it had bene a great number of shippes vnder saile, being indeed nothing els but the land which was full of Hummoks, some high some lowe, with high trees on them. We bare with the said land till we were within 3 leagues of the shore, and then we sounded, and found 28 fadome water, black oase. This day we saw much fish in sundry sculs swimming with their noses with the brim of the water.

Passing along this coast we might see two small round hils, seeming to vs about a league one from the other, which is the Cape, and betweene them are great store of trees, and in all our dayes sailing we saw no land so high as the said two hils.

The 19 day we came to an anker at the Cape, in a roade fast by the Westermost side of two hils in 10 fadome of water where you may ride in fiue or sixe fadome, for the ground is faire, and always you shall haue the winde off the shore. And as soone as we were all at an anker our Generall came aboord vs, and with him the master of the Admirall, whose name was William Bats, and with them the captaine of the Viceadmirall, whose name was master Edward Fenner, and Robert Curtise the master, and dined aboord of vs being in the George, wherein was Captaine Iohn Heiwood, and Iohn Smith of Hampton master, and there we concluded to goe a land, which was halfe a mile from vs: [Sidenote: The foolish rashness of Wil. Bats perswading company to land unarmed.] and by the counsel of William Bats both Captaine and marchants and diuers of the companie went without armour: for he sayd, that although the people were blacke and naked, yet they were ciuill: so that hee would needs giue the venter without the consent of the rest to go without weapon. Thus they rowed to shore, where we being in the shippe might see a great companie of Negros naked, walking to and fro by the sea side where the landing place was, waiting for the comming of our men, who came too soone, and landed to their losse as it fell out afterwards.

There went a shore the Admirals skiffe, and the May Flowers boate, and in them the number of 20 persons or thereabouts, as M. George Fenner the

Generall, his brother M. Edward Fenner, Thomas Valentine, Iohn Worme and
Francis Leigh marchants, Iohn Haward, William Bats, Nicholas Day, Iohn Thomson and others.

At their comming to the shore there were 100 Negros or vpward, with their bowes and arrowes: our Captaines and merchants talked with them, and according to the vse of the country, the one demanded pledges of the other, and they were content to deliuer 3 of their Negros for 5 of our men. Our 5 mens names were these, Iohn Haward, Wil. Bats, Nich. Day, Ioh. Tomson, and Iohn Curtise: these were deliuered them, and we receiued 3 Negros into our Admirals skiffe.

Our men being a shore among the Negros, began to talke with them, declaring what ware and marchandize we had, as woollen cloth, linnen cloth, iron, cheese and other things. The Negros answered againe, they had ciuet, muske, gold and graines, which pleased our captaines and marchants very well. Then the Negros desired to haue a sight of some of our wares, to the which our marchants were content, and foorthwith sent aboord one of the boats for part of their marchandise, and in the meane time while the boate went to the ship, our fiue men were walking on the shore with the Negros, and our Generall and marchants staied in the other boat by the sea side, hauing the 3 Negros with them.

Our boate then came againe and brought iron and other marchandise, with bread, wine, and cheese which they gave vnto him. Then two of the Negros (which were the pledges) made themselues sicke, desiring to goe a shore, promising to send other two for them. Captaine Haiward perceiuing that our men had let the Negros come a shore, asked what they meant, and doubting the worst began to drawe toward the boate, and two or three of the Negros folowed him. And when hee came to the boate they began to stay him, and he made signes vnto them that hee would fetch them more drinke and bread: notwithstanding, when he was entering into the boate, one of them caught him by the breeches and would haue staied him, but hee sprang from him and leapt into the boate, and as soone as hee was in, one of the Negros a shore beganne to blow a pipe, and presently the other Negro that was in our boate sitting on the boates side, and master Wormes sword by him, suddenly drew the sword out of the scabberd, and cast himselfe into the Sea, and swamme a shore, and presently the Negros laied handes on our men that were on shore, and tooke three of them with great violence, and tore all their apparell from their backes and left them nothing to couer them, and many of them shot so thicke at our men in our boates, that they could scarse set hand to any Oare to rowe from the shore, yet (by the helpe of God) they got from them with their boates although many of them were hurt with their poysoned arrowes: and the poison is vncurable, if the arrow enter within the skin and drawe blood, and except the poison be presently suckt out, or the place where any man is hurt bee foorthwith cut away, he dieth within foure dayes, and within three houres after they bee hurt or pricked, wheresoeuer it be, although but at the litle toe, yet it striketh vp to the heart, and taketh away the stomacke, and causeth the partie marueilously to vomite, being able to brooke neither meat nor drinke.

The Negros hauing vsed our men with such cruelty, whose names were Nicholas Day, William Bats, and Iohn Tomson, led them away to a towne which was within a mile of the water side, or thereabout.

The 20 day we sent to land a boate or skiffe wherein were eight persons, and one of them was the foresayd Iohn Tomson and our interpreter which was a Frenchman, (for there was one of the Negros which spake good French:) and they caried with them two harquebusses, two targets and a mantell.

The cause of sending them was to learne what ransome they demaunded for Bats and Day whom they detained. And when they came to the shore and told the Negros what they desired, they went and fetched them from among the trees, and brought them loose among fortie or fiftie of them. And being come within a stones cast of the sea side, William Bats brake from them, and ran as fast as he could into the sea towards the boat, and he was not so soone in the water but hee fell downe, either breath or his foote failing him in the sand being soft: so that the Negros came and fell on him and tooke him and haled him, that we thought they had torne him in pieces: [Sidenote: The danger of poysoned arrowes.] for they tore againe all the apparell from his backe, so that some of them caried our men againe to the towne, and the rest shot at vs with their poisoned arrowes, and hurt one of our men called Androwes in the smal of the leg, who being come aboord, (for all that our Surgeons could do) we thought he would haue died.

Our Generall (notwithstanding all this villanie) sent agayne to them, and offered them any thing that they desired for the raunsome of our men, but they would not deliuer them: giuing vs this answere: That there was in the foresayd roade, three weekes before we came, an English shippe which had taken three of their people, and vntill we did bring or send them againe, wee should not haue our men although wee would giue our three shippes with their furniture.

The 21 day a French shippe of the burden of 80 tunnes (or thereabouts,) came to the place where we were, being bound to traffique at the Cape: we told them of the detaining of our two men by the Negros: and seeing that these Frenchmen were very well welcome to the Negros, we wished them to see whether they could procure them againe of the Negros, and bring them along with them, and our Generall promised the Frenchmen 100 li. to obtaine them. So wee committed the matter to the Frenchmen and departed.

Of our men that were hurt by the Negros arrowes, foure died, and one to saue his life had his arme cut off. Androwes that was last of all hurt, lay lame not able to helpe himselfe: onely two recouered of their hurts. So we placed other men in the roomes of those that we lost, and set saile.

The 26 day between Cape Verde and Bona vista we sawe many flying fishes of the bignesse of herrings, whereof two flew into our boat, which we towed at our sterne.

The 28 day we fell with an Iland called Bona vista, which is from Cape Verde 86 leagues. The Northside of the sayde Iland is full of white sandie hils and dales, and somewhat high land.

The sayd day wee came to an anker within the Westermost point, about a league within the point and found in our sounding faire sand in ten fadome water, but you may go neere till you be in fiue or six fadome, for the ground is faire.

As soone as we were at an anker, our Generall sent his pinnasse a land, and found fiue or sixe small houses, but the people were fled into the mountains: and the next day he sent a shore againe, and met with two Portugals, who willingly went aboord with his men, and at their comming he welcommed them, although they were but poore and simple, and gaue each of them a paire of shoes, and so set them a shore againe.

The 30 day we weighed and sailed into a Bay within a small Iland about a league from vs, and tooke plentie of diuers sortes of fishe. The foresayd Iland lieth in sixteene degrees. And if you meane to anker in the said Bay, you may borow in four or fiue fadome of the Southermost point of the sayd Iland, which you may see when you ride in the road. But beware of the middle of the Baie, for there lieth a ledge of rocks, which at lowe water breaketh, yet there is three fadome water ouer them.

The last day of Ianuarie our Generall with certaine of his men went a shore in the Baie to the houses, where be found 12 Portugals. In all the Iland there were not aboue 30 persons, which were banished men for a time, some for more yeeres, some for lesse, and amongst them there was one simple man which was their captaine.

They liue vpon goats flesh, cocks, hennes, and fresh water: other victuals they haue none, sauing fish, which they esteeme not, neither haue they any boats to take them.

They reported that this Iland was giuen by the king of Portugall to one of his gentlemen, who hath let it foorth to rent for one hundreth duckats a yeere, which rent is reared onely in goates skinnes. For by their speaches there hath bene sent foorth of the sayd Iland into Portugall 40000 skins in one yeere.

We were to these men marueilously welcome, and to their powers very wel entertained, and they gaue vs the flesh of as many hee-goates as wee would haue, and tooke much paines for vs in taking them, and bringing them from the mountains vpon their asses.

They haue there great store of the oyle of Tortoises, which Tortoise is a fish which swimmeth in the Sea, with a shell on his backe as broad as a target. It raineth not in this Iland but in three moneths of the yeere, from the midst of Iuly to the midst of October, and it is here always very hote. Kine haue bene brought hither, but by reason of the heate and drought they haue died.

The 3 of February wee departed from this Iland, and the same day fell with another Iland called the Iland of Maiyo, which is 14 leagues from the other Iland: there is in the midst of the way between these two Ilands a danger which is always to be seene.

We ankred in the Northwest side of the sayd Ile in a faire Baie of eight fadomes water and faire sand, but here we staied not, but the fourth day weighed and sailed to another Iland called S. Iago, which lieth off the said Iland of Maiyo East and by South, and about fiue leagues one from the other. Being come within the Westermost point, we saw a faire road, and a small towne by the water side, and also a fort or platforme by it: there we purposed to come to anker, and our marchants to make some sale. But before we came within their shot, they let flie at vs two pieces, whereupon we went roomer and sailed along the shore two or three leagues from the road, where we found a small Baie and two or three small houses, where we came to an anker in 14 fadome faire ground.

Within an houre after we had ankered we might see diuers horsemen and footmen on the land right against vs riding and running to and fro.

The next day being the fift of Februarie, a great companie of their horsemen and footmen appeared on the shoare side, vnto whom our Generall sent to vnderstande whether they would quietly trafike with vs: And they sent him worde againe, desiring that they might speake with him, promising that if he came to trafike as a marchant he should be welcome, and also that he should haue any thing that he or the marchant would with reason demaund.

When this answere was brought vnto our Generall he was very glad thereof and the whole companie, and presently (with as much speede as he could) he caused his boates to be made readie: but doubting the villanie of the Portugales, he armed his boates putting a double base in the head of his pinnesse, and two single bases in the head of the Skiffe, and so sent to the May-floure, and the George, and willed them in like sort to man their two boates.

These boates being thus manned and well appointed, our Generall entered into his Skiffe, and with the rest rowed to the shoare where were threescore horsemen or more, and two hundreth footemen readie to receiue them. Our Generall marueiled that they came in so great a number and all armed, and therefore with a flagge of truce sent to them to knowe their pleasure: and they answered him with many faire promises and othes, that their pretence was all true, and that they meant like Gentlemen and Marchantes to trafike with him, declaring also that their Captaine was comming to speake with him, and therefore desired our Generall to come and speake with him himselfe.

With this answere the boate returned, and then our Generall caused his pinnesse to rowe to them, and as he came neere the shoare they came in a great companie with much obeysance, opening their hands and armes abroade, bowing themselues with their bonnets off, with as much humble salutations outwardly as they might: earnestly desiring our Generall and Marchants to come on lande to them, wherevnto he would not agree without sufficient gages of Gentlemen and Marchants. At length they promised to sende two gages to our Generals contentment, promising fresh water, victuall, money, or Negroes for ware, if it were such as they liked: and therefore desired our Generall and Marchants to sende them a shoare in writing the quantitie of their wares, and the names of them: all which our Generall departed to performe, looking for their answere the morrowe following. And being gone a litle from the shoare, he caused his bases, curriers, and harquebusses to be shot off, and our ships in like case shot off fiue or sixe pieces of great ordinance, and so came aboord to prepare the note. The Portugales most of them departed, sauing those that were left to watch and to receiue the note, which about foure or five a clocke in the afternoone was sent, and it was receiued. [Sidenote: The treason of the Portugals in S. Iago to our men.] But all the purposes of the Portugal were villainously to betray vs, (as shal appeare hereafter) although we meant in truth and honestie, friendly to trafike with them.

There was to the Westward of vs and about two leagues from vs, a towne behinde a point fast by the sea side, where they had certaine carauels, or shippes and also two Brigandines, whereof they (with all the speede that they might) made readie foure Carauels, and both the brigandines which were like two Gallies, and furnished them both with men and ordinance as much at they could carrie, and as soone as it was night, they came rowing and falling towards vs: so that the land being high and the weather somewhat cloude or mystie, and they comming all the way close vnder the shoare we could not see them till they were right against one of our ships called the May-floure.

By this time it was about one or two of the clocke in the morning, and the May-floure roade neerer them then the other two by a base shotte, so they made a sure account either to haue taken her or burnt her. In the meane time our men that had the watch (litle thinking of such villainous treacheries after so many faire wordes) were singing and playing one with the other and made such a noyse, that (being but a small gale of winde, and riding neere the lande) they might heare vs from the shoare: so that we supposed that they made account that we had espyed them, which indeede we had not, neither had any one piece of ordinance primed, or any other thing in a readinesse.

They came so neere vs that they were within gunshot of vs, and then one of our men chanced to see a light, and then looking out spied the 4 ships, and suddenly cried out, Gallies, gallies, at which crie we were all amazed, and foorthwith they shot at vs all the great ordinance that they had, and their harquebusses, and curriers, and so lighted certaine tronkes or pieces of wilde fire, and all of them with one voice (as well they on the shoare as they in the shippes) gaue a great shoute, and so continued hallowing with great noyses, still approaching neerer and neerer vnto the May-floure. We (with all the speede that we might) made readie one piece of ordinance and shotte at them, which caused them somewhat to stay, so they charged their ordinance and shot at vs freshly againe, and while they shotte this second time at vs, we had made readie three pieces which we shot at them, but they approched still so neere, that at last we might haue shot a sheafe arrowe to them. Wherevpon we hauing a gale of winde off the shoare hoysed our foresayle, and cut our cable at the hawse, and went towarde our Admirall, and they continued following and shooting at vs, and sometime at our Admirall, but our Admirall shotte one such piece at them, that it made them to retire, and at length to worpe away like traiterous villaines, and although they thus suddenly shot all their shot at vs, yet they hurt neither man or boye of ours, but what we did to them we know not.

But seeing the villanie of these men we thought it best to stay there no longer, but immediately set sayle towardes an Iland, called Fuego, 12 leagues from the said Iland of S. Iago. At which Island of Fuego we came to an anker the 11 day of this moneth, against a white chappell in the West end of the sayd Iland, within half a league of a litle towne, and with in a league or thereabout of the vtternost point of the said Island.

In this Island is a marueilous high hill which doth burne continually, and the inhabitants reported that about three yeeres past the whole Island was like to be burned with the abundance of fire that came out of it.

About a league from the chappel to the Westward is a goodly spring of fresh water, where we had as much as we would. Wheate they haue none growing here, but a certaine seede that they call Mill, and certaine peason like Guinie peason, which Mill maketh good breade, but they haue here good store of rother beasts and goates. [Sidenote: Cotton in Fuego.] Their marchandize is cotton, which groweth there.

The inhabitants are Portugals which haue commandement from the king to trafike neither with Englishmen nor Frenchmen for victuall or any other thing, except they be forced so to doe.

There lieth off this Iland another called Ila Braua, which is not passing two leagues ouer, it hath good store of goates and many trees, but there are not passing three or four persons dwelling in it.

[Sidenote: They returne.] The 25 day of February we departed towardes the Islands at Azores: and on the 23 day March we had sight of one of them called Flores, and then wee might see another Island to the Northward of it called Cueruo, lying two leagues or thereabouts off the other.

The 27 we came to an anker in Cueruo ouer against a village of about twelue simple houses; but in the night by a gale of winde, which caused vs to drawe our anker after vs we hoysed sayle and went to the aforesayd Island of Flores, where we sawe strange streames of water running downe from the high cliffes by reason of the great abundance of raine that had suddenly fallen.

The 29 day we came againe to Cueruo and cast anker, but a storme arose and continued seuen or eight houres together, so that we let slip a cable and anker, and after the storme was alayed we came againe thinking to haue recouered the same, but the Portugals had either taken it, or spoiled it: the cable was new and neuer wet before, and both the cable and anker were better worth then 40 li. So that we accompt our selues much beholding to the honest Portugales.

The 18 day of April we tooke in water at the Island of Flores, and hauing ankered our cable was fretted in sunder with a rocke and so burst, where wee lost that cable and anker also, and so departed to our coast.

Then wee set sayle to an Islande named Faial, about the which lie three other Islands, the one catted Pico, the other Saint George, and the other Graciosa, which we had sight of on the eight and twentieth day.

The 29 we came to an anker in the Southwest side of Faial in a faire bay, and 22 fadom water against a litle towne where we had both fresh water and fresh victuall. In this Iland by the report of the inhabitants, there groweth certaine greene woad, which by their speeches is faire better then the woad of S. Michael or of Tercera.

The 8 day of May we came to Tercera where we met with a Portugall ship, and being destitute of a cable and anker, our Generall caused vs to keepe her companie, to see if she could conueniently spare vs any. The next morning we might see bearing with vs a great shippe and two Carauels, which we iudged to be of the king of Portugals Armada, and so they were, wherevpon we prepared our selues for our defence. [Sidenote: A Portugall Galiasse of 400 tunnes.] The said ship was one of the kings Galliasses, about the burden of foure hundred tunnes, with about three hundred men in her, the shippe being well appointed with brasse pieces both great and small, and some of them so bigge that their shot was as great as a mans head, the other two Carauels were also very warlike and well appointed both with men and munition.

[Sidenote: A fight betweene one English ship and 7 Portugals.] As soone as they were within shotte of vs, they waued vs amaine with their swords, we keeping our course, the greatest shippe shot at vs freely and the carauell also, and we prepared our selues, and made all things cleare for our safegard as neere as we could. Then the great shippe shot at vs all her broad side, and her foure greatest pieces that lay in her sterne, and therewith hurt some of our men, and we did the best we could with our shot to requite it. At last two other Carauels came off the shoare, and two other pinnesses full of men, and deliuered them aboord the great shippe, and so went backe againe with two men in a piece of them. The ship and the Carauell gave vs the first day three fights, and when the night was come they left off shooting, yet notwithstanding kept hard by vs all the night. In the meane time we had as much as wee could doe all the night to mende our ropes, and to strengthen our bulwarkes, putting our trust in God, and resoluing our selues rather to die in our defence then to bee taken by such wretches.

The next day being the 10 of May in the morning, there were come to the aide the said Portugals foure great Armadas or Carauels more which made seuen, of which 4 three of them were at the least 100 tunnes a piece, the other not so bigge, but all well appointed and full of men. All these together came bearing with vs being in our Admirall, and one of the great Carauels came to lay vs aboorde (as we iudged) for they had prepared their false nettings, and all things for that purpose, so that the Gallias came vp in our larboord side, and the Carauell in our starboord side.

Our Captaine and master perceiuing their pretence, caused our gunners to make all our ordinance readie with crossebarres, chaineshotte and haileshot: so the ship and Carauell came vp, and as soone as they were right in our sides, they shotte at vs as much ordinance as they could, thinking to haue layde vs presently aboord: whereupon we gaue them such a heate with both our sides, that they were both glad to fall asterne of vs, and so paused the space of two or three houres being a very small gale of winde.

Then came vp the other fiue and shot all at vs, and so fell all asterne of vs, and then went to counsell together.

Then our small barke named the George came to vs, and wee confered together a great space. And as the Portugall shippes and Carauels were comming to vs againe, our barke minding to fall asteme of vs and so to come vp againe, fell quickly vpon the lee, and by reason of the litle winde, it was so long before she could fill her sailes againe, that both the shippe and Carauels were came vp to vs, and she falling in among them made reasonable shift with them, but they got a head of her, so that she could not vs: then 5 of the Carauels followed her, but we saw she defended her selfe against them all.

Then came the great shippe and the Carauell to vs, and fought with vs all that day with their ordinance.

The May-floure our other consort being very good by the winde, tooke the benefite thereof and halde all that day close by the winde, but could not come neere vs. So when night againe was come, they gaue ouer their fight and followed vs all the night.

In these many fights it could not otherwise be but needes some of our men must be slaine, (as they were indeede) and diuers hurt, and our tackle much spoyled: yet for all this we did our best indeuour to repaire all things, and to stand to it to the death with our assured trust in the mercie and helpe of God.

This night the May-floure came vp to vs, and our Captaine tolde them his harmes and spoyles, and wished them if they could spare halfe a dosen fresh men to hoyse out their boate and sende them to him, but they could not spare any, and so bare away againe. Which when our enemies sawe in the next morning that we were one from another, they came vp to vs againe and gaue vs a great fight with much hallowing and hooping, making accompt either to boorde vs or els to sinke vs: but although our companie was but small, yet least they should see vs any whit dismayed, when they hallowed we hallowed also as fast as they, and waued to them to come and boorde vs if they durst, but that they would not, seeing vs still so couragious: [Sidenote: The 7 Portugals depart with shame from one English ship.] and hauing giuen vs that day foure fights, at night they forsooke vs with shame, as they came to vs at the first with pride.

They had made in our ship some leakes with their shot which we againe stopped with al speed, and that being done, we tooke some rest after our long labour and trouble.

The next day in the morning the May-floure came to vs, and brought vs sixe men in her boate which did vs much pleasure, and we sent to them some of our hurt men.

Then we directed our course for our owne countrey, and by the second day of
Iune we were neere to our owne coast and sounded being thwart the Lyzard.

The third day we had sight of a shippe which was a Portugall, who bare with vs, and at his comming to vs (the weather being calme) our Captaine caused him to hoyse foorth his boate to come aboord to speake with him, and at their comming our Captaine and Marchants demanded of them what ware they had, and whether they were bound, and they made answere that their lading was sugar and cotton. Then our Captaine and Marchants shewed them fiue Negroes that we had, and asked them whither they would buy them, which they were very desirous to doe, and agreed to giue for them 40 chests of sugar, which chests were small hauiug not aboue 26 loaues in a piece: so they with their boate did fetch fiue of the chestes and deliuered them and went for more, and when they had laden their boate and were come againe, we might see bearing with vs a great ship and a small, which our Captaine supposed to be men of warre or Rouers, [Marginal Note: A Portugall ship (notwithstanding all their villanies) defended by our men from Rouers.] and then willed the Portugales to carie their sugar to their ship againe, purposing to make our selues readie for our defence. But the Portugales earnestly intreated our Captaine not so to forsake them, and promised him (if he would safegard them) to giue him aboue the bargain ten chests of sugar: whereupon our Captaine was content, and the Portugall not being good of sayle, we spared our topsayles for her; so at last the foresaid ship bare with vs, and (seeing that we did not feare them) gaue vs ouer. And the next morning came two others bearing with vs, and seeing vs not about to flie a iot from them forsooke vs also.

The 5 day of Iune we had sight of the Stert, and about noone we were thwart of the bay of Lime, and so sounded and had 35 fadom water.

The sixt day we came in at the Needles and so came to an anker vnder the Isle of Wight at a place called Meadhole, and from thence sayled to Southampton where we made an ende of this voyage.

* * * * *

The Ambassage of M. Edmund Hogan, one of the sworne Esquires of her Maiesties person, from her Highnesse to Mully Abdelmelech Emperour of Marocco, and king of Fes and Sus: in the yeere 1577, written by himselfe.

I Edmund Hogan being appointed Ambassadour from the Queenes Maiestie to the aboue named Emperour and King Mully Abdelmelech, departed with my company and seruants from London the two and twentie day of April 1577, being imbarked in the good ship called the Gallion of London, and arriued in Azafi a port of Barbarie the one and twentie day of May next following. Immediatly I sent Leonell Edgerton a shoare with my letters directed to Iohn Williams and Iohn Bampton, who dispatched a Trottero to Marocco to knowe the kings pleasure for my repaire to the Court, which letters came to their hands on the Thursday night.

They with all speede gaue the king understanding of it, who being glad thereof speeded the next day certaine Captaines with souldiers and tents, with other prouision to Azafi, so that vpon Whitsunday at night the said Captaines with Iohn Bambton, Robert Washborne, and Robert Lion, and the kings officers came late to Azafi.

In the meane time I remained a boord, and caused some of the goods to be discharged for lightning of the shippe, and I wrote in my letter that I would not lande, till I knewe the Kings pleasure.

The 22 day being Saturday, the Make-speede arriued in the roade about two of the clocke in the afternoone.

The 27 day, being Whitsunday, came aboord the Gallion Iohn Bampton, and others, giuing me to vnderstande how much the King reioyced of my safe arriuall, comming from the Queenes Maiestie, and how that for my safe conduct to the Court he had sent foure Captaines and an hundred souldiers well appointed, with a horse furnished which he vsed himselfe to ride on with all other furniture accordingly: they wished mee also to come on lande in the best order I could, as well for my selfe as my men, which I did, hauing to the number of tenne men, whereof three were trumpetters.

The ships being foure appointed themselues in the best order they could for the best shew, and shot off all their ordinance to the value of twentie Markes in powder.

At my comming a shoare, I found all the souldiers well appointed on horsebacke, the Captaines and the Gouernour of the towne standing as neere the water side as they could, with a Iennet of the kings, and receiued mee from the boate declaring how glad his maiestie was of my safe arriuall, comming from the Queenes Maiestie my Mistresse, and that hee had sent them to attend vpon me, it being his pleasure that I should tarie there on shore fiue or sixe dayes for my refreshing.

So being mounted vpon the Iennet, they conducted mee through the Towne into a faire fielde vpon the Sea-side where was a tent prouided for mee, and all the ground spread with Turkie carpets, and the Castle discharged a peale of ordinance, and all things necessarie were brought into my tent, where I both tooke my table and lodging, and had other conuenient tents for my seruants.

The souldiers enuironed the tents, and watched about vs day and night as long as I lay there, although I sought my speedier dispatch.

On the Wednesday towards night, I tooke my horse and traueiled ten miles to the first place of water that we could finde, [Marginal Note: In Barbarie they haue no Innes but they lodge in open fieldes where they can find water.] and there pitched our tents till the next morning, and so traueiled till ten of the clocke, and then pitched our tents till foure, and so traueiled as long as day light would suffer about 26 miles that day.

The next day being Friday I traueiled in like order but eight and twentie miles at the most, and by a Riuer being about sixe miles within sight of the Citie of Marocco we pitched our tents.

[Sidenote: The singular humanitie of the king to our Ambassadour.] Immediatly after came all our English marchants, and the French on horsebacke to meete me, and before night there came an Alcayde from the king with fiftie men, and diuers mules laden with victuall and banket, for my supper, declaring vnto me how glad the king shewed himselfe to heare of the Queenes Maiestie, and that his pleasere was I should be receiued into his country as neuer any Christian the like: and desired to knowe what time the next day I would come into his citie, because he would that all the Christians as also his nobilitie should meete me, and willed Iohn Bampton to be with him early in the morning, which he did.

About seuen of the clocke being accompanied with the French and English marchants, and a great number of souldiers, I passed towards the citie, and by that time I had traueiled 2 miles, there met me all the Christians of the Spaniards and Portugals to receiue me, which I knowe was more by the kings commandement then of any good wils of themselues: for some of them although they speake me faire hung downe their heads like dogs, and especially the Portugales, and I countenanced them accordingly. [Marginal Note: The Spaniards and Portugales were commanded by the king in paine of death, to meete the English Ambassadour.]

So I passed on till I came within two English miles of the Citie, and then Iohn Bampton returned, shewing me that the king was so glad of my comming, that hee could not deuise to doe too much, to shewe the good will that hee did owe to the Queenes Maiestie, and her Realme.

His counsellors met me without the gates, and at the entrie of the gates, his footmen and guard were placed on both sides of my horse, and so brought me to the kings palace.

The king sate in his chaire with his Counsell about him, as well the Moores as the Elchies, and according to his order giuen vnto me before, I there declared my message in Spanish, and made deliuerie of the Queenes Maiesties letters, and all that I spake at that present in Spanish, hee caused one of his Elchies to declare the same to the Moores present, in the Larbe tongue.

Which done, he answered me againe in Spanish, yeelding to the Queenes Maiestie great thankes, and offering himselfe and his countrey to bee at her Graces commaundement, and then commaunded certaine of his Counsellers to conduct mee to my lodging, not being farre from the Court.

The house was faire after the fashion of that countrey, being daily well furnished with al kind of victuall at the kings charge.

The same night he sent for mee to the Court, and I had conference with him about the space of two houres, where I throughly declared the charge committed vnto mee from her Maiestie, finding him conformable, willing to pleasure and not to vrge her Maiestie with any demaundes, more then conueniently shee might willingly consent vnto, hee knowing that out of his countrey the Realme of England might be better serued with lackes, then bee in comparison from vs.

[Sidenote: The king of Spaine sought to disgrace the Queene and her Ambassadour.] Further he gaue me to vnderstand, that the king of Spaine had sent vnto him for a licence, that an Ambassadour of his might come into his countrey, and had made great meanes that if the Queenes maiesty of England sent any vnto him, that he would not giue him any credit or intertainment, albeit (said he) I know what the king of Spaine is, and what the Queene of England and her Realme is: for I neither like of him nor of his religion, being so gouerned by the Inquisition that he can doe nothing of himselfe.

Therefore when he commeth vpon the licence which I haue granted, he shall well see how litle account I will make of him and Spaine, and how greatly will extoll you for the Queenes maiestie of England.

He shall not come to my presence as you haue done, and shall dayly: for I minde to accept of you as my companion and one of my house, whereas he shall attend twentie dayes after he hath done his message.

After the end of this speech I deliuered Sir Thomas Greshams letters, when as he tooke me by the hand, and led me downe a long court to a palace where there ranne a faire fountaine of water, and there sitting himselfe in a chaire, he commanded me to sit downe in another, and there called for such simple Musicians as he had.

[Sidenote: The king of Barbarie sent into England for Musicians.] Then I presented him with a great base Lute, which he most thankfully accepted, and then he was desirous to heare of the Musicians, and I tolde him that there was great care had to prouide them, and that I did not doubt but vpon my returne they should come with the first ship. He is willing to giue them good intertainment with prouision of victuall, and to let them liue according to their law and conscience wherein he vrgeth none to the contrary.

I finde him to be one that liueth greatly in the feare of God, being well exercised in the Scriptures, as well in the olde Testament as also in the New, and he beareth a greater affection to our Nation then to others because of our religion, which forbiddeth worship of Idols, and the Moores called him the Christian king.

[Sidenote: A rich gift bestowed upon our Ambassadour.] The same night being the first of Iune, I continued with him till twelue of the clocke, and he seemed to haue so good liking of me, that he tooke from his girdle a short dagger being set with 200 stones, rubies and turkies, and did bestow it vpon me, and so I being conducted returned to my lodging for that time.

The next day because he knew it to be Sunday and our Sabbath day he did let me rest. But on the Munday in the afternoone he sent for me, and I had conference with him againe, and musicke.

Likewise on the Tuesday by three of the clocke he sent for me into his garden, finding him layd vpon a silke bed complayning of a sore leg: yet after long conference he walked into another Orchard, where as hauing a faire banketting-house and a great water, and a new gallie in it, he went aboord the gallie and tooke me with him, and passed the space of two or three houres, shewing the great experience he had in Gallies, wherein (as he said) he had excercised himselfe eighteene yeeres in his youth.

After supper he shewed me his horses and other commodities that he had about his house, and since that night I haue not seene him, for that he hath kept in with his sore legge, but he hath sent to me daily.

The 13 of Iune at sixe of the clocke at night I had againe audience of the king, and I continued with him till midnight, hauing debated as well for the Queenes commission as for the well dealing, with her marchants for their traffike here in these parts, saying, he would do much more for the Queenes maiesty and the Realme offering that all English ships with her subiects may with good securitie enter into his ports and dominions as well in trade of marchandise, as for victuall and water, as also in time of warre with any her enemies to bring in prises and to make sales, as occasion should serue, or else to depart againe with them at their pleasure.

Likewise for all English ships that shall passe along his coast of Barbarie, and thorow the straites into the Leuant seas, that he would graunt safe conduct that the said ships and marchants with their goods might passe into the Leuant seas, and so to the Turks dominions, and the king of Argiers, as his owne, and that he would write to the Turke and to the king of Argier his letters for the well vsing of our ships and goods.

Also that hereafter no Englishmen that by any meanes be taken captiues, shall be solde within any of his dominions: whereupon I declared that the Queenes maiesty accepting of these his offers was pleased to confirme the intercourse and trade of our marchants within this his countrey, as also to pleasure him with such commodities as he should haue need of, to furnish the necessities and wants of his countrey in trade of marchandise, so as he required nothing contrarie to her honour and law, and the breach of league with the Christian princes her neighbours. [Sidenote: A good prouiso.]

The same night I presented the king with the case of combes, and desired his maiestie to haue special regard that the ships might be laden backe againe, for that I found litle store of saltpeter in readinesse in Iohn Bamptons hands. He answered me that I should haue all the assistance therein that he could, but that in Sus he thought to haue some store in his house there, as also that the Mountayners had made much in a readinesse: I requested that he would send downe, which he promised to doe.

The eighteene day I was with him againe and so continued there till night, and he shewed me his house with pastime in ducking with water-Spaniels, and baiting buls with his English dogges.

At this time I moued him againe for the sending downe to Sus, which he granted to doe, and the 24. day there departed Alcayde Mammie, with Lionell Edgerton, and Rowland Guy to Sus, and caried with them for our accompts and his company the kings letters to his brother Muly Hammet, and Alcayde Shauan, and the Viceroy.

The 23. day the king sent me out of Marocco to his garden called Shersbonare, with his gard, and Alcayde Mamoute, and the 24. at night I came to the court to see a Morris dance, and a play of his Elchies. He promised me audience the next day being Tuesday, but he put it off till Thursday: and the Thursday at night I was sent for to the king after supper, and then he sent Alcayde Rodwan, and Alcayde Gowry to conferre with me, but after a little talke I desired to be brought to the King for my dispatch. And being brought to him, I preferred two bils of Iohn Bamptons which he had made for prouision of Salt-peter: also two bils for the quiet traffique of our English marchants, and bils for sugars to be made by the Iewes, as well for the debts past, as hereafter, and for good order in the Ingenios. Also I mooued him againe for the Salt-peter, and other dispatches, which he referred to be agreed vpon by the two Alcaydes. But the Friday being the 20. the Alcaydes could not intend it, and vpon Saturday Alcayde Rodwan fell sicke, so on Sunday we made meanes to the King, and that afternoone I was sent for to conferre vpon the bargaine with the Alcaydes and others, but did not agree.

Vpon Tuesday I wrote a letter to the King for my dispatch, and the same afternoone I was called againe to the Court, and referred all things to the King, accepting his offer of Salt-peter.

That night againe the King had me into his Gallie, and the Spaniels did hunt the ducke.

The Thursday I was appointed to way the 300. kintals grosse of Salt-peter, and that afternoone the Tabybe came vnto mee to my lodging, shewing mee that the king was offended with Iohn Bampton for diuers causes.

The Sunday night late being the 7. of Iuly, I got the King to forgiue all to Iohn Bampton, and the King promised me to speake againe with me vpon Munday.

Vpon Tuesday I wrote to him againe for my dispatch, and then hee sent Fray
Lewes to mee, and said that he had order to write.

Vpon Wednesday I wrote againe, and he sent me word that vpon Thursday I should come and be dispatched, so that I should depart vpon Friday without faile, being the twelfth of Iuly.

[Sidenote: The Emperor of Maroco his priuileges to the English.] So the Friday after according to the kings order and appointment I went to the court, and whereas motion and petition was made for the confirmation of the demaunds which I had preferred, they were all granted, and likewise the priuileges which were on the behalfe of our English marchants requested, were with great fauour and readinesse yeelded vnto. And whereas the Iews there resident were to our men in certaine round summes indebted, the Emperors pleasure and commandement was, that they should without further excuse or delay, pay and discharge the same. And thus at length I was dismissed with great honour and speciall countenance, such as hath not ordinarily bene shewed to other Ambassadors of the Christians.

And touching the priuate affaires intreated vpon betwixt her Maiestie and the Emperour, I had letters from him to satisfie her highnesse therein. So to conclude, hauing receiued the like honourable conduct from his Court, as I had for my part at my first landing, I embarked my selfe with my foresaid company, and arriuing not long after in England, I repaired to her Maiesties court, and ended my Ambassage to her highnesse good liking, with relation of my seruice performed.

* * * * *

The voyage of Thomas Stukeley, wrongfully called Marques of Ireland, into Barbary 1578. Written by Iohannes Thomas Freigius in Historia de cæde Sebastiani Regis Lusitaniæ.

Venerant autem ad regem etiam sexcenti Itali, quos Papa subministrarat, Comiti Irlandiæ: qui cum Vlissiponem tribus instructis nauibus appulisset Regi operam suam condixit, eumque in bellum sequi promisit. Cap. 7.

Totum exercitum diuisit in quatuor acies quadratas: In dextro latere primum agmen erat Velitum et militum Tingitanorum, eosque ducebat Aluarus Peresius de Tauara: sinistram aciem seu mediam tenebant Germani et Ital, quibus imperabat Marchio Irlandiæ, etc. Cap 11.

Inter nobiles qui in hoc prælio ceciderunt, fuerunt, præter regem Sebastianum, dux de Auero, Episcopi Conimbricensis et Portuensis, Commissarius generalis à Papa missus Marchio Irlandiæ, Christophorus de Tauora, et plures alij. Cap. 13.

The same in English.

There came also to Don Sebastian the King of Portugal 600. Italians, whom the Pope sent vnder the conduct of the Marques of Irland: [Marginal note: Thomas Stukeley was wrongfully indued with this title.] who being arriued at Lisbone with three tall ships, proffered his seruice to the king, and promised to attend vpon him in the warres, &c.

He diuided the whole Armie into 4 squadrons: vpon the right wing stood the first squadron, consisting of men lightly armed or skirmishers and of the souldiers of Tangier, Generall of whom was Don Aluaro Perez de Tauara: the left or midle squadron consisted of Germanes and Italians, vnder the command of the Marques of Irland, &c. cap. 7.

Of Noblemen were slaine in this battel (besides Don Sebastian the king) the duke de Auero, the two bishops of Coimbra and of Porto, the Marques of Irland sent by the Pope as his Commissary generall, Christopher de Tauara, and many others, cap. 13.

It is further also to be remembred, that diuers other English gentlemen were in this battell, whereof the most part were slaine; and among others M. Christopher Lyster was taken captiue, and was there long detained in miserable seruitude. Which gentleman although at length he happily escaped the cruel hands of the Moores; yet returning home into England, and for his manifold good parts being in the yeere 1586. employed by the honourable the Earle of Cumberland, in a voyage intended by the Streights of Magellan for the South sea, as Viceadmirall, (wherein he shewed singular resolution and courage) and appointed afterward in diuers places of speciall command and credite, was last of all miserably drowned in a great and rich Spanish prize vpon the coast of Cornwall.

* * * * *

Certaine reports of the prouince of China learned through the Portugals there imprisoned, and chiefly by the relation of Galeotto Perera, a gentleman of good credit, that lay prisoner in that Countrey many yeeres. Done out of Italian into English by Richard Willes.

This land of China is parted into 13. Shires, the which sometimes were ech one a kingdome by it selfe, but these many yeeres they haue bene all subiect vnto one King. Fuquien is made by the Portugals the first Shire, because there their troubles began, and they had occasion thereby to know the rest. In the shire be 8 cities, but one principally more famous then others called Fuquieo, the other seuen are reasonably great, the best knowen whereof vnto the Portugals is Cinceo, in respect of a certaine hauen ioyning thereunto, whither in time past they were wont for marchandise.

Cantan is the second shire, not so great in quantitie, as well accompted of, both by the king thereof, and also by the Portugals, for that it lieth neerer vnto Malacca then any other part of China, and was first discried by the Portugals before any other shire in that prouince: this shire hath in it seuen Cities.

Chequeam is the third shire, the chiefest Citie therein is Donchion, therein also standeth Liampo, with other 13. or 14. boroughes: countrey townes therein are too too many to be spoken of.

The fourth shire is called Xutiamfu, the principall Citie thereof is great Pachin, where the King is always resident. In it are fifteene other very great Cities: of other townes therein, and boroughes well walled and trenched about, I will say nothing.

The fift shire hath name Chelim: the great Citie Nanquin chiefe of other fifteene cities was herein of ancient time the royall seat of the Chinish kings. From this shire, and from the aforesaid Chequeam forward bare rule the other kings, vntil the whole region became one kingdome.

[Sidenote: Quianci, or, Quinzi.] The 6. shire beareth the name Quianci, as also the principal City thereof, wherein the fine clay to make vessels is wrought. The Portugals being ignorant of this Countrey, and finding great abundance of that fine clay to be solde at Liampo, and that very good cheape, thought at the first that it had bene made there, howbeit in fine they perceiued that the standing of Quinzi more neere vnto Liampo then to Cinceo or Cantan was the cause of so much fine clay at Liampo: within the compasse of Quinci shire be other 12. cities.

The 7. shire is Quicin, the 8. Quansi, the 9. Confu, the 10. Vrnan, the 11. Sichiua. In the first hereof there be 16. Cities, in the next 15: how many Townes the other 3. haue, wee are ignorant as yet, as also of the proper names of the 12. and 13. shires, and the townes therein.

This finally may be generally said hereof, that the greater shires in China prouince may bee compared with mightie kingdomes.

In eche one of these shires bee set Ponchiassini and Anchiassini, before whom are handled the matters of other Cities. There is also placed in ech one a Tutan, as you would say, a gouernour, and a Chian, that is a visiter, as it were: whose office is to goe in circuit, and to see iustice exactly done. By these meanes so vprightly things are ordered there, that it may be worthily accompted one of the best gouerned prouinces in all the world.

The king maketh alwayes his abode in the great city Pachin, as much to say in our language, as by the name thereof I am aduertised, the towne of the kingdome. This kingdome is so large, that vnder fiue monethes you are not able to trauaile from the Townes by the Sea side to the Court, and backe againe, no not vnder three monethes in poste at your vrgent businesse. The post-horses in this Countrey are litle of body, but swift of foote. Many doe traueile the greater part of this iourney by water in certaine light barkes, for the multitude of Riuers commodious for passage from one Citie to another.

The king, notwithstanding the hugenesse of his kingdome, hath such a care thereof, that euery Moone (for by the Moones they reckon their monethes) hee is aduertised fully of whatsoeuer thing happeneth therein, by these meanes following.

The whole prouince being diuided into shires, and each shire hauing in it one chiefe and principall Citie, whereunto the matters of all the other Cities, Townes and boroughes, are brought, there are drawen in euery chiefe Citie aforesaid intelligences of such things as doe monethly fall out, and be sent in writing to the Court. If happely in one moneth euery Post be not able to goe so long a way, yet doeth there notwithstanding once euery moneth arriue one Poste out of the shire. Who so commeth before the new moone stayeth for the deliuery of his letters vntil the moone be changed. Then likewise are dispatched other Posts backe into all the 13. shires againe.

Before that we doe come to Cinceo wee haue to passe through many places, and some of great importance. For this Countrey is so well inhabited neere the Sea side, that you cannot goe one mile but you shall see some Towne, borough or hostry, the which are so aboundantly prouided of all things, that in the Cities and townes they liue ciuily. Neuertheles such as dwel abroad are very poore, for the multitude of them euery where is so great, that out of a tree you shall see many times swarme a number of children, where a man would not haue thought to haue found any one at all.

From these places in number infinite, you shall come vnto wo Cities very populous, and, being compared with Cinceo, not possibly to be discerned which is the greater of them. These Cities are as well walled as any Cities in all the world. As you come into either of them, there standeth so great and mighty a bridge, that the like thereof I haue neuer seene in Portugal nor else where. I heard one of my fellowes say, that hee tolde in one bridge 40. arches. The occasion wherefore these bridges are made so great is, for that the Countrey is toward the sea very plaine and low, and ouerflowed euer as the sea water encreaseth. The breadth of the bridges, although it bee well proportioned vnto the length thereof, yet are they equally built no higher in the middle then at either ende, in such wise that you may see directly from the one ende to the other: the sides are wonderfully well engraued after the maner of Rome-workes. But that we did most marueile at was therewithall the hugenesse of the stones, the like whereof, as we came into the Citie, we did see many set vp in places dis-habited by the way, to no small charges of theirs, howbeit to little purpose, whereas no body seeth them but such as doe come by. The arches are not made after our fashion, vauted with sundry stones set together: but paued, as it were, whole stones reaching from one piller to an other, in such wise that they lye both for the arches heads, and galantly serue also for the highway. I haue bene astonied to beholde the hugenesse of the aforesaid stones: some of them are xii. pases long and vpward, the least ii. good pases long, and an halfe.

The wayes echwhere are galantly paued with fouresquare stone, except it be where for want of stone they vse to lay bricke: in this voyage wee trauailed ouer certaine hilles, where the wayes were pitched, and in many places no worse paued then in the plaine ground. This causes vs to thinke, that in all the world there bee no better workemen for buildings, then the inhabitants of China. The Countrey is so well inhabited, that no one foote of ground is left vntilled: small store of cattell haue we seene this day, we sawe onely certaine oxen wherewithall the countrey, men do plow their ground. One oxe draweth the plough alone not onely in this shire, but in other places also, wherein is greater store of cattell. These countreymen by arte do that in tillage, which we are constrained to doe by force. Here be solde the voydings of close stooles, although there wanteth not the dung of beastes:

and the excrements of man are good marchandise throughout all China. The dungfermers seek in euery streete by exchange to buy this dirtie ware for herbs and wood. The custome is very good for keeping the Citie cleane. There is great aboundance of hennes, geese, duckes, swine, and goates, wethers haue they none: the hennes are solde by weight, and so are all other things. Two pound of hennes flesh, geese, or ducke, is worth two foi of their money, that is, d. ob. sterling. Swines flesh is sold at a penie the pound. Beefe beareth the same price, for the scarcitie thereof, howbeit Northward from Fuquieo and farther off from the seacoast, there is beefe more plentie and solde better cheape; We haue had in all the Cities we passed through, great abundance of all these victuals, beefe onely excepted. And if this Countrey were like vnto India, the inhabitants whereof eate neither henne, beefe, nor porke, but keepe that onely for the Portugals and Moores, they would be sold here for nothing. But it so falling out, that the Chineans are the greatest eaters in all the world, they do feed vpon all things, specially on porke, which, the fatter it is, is vnto them the lesse lothsome. The highest price of these things aforesaid I haue set downe, better cheap shal you sometimes buy them for the great plentie thereof in this countrey. Frogs are solde at the same price that is made of hennes, and are good meate amongst them, as also dogs, cats, rats, snakes, and all other vncleane meates.

The Cities be very gallant, specially neere vnto the gates, the which are marueilously great, and couered with iron. The gate houses are built on high with towers, and the lower part thereof is made of bricke and stone, proportionally with the walls, from the walles vpward the building is of timber, and many stories in it one aboue the other. The strength of their townes is in the mightie walles and ditches, artillerie haue they none.

The streetes in Cinceo, and in all the rest of the Cities we haue seene are very faire, so large and so straight, that it is wonderfull to behold. Their houses are built with timber, the foundations onely excepted, the which are layed with stone: in ech side of the streetes are pentises or continuall porches for the marchants to walke vnder: the breadth of the streets is neuertheless such, that in them 15. men may ride commodiously side by side. As they ride they must needs passe vnder many high arches of triumph that crosse ouer the streetes made of timber, and carued diuersly, couered with tiles of fine clay: vnder these arches the Mercers do vtter their smaller wares, and such as list to stand there are defended from raine and the heate of the Sunne. The greater gentlemen haue these arches at their doores: although some of them be not so mightily built as the rest.

I shall haue occasion to speake of a certaine order of gentlemen that are called Louteas. I wil first therefore expound what this word signifieth. Loutea is as much to say in our language as Sir, and when any of them calleth his name, he answereth Sir: and as we do say, that the king hath made some gentlemen, so say they, that there is made a Loutea. And for that amongst them the degrees are diuers both in name and office, I will tell you onely of some principals, being not able to aduertise you of all.

The maner how gentlemen are created Louteas, and do come to that honour and title, is by the giuing of a broad girdle, not like to the rest, and a cap, at the commaundement of the king. The name Loutea is more generall and common vnto mo, then the qualitie of honour thereby signified agreeth withall. Such Louteas as doe serue their prince in weightie matters for iustice, are created after trial made of their learning: but the other which serue in smaller affaires, as Captaines, constables, sergeants by land and sea, receiuers and such like, whereof there be in euery citie, as also in this, very many, are made for fauour: the chiefe Louteas are serued kneeling.

The whole prouince of China is diuided, as I haue said, into 13. shires, in euery shire at the least is one gouernour called there Tutan, in some shires there be two.

[Sidenote: Chian, or, Chaen.] Chiefe in office next vnto them be certaine other named Chians, that is, high Commissioners as you would say, visiters, with full authoritie in such wise, that they doe call vnto an accompt the Tutans themselues, but their authoritie lasteth not in any shire longer then one yere. Neuerthelesse in euery shire being at the least 7. cities, yea, in some of them 15. or 16. beside other boroughes and townes not well to be numbred, these visiters where they come are so honoured and feared, as though they were some great princes. At the yeres end, their circuit done, they come vnto that Citie which is chiefe of others in the shire, to do iustice there: finally busying themselues in the searching out of such as are to receiue the order of Louteas, whereof more shalbe said in another place.

Ouer and beside these officers, in the chiefe Citie of ech one of these aforesaid 13. prouinces, is resident one Ponchiassi, Captaine thereof, and treasurer of all the kings reuenues. This Magistrate maketh his abode in one of the foure greatest houses that be in all these head Cities. And although the principall part of his function be to be Captaine, to be treasourer of the reuenues in that prouince, and to send these reuenues at appointed times to the Court: yet hath he notwithstanding by his office also to meddle with matters appertaining vnto iustice.

[Sidenote: Anchiassi, or Hexasi.] In the second great house dwelleth an other Magistrate called Anchiassi, a great officer also, for he hath dealings in all matters of iustice. Who although he be somewhat inferior in dignitie vnto the Ponchiassi, yet for his great dealings and generall charge of iustice, whosoeuer seeth the affaires of the one house and the other might iudge this Anchiassi to be the greater.

Tuzi, an other officer so called, lieth in the thirde house, a magistrate of importance, specially in things belonging vnto warfare, for thereof hath he charge.

There is resident in the 4 house a fourth officer, bearing name Taissu. In this house is the principall prison of all the Citie. Ech one of these Magistrates aforesaide may both lay euill doers in prison, and deliuer them out againe, except the fact be heinous and of importance: in such a case they can do nothing, except they do meet al together. And if the deed deserueth death, all they together cannot determine thereof, without recourse made vnto the Chian wheresoeuer hee be, or to the Tutan; and eft soones it falleth put, that the case is referred vnto higher power. In all Cities, not onely chiefe in ech shire, but in the rest also, are meanes found to make Louteas. Many of them do study at the prince his charges, wherefore at the yeeres ende they resort vnto the head Cities, whither the Chians doe come, as it hath bene earst aside, as well to giue these degrees, as to sit in iudgement ouer the prisoners.

The Chians go in circuit euery yeere, but such as are to be chosen to the greatest offices meete not but from three yeeres to three yeeres, and that in certaine large halles appointed for them to be examined in. Many things are asked them, whereunto if they doe answere accordingly, and be found sufficient to take their degree, the Chian by and by granteth it them: but the Cap and girdle, whereby they are knowen to be Louteas, they weare not before that they be confirmed by the king. Their examination done, and triall made of them, such as haue taken their degree wont to be giuen them with all ceremonies, vse to banquet and feast many dayes together (as the Chineans fashion is to ende all their pleasures with eating and drinking) and so remaine chosen to do the king seruice in matters of learning. The other examinates founde insufficient to proceed are sent backe to their studie againe. Whose ignorance is perceiued to come of negligence and default, such a one is whipped, and sometimes sent to prison, where lying that yere when this kinde of acte was, we found many thus punished, and demaunding the cause thereof, they saide it was for that they knew not how to answere vnto certaine things asked them. It is a world to see how these Louteas are serued and feared, in such wise, that in publike assemblies at one shrike they giue, all the seruitors belonging vnto iustice tremble thereat. At their being in these places, when they list to mooue, be it but euen to the gate, these seruitors doe take them vp, and carry them in seates of beaten gold. After this sort are they borne when they goe in the City, either for their owne businesse abroad, or to see ech other at home. For the dignitie they haue, and office they doe beare, they be all accompanied: the very meanest of them all that goeth in these seates is vshered by two men at the least, that cry vnto the people to giue place, howbeit they neede it not, for that reuerence the common people haue vnto them. They haue also in their company certaine Sergeants with their maces either siluered or altogether siluer, some two, some foure, other sixe, other eight, conueniently for ech one his degree. The more principal and chiefe Louteas haue going orderly before these Sergeants, many other with staues, and a great many catchpoules with rods of Indish canes dragged on the ground, so that the streets being paued, you may heare affarre off as well the noyse of the rods, as the voyce of the criers. These fellowes serue also to apprehend others, and the better to be knowen they weare liuery red girdles, and in their caps peacocks feathers. Behinde these Louteas come such as doe beare certaine tables hanged at staues endes, wherein is written in siluer letters, the name, degree, and office of that Loutea, whom they follow. In like maner they haue borne after them hattes agreeable vnto their titles: if the Loutea be meane, then hath he brought after him but one hat, and that may not be yealowe: but if he be of the better sort, then may he haue two, three, or foure: the principall and chiefe Louteas may haue all their hats yealow, the which among them is accompted great honour. The Loutea for warres, although he be but meane, may notwithstanding haue yealow hats. The Tutans and Chians, when they goe abroad, haue besides all this before them ledde three or foure horses with their guard in armour.

Furthermore the Louteas, yea and all the people of China, are wont to eate their meate sitting on stooles at high tables as we doe, and that very cleanely, although they vse neither tableclothes nor napkins. Whatsoeuer is set downe vpon the boord is first carued before that it be brought in: they feede with two sticks, refraining from touching their meate with their hands, euen as we do with forkes: for the which respect they lesse do need any table clothes. Ne is the nation only ciuill at meate, but also in conuersation, and in courtesie they seeme to exceede all other. Likewise in their dealings after their maner they are so ready, that they farre passe all other Gentiles and Moores: the greater states are so vaine, that they line their clothes with the best silke that may be found. The Louteas are an idle generation, without all maner of exercises and pastimes, except it be eating and drinking. Sometimes they walke abroad in the fields to make the souldiers shoot at pricks with their bowes, but their eating passeth: they will stand eating euen when the other do draw to shoot. The pricke is a great blanket spread on certaine long poles, he that striketh it, hath of the best man there standing a piece of crimson Taffata, the which is knit about his head: in this sort the winners be honoured, and the Louteas with their bellies full returne home againe. The inhabitants of China be very great Idolaters, all generally doe worship the heauens: and, as wee are wont to say, God knoweth it: so say they at euery word, Tien Tautee, that is to say, The heauens doe know it. Some doe worship the Sonne, and some the Moone, as they thinke good, for none are bound more to one then to another. [Sidenote: After the Dutch fashion.] In their temples, the which they do call Meani, they haue a great altar in the same place as we haue, true it is that one may goe round about it There set they vp the image of a certaine Loutea of that countrey, whom they haue in great reuerence for certaine notable things he did. At the right hand standeth the diuel much more vgly painted then we doe vse to set him out, whereunto great homage is done by such as come into the temple to aske counsell, or to draw lottes: this opinion they haue of him, that he is malicious and able to do euil. If you aske them what they do thinke of the souls departed, they will answere that they be immortall, and that as soone as any one departeth out of this life, he becommeth a diuel if he haue liued well in this world, if otherwise, that the same diuel changeth him into a bufle, oxe, or dogge. [Marginal note: Pythagorean like.] Wherefore to this diuel they doe much honour, to him doe they sacrifice, praying him that he will make them like vnto himselfe, and not like other beastes. They haue moreouer another sort of temples, wherein both vpon the altars and also on the walls do stand many idols well proportioned, but bare headed; these beare name Omithofon, accompted of them spirits, but such as in heauen doe neither good nor euill, thought to be such men and women as haue chastly liued in this world in abstinence from fish and flesh, fed onely with rise and salates. Of that diuel they make some accompt: for these spirits they care litle or nothing at all. Againe they hold opinion that if a man do well in this life, the heauens will giue him many temporall blessings, but if he doe euil, then shall he haue infirmities, diseases, troubles, and penurie, and all this without any knowledge of God. Finally, this people knoweth no other thing then to liue and die, yet because they be reasonable creatures, all seemed good vnto them we speake in our language, though it were not very sufficient; our maner of praying especially pleased them, and truely they are well ynough disposed to receiue the knowledge of the trueth. Our Lord grant for his mercy all things so to be disposed, that it may sometime be brought to passe, that so great a nation as this is perish not for want of helpe.

Our maner of praying so well liked them, that in prison importunately they besought vs to write for them somewhat as concerning heauen, the which we did to their contentation with such reasons as we knew, howbeit not very cunningly. As they do their idolatry they laugh at themselues. If at any time this countrey might be ioyned in league with the kingdome of Portugale, in such wise that free accesse were had to deale with the people there, they might all be soone conuerted. The greatest fault we doe finde in them is Sodomie, a vice very common in the meaner sort, and nothing strange among the best. This sinne were it left of them, in all other things so well disposed they be, that a good interpreter in a short space might do there great good: If, as I said, the countrey were ioyned in league with vs.

Furthermore the Louteas, with all the people of China, are wont to solemnise the dayes of the new and full Moones in visiting one an other, and making great banquets: for to that end, as I earst said, do tend all their pastimes, and spending their dayes in pleasure. They are wont also to solemnise ech one his birth day, whereunto their kindred and friends do resort of custome with presents of iewels or money, receiuing againe for their reward good cheare. They keepe in like maner a generall feast with great banquets that day their king was borne. But their most principall and greatest feast of all, and best cheare, is the first day of new yeere, namely the first day of the new Moone of February, so that their first moneth is March, and they reckon the times accordingly, respect being had vnto the reigne of their princes: as when any deed is written, they date it thus, Made such a day of such a moone, and such a yeere of the reigne of such a king. And their ancient writings beare date of the yeeres of this or that king.

Now will I speake of the maner which the Chineans doe obserue in doing of iustice, that it be knowen how farre these Gentiles do herein exceed many Christians, that be more bounden then they to deale iustly and in trueth. Because the Chinish king maketh his abode continually in the city of Pachin, his kingdome is so great, and the shires so many, as tofore it hath bene said: in it therefore the gouernours and rulers, much like vnto our Shireffs, be appointed so suddenly and speedily discharged againe, that they haue no time to grow naught. Furthermore to keepe the state in more securitie, the Louteas that gouerne one shire are chosen out of some other shire distant farre off, where they must leaue their wiues, children and goods, carying nothing with them but themselues. True it is, that at their comming thither they doe finde in a readinesse all things necessary, their house, furniture, seruants, and all other things in such perfection and plentie, that they want nothing. Thus the king is well serued without all feare of treason.

In the principall Cities of the shires be foure chiefe Louteas, before whom are brought all matters of the inferiour Townes, throughout the whole Realme. Diuers other Louteas haue the managing of iustice, and receiuing of rents, bound to yeelde an accompt thereof vnto the greater officers. Other do see that there be no euil rule kept in the Citie: ech one as it behoueth him. [Sidenote: The Italians call it the strapado.] Generally all these doe imprison malefactors, cause them to be whipped and racked, hoysing them vp and downe by the armes with a cord, a thing very vsuall there, and accompted no shame. These Louteas do vse great diligence in the apprehending of theeues, so that it is a wonder to see a theefe escape away in any City, towne or village. Vpon the sea neere vnto the shoare many are taken, and looke euen as they are taken, so be they first whipped, and afterward layde in prison, where shortly after they all die for hunger and cold. At that time when we were in prison, there died of them aboue threescore and ten. If happely any one, hauing the meanes to get food, do escape, he is set with the condemned persons, and prouided for as they be by the King, in such wise as hereafter it shalbe said.

Their whips be certaine pieces of canes, cleft in the middle, in such sort that they seeme rather plaine then sharpe. He that is to be whipped lieth groueling on the ground: vpon his thighes the hangman layeth on blowes mightily with these canes, that the standers by tremble at their crueltie. Ten stripes draw a great deale of blood, 20. or 30. spoile the flesh altogether, 50. or 60. will require long time to bee healed, and if they come to the number of one hundred, then are they incurable.

The Louteas obserue moreouer this: when any man is brought before them to be examined, they aske him openly in the hearing of as many as be present, be the offence neuer so great. Thus did they also behaue themselues with vs: For this cause amongst them can here be no false witnesse, as daily amongst vs it falleth out. This good commeth thereof, that many being alwayes about the Iudge to heare the euidence, and beare witnesse, the processe cannot be falsified, as it happeneth sometimes with vs. The Moores, Gentiles, and Iewes haue all their sundry othes, the Moores do sweare by their Mossafos, the Brachmans by their Fili, the rest likewise by the things they do worship. The Chineans though they be wont to sweare by heauen, by the Moone, by the Sunne, and by all their Idoles, in iudgement neuertheless they sweare not at all. If for some offence an othe be vsed of any one, by and by with the least euidence he is tormented, so be the witnesses he bringeth, if they tell not the trueth, or do in any point disagree, except they be men of worship and credit, who are beleeued without any further matter: the rest are made to confesse the trueth by force of torments and whips. Besides this order obserued of them in examinations, they do feare so much their King, and he where he maketh his abode keepeth them so lowe, that they dare not once stirre. Againe, these Louteas as great as they be, notwithstanding the multitude of Notaries they haue, not trusting any others, do write all great processes and matters of importance themselues. Moreouer one vertue they haue worthy of great praise, and that is, being men so wel regarded and accompted as though they were princes, yet they be patient aboue measure in giuing audience. We poore strangers brought before them might say what we would, as all to be lyes and fallaces that they did write, ne did we stand before them with the usuall ceremonies of that Countrey, yet did they beare with vs so patiently, that they caused vs to wonder, knowing specially how litle any aduocate or Iudge is wont in our Countrey to beare with vs. For wheresoeuer in any Towne of Christendome should be accused vnknowen men as we were, I know not what end the very innocents cause would haue: but we in a heathen Countrey, hauing our great enemies two of the chiefest men in a whole Towne, wanting an interpreter, ignorant of that Countrey language, did in the end see our great aduersaries cast into prison for our sake, and depriued of their Offices and honour for not doing iustice, yea not to escape death: for, as the rumour goeth, they shalbe beheaded. Somewhat is now to be said of the lawes that I haue bene able to know in this Countrey, and first, no theft or murther is at any time pardoned: adulterers are put in prison, and the fact once prooued, are condemned to die, the womans husband must accuse them: this order is kept with men and women found in that fault, but theeues and murderers are imprisoned as I haue said, where they shortly die for hunger and cold. If any one happely escape by bribing the Gailer to giue him meate, his processe goeth further, and commeth to the Court where he is condemned to die. [Sidenote: A pillory boord.] Sentence being giuen, the prisoner is brought in publique with a terrible band of men that lay him in Irons hand and foot, with a boord at his necke one handfull broad, in length reaching downe to his knees, cleft in two parts, and with a hole one handfull downeward in the table fit for his necke, the which they inclose vp therein, nailing the boord fast together; one handfull of the boord standeth vp behinde in the necke: The sentence and cause wherefore the fellon was condemned to die, is written in that part of the table that standeth before.

This ceremony ended, he is laid in a great prison in the company of some other condemned persons, the which are found by the king as long as they do liue. The bord aforesaid so made tormenteth the prisoners very much, keeping them both from rest, and eke letting them to eat commodiously, their hands being manacled in irons vnder that boord, so that in fine there is no remedy but death. In the chiefe Cities of euery shire, as we haue erst said, there be foure principall houses, in ech of them a prison: but in one of them, where the Taissu maketh his abode, there is a greater and a more principall prison then in any of the rest: and although in euery City there be many, neuerthelesse in three of them remaine onely such as be condemned to die. Their death is much prolonged, for that ordinarily there is no execution done but once a yeere, though many die for hunger and cold, as we haue seene in this prison. Execution is done in this maner. The Chian, to wit, the high Commissioner or Lord chiefe Iustice, at the yeres end goeth to the head City, where he heareth againe the causes of such as be condemned. Many times he deliuereth some of them, declaring that boord to haue bene wrongfully put about their necks: the visitation ended, he choseth out seuen or eight, not many more or lesse of the greatest malefactors, the which, to feare and keepe in awe the people, are brought into a great market place, where all the great Louteas meete together, and after many ceremonies and superstitions, as the vse of the Countrey is, are beheaded. This is done once a yeere: who so escapeth that day, may be sure that he shall not be put to death all that yeere following, and so remaineth at the kings charges in the greater prison. In that prison where we lay were alwayes one hundred and mo of these condemned persons, besides them that lay in other prisons.

These prisons wherein the condemned caytifes do remaine are so strong, that it hath not bene heard, that any prisoner in all China hath escaped out of prison, for in deed it is a thing impossible. The prisons are thus builded. First all the place is mightily walled about, the walles be very strong and high, the gate of no lesse force: within it three other gates, before you come where the prisoners do lye, there many great lodgings are to be seene of the Louteas, Notaries, Parthions, that is, such as do there keepe watch and ward day and night, the court large and paued, on the one side whereof standeth a prison, with two mighty gates, wherein are kept such prisoners as haue committed enormious offences. This prison is so great, that in it are streets and Market places wherein all things necessary are sold. Yea some prisoners liue by that kind of trade, buying and selling, and letting out beds to hire: some are dayly sent to prison, some dayly deliuered, wherefore this place is neuer void of 7. or eight hundred men that go at libertie.

Into one other prison of condemned persons shall you go at three yron gates, the court paued and vauted round about, and open aboue as it were a cloister. In this cloister be eight roomes with yron doores, and in ech of them a large gallerie, wherein euery night the prisoners do lie at length, their feet in the stocks, their bodies hampered in huge wooden grates that keep them from sitting, so that they lye as it were in a cage, sleepe if they can: in the morning they are losed againe, that they may go into the court. Notwithstanding the strength of this prison, it is kept with a garrison of men, part whereof watch within the house, part of them in the court, some keepe about the prison with lanterns and watch-bels answering one another fiue times euery night, and giuing warning so lowd, that the Loutea resting in a a chamber not neere thereunto, may heare them. In these prisons of condemned persons remaine some 15, other 20. yeres imprisoned, not executed, for the loue of their honorable friends that seeke to prolong their liues. Many of these prisoners be shoomakers, and haue from the king a certaine allowance of rise: some of them worke for the keeper, who suffreth them to go at libertie without fetters and boords, the better to worke. Howbeit when the Loutea called his checke roll, and with the keeper vieweth them, they all weare their liuerses, that is, boords at their necks, yronned hand and foot. When any of these prisoners dieth, he is to be seene of the Loutea and Notaries, brought out of a gate so narrow, that there can but one be drawen out there at once. The prisoners being brought forth, one of the aforesaid Parthions striketh him thrise on the head with an yron sledge, that done he is deliuered vnto his friends, if he haue any, otherwise the king hireth men to cary him to his buriall in the fields.

Thus adulterers and theeues are vsed. Such as be imprisoned for debt once knowen, lie there vntill it be paied. [Sidenote: Of like the first lenders be the more wealthie.] The Taissu or Loutea calleth them many times before him by the vertue of his office, who vnderstanding the cause wherefore they do not pay their debts, appointeth them a certaine time to do it, within the compasse whereof if they discharge not their debts being debtors in deed, then they be whipped and condemned to perpetuall imprisonment: if the creditors be many, and one is to be paied before another, they do, contrary to our maner, pay him first of whom they last borrowed, and so ordinarily the rest, in such sort that the first lender be the last receiuer. The same order is kept in paying legacies: the last named receiueth his portion first. They accompt it nothing to shew fauour to such a one as can do the like againe: but to do good to them that haue litle or nothing, that is worth thanks, therefore pay they the last before the first, for that their intent seemeth rather to be vertuous then gainefull.

When I said, that such as be committed to prison for theft and murther were iudged by the Court, I ment not them that were apprehended in the deed doing, for they need no triall, but are brought immediatly before the Tutan, who out of hand giueth sentence. Others not taken so openly, which do need trial, are the malefactors put to execution once a yere in the chiefe cities, to keepe in awe the people: or condemned, do remaine in prison, looking for their day. Theeues being taken are caried to prison from one place to another in a chest vpon mens shoulders, hired therefore by the king, the chest is 6. handfuls high, the prisoner sitteth therein vpon a bench, the couer of the chest is two boords, amid them both a pillery-like hole, for the prisoners necke, there sitteth he with his head without the chest, and the rest of his body within, not able to mooue or turne his head this way or that way, nor to plucke it in; the necessities of nature he voydeth at a hole in the bottome of a chest, the meate he eateth is put into his mouth by others. There abideth he day and night during his whole iourney: if happily his porters stumble, or the chest do iogge or be set down carelessly, it turneth to his great paines that sitteth therein, al such motions being vnto him hanging as it were. Thus were our companions carried from Cinceo, 7. dayes iourney, neuer taking any rest as afterward they told vs, and their greatest griefe was to stay by the way: as soone as they came, being taken out of the chests, they were not able to stand on their feet, and two of them died shortly after. When we lay in prison at Fuquieo, we came many times abroad, and were brought to the pallaces of noble men, to be seene of them and their wiues, for that they had neuer seene any Portugale before. Many things they asked vs of our Countrey, and our fashions, and did write euery thing, for they be curious in nouelties aboue measure. The gentlemen shew great curtesie vnto strangers, and so did we finde at their hands, and because that many times we were brought abroad into the City, somewhat wil I say of such things as I did see therein, being a gallant City, and chiefe in one of the 13. shires aforesaid. The City Fuquieo is very great, and mightily walled with square stone both within and without, and, as it may seeme by the breadth thereof, filled vp in the middle with earth, layd ouer with brick and couered with tyle, after the maner of porches or galleries, that one might dwel therein. The staires they vse are so easily made, that one may go them vp and downe a horse-backe, as eftsoones they do: the streets are paued, as already it hath bin said: there be a great number of Marchants, euery one hath written in a great table at his doore such things as he hath to sel. In like maner euery artisane painteth out his craft: the market places be large, great abundance of al things there be to be sold. The city standeth vpon water, many streames run through it, the banks pitched, and so broad that they serue for streets to the cities vse. Ouer the streams are sundry bridges both of timber and stone, which being made leuel with the streets, hinder not the passage of the barges too and fro, the chanels are so deepe. Where the streames come in and go out of the city, be certaine arches in the wal, there go in and out their Parai, that is a kind of barges they haue, and that in the day time only: at night these arches are closed vp with gates, so do they shut vp al the gates of the City. These streames and barges do ennoblish very much the City, and make it as it were to seeme another Venice. The buildings are euen, wel made, high, not lofted, except it be some wherein marchandize is laid. It is a world to see how great these cities are, and the cause is, for that the houses are built euen, as I haue said, and do take a great deale of roome. One thing we saw in this city that made vs al to wonder, and is worthy to be noted: namely, ouer a porch at the comming in to one of the aforesaid 4. houses, which the king hath in euery shire for his gouernors, as I haue erst said, standeth a tower built vpon 40. pillers, ech one whereof is but one stone, ech one 40. handfuls or spans long: in bredth or compasse 12, as many of vs did measure them. Besides this, their greatnesse is such in one piece, that it might seeme impossible to worke them: they be moreouer cornered, and in colour, length and breadth so like, that the one nothing differeth from the other. This thing made vs all to wonder very much.

We are wont to cal this country China, and the people Chineans, but as long as we were prisoners, not hearing amongst them at any time that name, I determined to learne how they were called: and asked sometimes by them thereof, for that they vnderstood vs not when we called them Chineans, I answered them, that al the inhabitants of India named them Chineans, wherefore I praied them that they would tel me, for what occasion they are so called, whether peraduenture any city of theirs bare that name. Hereunto they alwayes answered me, that they haue no such name, nor euer had. Then did I aske them what name the whole Country bareth, and what they would answere being asked of other nations what countrymen they were? It was told me that of ancient time in this country had bin many kings, and though presently it were al vnder one, ech kingdom neuertheles enioyed that name it first had, these kingdomes are the prouinces I spake of before. [Sidenote: Tamen the proper name of China.] In conclusion they said, that the whole country is called Tamen, and the inhabitants Tamegines, so that this name China or Chineans, is not heard of in that country. I thinke that the neernesse of another prouince thereabout called Cochinchina, and the inhabitants thereof Cochinesses, first discouered before China was, lying not far from Malacca, did giue occasion to ech of the nations, of that name Chineans, as also the whole country to be named China. But their proper name is that aforesaid.

I haue heard moreouer that in the City of Nanquim remaineth a table of gold, and in it written a kings name, as a memory of that residence the kings were wont to keepe there. This table standeth in a great pallace, couered alwayes, except it be on some of their festiuall dayes, at what time they are wont to let it be seene, couered neuertheless as it is, all the nobilitie of the City going of duetie to doe it euery day reuerence. The like is done in the head Cities of all the other shires in the pallaces of the Ponchiassini, wherein these aforesaid tables doe stand with the kings name written in them, although no reuerence be done thereunto but in solemn feastes.

[Sidenote: Pochan, or Pachin.] I haue likewise vnderstood that the city Pachin, where the king maketh his abode, is so great, that to go from one side to the other, besides the Suburbs, the which are greater then the City it selfe, it requireth one whole day a horseback, going hackney pase. In the suburbs be many wealthy marchants of all sorts. They tolde me furthermore that it was moted about, and in the moates great store of fish, whereof the King maketh great gaines.

[Sidenote: Their enemies.] It was also told me that the king of China had no kings to wage battel withall, besides the Tartars, with whom he had concluded a peace more then 80. yeres ago. Neuerthelesse their friendship was not so great, that the one nation might marry with the other. [Sidenote: Marriage of the kings children.] And demanding with whom they married, they said, that in olde time the Chinish kings when they would marry their daughters, accustomed to make a solemne feast, whereunto came all sorts of men. The daughter that was to be married, stood in a place where she might see them all, and looke whom she liked best, him did she chuse to husband, and if happely he were of a base condition, hee became by and by a gentleman: but this custome hath bene left long since. Now a dayes the king marrieth his daughters at his owne pleasure, with great men of the kingdome: the like order he obserueth in the marriage of his sonnes.

They haue moreouer one thing very good, and that which made vs all to maruelle at them being Gentiles: namely, that there be hospitals in all their Cities, always full of people, we neuer saw any poore body begge. [Marginal note: He speaketh not here of all China, but of the Cities, for in other places there be beggers, as you haue seene already, swarming out of trees.] We therefore asked the cause of this: answered it was, that in euery City there is a great circuit, wherein be many houses for poore people, for blinde, lame, old folke, not able to trauaile for age, nor hauing any other meanes to liue. These folke haue in the aforesaid houses euer plentie of rice during their liues, but nothing else. Such as be receiued into these houses, come in after this maner. When one is sicke, blinde or lame, he maketh a supplication to the Ponchiassi, and prouing that to be true he writeth, he remaineth in the aforesaid great lodging as long as he liueth: besides this they keepe in these places swine and hennes, whereby the poore be relieued without going a begging.

I said before that China was full of riuers, but now I minde to confirme the same anew: for the farther we went into the Countrey, the greater we found the riuers. Sometimes we were so farre off from the sea, that where we came no sea fish had bene seene, and salt was there very deare, of fresh water fish yet was there great abundance, and that fish very good: they keep it good after this maner. Where the riuers do meete, and so passe into the sea, there lieth great store of boats, specially where no salt-water commeth, and that in March and April. These boates are so many that it seemeth wonderfull, ne serue they for other then to take small fish. By the riuers sides they make leyres of fine and strong nettes, that lye three handfulls vnder water, and one aboue to keepe and nourish their fish in, vntill such time as other fishers do come with boates, bringing for that purpose certaine great chests lined with paper, able to holde water, wherein they cary their fish vp and downe the riuer, euery day renuing the chest with fresh water, and selling their fish in euery City, towne and village where they passe, vnto the people as they neede it: most of them haue net leyres to keepe fish in always for their prouision. Where the greater boates cannot passe any further forward, they take lesser, and because the whole Countrey is very well watered, there is so great plenty of diuers sorts of fish, that it is wonderfull to see: assuredly we were amazed to behold the maner of their prouision. [Sidenote: Meanes to fat fish.] Their fish is chiefly nourished with the dung of Bufles and oxen, that greatly fatteth it. Although I said their fishing to be in March and April at what time we saw them do it, neuerthelesse they told vs that they fished at all times, for that vsually they do feed on fish, wherefore it behoueth them to make their prouision continually.

When we had passed Fuquien, we went into Quicin shire, [Sidenote: He speaketh of Fuquien shire.] where the fine clay vessell is made, as I said before: and we came to a City, the one side whereof is built vpon the the foote of a hill, whereby passeth a riuer nauigable: there we tooke boat, and went by water toward the Sea: on ech side of the riuer we found many Cities, Townes and villages, wherein we saw great store of marchandize, but specially of fine clay: there did we land by the way to buy victuals and other necessaries. Going downe this riuer Southward, we were glad that wee drew neere vnto a warmer Countrey, from whence we had bene farre distant: this Countrey we passed through in eight dayes, for our iourney lay downe the streame. Before that I doe say any thing of that shire we came into, I will first speake of the great City of Quicin, wherein alwayes remaineth a Tutan, that is a gouernour, as you haue seene, though some Tutans do gouerne two or three shires.

That Tutan that was condemned for our cause, of whom I spake before, was borne in this Countrey, but he gouerned Foquien shire: nothing it auailed him to be so great an officer. This Countrey is so great, that in many places where we went, there had bene as yet no talke of his death, although he were executed a Whole yere before. [Sidenote: Aliàs Cenchi.] At the Citie Quanchi whither we came, the riuer was so great it seemed a Sea, though it were so litle where we tooke water, that we needed small boats. One day about nine of the clocke, beginning to row neere the walls with the streame, we came at noone to a bridge made of many barges, ouerlinked al together with two mightie cheines. There stayed we vntill it was late, but we saw not one go either vp thereon or downe, except two Louteas that about the going downe of the Sunne, came and set them down there, the one on one side, the other on the other side. Then was the bridge opened in many places, and barges both great and small to the number of sixe hundred began to passe: those that went vp the streame at one place, such as came downe at an other. When all had thus shot the bridge, then was it shut vp againe. [Sidenote: The kings reuenues.] We heare say that euery day they take this order in all principall places of marchandize, for paying of the Custome vnto the king, specially for salt, whereof the greatest reuenues are made that the king hath in this Countrey. The passage of the bridge where it is opened, be so neere the shoare, that nothing can passe without touching the same. To stay the barges at their pleasure, that they goe no further forward, are vsed certaine iron instruments The bridge consisteth of 112. barges, there stayed we vntill the euening that they were opened, lothsomely oppressed by the multitude of people that came to see vs, so many in number, that we were enforced to go aside from the banke vntil such time as the bridge was opened: howbeit we were neuerthelesse thronged about with many boates full of people. And though in other Cities and places where we went, the people came so importunate vpon vs, that it was needfull to withdraw our selues: yet were we here much more molested for the number of people: and this bridge is the principall way out of the Citie vnto another place so wel inhabited, that were it walled about, it might be compared to the Citie. When we had shot the bridge, we kept along the Citie vntil it was night, and then met we with another riuer that ioyned with this, we rowed vp that by the walls vntill we came to another bridge gallantly made of barges, but lesser a great deale then that other bridge ouer the greater streame: here stayed we that night, and other two dayes with more quiet, being out of the preasse of the people. These riuers do meet without at one corner point of the City. In either of them were so many barges great and small, that we all thought them at the least to be aboue three thousand: the greater number thereof was in the lesser riuer, where we were. Amongst the rest here lay certaine greater vessels, called in their language Parai, that serue for the Tutan, when he taketh his voyage by other riuers that ioyne with this, towards Pachin, where the king maketh his abode. For, as many times I haue erst said, all this Countrey is full of riuers. Desirous to see those Parai we got into some of them, where we found some chambers set foorth with gilded beds very richly, other furnished with tables and seats, and all other things so neat and in perfection, that it was wonderfull.

Quiacim shire, as farre as I can perceiue, lieth vpon the South. On that side we kept at our first entry thereinto, trauayling not farre from the high mountaines we saw there. Asking what people dwelleth beyond those monntaines, it was told me that they be theeues and men of a strange language. And because that vnto sundry places neere this riuer the mountaines doe approch, whence the people issuing downe do many times great harme, this order is taken at the entry into Quiacim shire. To guard this riuer whereon continually go to and fro Parai great and small fraught with salt, fish poudred with peper, and other necessaries for that countrey, they do lay in diuers places certaine Parai, and great barges armed, wherin watch and ward is kept day and night on both sides of the riuer, for the safety of the passage, and securitie of such Parai as do remaine there, though the trauailers neuer go but many in company. In euery rode there be at the least thirtie, in some two hundred men, as the passage requireth. This guard is kept vsually vntill you come to the City Onchio, where continually the Tutan of this shire, and eke of Cantan, maketh his abode. From that City vpward, where the riuer waxeth more narrow, and the passage more dangerous, there be alwayes armed one hundred and fiftie Parai, to accompany other vessels fraught with marchandize, and all this at the Kings charges. This seemed to me one of the strangest things I did see in this Countrey.

When we lay at Fuquien, we did see certaine Moores, who knew so litle of their secte, that they could say nothing else but that Mahomet was a Moore, my father was a Moore, and I am a Moore, with some other wordes of their Alcoran, wherewithall, in abstinence from swines flesh, they liue vntill the diuel take them all. This when I saw, and being sure that in many Chinish Cities the reliques of Mahomet are kept, as soone as we came to the City where these fellowes be, I enfourmed my selfe of them, and learned the trueth.

[Sidenote: Great ships comming from the North.] These Moores, as they tolde me, in times past came in great ships fraught with marchandise from Pachin ward, to a port granted vnto them by the king, as hee is wont to all them that traffique into this Countrey, where they being arriued at a litle Towne standing in the hauens mouth, in time conuerted vnto their sect the greatest Loutea there. When that Loutea with all his family was become Moorish, the rest began likewise to doe the same. In this part of China the people be at libertie, euery one to worship and folow what him liketh best. Wherefore no body tooke heede thereto, vntil such time as the Moores perceiuing that many followed them in superstition, and that the Loutea fauoured them, they began to forbid wholy the eating of swines flesh. But all these countreymen and women chosing rather to forsake father and mother, then to leaue off eating of porke, by no meanes would yeeld to that proclamation. For besides the great desire they all haue to eate that kinde of meate, many of them do liue thereby: and therefore the people complained vnto the Magistrates, accusing the Moores of a conspiracie pretended betwixt them and the Loutea against their king. In this countrey, as no suspition, no not one traiterous word is long borne withall, so was the king speedily aduertised thereof, who gaue commandement out of hand that the aforesaid Loutea should be put to death, and with him the Moores of most importance: the other to be layde first in prison, and afterward to be sent abroad into certaine Cities, where they remained perpetuall slaues vnto the king. To this City came by happe men and women threescore and odde, who at this day are brought to fiue men and foure women, for it is how twenty yeeres since this happened. [Sidenote: That is their temples.] Their offspring passeth the number of two hundreth, and they in this City, as the rest in other Cities whither they were sent, haue their Moscheas, whereunto they all resort euery Friday to keepe their holy day. But, as I thinke, that will no longer endure, then whiles they doe liue that came from thence, for their posteritie is so confused, that they haue nothing of a Moore in them but abstinence from swines flesh, and yet many of them doe eate thereof primly. [Sidenote: It should seeme by their voyage to be Cardandan in

Ortelius.] They tell mee that their natiue Countrey hath name Camarian, a firme land wherein be many kings, and the Indish countrey well knowen vnto them. It may so be: for as soone as they did see our seruants (our seruants were Preuzaretes) they iudged them to be Indians: many of their wordes sounded vpon the Persian tongue, but none of vs coulde vnderstand them. I asked them whether they conuerted any of the Chinish nation vnto their secte: they answered mee, that with much a doe they conuerted the women with whom they doe marry, yeelding me no other cause thereof, but the difficultie they finde in them to be brought from eating swines flesh and drinking of wine. I am perswaded therefore, that if this Countrey were in league with vs, forbidding them neither of both, it would be an easie matter to draw them to our Religion, from their superstition, whereat they themselues do laugh when they do then idolatry.

[Sidenote: A Northerne Sea.] I haue learned moreouer that the Sea, whereby these Moores that came to China were wont to trauaile, is a very great gulfe, that falleth into this Countrey out from Tartaria and Persia, leauing on the other side all the Countrey of China, and land of the Mogores, drawing alwayes toward the South: and of all likelyhood it is euen so, because that these Moores, the which we haue seene, be rather browne then white, whereby they shewe themselues to cone from some warmer Countrey then China is neere to Pachin, where the riuers are frosen in the Winter for colde, and many of them so vehemently that carts may passe ouer them.

We did see in this Citie many Tartars, Mogores, Brames, and Laoynes, both men and women. The Tartars are men very white, good horsemen and archers, confining with China on that side where Pachin standeth, separated from thence by great mountaines that are bewixt these kingdomes. Ouer them be certaine wayes to passe, and for both sides, Castles continually kept with Souldiers: in time past the Tartars were wont alwayes to haue warres with the Chineans, but these fourescore yeeres past they were quiet, vntill the second yeere of our imprisonment. The Mogores be in like maner white, and heathen, we are aduertised that of one side they border vpon these Tartars, and confine with the Persian Tartars on the other side, whereof we sawe in them some tokens, as their maner of clothes, and that kinde of hat the Saracens doe weare. The Moores affirmed, that where the king lyeth, there be many Tartars and Mogores, that brought into China certaine blewes of great value: all we thought it to be Vanil of Cambaia wont to be sold at Ormus. So that this is the true situation of that Countrey, not in the North parts, as many times I haue heard say, confining with Germanie.

As for the Brames we haue seene in this city Chenchi certaine men and women, amongst whom there was one that came not long since, hauing as yet her haire tied vp after the Pegues fashion: this woman, and other mo with whom a black Moore damsel in our company had conference, and did vnderstand them wel ynough, had dwelt in Pegu. This new come woman, imagining that we ment to make our abode in that citie, bid vs to be of good comfort, for that her countrey was not distant from thence aboue fiue dayes iourney, and that out of her countrey there lay a high way for vs home into our owne. Being asked the way, she answered that the first three daies the way lieth ouer certaine great mountaines and wildernesse, afterward people are met withall againe. [Sidenote: Southward from Chenchi to the sea.] Thence two dayes iourney more to the Brames countrey. Wherefore I doe conclude, that Chenchi is one of the confines of this kingdome, separated by certaine huge mountaines, as it hath bene alreadie said, that lie out towards the South. In the residue of these mountaines standeth the prouince of Sian, the Laoyns countrey, Camboia, Campaa, and Cochinchina.

This citie chiefe of other sixteene is situated in a pleasant plaine abounding in all things necessarie, sea-fish onely excepted, for it standeth farre from the sea: of fresh fish so much store, that the market places are neuer emptie. The walles of this city are very strong and high: one day did I see the Louteas thereof go vpon the walles to take the view thereof, borne in their seates which I spake of before, accompanied with a troupe of horsemen that went two and two: It was tolde me they might haue gone three and three. We haue seene moreouer, that within this aforesayd Citie: the king hath moe then a thousande of his kinne lodged in great pallaces, in diuers partes of the Citie: their gates be redde, and the entrie into their houses, that they may be knowen, for that is the kings colour. These Gentlemen, according to their neerenesse in blood vnto the king, as soone as they be married receiue their place in honour: this place neither increaseth nor diminisheth in any respect as long as the king liueth, the king appointeth them their wiues and familie, allowing them by the moneth all things necessarie abundantly, as he doth to his gouernours of shires and Cities, howbeit, not one of these hath as long as he liueth any charge or gouernement at all. They giue themselues to eating and drinking, and be for the most part burly men of bodie, insomuch that espying any one of them whom we had not seene before, we might knowe him to be the King his cosin. They be neuerthelesse very pleasant, courteous, and faire conditioned: neither did we find, all the time wee were in that citie, so much honour and good intertainement any where as at their hands. They bid vs to their houses to eate and drinke, and when they found vs not, or we were not willing to go with them, they bid our seruants and slaues, causing them to sit downe with the first. Notwithstanding the good lodging these Gentlemen haue, so commodious that they want nothing, yet are they in this bondage, that during life they neuer goe abroad. The cause, as I did vnderstand, wherefore the king so vseth his cosins is, that none of them at any time may rebell against him: and thus he shutteth them vp in three or foure other cities. Most of them can play on the Lute, and to make that kinde of pastime peculiar vnto them onely, all other in the cities where they doe liue be forbidden that instrument, the Curtisans and blinde folke onely accepted, who be musicians and can play.

This king furthermore, for the greater securitie of his Realme and the auoiding of tumults, letteth not one in all his countrey to be called Lord, except he be of his blood. Manie great estates and gouernours there be, that during their office are lodged Lord-like, and doe beare the port of mightie Princes: but they be so many times displaced and other placed a new, that they haue not the time to become corrupt. True it is that during their office they be well prouided for, as afterward also lodged at the kings charges, and in pension as long as they liue, payed them monethly in the cities where they dwell by certaine officers appointed for that purpose. The king then is a Lord onely, not one besides him as you haue seene, except it be such as be of his blood. A Nephew likewise of the king, the kings sisters sonne, lyeth continually within the walles of the citie in a strong pallace built Castlewise, euen as his other cousins do, remayning alwayes within doores, serued by Eunuches, neuer dealing with any matters. On their festiuall dayes, new moones, and full moones the magistrates make great bankets, and so do such as be of the king his blood. [Sidenote: Goa is a city of the Portugals in the East Indies.] The kings Nephew hath to name Vanfuli, his pallace is walled about, the wall is not high but fouresquare, and in circuit nothing inferiour to the wals of Goa, the outside is painted red, in euery square a gate, and ouer each gate a tower made of timber excellently well wrought: before the principall gate of the foure that openeth in to the high street no Loutea, be he neuer so great, may passe on horsebacke, or carried in his seat. Amidst this quadrangle standeth the pallace where that Nobleman lyeth, doubtlesse worth the sight, although we came not in to see it. By report the roofes of the towers and houses are glased greene, and the greater part of the quadrangle set with sauage trees, as Okes, Chesnuts, Cypresse, Pineapples, Cedars, and other such like that we do want, after the manner of a wood, wherein are kept Stags, Oxen, and other beasts, for that Lord his recreation neuer going abroad as I haue sayd. One preheminence this citie hath aboue the rest where we haue bene, and that of right, as we do thinke, that besides the multitude of market places wherein all things are to be sold through euery streete continually are cryed all things necessary, as flesh of all sortes, freshfish, hearbes, oyle, vineger, meale, rise: in summa, all things so plentifully, that many houses neede no servants, euery thing being brought to their doores. Most part of the marchants remaine in the suburbes, for that the cities are shut vp euery night, as I haue said. The marchants therefore, the better to attend their businesse, do chuse rather to make their abode without in the suburbes then within the citie. I haue seene in this riuer a pretie kinde of fishing, not to be omitted in my opinion, and therefore I will set it downe. [Marginal note: Odeicus writeth of the like.] The king hath in many riuers good store of barges full of sea-crowes that breede, are fedde and doe die therein, in certaine cages, allowed monethely a certaine prouision of rise. These barges the king bestoweth vpon his greatest magistrates, giuing to some two, to some three of them as be thinketh good, to fish therewithal after this manner. At the houre appointed to fish, all the barges are brought together in a circle, where the riuer is shalow, and the crowes tyed together vnder the wings are let leape downe into the water some vnder, some aboue, woorth the looking vpon: each one as he hath filled his bagge, goeth to his owne barge and emptieth it, which done, he returneth to fish againe. Thus hauing taken good store of fish, they set the crowes at libertie, and do suffer them to fish for their owne pleasure. There were in that city where I was, twentie barges at the least of these aforesayd crowes. I went almost euery day to see them, yet could I neuer be throughly satisfyed to see so strange a kind of fishing.

* * * * *

Of the Iland Iapan, and other litle Iles in the East Ocean.

By R. Willes.

The extreame part of the knowen world vnto vs is the noble Iland Giapan, written otherwise Iapon and Iapan. This Island standeth in the East Ocean, beyond all Asia, betwixt Cathayo and the West Indies sixe and thirtie degrees Northward from the Equinoctial line, in the same clime with the South part of Spain and Portugall, distant from thence by sea sixe thousand leagues: the trauile thither, both for ciuill discord, great pyracie, and often shipwracks is very dangerous. This countrey is hillie and pestered with snow, wherefore it is neither so warme as Portugall, nor yet so wealthy, as far as we can learne, wanting oyle, butter, cheese, milke, egges, sugar, honny, vinegar, saffron, cynamom and pepper. Barleybranne the Ilanders doe vse in stead of salt: medicinable things holsome for the bodie haue they none at all. Neuerthelesse in that Iland sundry fruites doe growe, not much vnlike the fruites of Spaine: and great store of Siluer mynes are therein to be seene. The people are tractable, ciuill, wittie, courteous, without deceit, in vertue and honest conuersation exceeding all other nations lately discouered, but so much standing vpon their reputation, that their chiefe Idole may be thought honour. The contempt thereof causeth among them much discord and debate, manslaughter and murther: euen for their reputation they doe honour their parents, keepe their promises, absteine from adulterie and robberies, punishing by death the least robbery done, holding for a principle, that whosoeuer stealeth a trifle, will, if he see occasion, steale a greater thing. It may be theft is so seuerely punished of them, for that the nation is oppressed with scarcitie of all things necessary, and so poore, that euen for miserie they strangle their owne children, preferring death before want. These fellowes doe neither eate nor kill any foule. They liue chiefely by fish, hearbes, and fruites, so healthfully, that they die very old. Of Rice and Wheat there is no great store. No man is ashamed there of his pouertie, neither be their gentlemen therefore lesse honoured of the meaner people, neither will the poorest gentleman there matche his childe with the baser sort for any gaine, so much they do make more account of gentry then of wealth. The greatest delight they haue is in armour, each boy at fourteene yeeres of ages, be he borne gentle or otherwise, hath his sword and dagger: very good archers they be, contemning all other nations in comparison of their manhood and prowesse, putting not vp one iniurie be it neuer so small in worde or deede, among themselues. They feede moderately, but they drinke largely. The vse of vines they knowe not, their drinke they make of Rice, vtterly they doe abhorre dice, an all games, accounting nothing more vile in a man, then to giue himselfe vnto those things that make vs greedy and desirous to get other mens goods. If at any time they do sweare, for that seldome they are wont to doe, they sweare by the Sunne: many of them are taught good letters, wherfore they may so much the sooner be brought vnto Christianitie. Each one is contented with one wife: they be all desirous to learne, and naturally inclined vnto honesty and courtesie: godly talke they listen vnto willingly, especially when they vnderstand it throughly. Their gouernment consisteth of 3 estates. The first place is due vnto the high Priest, by whose laws and decrees all publike and priuate matters appertayning to religion are decided. The sects of their clergie men, whom they doe call Bonzi, be of no estimation or authoritie except the high Priest by letters patent doe confirme the same: he confirmeth and alloweth of their Tundi, who be as it were Bishops, although in many places they are nominated by sundry Princes. These Tundi are greatly honoured of all sorts: they doe giue benefices vnto inferiour ministers, and do grant licences for many things as to eate flesh vpon those dayes they goe in pilgrimage to their Idoles with such like priuileges. Finally, this High Priest wont to be chosen in China for his wisedome and learning, made in Iapan for his gentry and birth, hath so large a Dominion and reuenues so great, that eftsones he beardeth the petie Kings and Princes there.

Their second principal Magistrate, in their language Vo, is the chiefe Herehaught, made by succession and birth, honoured as a God. This gentleman neuer toucheth the ground with his foote without forfaiting of his office, he neuer goeth abroad out of his house, nor is at all times to be seene. At home he is either carried about in a litter, or els he goeth in wooden Choppines a foote high from the ground: commonly he sitteth in his chaire with a sword in one side, and a bow and arrows in the other, next his bodie he wearth blacke, his outward garments be red, all shadowed ouer with Cypresse, at his cappe hang certaine Lambeaux much like vnto a Bishop Miter, his forehead is painted white and red, he eateth his meat in earthen dishes. This Herehaught determineth in all Iapan the diuerse titles of honour, whereof in that Iland is great plentie, each one particularly knowen by his badge, commonly seene in sealing vp their letters, and dayly altered according to their degrees. About this Vo euery Noble man hath his Solicitor, for the nation is so desirous of praise and honour, that they striue among themselues who may bribe him best. By these meanes the Herehaught groweth so rich, that although hee haue neither land nor any reuenues otherwise, yet may he be accounted the wealthiest man in all Iapan. For three causes this great Magistrate may loose his office: first, if he touch the ground with his foote, as it hath beene alreadie said: next, if he kill any body: thirdly, if he be found an enemie vnto peace and quietnesse, howbeit neither of these aforesaid causes is sufficient to put him to death.

Their third chiefe officer is a Iudge, his office is to take vp and to end matters in controuersie, to determine of warres and peace, that which he thinketh right, to punish rebels, wherein he may commaund the noble men to assist him vpon paine of forfeiting their goods: neuerthelesse at all times he is not obeyed, for that many matters are ended rather by might and armes, then determined by law. Other controuersies are decided either in the Temporall Court, as it seemeth good vnto the Princes, or in the Spirituall consistorie before the Tundi.

Rebelles are executed in this manner, especially if they be noble men or officers. The king looke what day he giueth sentence against any one, the same day the partie, wheresoeuer he be, is aduertised thereof, and the day told him of his execution. The condemned person asketh of the messenger whether it may bee lawful for him to kill himselfe: the which thing when the king doeth graunt, the partie taking it for an honour, putteth on his best apparel and launcing his body a crosse from the breast downe all the belly, murthereth himselfe. This kind of death they take to be without infamie, neither doe their children for their fathers crime so punished, loose their goods. But if the king reserue them to be executed by the hangman, then flocketh he together his children, his seruants, and friends home to his house, to preserue his life by force. The king committeth the fetching of him out vnto his chiefe Iudge, who first setteth vpon him with bow and arrowes, and afterward with pikes and swords, vntill the rebell and family be slaine to their perpetuall ignominie and shame.

The Indie-writers make mention of sundry great cities in this Iland, as Cangoxima a hauen towne in the South part thereof, and Meaco distant from thence three hundred leagues northward, the royall seat of the king and most wealthy of all other townes in that Iland. The people thereabout are very noble, and their language the best Iaponish. In Maco are sayd to be ninetie thousande houses inhabited and vpward, a famous Vniuersitie, and in it fiue principall Colleges, besides closes and cloysters of Bonzi, Leguixil, and Hamacata, that is, Priests, Monks and Nunnes. Other fiue notable Vniuersities there be in Iapan, namely, Coia, Negru, Homi, Frenoi, and Bandu. The first foure haue in them at the least three thousand and fiue hundred schollers: in the fift are many mo. For Bandu prouince is very great and possessed with six princes, fiue whereof are vassals vnto the sixt, yet he himselfe subiect vnto the Iaponish king, vsually called the great king of Meaco: lesser scholes there be many in diuers places of this Ilande. And thus much specially concerning this glorious Iland, among so many barbarous nations and rude regions, haue I gathered together in one summe, out of sundry letters written from thence into Europe, by no lesse faithfull reporters than famous trauellers. [Sidenote: Petrus Maffeius de rebus Iaponicis.] For confirmation wherof, as also for the knowledge of other things not conteyned in the premisses, the curious readers may peruse these 4 volumes of Indian matters written long ago in Italian, and of late compendiously made Latine, by Petrus Maffeius my old acquainted friend, entituling the same, De rubus Iaponicis. One whole letter out of the fift booke thereof, specially intreating of that countrey, I haue done into English word for word in such wise as followeth.

Aloisius Froes to his companions in Iesus Christ that remaine in China and India.

The last yeere, deare brethren, I wrote vnto you from Firando, how Cosmus Turrianus had appointed me to trauile to Meaco to helpe Gaspar Vilela, for that there the haruest was great, the labourers few, and that I should haue for my companion in that iourney Aloisius Almeida. It seemeth now my part, hauing by the helpe of God ended so long a voiage, to signifie vnto you by letter such things specially as I might thinke you would most delight to know. And because at the beginning Almeida and I so parted the whole labour of writing letters betwixt vs, that he should speake of our voyage, and such things as happened therein, I should make relation of the Meachians estate, and write what I could well learne of the Iapans manners and conditions: setting aside all discourses of our voyage, that which standeth me vpon I will discharge in this Epistle, that you considering how artificially, how cunningly, vnder the pretext of religion, that craftie aduersary of mankind leadeth and draweth vnto perdition the Iapanish mindes, blinded with many superstitions and ceremonies, may the more pitie this Nation.

The inhabiters of Iapan, as men that had neuer had greatly to doe with other Nations, in their Geography diuided the whole world into three parts,

Iapan, Sian, and China. And albeit the Iapans receiued out of Sian and China their superstitions and ceremonies, yet doe they neuertheless contemne all other Nations in comparison of themselues, and standing in their owne conceite doe far preferre themselues before all other sorts of people in wisedome and policie.

Touching the situation of the countrey and nature of the soyle, vnto the things eftsoones erst written, this one thing I will adde: in these Ilands, the sommer to be most hot, the winter extreme cold. In the kingdom of Canga, as we call it, falleth so much snow, that the houses being buried in it, the inhabitants keepe within doores certaine moneths of the yeere, hauing no way to come foorth except they break vp the tiles. Whirlewindes most vehement, earthquakes so common, that the Iapans dread such kind of feares litle or nothing at all. The countrey is ful of siluer mines otherwise barren, not so much by fault of nature, as through the slouthfulnesse of the inhabitants: howbeit Oxen they keepe and that for tillage sake onely. The ayre is holesome, the waters good, the people very faire and well bodied: bare headed commonly they goe, procuring baldnesse with sorrow and teares, eftsoones rooting vp with pinsars all the haire of their heads as it groweth, except it be a litle behind, the which they knot and keepe with all diligence. Euen from their childhood they weare daggers and swords, the which they vse to lay vnder their pillowes when they goe to bed: in shew courteous and affable, in deede haughtie and proud. They delight most in warlike affaires, and their greatest studie is armes. Mens apparel diuersely coloured is worne downe halfe the legges and to the elbowes: womens attire made handsomely like vnto a vaile, is somewhat longer: all manner of dicing and theft they do eschewe. The marchant although he be wealthy, is not accounted of. Gentlemen, be they neuer so poore, retaine their place: most precisely they stand vpon their honour and worthinesse, ceremoniously striuing among themselues in courtesies and faire speeches. Wherein if any one happily be lesse carefull than he should be, euen for a trifle many times he getteth euill will. Want though it trouble most of them, so much they doe detest, that poore men cruelly taking pittie of their infantes newly borne, especially girles, do many times with their owne feete strangle them. Noble men, and other likewise of meaner calling generally haue but one wife a peece, by whom although they haue issue, yet for a trifle they diuorse themselues from their wiues, and the wiues also sometimes from their husbands, to marry with others. After the second degree cousins may there lawfully marry. Adoption of other mens children is much vsed among them. In great townes most men and women can write and reade.

This Nation feedeth sparingly, their vsuall meat is rice and salets, and neere the sea side fish. They feast one another many times, wherein they vse great diligence, especially in drinking one to another, insomuch that the better sort, least they might rudely commit some fault therein, does vse to reade certaine bookes written of duties and ceremonies apperteyning vnto banquets. To be delicate and fine, they put their meate into their mouthes with litle forkes, accounting it great rudenesse to touch it with their fingers: winter and sommer they drinke water as hot as they may possibly abide it. Their houses are in danger of fire, but finely made and cleane, layde all ouer with strawe-pallets, whereupon they doe both sit in stead of stooles, and lie in their clothes with billets under their heads. For feare of defiling these pallets, they goe either bare foote within doores, or weare strawe pantofles on their buskins when they come abroad, the which they lay aside at their returne home againe. Gentlemen for the most part do passe the night in banketting, musicke, and vaine discourses, they sleepe the day time. In Meaco and Sacaio there is good store of beds, but they be very litle, and may be compared vnto our pues.

In bringing vp children they vse words only to rebuke them, admonishing as diligently and aduisedly boyes of sixe or seuen yeeres of age, as though they were olde men. They are giuen very much to intertaine strangers, of whom most curiously they loue to aske euen in trifles what forraine nations doe, and their fashions. Such arguments and reasons as be manifest, and are made plaine with examples, doe greatly persuade them. They detest all kinde of theft, whosoeuer is taken in that fault may be slaine freely of any bodie. No publike prisons, no common gayles, no ordinary Iusticers: priuately each householder hath the hearing of matters at home in his owne house, and the punishing of greater crimes that deserue death without delay. Thus vsually the people is kept in awe and feare.

About foure hundred yeeres past (as in their olde recordes we finde) all Iapan was subiect vnto one Emperour whose royall seat was Meaco, in the Iaponish language called Cubucama. But the nobtlitie rebelling against him, by litle and litle haue taken away the greatest part of his dominion, howbeit his title continually remayneth, and the residue in some respect doe make great account of him still, acknowledging him for their superior. Thus the Empyre of Iapan, in times past but one alone, is now diuided into sixtie six kingdomes, the onely cause of ciuill warres continually in that Iland, to no small hinderance of the Gospell, whilest the kings that dwell neare together inuade one another, each one coueting to make his kingdome greater. Furthermore in the citie Meaco is the pallace of the high Priest, whom that nation honoureth as a God, he hath in his house 306 Idoles, one whereof by course is euery night set by his side for a watchman. He is thought of the common people so holy, that it may not be lawfull for him to goe vpon the earth: if happily he doe set one foote to the ground, he looseth his office. He is not serued very sumptuously, he is maintained by almes. The heads and beards of his ministers are shauen, they haue name Cangues, and their authoritie is great throughout all Iapan. The Cubucama vseth them for Embassadores to decide controuersies betwixt princes, and to end their warres, whereof they were wont to make very great game. It is now two yeres since or there about, that one of them came to Bungo, to intreate of peace betwixt the king thereof and the king of Amanguzzo. This Agent fauouring the king of Bungo his cause more then the other, brought to passe that the foresayd king of Bungo should keepe two kingdomes, the which he had taken in warres from the king of Amanguzzo. Wherefore he had for his reward of the king of Bungo aboue 30000 ducats. And thus farre hereof.

I come now to other superstitions and ceremonies, that you may see, deare brethren, that which I said in the beginning, how subtilly the diuell hath deceiued the Iaponish nation, and how diligent and readie they be to obey and worship him. And first, al remembrance and knowledge not onely of Christ our Redeemer, but also of that one God the maker of all things is cleane extinguished and vtterly abolished out of the Iapans hearts. Moreouer their superstitious sects are many, whereas it is lawfull for each one to follow that which liketh him best: but the principall sects are two, namely the Amidans and Xacaians. Wherefore in this countrey shall you see many monasteries, not onely of Bonzii men, but also of Bonziæ women diuersely attired, for some doe weare white vnder, and blacke vpper garments, other goe apparelled in ash colour, and their idole hath to name Denichi: from these the Amidanes differ very much. Againe the men Bonzii for the most part dwell in sumptuous houses, and haue great reuenues. These fellowes are chaste by commandement, marry they may not vpon paine of death. In the midst of their temple is erected an altar, whereon standeth a woodden Idole of Amida, naked from the girdle vpward, with holes in his eares after the manner of Italian gentlewomen, sitting on a wooden rose goodly to behold. They haue great libraries, and halles for them all to dine and sup together, and bels wherewith they are at certaine houres called to prayers. In the euening the Superintendent giueth each one a theame for meditation. After midnight before the altar in their Temple they do say Mattens at it were out of Xaca his last booke, one quier one verse, the other quier another. Early in the morning each one giueth himselfe to meditation one houre: they shaue their heads and beards. Their cloysters be very large, and within the precinct thereof, Chappels of the Fotoquiens, for by that name some of the Iapanish Saints are called: their holydaies yeerely be very many. Most of these Bonzii be gentlemen, for that the Iapanish nobility charged with many children, vse to make most of them Bonzii, not being able to leaue for each one a patrimony good enough. The Bonzii most coueteously bent, know all the wayes how to come by money. They sell vnto the people many scrolles of paper, by the helpe whereof the common people thinketh it selfe warranted from all power of the deuils. They borrow likewise money to be repayed with great vsury in an other worlde, giuing by obligation vnto the lender an assurance thereof, the which departing out of his life he may carry with him to hell.

There is another great company of such as are called Inambuxu, with curled and staring haire. They make profession to finde out againe things either lost or stolen, after this sort. They set before them a child whom the deuill inuadeth, called vp thither by charmes: of that child then doe they ask that which they are desirous to know.

These mens prayers both good and bad are thought greatly to preuaile, insomuch that both their blessings and their curses they sell vnto the people. The nouices of this order, before they be admitted, goe together two or three thousand in a company, vp a certaine high mountaine to doe pennance there, threescore dayes voluntarily punishing themselues. In this time the deuill sheweth himselfe vnto them in sundry shapes: and they like young graduats, admitted as it were fellowes into some certaine companie, are set foorth with white tassels hanging about their neckes, and blacke Bonnets that scarcely couer any more then the crawne of their heads. Thus attyred they range abroade in all Iapan, to set out themselues and their cunning to sale, each one beating his bason which he carieth always about with him, to giue notice of their comming in al townes where they passe.

There is also an other sort called Genguis, that make profession to shewe by soothsaying where stollen things are, and who were the theeues. These dwell in the toppe of an high mountaine, blacke in the face: for the continuall heate of the sunne, for the cold windes, and raines they doe continually endure. They marry but in their owne tribe and line: the report goeth that they be horned beasts. They climbe vp most high rockes and hilles, and go ouer very great riuers by the onely arte of the deuill, who to bring those wretches the more into errour, biddeth them to goe vp a certaine high mountaine, where they stande miserably gazing and earnestly looking for him as long as the deuill appointeth them. At the length at noonetide or in the euening commeth that deuill, whom they call Amida among them to shew himselfe vnto them: this shew breedeth in the braines and hearts of men such a kinde of superstition, that it can by no meanes be rooted out of them afterward.

The deuill was wont also in another mountaine to shew himselfe vnto the Iapanish Nation. Who so was more desirous than other to go to heauen and to enioy Paradise, thither went he to see that sight, and hauing seene the deuill followed him (so by the deuill persuaded) into a denne vntil he came to a deepe pit. Into this pit the deuill was wont to leape and to take with him his worshipper whom he there murdred. This deceit was thus perceiued. An old man blinded with this superstition, was by his sonne diswaded from thence, but all in vaine. Wherefore his sonne followed him priuily into that denne with his bow and arrows, where the deuill gallantly appeared vnto him in the shape of a man. Whilest the old man falleth downe to worshippe the deuill, his sonne speedily shooting an arrow at the spirit so appearing, strooke a Foxe in stead of a man so suddenly was that shape altered. This olde manne his sonne tracking the Foxe so running away, came to that pit whereof I spake, and in the bottome thereof he found many bones of dead men, deceiued by the deuill after that sort in time past. Thus deliuered he his father from present death, and all other from so pestilent an opinion.

There is furthermore a place bearing name Coia, very famous for the multitude of Abbyes which the Bonzii haue therein. The beginner and founder whereof is thought to be one Combendaxis a suttle craftie fellowe, that got the name of holinesse by cunning speech, although the lawes and ordinances he made were altogether deuillish: he is said to haue found out the Iapanish letters vsed at this day. In his latter yeeres this Sim suttle buried himselfe in a fouresquare graue, foure cubites deepe, seuerely forbidding it to be opened, for that then he died not, but rested his bodie wearied with continuall businesse, vntill many thousand thousands of yeeres were passed, after the which time a great learned man named Mirozu should come into Iapan, and then would he rise vp out of his graue againe. About his tombe many lampes are lighted, sent thither out of diuerse prouinces, for that the people are perswaded that whosoeuer is liberall and beneficiall towardes the beautifying of that monument shall not onely increase in wealth in this world, but in the life to come be safe through Combendaxis helpe. Such as giue themselues to worship him, liue in those Monasteries or Abbyes with shauen heads, as though they had forsaken all secular matters, whereas in deede they wallow in all sortes of wickednesse and lust. In these houses, the which are many (as I sayd) in number, doe remaine 6000 Bonzii, or thereabout besides the multitude of lay men, women be restrained from thence vpon paine of death. Another company of Bonzii dwelleth at Fatonochaiti. They teach a great multitude of children all tricks and sleights of guile and theft: whom they do find to be of great towardnes, those do they instruct in al the petigrues of princes, and fashions of the nobilitie, in chiualrie and eloquence, and so send them abroad into other prouinces, attired like yong princes, to this ende, that faining themselues to be nobly borne, they may with great summes of money borowed vnder the colour and pretence of nobilitie returne againe. Wherefore this place is so infamous in all Iapan, that if any scholer of that order be happily taken abroad, he incontinently dieth for it. Neuerthelesse these cousiners leaue not daily to vse their woonted wickednesse and knauerie.

[Sidenote: A warrelike people 300 leagues to the North of Meaco.] North from Iapan, three hundred leagues out of Meaco, lieth a great countrey of sauage men clothed in beasts skinnes, rough bodied, with huge beards and monstrous muchaches, the which they hold vp with litle forkes as they drinke. These people are great drinkers of wine, fierce in warres, and much feared of the Iapans: being hurt in fight, they wash their wounds with salt water, other Surgerie haue they none. In their breasts they are sayd to cary looking glasses: their swordes they tie to their heads, in such wise, that the handle doe rest vpon their shoulders. Seruice and ceremonies haue they none at all, onely they are woont to worship heauen. To Aquita a great towne in that Iaponish kingdom, which we call Geuano, they much resort for marchandise, and the Aquitanes likewise doe trauell in to their countrey, howbeit not often, for that there many of them are slaine by the inhabiters.

Much more concerning this matter I had to write: but to auoyd tediousnesse I will come to speake of the Iapans madnesse againe, who most desirous of vaine glory doe thinke then specially to get immortall fame, when they procure themselues to be most sumptuously and solemnly buried: their burials and obsequies in the citie Meaco are done after this maner. [Sidenote: The Iapanish funerals.] About one houre before the dead body be brought fourth, a great multitude of his friends apparelled in their best aray goe before vnto the fire, with them goe their kinswomen and such as bee of their acquaintance, clothed in white, (for that is the mourning colour there) with a changeable coloured vaile on their heads. Each woman hath with her also, according to her abilitie, all her familie trimmed vp in white mockado: the better sort and wealthier women goe in litters of Cedar artificially wrought and richly dressed. In the second place marcheth a great company of footemen sumptuously apparelled. Then afarre off commeth one of these Bonzii master of the ceremonies for that superstition, brauely clad in silkes and gold, in a large and high litter excellently well wrought, accompanied with 30 other Bonzii or thereabout, wearing hats, linnen albes, and fine blacke vpper garments. Then attired in ashe colour (for this colour also is mourning) with a long torch of Pineaple, he sheweth the dead body the way vnto the fire, lest it either stumble or ignorantly go out of the way. Well neere 200 Bonzii folow him singing the name of that deuill the which the partie deceassed chiefly did worship in his life time, and therewithall a very great bason is beaten euen to the place of fire instead of a bell. Then follow two great paper baskets hanged open at staues endes full of paper roses diuersly coloured, such as beare them doe march but slowly, shaking euer now and then their staues, that the aforesayd flowers may fall downe by litle and litle as it were drops of raine: and be whirled about with wind. This shower say they is an argument that the soule of the dead man is gone to paradise. After al this, eight beardles Bonzii orderly two and two drag after them on the ground long speares, the points backward, with flags of one cubite a piece, wherein the name also of that idole is written. Then there be caried 10 lanterns trimmed with the former inscription, ouercast with a fine vaile, and candles burning in them. [Sidenote: They burne their dead.] Besides this, two yoong men clothed in ashe colour beare pineaple torches, not lighted, of three foote length, the which torches serue to kindle the fire wherein the dead corpes is to bee burnt. In the same colour follow many other that weare on the crownes of their heads faire, litle, threesquare, blacke Lethren caps tied fast vnder their chinnes (for that is honorable amongst them) with papers on their heads, wherein the name of the deuill I spake of, is written. And to make it the more solemne, after commeth a man with a table one cubite long, one foot broad, couered with a very fine white vaile, in both sides whereof is written in golden letters the aforesayd name. At the length by foure men is brought fourth the corps sitting in a gorgeous litter clothed in white, hanging downe his head and holding his hands together like one that prayed: to the rest of his apparell may you adde an vpper gowne of paper, written full of that booke the which his God is sayd to haue made, when he liued in the world, by whose helpe and merites commonly they doe thinke to be saued. The dead man his children come next after him most gallantly set foorth, the yongest wherof carieth likewise a pineaple torch to kindle the fire. Last of all foloweth a great number of people in such caps as I erst spake of.

When they are al come to the place appointed for the obsequie, al the Bonzii with the whole multitude for the space of one houre, beating pannes and basons with great clamours, call vpon the name of that deuill, the which being ended, the Obsequie is done in this maner. In the midst of a great quadrangle railed about, hanged with course linnen, and agreeably vnto the foure partes of the world made with foure gates to goe in and out at, is digged a hole: in the hole is laied good store of wood, whereon is raised gallantly a waued roofe; before that stand two tables furnished with diuers kindes of meates, especially drie Figs, Pomegranates and Tartes good store, but neither Fish nor Flesh: vpon one of them standeth also a chafer with coales, and in it sweete wood to make perfumes. When all this is readie, the corde wherewith the litter was caried, is throwen by a long rope into the fire: as many as are present striue to take the rope in their handes, vsing their aforesayd clamours, which done, they goe in procession as it were round about the quadrangle thrise. Then setting the litter on the wood built vp ready for the fire that Bonzius who then is master of the ceremonies, saieth a verse that no bodie there vnderstandeth, whirling thrise about ouer his head a torch lighted, to signifie thereby that the soule of the dead man had neither any beginning, ne shall haue at any time an ende, and throweth away the torch. Two of the dead man his children, or of his neere kinne, take it vp againe, and standing one at the East side of the litter, the other at the West, doe for honour and reuerence reach it to each other thrise ouer the dead corps, and so cast it into the pile of wood: by and by they throw in oyle, sweete wood, and other perfumes, accordingly as they haue plentie, and so with a great flame bring the corps to ashes: his children in the meane while putting sweete wood into the chafer at the table with odours, doe solemnly and religiously worship their father as a Saint: which being done, the Bonzii are paied each one in his degree. The master of the ceremonies hath for his pact fiue duckats, sometimes tenne, sometimes twentie, the rest haue tenne Iulies a piece, or els a certaine number of other presents called Caxæ. The meate that was ordained, as soone as the dead corps friends and all the Bonzii are gone, is left for such as serued at the obsequie, for the poore and impotent lazars.

The next day returne to the place of obsequie the dead man his children, his kindred and friends, who gathering vp his ashes, bones, and teeth, doe put them in a gilded pot, and so carie them home, to bee set vp in the same pot couered with cloth, in the middest of their houses. Many Bonzii returne likewise to these priuate funerals, and so do they againe the seuenth day: then cary they out the ashes to be buried in a place appointed, laying thereupon a fouresquare stone, wherein is written in great letters drawen all the length of the stone, the name of that deuil the which the dead man worshipped in his life time. Euery day afterward his children resort vnto the graue with roses and warme water that the dead corps thirst not. Nor the seuenth day onely, but the seuenth moneth and yeere, within their owne houses they renue this obsequie, to no small commodities and gaine of the Bonzii: great rich men doe spend in these their funerals 3000 duckats or thereabout, the meaner sort two or three hundred. Such as for pouertie be not able to go to that charges, are in the night time darke long without all pompe and ceremonies buried in a dunghill.

They haue another kinde of buriall, especially neere the Sea side, for them that bee not yet dead. These fellowes are such, as hauing religiously with much deuotion worshipped Amida, now desirous to see him, doe slay themselues. And first they goe certaine dayes begging almes, the which they thrust into their sleeues, then preach they in publique a sermon vnto the people, declaring what they mind to doe, with the great good liking of all such as doe heare them: for euery body wondreth at such a kinde of holinesse. Then take they hookes to cut downe briars and thornes that might hinder them in their way to heauen, and so embarke themselues in a new vessell, tying great stones about their neckes, armes, loines, thighes, and feete: thus they launching out into the main Sea be either drowned there, their shippe bouged for that purpose, or els doe cast themselues ouer-boord headlong into the Sea. The emptie barke is out of hand set a fire for honours sake by their friends that folow them in another boat of their owne, thinking it blasphemie that any mortall creature should afterward once touch the barke that had bene so religiously halowed.

Truly when we went to Meaco, eight dayes before we came to the Ile of Hiu at Fore towne, sixe men and two women so died. To all such as die so the people erecteth a Chappell, and to each of them a pillar and a pole made of Pineaple for a perpetuall monument, hanging vp many shreds of paper in stickes all the roofe ouer, with many verses set downe in the walles in commendation of that blessed company. Wherefore vnto this place both day and night many come very superstitiously in pilgrimage. It happened euen then as Aloisius Almeida and I went to christen a childe wee traueiled that way at what time foure or fiue olde women came foorth out of the aforesayd chappell with beades in their handes (for in this point also the deuill counterfeiteth Christianitie) who partly scorned at vs for follie, partly frowned and taunted at our small deuotion, for passing by that holy monument without any reuerence or worship done thereunto at all.

It remaineth now we speake two or three wordes of those Sermons the Bonzii are woont to make, not so many as ours in number, but assuredly very well prouided for. The Pulpit is erected in a great temple with a silke Canopie ouer it, therein standeth a costly seate, before the seate a table with a bell and a booke. At the houre of Sermon each sect of the Iapans resorteth to their owne doctors in diuers Temples. Vp goeth the doctor into the Pulpit, and being set downe, after that hee hath lordlike looked him about, signifieth silence with his bell, and so readeth a fewe wordes of that booke we spake of, the which he expoundeth afterward, more at large. These preachers be for the most part eloquent, and apt to drawe with their speach the mindes of their hearers. Wherefore to this ende chieflie (such is their greedinesse) tendeth all their talke, that the people bee brought vnder the colour of godlinesse to enrich their monasteries, promising to each one so much the more happinesse in the life to come, how much the greater costes and charges they bee at in Church matters and obsequies: notwithstanding this multitude of superstitious Sects and companies, and the diuersities thereof amongst themselues: yet in this principally all their Superintendents doe trauell so to perswade their Nouices in their owne tales and lies, that they thinke nothing els trueth, nothing els sure to come by euerlasting saluation, nothing els woorth the hearing. Whereunto they adde other subtleties, as in going grauitie, in countenance, apparell, and in all outward shew, comelinesse. Whereby the Iapans mindes are so nousled in wicked opinions, and doe conceiue thereby such trust and hope of euerlasting saluation, that not onely at home, but also abroad in euery corner of the towne continually almost they run ouer their beades, humbly asking of Amida and Xaca, wealth, honour, good health, and euerlasting ioyes. Thus then, deare brethren, may you thinke how greatly they need the helpe of God, that either doe bring the Gospell into this countrey, or receiuing it brought vnto them, doe forsake idolatrie and ioine themselues with Christ, being assaulted by so many snares of the deuill, troubled with the daily dissuasions of their Bonzii, and finally, so iniuriously, so hardly, so sharpely vexed of their kinred and friends, that except the grace of God obtained by the sacrifices and prayers of the Catholique church doe helpe vs, it cannot be chosen but that the faith and constancie of many, if not of all, in these first beginnings of our churches, will greatly be put in ieopardie. So much the more it standeth you vpon that so earnestly long for the health of soules, to commend specially these Iapanish flocks vnto our Lord.

We came to Sacaio the eight and twentie day of Ianuary: Aloisius Almeida first for businesse, but afterward let by sicknesse, staied there some while, but I parting the next day from thence came thirteene leagues off to Meaco the last of Ianuarie. Of my comming all the Christians tooke great comfort, but specially Gaspar Vilela who in 6 yeres had seen none of our companie at Meaco: his yeeres are not yet fortie, but his grey haires shew him to be seuentie, so vehemently is his litle body afflicted and worne with extreme cold. Hee speaketh Iapanish so skilfully after the phrase of Meaco (the which for the renowne of this people and royal seat of the king is best accounted of) that hee doeth both confesse and preach in that language. Certaine godly bookes also he hath done into that speach, not omitting to translate other as laisure suffreth him. To make an ende, our Lord for his goodnesse vouchsafe to preserue vs all continually, and to giue vs ayde both rightly to interprete his will, and well to doe the same. From Meaco the 19 of February 1565.

Other such like matter is handled both in other his letters, and also in the Epistles written by his companions to be seene at large in the aforesaid volume. Amongst the rest this seemed in my iudgement one of the principall, and therefore the rather I tooke vpon me to doe it into English.

* * * * *

Of the Iles beyond Iapan in the way from China to the Moluccas.

Amongst other Iles in the Asian sea betwixt Canton a Chinish hauen in Cathaio and the Moluccas, much spoken of in the Indian histories and painted out in Maps, Ainan and Santianum are very famous. Ainan standeth 19 degrees on this side of the Equinoctiall line neere China, from whence the Chinish nation haue their prouision for shipping and other necessaries requisite for their Nauie. There staied Balthasar Gagus a great traueiler 5 moneths, who describeth that place after this maner. [Sidenote: De reb. Iap. li. 4.] Ainan is a goodly countrey ful of Indian fruits and all kinds of victuals, besides great store of iewels and pearle, well inhabited, the townes built of stone, the people rude in conditions, apparelled in diuers coloured rugs, with two oxe hornes, as it were, made of fine cypres hanging downe about their eares, and a paire of sharpe cyzers at their foreheads.

The cause wherefore they go in such attire I could not vnderstand, except it bee for that they do counterfeit the deuil in the forme of a brute beast, offring themselues vp to him.

Santianum is an Ile neere vnto the hauen Cantan in the confines likewise of China, famous for the death of that worthy traueiler and godly professour and painfull doctor of the Indian nation in matters concerning religion, Francis Xauier, who after great labours, many iniuries, and calamities infinite suffred with much patience, singular ioy and gladnesse of mind, departed in a cabben made of bowes and rushes vpon a desert mountaine, no lesse voyd of all worldly commodities, then endued with all spirituall blessings, out of this life, the 2 day of December, the yeere of our Lord 1552. after that many thousand of these Easterlings were brought by him to the knowledge of Christ. Of this holy man, his particular vertues, and specially trauell, and wonderfull works in that region, of other many litle Iles (yet not so litle, but they may right wel be written of at laisure) all the latter histories of the Indian regions are full.

* * * * *

An excellent treatise of the kingdome of China, and of the estate and gouernment thereof: Printed in Latine at Macao a citie of the Portugals in China, An. Dom. 1590. and written Dialogue-wise. The speakers are Linus, Leo, and Michael.

LINUS.

Concerning the kingdome of China (Michael) which is our next neighbour, we haue heard and daily do heare so many reports, that we are to request at your hands rather a true then a large discourse and narration thereof. And if there be ought in your knowledge besides that which by continual rumours is waxen stale among vs, we will right gladly giue diligent eare vnto it.

MICHAEL. Because the report of this most famous kingdome is growen so common among vs, reducing diuers and manifold particulars into order, I will especially aime at the trueth of things receiued from the fathers of the societie, which euen now at this present are conuersant in China. [Sidenote: The situation and limites of China.] First of all therefore it is not vnknowen, that of all parts of the maine continent this kingdom of China is situate most Easterly: albeit certaine Ilands, as our natiue Iapon, and the Ile of Manilia stand more Easterly then China it selfe. As touching the limites and bounds of this kingdom, we may appoint the first towards the West to be a certaine Ile commonly called Hainan, which standeth in 19 degrees of Northerly latitude. For the continent next adioining vnto this Ile trendeth towardes the East, and that especially, where the promontorie of the citie called Nimpo or Liampo doeth extend it selfe. Howbeit, from that place declining Northward, it stretcheth foorth an huge length, insomuch that the farthest Chinian inhabitants that way doe behold the North pole eleuated, at least 50 degrees, and perhaps more also: whereupon a man may easilie coniecture (that I may speake like an Astronomer) how large the latitude of this kingdom is, when as it containeth about more then 540 leagues in direct extension towards the North. But as concerning the longitude which is accounted from East to West, it is not so exactly found out, that it may be distinguished into degrees. [Sidenote: Chinian Cosmographers.] Howbeit certaine it is, that according to the Map wherein the people of China describe the forme of their kingdom, the latitude thereof doeth not much exceed the longitude. This kingdom therefore is, without all peradventure, of all earthly kingdoms the most large and spacious: for albeit diuers other kings vnder their iurisdiction containing in dimensions more length and breadth then all China, do possesse very many kingdoms and far distant asunder: yet none of them all enioyeth any one kingdom so large and so ample, as the most puissant king of China doeth. [Sidenote: The rich reuenues of the king of China.] Now, if we shall make enquirie into his reuenues and tributes, true it is, that this king, of all others, is endued with the greatest and the richest, both in regard of the fertilitie and greatnes of his dominions, and also by reason of the seuere collection and exaction of his duties: yea, tributes are imposed vpon his subiects, not onely for lands, houses, and impost of marchandise, but also for euery person in each family. It is likewise to be understood, that almost no lord or potentate in China hath authoritie to leuie vnto himselfe any peculiar reuenues, or to collect any rents within the precincts of his seigniories, al such power belonging onely vnto the king: whereas in Europe the contrary is most commonly seen, as we haue before signified. In this most large kingdom are conteined 15 prouinces, euery one of which were in it selfe sufficient to be made one great kingdom. Six of these prouinces do border vpon the sea, namely (that I may vse the names of the Chinians themselues) Coantum, Foquien, Chequiam, Nanquin, Xantum, Paquin: the other 9 be in-land prouinces, namely, Quiansi, Huquam, Honan, Xiensi, Xansi, Suchuon, Queicheu, Iunan, Coansi. [Sidenote: The seats roiall of the king of China.] Amongst all the foresayd prouinces, two are allotted for the kings court and seat roial, that is to say, Paquin for his court in the North, and Nanquin for his court in the South. For the kings of China were woont to be resident altogether at the South court: but afterward by reason of the manifold and cruell warres mooued by the Tartars, they were constrained to defixe their princely seate and habitation in that extreme prouince of the North. Whereupon it commeth to passe, that those Northren confines of the kingdom doe abound with many moe fortresses, marciall engines, and garrisons of souldiers. LEO. I haue heard, amongst those munitions, a certaine strange and admirable wall reported of, wherewith the people of China doe represse and driue backe the Tartars attempting to inuade their territories. MICHAEL. Certes that wall which you haue heard tell of is most woorthie of admiration; for it runneth alongst the borders of three Northerlie prouinces, Xiensi, Xansit and Paquin, and is sayd to contayne almost three hundred leagues in length, and in such sort to bee built, that it hindereth not the courses and streames of any riuers, their chanels being ouerthwarted and fortified with wonderfull bridges and other defences. Yet is it not vnlikely, that the sayd wall is built in such sort, that onely lowe and easie passages bee therewith stopped and enuironed; but the mountaines running betweene those lowe passages are, by their owne naturall strength, and inaccessible heigth, a sufficient fortification agaynst the enemie. LINUS. Tell vs (Michael) whether the kingdome of China be so frequented with inhabitants, as wee haue often bene informed, or no? MICHAEL. It is (Linus) in very deed a most populous kingdom, as I haue bene certified from the fathers of societie: who hauing seene sundry prouinces of Europe renoumed for the multitude of their inhabitants, doe notwithstanding greatly admire the infinite swarmes of people in China. Howbeit these multitudes are not pel-mel and confusiuely dispersed ouer the land, but most conueniently and orderly distributed in their townes and famous cities: of which assemblies there are diuers kindes among the Chinians. For they haue certaine principal cities called by the name of Fu: other inferior cities called Cheu: and of a third kind also named Hien, which be indeed walled townes, but are not priuileged with the dignities and prerogatiues of cities. To these may be added two other kindes of lesser townes, which are partly villages, and partly garrisons of souldiers. Of the first and principall kind is that most noble citie standing neere vnto the port of Macao, called by the Chinians Coanchefu, but by the Portugals commonly termed Cantam, which is rather the common name of the prouince, then a word of their proper imposition. Vnto the third kind appertaineth a towne, which is yet nigher vnto the port of Macao, called by the Portugals Ansam, but by the Chinians Hiansanhien. Al the foresayd prouinces therefore haue their greater cities named Fu, and their lesser cities called Cheu, vnto both of which the other townes may be added. Moreouer in euery prouince there is a certain principal city which is called the Metropolitane thereof, wherein the chief magistrates haue their place of residence, as the principal citie by me last mentioned, which is the head of the whole prouince called Coantum. The number of the greater cities throughout the whole kingdom is more then 150, and there is the same or rather a greater multitude of inferiour cities. Of walled townes, not endued with the priuileges of cities there are mo then 1120: the villages and garrisons can scarce be numbred: ouer and besides the which conuents it is incredible what a number of countrie fames or granges there be: for it is not easie to find any place desert or void of inhabitants in all that land. [Sidenote: The Chinian riuers greatly inhabited.] Now in the sea, in riuers, and in barks there are such abundance of people, and of whole families inhabiting, that euen the Europæans themselues doe greatly wonder thereat: insomuch that some (albeit beyond measure) haue bene perswaded that there are as many people dwelling vpon the water as vpon the land. Neither were they induced so to thinke altogether without probabilitie: for whereas the kingdom of China is in all parts thereof interfused with commodious riuers, and in many places consisteth of waters, barges and boats being euery-where very common, it might easily bee supposed, that the number of watermen was equal vnto the land inhabitants. Howbeit, that is to be vnderstood by amplification, whereas the cities do swarme so ful with citizens and the countrie with peasants. [Sidenote: Holesome aire, plenty and peace in China.] LEO. The abundance of people which you tell vs of seemeth very strange: whereupon I coniecture the soile to be fertile, the aire to be holesome, and the whole kingdom to be at peace. MICHAEL. You haue (friend Leo) ful iudicially coniectured those three: for they do all so excel that which of the three in this kingdom be more excellent, it is not easie to discerne. And hence it is that this common opinion hath been rife among the Portugals, namely, that the kingdom of China was neuer visited with those three most heauy and sharpe scourges of mankind, warre, famine, and pestilence. But that opinion is more common then true: sithens there haue bene most terrible intestine and ciuile warres, as in many and most autenticall histories it is recorded: sithens also that some prouinces of the sayd kingdom, euen in these our dayes, haue bene afflicted with pestilence and contagious diseases, and with famine. [Sidenote: Chinian stories.] Howbeit, that the foresaid three benefits do mightily flourish and abound in China, it cannot be denied. For (that I may first speake of the salubritie of the aire) the fathers of the societie themselues are witnesses; that scarcely in any other realme there are so many found that liue vnto decrepite and extreme old age: so great a multitude is there of ancient and graue personages: neither doe they vse so many confections and medicines, nor so manifold and sundry wayes of curing diseases, as wee saw accustomed in Europe. For amongst them they haue no Phlebotomie or letting of blood: but all their cures, as ours also in Iapon, are atchieued by fasting, decoctions of herbes, and light or gentle potions. But in this behalfe let euery nation please themselues with their owne customes. Now, in fruitfulnes of soile this kingdom certes doth excel, far surpassing all other kingdoms of the East: yet it is nothing comparable vnto the plentie and abundance of Europe, as I haue declared at large in the former treatises. But the kingdom of China is, in this regard, so highly extolled, because there is not any region in the East partes that aboundeth so with marchandise, and from whence so much traffique is sent abroad. [Sidenote: The city of Coanchefu, *aliàs* Cantam.] For whereas this kingdome is most large and full of nauigable riuers, so that commodities may easilie be conueyed out of one prouince into another: the Portugals doe find such abundance of wares within one and the same Citie, (which perhaps is the greatest Mart throughout the whole kingdome) that they are verily perswaded, that the same region, of all others, most aboundeth with marchandise: which notwithstanding is to be vnderstood of the Orientall regions: albeit there are some kindes of marchandise, wherewith the land of China is better stored then any other kingdom. [Sidenote: Great abundance of gold in China.] This region affordeth especially sundry kinds of mettals, of which the chiefe, both in excellencie and in abundance, is gold, whereof so many Pezoes are brought from China to India, and to our countrey of Iapon, that I heard say, that in one and the same ship, this present yeere, 2000 such pieces consisting of massie gold, as the Portugals commonly call golden loaues, were brought vnto vs for marchandise: and one of these loaues is worth almost 100 duckats. Hence it is that in the kingdom of China so many things are adorned with gold, as for example, beds, tables, pictures, images, litters wherein nice and daintie dames are caried vpon their seruants backes. Neither are these golden loaues onely bought by the Portugals, but also great plentie of gold-twine and leaues of gold: for the Chinians can very cunningly beate and extenuate gold into plates and leaues. [Sidenote: Great store of siluer.] There is also great store of siluer, whereof (that I may omit other arguments) it is no small demonstration, that euery yeere there are brought into the citie commonly called Cantam by the Portugal marchants to buie wares, at the least 400 Sestertium thereof, and yet nothing in a maner is conueied out of the Chinian kingdom: because the people of China abounding with all necessaries, are not greatly inquisitiue or desirous of any marchandise from other kingdomes. I doe here omit the Siluer mines whereof there are great numbers in China, albeit there is much circumspection vsed in digging the siluer thereout: for the king standeth much in feare least it may bee an occasion to stirre vp the couetous and greedie humour of many. Nowe their siluer which they put to vses is for the most part passing fine, and purified from all drosse, and therefore in trying it they vse great diligence. What should I speake of their iron, copper, lead, tinne, and other mettals, and also of their quick-siluer. Of all which in the realme of China there is great abundance, and from thence they are transported into diuers countreys. Hereunto may bee added the wonderfull store of pearles, which, at the Ile of Hainan, are found in shell-fishes taken very cunningly by certaine Diuers, and doe much enlarge the kings reuenues. [Sidenote: Great store of silke in China.] But now let vs proceed vnto the Silke or Bombycine fleece, whereof there is great plentie in China: so that euen as the husbandmen labour in manuring the earth, and in sowing of Rice; so likewise the women doe employ a great part of their time in preseruing of silke-wormes, and in keeming and weauing of Silke. Hence it is that euery yeere the King and Queene with great solemnitie come foorth into a publique place, the one of them touching a plough, and the other a Mulberie tree, with the leaues whereof Silke-wormes are nourished: and both of them by this ceremonie encouraging both men and women vnto their vocation and labour: whereas otherwise, all the whole yeere throughout, no man besides the principall magistrates, may once attaine to the sight of the king. [Sidenote: Silke brought into Iapon.] Of this Silke or Bombycine fleece there is such abundance, that three shippes for the most part comming out of India to the port of Macao, and at the least one euery yeere comming vnto vs, are laden especially with this fraight, and it is vsed not onely in India, but caried euen vnto Portugal. Neither is the Fleece it selfe onely transported thence, but also diuers and sundry stuffes wouen thereof, for the Chinians do greatly excel in the Art of weauing, and do very much resemble our weauers of Europe. Moreouer the kingdom of China aboundeth with most costlie spices and odours, and especially with cynamom (albeit not comparable to the cynamom of Zeilan) with camphire also and muske, which is very principal and good. Muske deriueth his name from a beast of the same name (which beast resembleth a Beuer) from the parts whereof bruseda and putrified proceedeth a most delicate and fragrant smel which the Portugals highly esteem, commonly calling those parts of the foresaid beasts (because they are like vnto the gorges of foules) Papos, and conuey great plenty of them into India, and to vs of Iapon. [Sidenote: Cotton wooll, whereof Calicut-cloth is made.] But who would beleeue, that there were so much gossipine or cotton-wool in China; whereof such variety of clothes are made like vnto linnen; which we our selues do so often vse, and which also is conueied by sea into so many regions? Let vs now intreat of that earthen or pliable matter commonly called porcellan, which is pure white, and is to be esteemed the best stuffe of that kind in the whole world: whereof vessels of all kinds are very curiously framed. I say, it is the best earthen matter in all the world, for three qualities; namely, the cleannesse, the beauty, and the strength thereof. There is indeed other matter to be found more glorious, and more costly, but none so free from vncleannes, and so durable: this I adde, in regard of glasse, which indeed is immaculate and cleane, but may easily be broken in pieces. This matter is digged, not thorowout the whole region of China, but onely in one of the fifteene prouinces called Quiansi, wherein continually very many artificers are employed about the same matter: neither doe they only frame thereof smaller vessels, as dishes, platters, salt sellers, ewers, and such like, but also certaine huge tunnes, and vessels of great quantity, being very finely and cunningly wrought, which, by reason of the danger and difficulty of carriage, are not transported out of the realme, but are vsed onely within it, and especially in the kings court. The beauty of this matter is much augmented by variety of picture, which is layed in certaine colours vpon it, while it is yet new, golde also being added thereunto, which maketh the foresayd vessels to appeare most beautifull. It is wonderfull how highly the Portugals do esteeme thereof, seeing they do, with great difficulty transport the same, not onely to vs of Iapon and into India, but also into sundry prouinces of Europe. Vnto the marchandize aboue-mentioned may be added diuers and sundry plants, the rootes whereof be right holesome for mens bodies, and very medicinable, which are brought vnto our Iles of Iapon, and vnto many other Ilands, amongst the which that wood may be reckoned, which (by a synechdoche) is called The Wood of China, being of notable force to expell out of mens bodies those humours, which would breed contagious diseases. To these you may adde sugar-canes (for in the realme of China there is great store of excellent sugar) which is conueyed by the Portugals very plentifully, both into our countrey, and also into India. My speeches vttered immediatly before concerned marchandize onely, in regard whereof this kingdome is beneficiall not to itselfe alone, but most profitable to many other nations also. [Sidenote: China in a maner destitute of corne, wine, and oile.] As for those fruits which pertaine to yerely sustenance and common food, they can scarse be numbred: albeit, of those three commodities which they of Europe so greatly account of; namely of cornes, vines, and oliues the land of China is not very capable: for the Chinians know not so much as the name of an Oliue tree (out of the fruit whereof oile is expressed) neither yet the name of a vine. The prouince of Paquin is not altogether destitute of wine, but whether it be brought from other places, or there made, I am not able to say: although it aboundeth with many other, and those not vnpleasant liquors, which may serue in the stead of wine it selfe. Now, as touching corne, there is indeed wheat sowen in all the prouinces, howbeit rise is in farre more vse and request then it: and so in regard of these two commodities profitable for mans life; namely, wine and corne; the kingdome of China and our countrey of Iapon may be compared together.

LEO. You haue discoursed (Michael) of the fruitfulnesse of China, whereof I haue often heard, that it is no lesse pleasant than fruitful, and I haue bene especially induced so to thinke, at the sight of the Chinian maps. MICHAEL. The thing it selfe agrees right well with the picture: for they that haue seene the mediterran or inner parts of the kingdome of China, do report it to be a most amiable countrey, adorned with plenty of woods, with abundance of fruits and grasse, and with woonderfull variety of riuers, wherewith the Chinian kingdome is watered like a garden; diuers of which riuers doe naturally flowe, and others by arte and industry are defined into sundry places. But now I will intreat of the tranquility and peace of China, after I haue spoken a word or two concerning the maners of the inhabitants. [Sidenote: The disposition and maners of the Chinians.] This nation is indued with excellent wit and dexterity for the attaining of all artes, and being very constant in their owne customes, they lightly regard the customes or fashions of other people. They vse one and the same kinde of vesture, yet so, that there is some distinction betweene the apparell of the magistrate and of the common subiect. They all of them do weare long haire vpon their heads, and, after the maner of women, do curiously keame their dainty locks hanging downe to the ground, and, hauing twined and bound them vp, they couer them with calles, wearing sundry caps thereupon, according to their age and conditon. It seemeth that in olde time one language was common to all the prouinces: notwithstanding, by reason of variety of pronunciation, it is very much altered, and is diuided into sundry idiomes or proprieties of speech, according to the diuers prouinces: howbeit, among the magistrates, and in publike assemblies of iudgement, there is one and the very same kinde of language vsed thorowout the whole realme, from the which (as I haue sayd) the speech of ech prouince differeth not a little. [Sidenote: Their loyaltie vnto their superiours.] Moreouer this people is most loyall and obedient vnto the king and his magistrates, which is the principall cause of their tranquility and peace. For whereas the common sort doe apply themselues vnto the discretion and becke of inferiour magistrates, and the inferiour magistrates of the superiour, and the superiour magistrates of the king himselfe, framing and composing all their actions and affaires vnto that leuell: a world it is to see, in what equability and indifferency of iustice all of them do leade their liues, and how orderly the publike lawes are administred. Which thing notwithstanding shall be handled more at large, when we come to intreat of the gouernment. LINUS. Tell vs now (Michael) of the industry of that people, whereof we haue heard great reports. MICHAEL. Their industry is especially to be discerned in manuary artes and occupations, and therein the Chinians do surpasse most of these Easterly nations. For there are such a number of artificers ingeniously and cunningly framing sundry deuices out of golde, siluer, and other mettals, as likewise of stone, wood and other matters conuenient for mans vse, that the streets of cities being replenished with their shops and fine workemanship, are very woonderfull to beholde. Besides whom also there are very many Painters, vsing either the pensill or the needle (of which the last sort are called Embrotherers) and others also that curiously worke golde-twine vpon cloth either of linnen or of cotton: whose operations of all kinds are diligently conueyed by the Portugals into India. Their industry doth no lesse appeare in founding of gunnes and in making of gun-powder, whereof are made many rare and artificiall fire-works. To these may be added the arte of Printing, albeit their letters be in maner infinite and most difficult, the portraitures whereof they cut in wood or in brasse, and with maruellous facilitie they dayly publish huge multitudes of books. Vnto these mechanicall and illiberall crafts you may adde two more; that is to say, nauigation and discipline of warre; both of which haue bene in ancient times most diligently practised by the inhabitants of China: for (as we haue before signified in the third dialogue) the Chinians sailing euen as farre as India, subdued some part thereof vnto their owne dominion: howbeit afterward, least they should diminish the forces of their realme by dispersing them into many prouinces, altering their counsell, they determined to containe themselues within their owne limits: within which limits (as I haue sayd) there were in olde time vehement and cruell wares, both betweene the people of China themselues, and also against the Tartarian king, who inuaded their kingdome, and by himselue and his successours, for a long season, vsurped the gouernment thereof. Howbeit the kings of the Tartarian race being worne out, and their stocke and family being vtterly abolished, the Chinians began to lift vp their heads, and to aduance themselues, inioying for these 200 yeeres last past exceeding peace and tranquility, and at this day the posterity of the same king that expelled the Tartars, with great dignity weareth the crowne, and wieldeth the royall scepter. Albeit therefore the people of China (especially they that inhabit Southerly from the prouince of Paquin) are, for the most part, by reason of continuall ease and quiet, growen effeminate, and their courage is abated, notwithstanding they would prooue notable and braue souldiers, if they ioyned vse and exercise vnto their naturall fortitude. As a man may easily obserue in them, that maintaine continuall warres against the most barbarous and cruell Tartars. Howbeit in this kingdome of China there is so great regard of military discipline, that no city nor towne there is destitute of a garison, the captaines and gouernours keeping ech man his order; which all of them, in euery prouince, are subiect vnto the kings lieutenant generall for the warres, whom they call Chumpin, and yet he himselfe is subiect vnto the Tutan or viceroy. Let vs now come vnto that arte, which the Chinians do most of all professe, and which we may, not vnfitly, call literature or learning. For although it be commonly reported, that many liberall sciences, and especially naturall and morall phylosophy are studied in China, and that they haue Vniuersities there, wherein such ingenuous artes are deliuered and taught, yet, for the most part this opinion is to be esteemed more popular then true; but I will declare, vpon what occasion this conceit first grew. The people of China doe, aboue all things, professe the arte of literature; and learning it most diligently, they imploy themselues a long time and the better part of their age therein. For this cause, in all cities and townes, yea, and in pety villages also, there are certaine scholemasters hired for stipends to instruct children: and their literature being (as ours in Iapon is also) in maner infinite, their children are put to schole euen from their infancy and tender yeeres, from whence notwithstanding such are taken away, as are iudged to be vnfit for the same purpose, and are trained vp to marchandize or to manuary sciences: but the residue do so dedicate themselues to the study of learning, that (a strange thing it is to consider) being conuersant in the principall books, they will easily tel you, if they be asked the question, how many letters be conteined in euery page, and where ech letter is placed. Now, for the greater progresse and increase of learning, they (as the maner is in Europe) do appoint three degrees to the attaining of noble sciences; that is to say, the lowest, the middle degree, and the highest. Graduates of the first degree are called Siusai, of the second Quiugin, and of the third Chinzu. And in each city or walled towne there is a publique house called the Schoole, and vnto that all they doe resort from all priuate and pety-schooles that are minded to obtain the first degree; where they do amplifie a sentence or theame propounded vnto them by some magistrate: and they, whose stile is more elegant and refined, are, in ech city, graced with the first degree. Of such as aspire vnto the second degree triall is made onely in the metropolitan or principall city of the prouince, whereunto, they of the first degree, euery third yere, haue recourse, and, in one publike house or place of assembly, doe, the second time, make an oration of another sentence obscurer then the former, and doe vndergo a more seuere examination. Now, there is commonly such an huge multitude of people, that this last yere, in the foresayd famous city of Cantam, by reason of the incredible assembly of persons flocking to that publike act or commencement, at the first entrance of the doores, there were many troden vnder foot, and quelled to death, as we haue bene most certainly informed. Moreouer they that sue for the highest degree are subiect vnto a most seuere and exact censure, whereby they are to be examined at the Kings Court onely, and that also euery third yere next ensuing the sayd yere wherein graduates of the second degree are elected in ech prouince, and, a certaine number being prescribed vnto euery particular prouince, they do ascend vnto that highest pitch of dignity, which is in so great regard with the king himselfe, that the three principall graduates do, for honours sake, drinke off a cup filled euen with the Kings owne hand, and are graced with other solemnities. [Marginal note: Note the extraordinary honor vouchsafed by the great King of China vpon his learned graduates.] Out of this order the chiefe magistrates are chosen: for after that they haue attained vnto this third degree, being a while trained vp in the lawes of the realme, and in the precepts of vrbanity, they are admitted vnto diuers function. Neither are we to thinke that the Chinians be altogether destitute of other artes. For, as touching morall philosophy, all those books are fraught with the precepts thereof, which, for their instructions sake, are always conuersant in the hands of the foresayd students, wherein such graue and pithy sentences are set downe, that, in men void of the light of the Gospell, more can not be desired. [Sidenote: Naturall philosophy.] They haue books also that intreat of things and causes naturall, but herein it is to be supposed, that aswell their books as ours do abound with errors. There be other books among them, that discourse of herbs and medicines, and others of chiualry and martiall affaires. Neither can I here omit, that certaine men of China (albeit they be but few, and rare to be found) are excellent in the knowledge of astronomy, by which knowledge of theirs the dayes of the new moone incident to euery moneth are truly disposed and digested, and are committed to writing and published: besides, they doe most infallibly foretell the eclipses of the Sun and Moone: and whatsoeuer knowledge in this arte we of Iapon haue, it is deriued from them. LEO. We doe freely confesse that (Michael) sithens our books intreating of the same arte are a great part of them, written in the characters or letters of China. [Sidenote: The politike gouernment of China.] But now, instruct you vs as touching their maner of gouernment, wherein the Chinians are sayd greatly to excell. MICHAEL. That, that, in very deed, is their chiefe arte, and vnto that all their learning and exercise of letters is directed. Whereas therefore, in the kingdome of China, one onely king beares rule ouer so many prouinces, it is strange what a number of Magistrates are by him created to admister publique afiaires. For (to omit them which in ech Towne and City haue iurisdiction ouer the townesmen and citizens) there are three principall Magistrates in euery prouince. The first is he that hath to deale in cases criminall, and is called Ganchasu: the second is the Kings Fosterer, and is called Puchinsu: the third is the Lieutenant-generall for the warres, named, as we sayd before, Chumpin.

These three therefore haue their place of residence in the chiefe City of the prouince: and the two former haue certaine associates of their owne order, but of inferiour authority, appointed in diuers Cities and Townes, vnto whom, according to the variety of causes, the Gouernours of Townes and the Maiors of Cities doe appeale. Howbeit the three forenamed Magistrates are in subjection vnto the Tutan, that is, the Vice-roy, ordained in ech prouince. And all these Magistrates beare office for the space of three yeeres together: yet so, that for the gouerning of ech province, not any of the same prouince, but strangers, that is, men of another prouince, are selected: whereof it commeth to passe, that the Iudges may giue sentence with a farre more entire and incorrupt minde, then if they were among their owne kinesfolke and allies. Ouer and besides all these, there is an annuall or yeerely Magistrate, which is called Chaien, whose duety it is to make inquisition of all crimes, and especially the crimes of Magistrates, and also to punish common offences: but concerning the faults of the great magistrates to admonish the king himselfe. Of this order, euery yere, are sent out of the Kings Court, for ech prouince, one; and going ouer all the Cities and Townes thereof, they do most diligently ransacke and serch out all crimes, and vpon them which are imprisoned they inflict due punishment, or, being found not guilty, they dismisse them vnpunished. Hence it is, that all Magistrates greatly fearing to be called in question by the Chaien are well kept within the limits of their callings. [Sidenote: Two Senates or Counsels continually holden in China.] Besides all these Magistrates there is at either Court, namely in the North, and in the South, a Senate or honourable assembly of graue counsellors, vnto the which, out of all prouinces, according to the neerenesse and distance of the place, affaires of greater weight and moment are referred, and by their authority diuers Magistrates are created: howbeit the managing and expedition of principall affaires is committed vnto the Senate of Paquin. Moreouer there are euery yeere certaine Magistrates appointed in ech prouince, to goe vnto the king; and euery third yeere all the Gouernours of Cities and of Townes do visit him at once, what time triall is made of them that aspire vnto the third degree: vpon which occasion there is at the same time an incredible number of people at the Kings Court. [Sidenote: The causes of peace in China.] By reason of this excellent order and harmony of Magistrates placed one vnder another, it can scarse be imagined, what sweete peace and tranquility flourisheth thorowout the whole realme, especially sithens, after speedy inquisition, persons that are guilty be put (as the maner is there) to the punishment of the bastinado: neither yet are suits or actions any long time delayed. [Sidenote: Learning the only step to honour in China.] Also it is not to be omitted, that for the obtaining of any dignity or magistracy, the way is open, without all respect of gentry or blood, vnto all men, if they be learned, and especially if they haue attained vnto the third and highest degree aforesaid. [The stately and formidable procession of the Chinian magistrates.] Neither can it be expressed how obedient and duetifull the common sort are vnto their Magistrates, and with what magnificence and pompe the sayd Magistrates come abroad: for the most part of them haue fiftie or threescore Sergeants attending vpon them, and going before them, two and two in a ranke: some of them carrying Halberds, Maces and Battle-axes: some trailing yron chaines vpon the ground: others holding great roddes or staues of a certaine kinde of reede, wherewith malefactours are punished, in their hands: and two there are that carry, inclosed in a case, the Kings seale peculiar for ech office: and many others also, that shew sundry spectacles vnto the people: whereunto may be added the horrible out-cries and showtes, which betweene whiles they vtter, to strike a terrour into the hearts of all men: and at length come the Magistrates themselues, being carried in a throne vpon the backs of foure men, sixe men, or eight men, according to the dignity of their office. [Sidenote: The houses of the Chinian magistrates.] Now, as concerning their houses, they are very large and stately, being built and furnished with all necessary stuffe, at the Kings owne cost, in the which, so long as their magistracy lasteth, they leade a braue and an honourable life. The sayd houses are without variety of stories one aboue another, which in the kingdome of China and in our Iles of Iapon also are not ordinarily vsed for habitation, but either to keepe watch and ward, or els for solace and recreations sake (for the which purposes, eight most lofty turrets of nine stories high are built) or els for the defence of Cities. Howbeit in other regardes these buildings doe shew foorth no small magnificence: for they haue their cisternes for the receit of raine-water, which are adorned with beautifull trees, set in order, round about them: and they haue also their places designed for the administration of iustice, and diuers other conuenient roomes to bestow their wiues and families in. Within the doores of the foresayd habitations a certain number of Sergeants and officers, hauing cabbins or little houses allotted them on both sides, doe alwayes giue their attendance; and so long as matters of iudgement are in deciding, they be alwayes ready at hand, that, at the direction of the Magistrates they may either beat malefactours, or by torments constraine them to tell the trueth. [Sidenote: The magistrates barges.] The sayd Magistrates also haue their peculiar barges wherein to take the water; being in breadth and length not much vnlike to galleys of Europe, but for swiftnesse and multitude of orres, farre inferiour vnto them. The rowers, sitting vpon galleries without the hatches or compasse of the barge, doe mooue it on forward with their oares: whereupon it commeth to passe, that the middle part of the barge affordeth sufficient roome for the Magistrates themselues to abide in, containing chambers therein almost as conuenient and handsome, as in any of their foresayd publique houses, together with butteries and kitchins, and such other places necessary for the prouision and stowage of victuals. LEO. All these things agree right well with the reports, which we haue heard of the stately and renowmed kingdome of China: I would now right gladly know somewhat concerning the order which is obserued in the obtaining of magistracies.

MICHAEL. You haue enquired of a matter most woorthy to be knowen, which I had almost omitted to entreat of. [Sidenote: The maner of electing magistrates in China.] The Chinians therefore doe vse a kinde of gradation in aduancing men vnto sundry places of authority, which for the most part is performed by the Senatours of Paquin. For first they are made iudges of townes: then of Cities: afterward they are elected to be of that order, which decreeth punishments in cases criminall without further appeale, or of their order, that are the kings fosterers. [Sidenote: Degrees vnto honour.] And in both of these Orders, which are very honourable, there are many places and degrees, so that from the inferiour place they must ascend vnto the superiour, vntill they haue attained vnto the highest dignity of all: and immediatly after that they come to be Vice-royes, howbeit this gradation is not alwayes accomplished in one and the same prouince, but in changing their offices they change places and prouinces also. Moreouer, next after the office of Vice-roy they are capable to be chosen Senatours of Nanquin, and last of all to be elected into the Senate of Paquin. Now, there is such an order and methode obserued in the ascending vnto these dignities, that all men may easily coniecture, what office any one is to vndertake. [Sidenote: Riding post.] And there is so great diligence and celerity vsed for the substitution of one into the roome of another, that for the same purpose, messengers are dispatched by land, vpon swift post-horses, vnto diuers prouinces, almost twenty dayes iourney from the Kings Court. And, to be short, there is such district seuerity in degrading those that vniustly or negligently demeane themselues, from an honourable vnto an inferiour and base office, or altogether in depriuing them of the kings authority: that all Magistrates doe stand in feare of nothing in the world more then of that. [Sidenote: Martiall dignities.] The same order, almost, is obserued among the Captaines and Lieu-tenants generall for the warres: except onely in them, that their birth and offspring is respected: for many there be, who descending by parentage from such men as haue in times past atchieued braue exploits in warfare, so soone as they come to sufficient yeeres, are created Centurions, Colonels, and Gouernours, vntill at last they attaine to be Lieu-tenants generall and Protectours of some whole prouince; who notwithstanding (as I haue sayd) are in all things subiect vnto the Vice-roy. All the foresayd Magistrates both of warre and of peace haue a set number of attendants allotted vnto them, enioying a stipend, and carying certaine ensignes and peculiar badges of their office: and (besides the ordinary watch, which souldiers appointed for the same purpose doe in the night season, after the City gates be shut, keepe in their forts) wheresoeuer any

Magistrate is, either at his house or in his barge, the sayd attendants striking vpon a cymball of brasse, at certaine appointed times, do keepe most circumspect and continuall watch and ward about his person. LINUS. You haue (Michael) sufficiently discoursed of the Magistrates: informe vs now of the king himselfe, whose name is so renowmed and spread abroad. [Sidenote: The king of China.] MICHAEL. Concerning this matter I will say so much onely as by certaine rumours hath come to my knowledge; for of matters appertaining vnto the kings Court we haue no eye-witnesses, sithens the fathers of the society haue not as yet proceeded vnto Paquin, who so soone as (by Gods assistance) they shall there be arriued, will by their letters more fully aduertise vs. [Sidenote: Van-Sui.] The king of China therefore is honoured with woonderfull reuerence and submission thorowout his whole realme; and whensoeuer any of his chiefe Magistrates speaketh vnto him, he calleth him VAN-SVI, signifying thereby that be wisheth tenne thousands of yeeres vnto him. [Sidenote: The succession of the crowne.] The succession of the kingdome dependeth vpon the bloud royall: for the eldest sonne borne of the kings first and lawfull wife obtaineth the kingdome after his fathers decease: neither doe they depriue themselues of the kingly authority in their life time (as the maner is in our Ilands of Iapon) but the custome of Europe is there obserued. [Sidenote: The kings yonger brethren.] Now, that the safety and life of the king may stand in more security, his yoonger brethren, and the rest borne of concubines are not permitted to liue in the kings Court: but places of habitation are by the king himselfe assigned vnto them in diuers prouinces farre distant asunder, where they dwell most commodiously, being comparable vnto kings for their buildings and revenues: howbeit they exercise no authority ouer the people, but all the gouernment of those cities wherein they dwell concerneth the Magistrates, who notwithstanding haue the sayde Princes in high regard and honour, and doe visit them twise in a moneth, and salute them kneeling vpon their knees, and bowing their faces downe to the earth: and yet they communicate nothing vnto them as touching the administration of the Common-wealth. These are they which may properly be called the Peeres or Princes of the Realme of China: for they deriue their houses and reuenues vnto their posterity, and so are these royall families continually preserued. But to returne vnto the king himselfe, hee is most chary in obseruing the Chinian lawes and customes, and diligently exerciseth himselfe in learning so much as concernes his estate, sheweth himselfe dayly vnto his chiefe Magistrates, and communeth of matters appertaining to the publique commodity of the Realme. [Sidenote: Twelue chariots.] His palace is of woonderfull largenesse and capacity, out of the which he very seldome takes his progresse; and whensoeuer he doeth so, there are twelue chariots brought foorth, all of them most like one to another both in workemanship and in value, that no man may discerne in which the king himselfe is placed. [Sidenote: The idolatrous religion of the king.] He followeth in religion especially the opinions of the Magistrates, attributing diuine power vnto heauen and earth as vnto the parents of all, and with great solemnity sacrificing vnto them. He hath diuers most sumptuous Temples dedicated vnto his ancestours, whereunto likewise he ascribeth diuine honour, and yet ceaseth hee not to fauour Priests of other sects, yea, hee erecteth Temples vnto their Patrons, endowing them with most rich reuenues; and so often as any vrgent necessity requireth, he enioynes continuall fastings and prayers vnto them: and after this sort he doeth in a maner patronize all the idolatrous sects of his Realme, and shewing himselfe ready to embrace any false religion whatsoeuer, be liueth in sundry and manifolde kindes of superstition. [Sidenote: The ciuill gouernment of China most agreeable to the instinct of nature.] Out of all the former particulars by me alledged, you may easily coniecture that the administration of kingdome of China doeth, for the most parts agree with the instinct of nature, authority being committed, not vnto rude and vnskilfull persons, but vnto such as haue beene conuersant in the vse and exercise of learning, yea, and in promoting learned men vnto magistracies, great consideration is had of their wisedom, justice, and of other virtues esteemed by the Chinian: wherefore the way being open for all men, without any respect of degree or parentage, to obtaine any of the foresayd dignities, it can not be but that this most mighty and famous kingdome must needes enioy exceeding peace and tranquility. LEO. I would nowe (Michael) right gladly vnderstand, what kinde of vrbanity or ciuill demeanour both the common people and the Magistrates doe vse one towardes another: for it is not likely that where such due administration of iustice is, common ciuility, which so well beseemeth all men, should be wanting. [Sidenote: The fiue vertues principally esteemed among the Chinians.] MICHAEL. You haue hit euen the very naile on the head: for among the fiue vertues, which the Chinians principally regard, vrbanity or courtesy is one, the rest are piety, a thankefull remembrance of benefites, true dealing in contracts or bargaines, and wisedome in atchieuing of matters: with the praises and commendations of which vertues the Chinian bookes are full fraught. [Sidenote: Vrbanity.] Now as touching their vrbanity, it is much vnlike vnto ours in Iapan, and vnto that of Europe: howbeit vnder two principall kindes the rule of their vrbanity or courtesie may be comprehended: whereof one is obserued betweene equals, and the other betweene superiours and inferiours. For when men of equall dignity meet together, they stand bending their backes, and bowing their heads downe to the ground, and this they doe either once or twice, or sometimes thrise. Now when the inferiour meets with his superiour, the sayd inferiour, for the most part kneeling lowly on his knees, enclineth his countenance downe to the earth. But how often and when this obeizance is to be performed it is woonderfull what a number of rules and prescriptions are set downe, which to recount would require a long time. [Sidenote: The Chinians great piety towards their parents.] Somewhat also I wil say as touching their piety, and especially of the piety which they vse towards their parents, which verily is so exceeding great, that for the space of three whole yeres together, the sonnes being cladde in mourning vestures doe bewaile the death of their parents, which duety is performed not onely by the common sort, but euen by all the Magistrates themselues, and that most curiously and diligently. And that all men may wholly giue their attendance vnto this businesse, it is prouided by a most inuiolable law among the Chinians, that Magistrates, vpon the death of their parents, must foorthwith renounce their authority, and three whole yeeres, for the performance of their fathers exequies, must betake themselues vnto a priuate kinde of liuing: which also is most duely put in practise by the Senatours of the Kings owne Councell. For albeit a man be right gracious in the eyes of his Prince, yea, and such an one, as vpon whom the administration of the Realme doeth principally depend; yet hauing heard of the death of his parents, that is, of his father or his mother, he hies himselfe immediately home to solemnise their funerals: insomuch that if the king would retaine him still in his office, he should be esteemed by the people, as a transgressour of the lawes and customes of China: which accident (as it is recorded) in ancient times fel out euen so. [Sisdenote: A memorable story.] For whenas a certain king most familiarly vsed a certaine Senatour of his about the managing and expedition of publike affaires, and vnderstanding well how necessary the helpe of his foresayd Senatour was, would gladly, after the death of his father, haue retained him still in his office: yet a certaine other man, being a welwiller vnto the Chinian lawes, could in no case abide it, but checking his Prince with sharpe rebukes, obiected the transgression of the law against him. The king waxing wroth menaced present death vnto the man; but when the party being no wit danted with the terrour of death, persisted still in his sayings, the king changing his determination dismissed the Senatour to mourne for his father, but as for his reprehender be aduanced him vnto an higher dignity. LINUS. I perceiue (Michael) that drawing to an end of these dialogues, and being weary of your long race, you begin to affect breuity: yet let it not seeme troublesome vnto you to speake somewhat of the religion of China, which onely thing seemes to be wanting in this present dialogue. [Sidenote: The religion of China.] MICHAEL. I confesse indeed that I endeuour to be briefe, not so much in regard of wearisomnesse, as for feare least I haue bene ouer tedious vnto you: howbeit I will not faile but accomplish that which I haue vndertaken, and (according to your request) adde somewhat more concerning religion. Whereas therefore the kingdome of China hath hitherto bene destitute of true religion, and now the first beginnings thereof are included in most narrow bounds, that nation being otherwise a people most ingenious, and of an extraordinory and high capacity, hath alwayes liued in great errours and ignorance of the trueth, being distracted into sundry opinions, and following manifolde sects. [Sidenote: Three principall sectes among the Chinians.] And among these sects there are three more famous then the rest: [Sidenote: Confucius authour of the first sect.] the first is of them that professe the doctrine of one Confucius a notable philosopher. This man (as it is reported in the history of his life) was one of most vpright and incorrupt maners, whereof he wrote sundry treatises very pithily and largely, which aboue all other books, are seriously read and perused by the Chinians. The same doctrine do all Magistrates embrace, and others also that giue their mindes to the study of letters, a great part whereof Confucius is sayd to haue inuented: and he is had in so great honour, that all his followers and clients, vpon the dayes of the new and full Moone, doe assemble themselues at the common Schoole, which I haue aboue mentioned, and before his image, which is worshipped with burning of incense and with tapers, they doe thrise bend their knees, and bow their heads downe to the ground; which not onely the common scholars, but the chiefe Magistrates do performe. [The summe of Confucius his doctrine.] The summe of the foresayd doctrine is, that men should follow the light of nature as their guide, and that they should diligently endeuour to attaine vnto the vertues by me before mentioned: and lastly, that they should employ their labour about the orderly gouernment of their families and of the Common-wealth. All these things are in very deed praise-worthy, if Confucius had made any mention of almighty God and of the life to come, and had not ascribed so much vnto the heauens, and vnto fatall necessity, nor yet had so curiously intreated of worshipping the images of their forefathers. In which regard he can very hardly or not at all be excused from the crime of idolatry: notwithstanding it is to be granted, that none other doctrine among the Chinians approacheth so neere vnto the trueth as this doeth. [Sidenote: Xequiam author of the second sect, whose followers are called Cen or Bonzi.] The second sect is of them which followethe the instructions of Xaquam, or as the Chinians call him Xequiam, whose opinions, because they are well knowen amongst vs, it were bootlesse for me to repeat; especially sithens, in the Catechisme composed by our graue visitour, they are notably refuted. This doctrine doe all they embrace, which are in China called Cen, but with vs at Iapon are named Bonzi. [Sidenote: Note.] For this I doe briefly and by the way giue you to vnderstand, that all words of the Chinians language are of one sillable onely, so that if there be any word that consisteth of more sillables then one, it consisteth also of more wordes then one. These sectaries called Cen doe shaue their beards and their heads, and doe for the most part, together with diuers of their associates, inhabit the Temples of Xaquam, or of others which in regard of the same profession haue in their Kalenders beene canonized for Saints, and doe rehearse certaine prayers after their maner, either vpon books or beads, vsing other ceremonies after the maner of our Bonzi. These men haue some inckling of the life to come, and of the rewardes of good men, and the punishments of the wicked: howbeit all their assertions are fraught with errours. [Sidenote: The third sect.] The third sect is of them which are called Tauzu: and those doe imitate a certaine other man, to be adored, as they thinke, for his holinesse. These also are Priests after their kinde, howbeit they let their haire grow, and doe in other obseruations differ from the former. Now, because the sect of Confucius is the most famous of all the three, and the two other sects called Cen and Tauzu are not much adicted vnto learning, their religion preuailing onely among the common sort, the Priests of both the sayd sects doe leade a most base and seruile life amongst the Chinians, insomuch that they kneele downe before the Magistrates, and are not permitted to sit beside them, sometimes, if the Magistrate please, are abased vnto the punishment of the bastonado: whereas in our Iles of Iapon it is farre otherwise, Priests, euen of false religion, being had in so great honour among vs. [Sidenote: The superstition of the Saracens.] LEO. I heard also (Michael) that the Saracens superstition takes place in China: now, whether it doth or no, you can resolue vs. MICHAEL. That forren superstition was brought into China what time the Tartars inuaded the kingdome, and vsurped the gouernment thereof. All the Saracens therefore in China are originally descended of the Tartars, who, because they were an infinite number, could not vtterly be expelled and rooted out of the kingdome, but remaining still there, haue propagated their posterity, though not their religion. These therefore are souldiers for the greater part of them, and sometimes doe obtaine martiall dignities: and except a few ceremonies of their superstition which is nowe become stale and almost worne out, they doe liue, altogether after the Chinians fashion, their predecessours being brought into the same kingdome about foure hundred yeeres agoe. [Sidenote: Christian religion planted in China.] LINUS. Now (Michael) let vs heare you say somewhat of the Christian religion, which as we hope hath set most happy footing in that kingdome. MICHAEL. I could say much concerning those most wished and acceptable beginnings were they not already published in Iapon by the letters of the fathers: howbeit I will make a briefe rehearsall of all things, that I may not seem altogether to haue abandoned this labour. You know that from the time wherein the fathers of the society arriued in our Ilands, to the end they might augment Christian religion, they were in like sort most carefull how they might insinuate themselues into the innermost parts of the kingdome of China. In the middst of this endeauour and trauell Francis Xauier, a most deuout man of the foresayd society, departed out of this present life at the Ile of Sancian (which some call Sangiam) leauing an example vnto the rest of his associates, how they should likewise doe their best to plant the religion of Christ in that nation. [Sidenote: An ancient custome worthy the obseruation.] This man was seconded by others, who vsed all meanes, and left no practise vnattempted, that they might bring these good beginnings vnto a prosperours issue: howbeit they were greatly hindered by reason of an ancient custome in China, in regard whereof they doe not without great difficulty and circumspection admit any strangers into their dominions, except those which hauing a long time executed the office of ambassadours doe ordinarily euery third yeere present themselues before the king: in the admission of whom likewise there is maruellous care vsed, that they may not easily espie and become acquainted with the affaires of the Realme. [Sidenote: The Chinians contemne other nations.] Hereunto may be added, that the Chinians are great contemners of other nations, and most constant obseruers of their owne lawes and customes: in all which respects it came to passe that there was wonderfull labour and diligence employed aboue thirty yeeres together, onely to get an entrance, vntill in the yeere one thousand fiue hundred fourescore and three, two fathers of the foresayd society, that had pretty skill in the letters and language of China, vtterly despairing of mans helpe, and depending vpon the prouidence of almighty God, obtained licence of the Tutan or Vice-roy to build them an house and a Church in the City of Xauquin, which by reason of the commodiousnesse thereof is the seat of the Viceroy himselue. This worke being begunne, the sayd fathers of the society, for the nouelty therof, were a few yeeres right well entreated by the Magistrates: inasmuch that two others out of India had free and easie accesse vnto them, one couple remaining still in their foresayd house at Xauquin, and the other two taking their iourney for the inner prouinces, to conuert more people vnto the faith: who notwithstanding afterward, other Magistrates not approouing of their attempts, were constrained to retire. Nowe all the time wherein the foresayd fathers abode at Xauquin (being more then fiue yeeres) certaine of the common people were restrained from false superstition to Christian religion, and seuenty persons were baptised. But the enemy of mankinde, who omitteth none opportunity for the hinderance of Christian religion, suggested into the mindes of the Chinians (being, as I sayd, of their owne nature, a people estranged from the traffique and acquaintance of other nations, and always being too suspicious of strangers) that they should exhibit letters of supplication vnto the Caien and the Tutan their principall Magistrates, to haue the fathers expelled out of Xauquin: which Magistrates repairing vnto their foresayed house and Church entered consultation how they might bannish them out of the sayd City of Xauquin: in which thing verily they vsed great moderation, not any way offending or exasperating the mindes of the fathers, but onely signifying that they had regard vnto the estate of their Common-wealth. For the Tutan or Vice-roy calling the fathers vnto him, and (to let passe other accidents) vsing courteous and familiar conference with them, declared by many arguments, that their habitation in the City of Xauquin was not conuenient, especially sithens so many Magistrates resorted vnto that City, who would take great offence at the presence of strangers. For the which cause he perswaded them to accept some part of the money which they had bestowed in the building of their house, and so to returne either home into their own countrey, or vnto the port of Macao. Howbeit, such was the instant supplication of the fathers, and so woorthy of compassion, that the Tutan or Vice-roy, in the extreame and mediterrane borders of the prouince of Coantum, assigned vnto them a new habitation at the city called Xaucheo, commending them also to a certaine Magistrate, who was come from the same place to salute him. Thither therefore the sayd others, not without great sorrow and griefe of the Christians, hied themselues, and as we are informed by their last letters, they haue euen now layed the foundation of their first building, and haue also written that they are like to liue much more peaceably and conueniently for the propagating of Christian religion. These be the first beginnings of Christianity in China, where, euen as in other places of the Christian Common-wealth, the seed is to be sowen with great labour and teares, that acceptable fruits may be reaped with gladnesse. LEO. It is euen as you haue sayd (Michael) and nowe for this your pleasant and eloquent discourse we do acknowledge our selues much bounden vnto you.

* * * * *

A Letter written from Goa, the principall City of all the East Indies, by one Thomas Steuens an English man, and sent to his father, M. Thomas Steuens: Anno 1579.

After most humble commendations: These shall be to crave your dayly blessing, with like commendations vnto my mother; and withall, to certifie you of my being: according to your will and my duety. I wrote vnto you taking my iourney from Italy to Portugall, which letters I thinke are come to your hands, so that presuming therupon, I thinke I haue the lesse need at this time to tell you the cause of my departing, which nevertheless in one word I may conclude, if I do but name obedience. I came to Lisbon toward the end of March, eight dayes before the departure of the shippes, so late that if they had not bene stayed about some weighty matters, they had bene long gone before our comming: insomuch that there were others ordained to goe in our places, that the kings prouision and ours also might not be in vaine. Neuerthelesse our sudden comming tooke place, and the fourth of Aprill fiue ships departed for Goa, wherein besides shipmen and souldiers, there were a great number of children which in the seas beare out better than men, and no maruell, when that many women also passe very well. The setting foorth from the port I need not to tell how solemne it is with trumpets, and shooting of ordinance, you may easily imagine it, considering that they go in the maner of warre. The tenth of the foresayd moneth we came to the sight of Porto Santo neere vnto Madera, where an English shippe set vpon ours (which was then also alone) with a few shots, which did no harme, but after that our ship had layed out her greatest ordinance, they straight departed as they came. The English shippe was very faire and great, which I was sorry to see so ill occupied, for she went rouing about, so that we saw her againe at the Canarian Iles, vnto the which we came the thirteenth of the sayd moneth, and good leisure we had to woonder at the high mountaine of the Iland Tenerif, for we wandred betweene that and great Canaria foure dayes by reason of contrary windes: and briefly, such euill weather we had vntill the foureteenth of May, that they despaired, to compasse the Cape of Good hope that yeere. Neuertheless, taking our voyage betweene Guinea and the Ilands of Capo Verde, without seeing of any land at all, we arriued at length vnto the coast of Guinie, which the Portugals so call, chiefly that part of the burning Zone, which is from the sixt degree vnto the Equinoctiall, in which parts they suffered so many inconueniences of heats, and lacke of windes, that they thinke themselues happy when they haue passed it: for sometimes the ship standeth there almost by the space of many dayes, sometimes she goeth, but in such order that it were almost as good to stand still. And the greatest part of this coast not cleare, but thicke and cloudy, full of thunder and lightening, and raine so vnholesome, that if the water stand a little while, all is full of wormes, and falling on the meat which is hanged vp, it maketh it straight full of wormes. Along all that coast we often times saw a thing swimming vpon the water like a cocks combe (which they call a ship of Guinea) but the colour much fairer; which combe standeth vpon a thing almost like the swimmer of a fish in colour and bignesse, and beareth vnderneath in the water, strings which saue it from turning ouer. This thing is so poisonous, that a man cannot touch it without great perill. In this coast, that is to say, from the sixt degree vnto the Equinoctiall, we spent no lesse than thirty dayes, partly with contrary windes, partly with calme. The thirtieth of May we passed the Equinoctiall with contentation, directing our course as well as we could to passe the promontory, but in all that gulfe, and in all the way beside, we found so often calmes, that the expertest mariner wondred at it. And in places where there are always woont to be most horrible tempests, we found most quiet calmes which was very troublesome to those ships which be the greatest of all other, and cannot go without good windes. Insomuch, that when it is tempest almost intollerable for other ships, and maketh them maine all their sailes, these hoise vp, and saile excellent well, vnlesse the waters be too furious, which seldome happened in our nauigation. You shall vnderstand, that being passed the line, they cannot straightway go the next way to the promontory: but according to the winde, they draw always as neere South as they can to put themselues in the latitude of the point, which is 35 degrees and an halfe, and then they take their course towards the East, and so compass the point. But the winde serued vs so, that at 33 degrees we did direct our course toward the point or promontory of Good hope.

You know that it is hard to saile from East to West, or contrary, because there is no fixed point in all the skie, whereby they may direct their course, wherefore I shall tell you what helps God prouided for these men. There is not a fowle that appereth, or signe in the aire, or in the sea, which they haue not written, which haue made the voyages heretofore. [Sidenote: The variation of the compasse.] Wherfore, partly by their owne experience, and pondering withall what space the ship was able to make with such a winde, and such direction, and partly by the experience of others, whose books and nauigations they haue, they gesse whereabouts they be, touching degrees of longitude, for of latitude they be alwayes sure: but the greatest and best industry of all is to marke the variation of the needle or compasse, which in the Meridian of the Iland of S. Michael, which is one of the Azores in the latitude of Lisbon, is iust North, and thence swarueth towards the East so much, that betwixt the Meridian aforesayd, and the point of Africa it carrieth three or foure quarters of 32. And againe in the point of Afrike, a little beyond the point that is called Cape das Agulias (in English the needles) it returneth againe vnto the North, and that place passed, it swarueth againe toward the West, as it did before proportionally. [Sidenote: Signes about the Cape of Bona Speransa.] As touching our first signes, the neerer we came to the people of Afrike, the more strange kindes of fowles appeared, insomuch that when we came within no lesse then thirty leagues (almost an hundred miles) and six hundred miles as we thought from any Iland, as good as three thousand fowles of sundry kindes followed our ship: some of them so great that their wings being opened from one point to the other, contained seuen spannes, as the Mariners sayd. A maruellous thing to see how God prouided, so that in so wide a sea these fowles are all fat, and nothing wanteth them. The Portugals haue named them all according to some propriety which they haue: some they call Rushtailes, because their tailes be not proportionable to their bodies, but long and small like a rush, some forked tailes because they be very broad and forked, some Veluet sleeues, because they haue wings of the colour of veluet, and bowe them as a man boweth his elbow. This bird is always welcome, for he appeareth neerest the Cape. I should neuer make an end if I should tell all particulars: but it shall suffice briefly to touch a few, which yet shall be sufficient, if you marke them, to giue occasion to glorifie almighty God in his wonderfull works, and such variety in his creatures. [Sidenote: Fishes on sea coast of Africa.] And to speake somewhat of fishes in all places of calme, especially in the burning Zone, neere the line (for without we neuer saw any) there waited on our ship fishes as long as a man, which they call Tuberones, they come to eat such things as from the shippe fall into the sea, not refusing men themselues if they light vpon them. And if they finde any meat tied in the sea, they take it for theirs. These haue waiting on them six or seuen small fishes (which neuer depart) with gardes blew and greene round about their bodies, like comely seruing men: and they go two or three before him, and some on euery side. Moreouer, they haue other fishes which cleaue alwayes vnto their body, and seeme to take such superfluities as grow about them, and they are sayd to enter into their bodies also to purge them if they need. The Mariners in time past haue eaten of them, but since they haue seene them eate men their stomacks abhorre them. Neuerthelesse, they draw them vp with great hooks, and kill of them as many as they can, thinking that they haue made a great reuenge. There is another kind of fish as bigge almost as a herring, which hath wings and flieth, and they are together in great number. These haue two enemies, the one in the sea, the other in the aire. In the sea the fish which is called Albocore, as big as a Salmon, followeth them with great swiftnesse to take them. This poore fish not being able to swim fast, for he hath no finnes, but swimmeth with moouing of his taile, shutting his wings, lifteth himselue aboue the water, and flieth not very hie: the Albocore seeing that, although he haue no wings, yet he giueth a great leape out of the water, and sometimes catcheth him, or els he keepeth himselfe vnder the water going that way on as fast as he flieth. And when the fish being weary of the aire, or thinking himselue out of danger, returneth into the water, the Albocore meeteth with him: but sometimes his other enemy the sea-crow, catcheth him before he falleth. [Sidenote: Note.] With these and like sights, but alwayes making our supplications to God for good weather and saluation of the ship, we came at length vnto the point, so famous and feared of all men: but we found there no tempest, only great waues, where our Pilot was a little ouerseene: for whereas commonly al other neuer come within sight of land, but seeing signes ordinary, and finding bottome, go their way sure and safe, he thinking himselfe to haue wind at will, shot so nigh the land that the winde turning into the South, and the waues being exceeding great, rolled vs so neere the land, that the ship stood in lesse then 14 fadoms of water, no more then six miles from the Cape, which is called Das Agulias, and there we stood as vtterly cast away: for vnder vs were rocks of maine stone so sharpe, and cutting, that no ancre could hold the ship, the shore so euill, that nothing could take land, and the land itselfe so full of Tigers, and people that are sauage, and killers of all strangers, that we had no hope of life nor comfort, but onely in God and a good conscience. Notwithstanding, after we had lost ancres, hoising vp the sailes for to get the ship a coast in some safer place, or when it should please God, it pleased his mercy suddenly, where no man looked for helpe, to fill our sailes with wind from the land, and so we escaped, thanks be to God. And the day following, being in the place where they are alwayes wont to catch fish, we also fell a fishing, and so many they tooke, that they serued all the ship for that day, and part of the next. [Sidenote: Corall.] And one of them pulled vp a corall of great bignesse and price. For there they say (as we saw by experience) that the corals doe grow in the maner of stalks vpon the rocks in the bottome, and waxe hard and red. The day of perill was the nine and twentieth of Iuly. [Sidenote: Two wayes beyond the cape of Good hope.] And you shall vnderstand that, the Cape passed, there be two wayes to India: one within the Ile of S. Lawrence, which they take willingly, because they refresh themselues at Mosambique a fortnight or a moneth, not without great need, and thence in a moneth more land in Goa. The other is without the Ile of S. Lawrence, which they take when they set foorth so late, and come so late to the point, that they have no time to take the foresayd Mosambique, and then they goe heauily, because in this way they take no port. And by reason of the long nauigation, and want of food and water, they fall into sundry diseases, their gummes waxe great, and swell, and they are faine to cut them away, their legges swell and all the body becommeth sore, and so benummed, that they cannot stirre hand nor foot, and so they die for weaknesse, others fall into fluxes and agues, and die thereby. And this way it was our chance to make: yet though we had more then one hundred and fifty sicke, there died not past seuen and twentie; which losse they esteemed not much in respect of other times. Though some of ours were diseased in this sort, yet, thanks be to God, I had my health, contrary to the expectation of many: God send me my health so well in the land, if it may be to his honour and seruice. This way is full of priuy rocks and quicke-sands, so that sometimes we durst not saile by night, but by the prouidence of God we saw nothing, nor neuer found bottom vntill we came to the coast of India. When we had passed againe the line, and were come to the third degree or somewhat more, we saw crabs swimming on the water that were red as though they had bene sodden: but this was no signe of land. After about the eleuenth degree, the space of many days, more than ten thousand fishes by estimation followed round about our ship, whereof we caught so many, that for fifteene days we did eate nothing els, and they serued our turne very well: for at this time we had neither meate nor almost any thing els to eate, our nauigation growing so long that it drew neere to seuen moneths, where as commonly they goe it in fiue, I mean when they saile the inner way. [Sidenote: They commonly sail from Lisbon to Goa in 5 moneths.] But these fishes were not signe of land, but rather of deepe sea. At length we tooke a couple of Birds which were a kinde of Hawks, whereof they ioyed much, thinking that they had bene of India, but indeed they were of Arabia, as we found afterward. And we that thought we had bene neere India, were in the same latitude neere

Zocotoro, an Ile in the mouth of the Red sea. [Sidenote: Running seas very dangerous.] But there God sent vs great winds from the Northeast or Northnortheast, wherevpon vnwillingly they bare vp towards the East, and thus we went tenne dayes without seeing signe of land, whereby they perceived their errour: for they had directed their course before always Northeast, coueting to multiply degrees of latitude, but partly the difference of the Needle, and most of all the running seas, which at that time ran Northwest, had drawen vs to this other danger, had not God sent vs this winde, which at length waxed larger, and restored vs to our right course. These running seas be so perillous that they deceiue the most part of the gouernours, and some be so little curious, contenting themselues with ordinary experience, that they care not to seeke out any meanes to know when they swarue, neither by the compasse, nor by any other triall. [Sidenote: Certaine signs of land.] The first signe of land were certaine fowles which they knew to be of India: the second, boughes of palmes and sedges: the third, snakes swimming on the water, and a substance which they call by the name of a coine of money, as broad and as round as a groat, wonderfully printed and stamped of nature, like vnto some coine. And these two last signes be so certaine, that the next day after, if the winde serue, they see lande, which we did to our great joy, when all our water (for you know they make no beere in those parts) and victuals began to faile vs. [Sidenote: They arriued at Goa the 24 of October.] And to Goa we came the foure and twentieth day of October, there being receiued with passing great charity. The people be tawny, but not disfigured in their lips and noses, as the Moores and Cafres of Ethiopia. They that be not of reputation, or at least the most part, goe naked, sauing an apron of a span long, and as much in breadth before them, and a lace two fingers broad before them, girded about with a string and no more: and thus they thinke them as well as we with all our trimming. Of the fruits and trees that be here I cannot now speake, for I should make another letter as long as this. For hitherto I haue not seene a tree here whose like I haue seene in Europe, the vine excepted, which neuerthelesse here is to no purpose, so that all the wines are brought out of Portugall. The drinke of this countrey is good water, or wine of the Palme tree, or of a fruit called Cocos. And this shall suffice for this time. If God send me my health, I shall haue opportunity to write to you once againe. Now the length of my letter compelleth me to take my leaue, and thus I wish your most prosperous health. From Goa the tenth of Nouember, 1579.

Your louing sonne Thomas Steuens.

* * * * *

A briefe relation of the great magnificence and rich traffike of the kingdome of Pegu beyond the East India, written by Frey Peter of Lisbon, to his cousin Frey Diego of Lisbon, from Cochin.

[Sidenote: The coast of India greatly troubled with Moores.] I receiued your letters in the harbour of Damaon by a carauell of aduise that came from Malacca, which brought shot, powder, and other prouision for the furnishing of foure gallies and a great Gallion, which are now in building, to keepe our coast for feare of great store of men of warre, being Moores, which trouble vs very sore. At that instant when I receiued your letters I was newly come from the kingdome of Pegu, where I had remained one yeere and an halfe, and from thence I departed to the city of Cochin in October 1587. The newes which I can certifie you of concerning these countreys are: that this king of Pegu is the mightiest king of men, and the richest that is in these parts of the world: for he bringeth into the field at any time, when he hath warres with other princes, aboue a million of fightingmen: howbeit they be very leane and small people, and are brought vnto the field without good order. [Sidenote: Abundance of golde, siluer, pearles, and precious stones in Pegu.] He is lord of the Elephants, and of all the golde and siluer mines, and of all the pearles and precious stones: so that he hath the greatest store of treasure that euer was heard of in these parts. The countrey people call him the God of trueth and of iustice. I had great conference with this king, and with the head captaine of the Portugals, which is one of the countrey. They demanded of me many questions as touching the law and faith of Iesus Christ, and as touching the Ten Commandements. And the king gaue his consent that our Order should build a Church in his countrey, which was halfe builded; but our peruerse and malicious Portugals plucked it downe againe: [Sidenote: The great gaine of the Portugals in Pegu.] for whereas it is a countrey wherein our nation gaine very much by their commodities, they fearing that by the building of this Church there would be greater resort thither, and so their trade should be impaired if their great gaines should be knowen vnto others then those which found this countrey out first, therefore they were so vnwilling that the building of this church should goe forward. Our Portugals which are here in this realme are woorse people then the Gentiles. I preached diuers times among those heathen people; but being obstinate they say, that as their father beleeued so they will beleeue: for if their forefathers went to the diuell so they will. Whereupon I returned backe againe to our monastery to certifie our Father prouinciall of the estate of this new found countrey. It is the best and richest countrey in all this East India: and it is thought to be richer then China.

[Sidenote: Pegu the best and richest countrey in all the East Indies.] I am afrayd that the warres which his Maiestie hath with England will be the vtter vndoing and spoile of Spaine: for these countreys likewise are almost spoiled with ciull warres, which the Moores haue against the Gentiles: for the kings here are vp in armes all the countrey ouer. Here is an Indian which is counted a prophet, which hath prophesied that there will a Dragon arise in a strange countrey, which will do great hurt to Spaine. How it will fall out onely God doth know. And thus I rest: from this monastery of Cochin the 28 of December, 1589. [Sidenote: A prophesie of an Indian against Spaine.]

Your good cousin and assured friend

frier Peter of Lisbon.

* * * * *

A voyage with three tall ships, the Penelope Admirall, the Marchant royall Viceadmirall, and the Edward Bonaduenture Rereadmirall, to the East Indies, by the Cape of Buona Speransa, to Quitangone neere Mosambique, to the Iles of Comoro and Zanzibar on the backeside of Africa, and beyond Cape Comori in India, to the Iles of Nicubar and of Gomes Polo, within two leagues of Sumatra, to the Ilands of Pulo Pinaom, and thence to the maine land of Malacca, begunne by M. George Raymond, in the yeere 1591, and performed by M. Iames Lancaster, and written from the mouth of Edmund Barker of Ipswich, his lieutenant in the sayd voyage, by M. Richard Hakluyt.

Our fleet of the three tall ships abouenamed departed from Plimmouth the 10 of April 1591, and arrived at the Canarie-ilands the 25 of the same, from whence we departed the 29 of April. The second of May we were in the height of Cape Blanco. The fift we passed the tropique of Cancer. The eight we were in the height of Cape Verde. All this time we went with a faire winde at Northeast, alwayes before the winde vntil the 13 of the same moneth, when we came within 8 degrees of the Equinoctiall line, where we met with a contrary winde. Here we lay off and on in the sea vntil the 6 of Iune, on which day we passed the sayd line. While we lay thus off and on, we tooke a Portugal Carauel laden by merchants of Lisbon for Brasile, in which Carauel we had some 60 tunnes of wine, 1200 iarres of oyle, about 100 iarres of oliues, certaine barrels of capers, three fats of peason, with diuers other necessaries fit for our voyage; which wine, oyle, oliues and capers were better to vs then gold. [Sidenote: Three occasions of sicknes neere the line.] We had two men died before wee passed the line, and diuers sicke, which took their sicknesse in those hote climates: for they be wonderfull vnwholesome from 8 degrees of Northerly latitude vnto the line, at that time of the yeere: for we had nothing but Ternados, with such thunder, lightning, and raine, that we could not keep our men drie 3 houres together, which was an occasion of the infection among them, and their eating of salt victuals, with lacke of clothes to shift them. After we passed the line, we had the wind still at Eastsoutheast, which carried vs along the coast of Brasil 100 leagues from the maine, til we came in 26 degrees to the Southward of the line, where the wind came vp to the North, at which time we did account, that the Cape of Buona esperansa did beare off vs East and by South, betwixt 900 and 1000 leagues. Passing this gulfe from the coast of Brasil vnto the Cape we had the wind often variable as it is vpon our coast, but for the most part so, that we might lie our course. The 28 of Iuly we had sight of the foresayd Cape of Buona esperansa: vntill the 31 we lay off and on with the wind contrary to double the Cape, hoping to double it, and so to haue gone seuentie leagues further to a place called Agoada de S. Bras, before we would haue sought to haue put into any harbour. But our men being weake and sicke in all our shippes, we thought good to seeke some place to refresh them. With which consent we bare vp with the land to the Northward of the Cape, and going along the shoare, we espied a goodly Baie with an Iland lying to Seawards of it into which we did beare, and found it very commodious for our ships to ride in. [Sidenote: Agoada de Saldanha.] This Baie is called Agoada de Saldanha, lying 15 leagues Northward on the hither side of the Cape. The first of August being Sunday we came to an anker in the Baie, sending our men on land, and there came vnto them certaine blacke Saluages very brutish which would not stay, but retired from them. For the space of 15 or 20 dayes we could finde no reliefe but onely foules which wee killed with our pieces, which were cranes and geese: there was no fish but muskles and other shel-fish, which we gathered on the rockes. [Sidenote: Great store of Penguins and Seales.] After 15 or 20 dayes being here, our Admirall went with his pinnasse vnto the Iland which lieth off this Baie, where hee found great store of Penguines and Seales, whereof he brought good plenty with him. And twise after that we sent certain of our men, which at both times brought their bots lading vnto our ships. After we had bene here some time, we got here a Negro, whom we compelled to march into the countrey with vs, making signs to bring vs some cattel; but at this time we could come to the sight of none, so we let the Negro goe with some trifles. [Sidenote: Bullocks, oxen, and sheepe, dog-cheape.] Within 8 dayes after, he with 30 or 40 other Negroes, bought vs downe some 40 bullocks and oxen, with as many sheepe: at which time we brought but few of them. But within 8 dayes after they came downe with as many more, and then we bought some 24 oxen with as many sheepe. We bought an oxe for two kniues, a stirke for a knife, and a sheepe for a knife, and some we bought for lesse value then a knife. The oxen be very large and well fleshed, but not fat. The sheepe are very big and very good meat, they haue no woll on their backs but haire, and haue great tailes like the sheepe in Syria. There be diuers sorts of wild beests, as the Antilope, (whereof M. Lancaster killed one of the bignes of a yong colt) the red and fallow Deere, with other great beasts vnknowen vnto vs. Here are also great store of ouer-growen monkies. As touching our proceeding vpon our voyage, it was thought good rather to proceed with two ships wel manned, then with three euill manned: for here wee had of sound and whole men but 198, of which there went in the Penelope with the Admiral 101, and in the Edward with the worshipfull M. captaine Lancaster 97. We left behind 50 men with the Roiall marchant, whereof there were many pretily well recouered, of which ship was master and gouernour Abraham Kendal, which for many reasons we thought good to send home. The disease that hath consumed our men hath bene the skuruie. Our souldiers which haue not bene vsed to the Sea, haue best held out, but our mariners dropt away, which (in my iudgement) proceedeth of their euill diet at home.

[Sidenote: Cape de Buona Speransa doubled. Cape dos Corrientes.] Six dayes after our sending backe for England of the Marchant Roiall from Agoada de Saldanha, our Admirall M. captaine Raimond in the Penelope, and M. Iames Lancaster in the Edward Bonaduenture, set forward to double the Cape of Buona esperansa, which they did very speedily. [Sidenote: Here they are seuered from the Penelope.] But being passed as far as Cape dos Corrientes the 14 of September we were encountred with a mighty storme and extreme gusts of wind, wherein we lost our Generals companie, and could neuer heare of him nor his ship any more, though we did our best endeuour to seeke him vp and downe a long while, and staied for him certaine dayes at the Iland of Comoro, where we appointed to stay one for another. [Sidenote: Foure men slaine with a clap of thunder.] Foure days after this uncomfortable seperation in the morning toward ten of the clocke we had a terrible clap of thunder, which slew foure of our men ovtright, the necks being wrung in sonder without speaking any word, and of 94 men there was not one vntouched, whereof some were striken blind, others were bruised in their legs and armes, and others in their brests, so that they voided blood two days after, others were drawen out at length as though they had been racked. But (God be thanked) they all recouered sauing onely the foure which were slain out right. Also with the same thunder our maine maste was torn very grieuously from the head to the decke, and some of the spikes that were ten inches into the timber, were melted with the extreme heate thereof. [Sidenote: The Shoulds of S. Laurence.] From thence we shaped our course to the Northeast, and not long after we fell vpon the Northwest end of the mighty Iland of S. Laurence: which one of our men espied by Gods good blessing late in the euening by Moone light, who seeing afarre off the breaking of the Sea, and calling to certaine of his fellowes, asked them what it was: which eft soones told him that it was the breaking of the Sea vpon the Shoulds. Whereupon in very good time we cast about to auoyd the danger which we were like to haue incurred. [Sidenote: Quitangone neere Mozambique.] Thus passing on forward, it was our lucke to ouer-shoote Mozambique, and to fall with a place called Quitangone two leagues to the Northward of it, and we tooke three or foure Barkes of Moores, which Barkes in their language they call Pangaias, laden with Millio, hennes and ducks, with one Portugall boy, going for the prouision of Mozambique. [Sidenote: The Ile of Comoro.] Within few dayes following we came to an Iland an hundred leagues to, the Northeast of Mozambique called Comoro, which we found exceedingly full of people, which are Moores of tawnie colour and good stature, but they be very trecherous and diligently to be taken heed of. Here wee desired to store our selues with water, whereof we stood in great need, and sent sixteene of our men well armed on in our boate: whom the people suffred quietly to land and water, and diuers of them with their king came aboord our ship in a gowne of crimosine Sattin pinked after the Moorish fashion downe to the knee, whom we entertained in the best maner, and had some conference with him of the state of the place and marchandises, vsing our Portugall boy which we had taken before for our interpreter, and in the end licensed the king and his company to depart, and sent our men againe for more water, who then also dispatched their businesse and returned quietly: the third time likewise we sent them for more, which also returned without any harme. [Sidenote: 32 of our men betraid at the Ile of Comoro.] And though we thought our selues furnished, yet our master William Mace of Radcliffe pretending that it might be long before we might finde any good watering place, would needes goe himselfe on shore with thirtie men, much against the will of our captaine, and hee and 16 of his company, together with one boat which was all that we had, and 16 others that were a washing ouer against our ship, were betrayed of the perfidious Moores, and in our sight for the most part slaine, we being not able for want of a boat to yeeld them any succour. [Sidenote: Zanzibar Iland.] From thence with heauie hearts we shaped our course for Zanzibar the 7 of Nouember, where shortly after we arriued and made vs a new boat of such boards as we had within boord, and rid in the road vntill the 15 of February, where, during our aboad, we sawe diuers Pangaias or boates, which are pinned with wooden pinnes, and sowed together with Palmito cordes, and calked with the husks of Cocos shels beaten, whereof they made Occam. [Sidenote: A Portugall Factorie in Zanzibar.] At length a Portugal Pangaia comming out of the harborow of Zanzibar, where they haue a small Factorie, sent a Canoa with a Moore which had bene christened, who brought vs a letter wherein they desired to know what wee were, and what we sought. We sent them word we were Englishmen come from Don Antonio vpon businesse to his friends in the Indies: with which answere they returned, and would not any more come at vs. Whereupon not long after wee manned out our boat and tooke a Pangaia of the Moores, which had a priest of theirs in it, which in their language they call a Sherife: whom we vsed very courteously: which the king tooke in very good part, hauing his priests in great estimation, and for his deliuerance furnished vs with two moneths victuals, during all which time we detained him with vs. These Moores informed vs of the false and spitefull dealing of the Portugals towards vs, [Marginal note: The treason of the Portugals towards the English.] which made them beleeue that we were cruell people and men-eaters, and willed them if they loued their safetie in no case to come neere vs. Which they did onely to cut us off from all knowledge of the state and traffique of the countrey. While we road from the end of Nouember vntil the middle of February in this harborough, which is sufficient for a ship of 500 tuns to ride in, we set vpon a Portugall Pangaia with our boat, but because it was very litle, and our men not able to stirre in it, we were not able to take the sayd Pangaia which was armed with 10 good shot like our long fouling pieces. [Sidenote: An excellent place for refreshing.] This place for the goodnesse of the harborough and watering, and plentifull refreshing with fish, whereof we tooke great store with our nets, and for sundry sorts of fruits of the countrey, as Cocos and others, which were brought vs by the Moores as also for oxen and hennes, is carefully to be sought for by such of our ships, as shall hereafter passe that way. [Sidenote: A gallie Frigate.] But our men had need to take good heed of the Portugals: for while we lay here the Portugall Admiral of the coast from Melinde to Mozambique, came to view and betray our boat if he could haue taken at any time aduantage, in a gallie Frigate of ten tunnes with 8 or 9 oares on a side. Of the strength of which Frigate and their trecherous meaning we were aduertised by an Arabian Moore which came from the king of Zanzibar diuers times vnto vs about the deliuerie of the priest aforesayd, and afterward by another which we caried thence along with vs: for whersoeuer we came, our care was to get into our hands some one or two of the countreys to learne the languages and states of those partes where we touched. [Sidenote: Another thunder-clap.] Moreouer, here againe we had another clap of thunder which did shake our foremast very much, which wee fisht and repaired with timber from the shore, whereof there is good store thereabout of a kind of tree some fortie foot high, which is a red and tough wood, and as I suppose, a kind of Cedar. [Sidenote: Heat in the head deadly. Letting of blood very necessary.] Here our Surgeon Arnold negligently catching a great heate in his head being on land with the master to seeke oxen, fell sicke and shortly died, which might haue bene cured by letting of blood before it had bin settled. Before our departure we had in this place some thousand weight of pitch, or rather a kind of gray and white gumme like vnto frankincense, as clammie as turpentine, which in melting groweth as blacke as pitch, and is very brittle of it selfe, but we mingled it with oile, whereof wee had 300 iarres in the prize which we tooke to the Northward of the Equinoctiall, not farre from Guinie, bound for Brasil. Sixe days before wee departed hence, the Cape marchant of the Factorie wrote a letter vnto our capitaine in the way of friendship, as he pretended, requesting a iarre of wine and a iarre of oyle, and two or three pounds of gunpowder, which letter hee sent by a Negro his man, and Moore in a Canoa: we sent him his demaunds by the Moore, but tooke the Negro along with vs because we vnderstood he had bene in the East Indies and knew somewhat of the Countrey. [Sidenote: A Iunco laden with pepper and drugs.] By this Negro we were aduertised of a small Barke of some thirtie tunnes (which the Moores call a Iunco) which was come from Goa thither laden with Pepper for the Factorie and seruice of that kingdome. Thus hauing trimmed our shippe as we lay in this road, in the end we set forward for the coast of the East Indie, the 15 of February aforesayd, intending if we could to haue reached to Cape Comori, which is the headland or Promontorie of the maine of Malauar, and there to haue lien off and on for such ships as should haue passed from Zeilan, Sant Tome, Bengala, Pegu, Malacca, the Moluccos, the coast of China, and the Ile of Japan, which ships are of exceeding wealth and riches. [Sidenote: The currents set to the North-west.] But in our course we were very much deceiued by the currents that set into the gulfe of the Red sea along the coast of Melinde. [Sidenote: Zocotora.] And the windes shortening vpon vs to the Northeast and Easterly, kept vs that we could not get off, and so with the putting in of the currents from the Westward, set vs in further vnto the Northward within fourscore leagues of the Ile of Zocotora, farre from our determined course and expectation. But here we neuer wanted abundance of Dolphins, Bonitos, and flying fishes. Now while we found our selues thus farre to the Northward, and the time being so farre spent, we determined to goe for the Red sea, or for the Iland of Zocotora, both to refresh our selues, and also for some purchase. But while we were in this consultation, the winde very luckily came about to the Northwest and caried vs directly toward Cape Comori. [Sidenote: The Isles of Mamale.] Before we should haue doubled this Cape, we were determined to touch at the Ilands of Mamale, of which we had aduertisement, that one had victuals, standing in the Northerly latitude of twelue degrees. Howbeit it was not our good lucke to finde it, which fell out partly by the obstinacie of our master: for the day before we fell with part of the Ilands the wind came about to the Southwest, and then shifting our course we missed it. So the wind increasing Southerly, we feared we should not haue bene able to haue doubled the Cape, which would haue greatly hazarded our casting away vpon the coast of India, the Winter season and Westerne Monsons already being come in, which Monsons continue on that coast vntil August. [Sidenote: Cape Comori doubled 1592.] Neuertheless it pleased God to bring the wind more Westerly, and so in the moneth of May 1592, we happily doubled Cape Comori without sight of the coast of India. From hence thus hauing doubled this Cape, we directed our course for the Ilands of Nicubar, which lie North and South with the Westerne part of Sumatra, and in the latitude of 7 degrees to the Northward of the Equinoctiall. From which Cape of Comori vnto the aforesayd Ilands we ranne in sixe days with a very large wind though the weather were foule with extreme raine and gustes of winde. These Ilands were missed through our masters default for want of due obseruation of the South starre. [Sidenote: The Iles of Gomes Polo.] And we fell to the Southward of them within the sight of the Ilands of Gomes Polo, [Sidenote: Sumatra.] which lie hard vpon the great Iland of Sumatra the first of Iune, and at the Northeast side of them we lay two or three dayes becalmed, hoping to haue had a Pilote from Sumatra, within two leagues whereof we lay off and on. [Sidenote: The Iles of Pulo Pinauo.] Now the Winter coming vpon vs with much contagious weather, we directed our course from hence with the Ilands of Pulo Pinaou, (where by the way it is to be noted that Pulo in the Malaian tongue signifieth an Iland) at which Ilands wee arriued about the beginning of Iune, where we came to an anker in a very good harborough betweene three Ilands: at which time our men were very sicke and many fallen. Here we determined to stay vntil the Winter were ouerpast. This place is in 6 degrees and a halfe to the Northward, and some fiue leagues from the maine betweene Malacca and Pegu. Here we continued vntil the end of August. Our refreshing in this place was very smal, onely of oysters growing on rocks, great wilks, and some few fish which we tooke with our hookes. Here we landed our sicke men on these vninhabited Ilands for their health, neuertheless 26 of them died in this place, whereof John Hall our master was one, and M. Rainold Golding another, a marchant of great honestie and much discretion. [Sidenote: Trees fit for mastes.] In these Ilands are abundance of trees of white wood, so right and tall, that a man may make mastes of them being an hundred foote long. The winter passed and hauing watered our ship and fitted her to goe to Sea, wee had left vs but 33 men and one boy, of which not past 22 were sound for labour and helpe, and of them not past a third part sailers: [Sidenote: Malacca.] thence we made saile to seeke some place of refreshing, and went ouer to the maine of Malacca. The next day we came to an anker in a Baie in six fadomes water some two leagues from the shore. Then master Iames Lancaster our captaine, and M. Edmund Barker his lieutenant, and other of the companie manning the boat, went on shoare to see what inhabitants might be found. And comming on land we found the tracking of some barefooted people which were departed thence not long before: for we sawe their fire still burning, but people we sawe none, nor any other living creature, saue a certaine kind of foule called oxe birds, which are a gray kind of Sea-foule, like a Snite in colour, but not in beake. Of these we killed some eight dozen with haile-shot being very tame, and spending the day in search, returned toward night aboord. The next day about two of the clocke in the afternoone we espied a Canoa which came neere vnto vs, but would not come aboord vs, hauing in it some sixteen naked Indians, with whom neuertheles going afterward on land, we had friendly conference and promise of victuals. [Sidenote: Three ships of Pegu laden with pepper.] The next day in the morning we espied three ships, being all of burthen 60 or 70 tunnes, one of which wee made to strike with our very boate: and vnderstanding that they were of the towne of Martabam, [Sidenote: Martabam.] which is the chiefe hauen towne for the great citie of Pegu, and the goods belonging to certaine Portugal Iesuites and a Biscuit baker a Portugall we tooke that ship and did not force the other two, because they were laden for marchants of Pegu, but hauing this one at our command, we came together to an anker. The night folowing all the men except twelue, which we tooke into our ship, being most of them borne in Pegu, fled away in their boate, leauing their ship and goods with vs. [Sidenote: Pera.] The next day we weighed our anker and went to the Leeward of an Iland hard by, and tooke in her lading being pepper, which shee and the other two had laden at Pera, which is a place on the maine 30 leagues to the South. Besides the aforesaid three ships we tooke another ship of Pegu laden with pepper, and perceiuing her to bee laden with marchants goods of Pegu onely, wee dismissed her without touching any thing.

[Sidenote: Pulo Sambilam.] Thus hauing staied here 10 daies and discharged her goods into the Edward, which was about the beginning of September, our sicke men being somewhat refreshed and lustie, with such reliefe as we had found in this ship, we weighed anker, determining to runne into the streights of Malacca to the Ilands called Pulo Sambilam, which are some fiue and fortie leagues Northward of the citie of Malacca, to which Ilands the Portugals must needs come from Goa or S. Thome, for the Malucos, China, and Iapan. And when wee were there arriued, we lay too and agayne for such shipping as should come that way. [Sidenote: A ship of Negapatan taken.] Thus hauing spent some fiue dayes, vpon a Sunday we espied a saile which was a Portugall ship that came from Negapatan a towne on the maine of India ouer-against the Northeast part of the Ile of Zeilan; and that night we tooke her being of 250 tunnes: she was laden with Rice for Malacca. Captaine Lancaster commanded their captaine and master aboord our shippe, and sent Edmund Barker his lieutenant and seuen more to keepe this prize, who being aboord the same, came to an anker in thirtie fadomes water: for in that chanell, three or foure leagues from the shore you shall finde good ankorage. [Sidenote: A ship of S. Thome.] Being thus at an anker and keeping out a light for the Edward, another Portugall ship of Sant Thome of foure hundred tunnes, came and ankered hard by vs. The Edward being put to Leeward for lacke of helpe of men to handle her sailes, was not able the next morning to fetch her vp, vntil we which were in the prize with our boate, went to helpe to man our shippe. Then comming aboord we went toward the shippe of Sant Thome, but our ship was so foule that shee escaped vs. After we had taken out of our Portugall prize what we thought good, we turned her and all her men away except a Pilot and foure Moores. [Sidenote: The galeon of Malacca of 700 taken.] We continued here vntill the sixt of October, at which time we met with the ship of the captaine of Malacca of seuen hundred tunnes which came from Goa: we shot at her many shot, and at last shooting her maine-yard through, she came to an anker and yeelded. We commaunded her Captaine, Master, Pilot, and Purser to come aboord vs. But the Captaine accompanied by one souldier onely came, and after certaine conference with him, he made excuse to fetch the Master, and Purser, which he sayd would not come vnless he went for them: but being gotten from vs in the edge of the euening, he with all the people which were to the number of about three hundred men, women and children gote a shore with two great boates and quite abandoned the ship. [Sidenote: Wares fit to carry into the East India.] At our comming aboord we found in her sixteene pieces of brasse, and three hundred but of Canarie wine, and Nipar wine, which is made of the palme trees, and raisin wine which is also very strong: as also all kinds of Haberdasher wares, as hats, red caps knit of Spanish wooll, worsted stockings knit, shooes, veluets, taffataes, chamlets, and silkes, abundance of suckets, rice, Venice glasses, certaine paper full of false and counterfeit stones which an Italian brought from Venice to deceiue the rude Indians withall, abundance of playing cardes, two or three packs of French paper. Whatsoeuer became of the treasure which vsually is brought in roials of plate in this gallion, we could not find it. After that the mariners had disordredly pilled this rich shippe, the Captaine because they would not follow his commandement to vnlade those excellent wines into the Edward, abandoned her and let her driue at Sea, taking out of her the choisest things that she had. [Sidenote: The kingdom of Iunsaloam.] And doubting the forces of Malaca, we departed thence to a Baie in the kingdom of Iunsalaom, which is betweene Malacca and Pegu eight degrees to the Northward, to seeke for pitch to trimme our ship. Here we sent our souldier, which the captaine of the aforesaid galion had left behind him with vs, because he had the Malaian language, to deale with the people for pitch, which hee did faithfully, and procured vs some two or three quintals with promise of more, and certaine of the people came vnto vs. [Sidenote: Amber-greese. The hornes of Abath.] We sent commodities to their king to barter for Amber-griese, and for the hornes of Abath, whereof the king onely hath the traffique in his hands. [Sidenote: The female Vnicorne.] Now this Abath is a beast which hath one horne onely in her forehead, and is thought to be the female Vnicorne, and is highly esteemed of all the Moores in those parts as a most soueraigne remedie against poyson. We had only two or three of these hornes which are of the colour of a browne gray, and some reasonable quantitie of Amber-griese. At last the king went about to betray our Portugall with our marchandise: but he to get aboord vs, told him that we had gilt armour, shirtes of maile and halberds, which things they greatly desire: for hope whereof he let him returne aboord, and so he escaped the danger. [Marginal note: Some small quantitie hereof may be caried to pleasure those kings.] Thus we left this coast and went backe againe in sight of Sumatra, and thence to the Ilands of Nicubar, where we arriued and found them inhabited with Moores, [Sidenote: They arriue at the Iles of Nicubar, which are inhabited by Moores.] and after wee came to an anker, the people daily came aboord vs in their Canoas, with hennes, Cocos, plantans, and other fruits: and within two dayes they brought vnto vs roials of plate, giuing vs them for Calicut cloth: which roials they nude by diuing for them in the Sea, which were lost not long before in two Portugall ships which were bound for China and were cast away there. They call in their language the Coco Calambe, the Plantane Pison, a Hen Iam, a Fish Iccan, a Hog Babee. From thence we returned the 21 of Nouember to goe for the Iland of Zeilan, and arriued there about the third of December 1592, and ankered vpon the Southside in sixe fadomes water, where we lost our anker, the place being rockie and foule ground. Then we ranne along the Southwest part of the sayd Iland, to a place called Punta del Galle, where we ankered, determining there to haue remained vntill the comming of the Bengala Fleet of seuen or eight ships, and the Fleete of Pegu of two or three sailes, and the Portugall shippes of Tanaseri being a great Baie to the Southward of Martabam in the kingdome of Siam: which ships, by diuers intelligences which we had, were to come that way within foureteene daye to bring commodities to serue the Caraks, which commonly depart from Cochin for Portugall by the middest of Ianuarie. The commodities of the shippes which come from Bengala bee fine pauillions for beds, wrought quilts, fine Calicut cloth, Pintados and other fine workes, and Rice, and they make this voiage twise in the yeere. Those of Pegu bring the chiefest stones, as Rubies and Diamants, but their chiefe fraight is Rice and certaine cloth. Those of Tanaseri are chiefly freighted with Rice and Nipar wine, which is very strong, and in colour like vnto rocke water, somewhat whitish, and very hote in taste like vnto Aqua vitæ. Being shot vp to the place aforesayd, called Punta del Galle, wee came to an anker in foule ground and lost the same, and lay all that night a drift, because we had nowe but two ankers left vs, which were vnstocked and in hold. Whereupon our men tooke occasion to come home, our Captaine at that time lying very sicke more like to die then to liue. In the morning wee set our foresaile determining to lie vp to the Northward and there to keepe our selues to and againe out of the current, which otherwise would haue set vs off to the Southward from all knowen land. Thus hauing set our foresayle, and in hand to set all our other sayles to accomplish our aforesayd determination, our men made answere that they would take their direct course for England and would stay there no longer. Nowe seeing that they could not bee perswaded by any meanes possible, the captaine was constrained to giue his consent to returne, leauing all hope of so great possibilities. Thus the eight of December 1592, wee set sayle for the Cape of Buona Speransa, passing by the Ilands of Maldiua, and leauing the mightie Iland of S. Laurence on the starreboord or Northward in the latitude of 26 degrees to the South. In our passage ouer from S. Laurence to the maine we had exceeding great store of Bonitos and Albocores, which are a greater kind of fish; of which our captain, being now recouered of his sicknesse, tooke with a hooke as many in two or three howers as would serue fortie persons a whole day. And this skole of fish continued with our ship for the space of fiue or sixe weekes, all which while we tooke to the quantitie aforesayd, which was no small refreshing to vs. In February 1593 we fell with the Eastermost land of Africa at a place called Baia de Agoa some 100 leagues to the Northeast of the Cape of Good Hope: and finding the winds contrary, we spent a moneth or fiue weekes before we could double the Cape. After wee had doubled it in March following wee directed our course for the Iland of Santa Helena, and arriued there the third day of Aprill, where we staied to our great comfort nineteene dayes: in which meane space some one man of vs tooke thirtie goodly Congers in one day, and other rockie fishe and some Bonitos. After our arriual at Santa Helena, I Edmund Barker went on shore with foure or fiue Peguins or men of Pegu which we had taken, and our Surgion, where in an house by the Chappell I found an Englishman one Iohn Segar of Burie in Suffock, [Marginal note: Iohn Segar an Englishman left 18 moneths alone in the Ile of santa Helena.] who was left there eighteene moneths before by Abraham Kendall, who put in there with the Roiall marchant and left him there to refresh him on the Iland, being otherwise like to haue perished on shipboord: and at our comming wee found him as fresh in colour and in as good plight of body to our seeming as might be, but crazed in minde and halfe out of his wits, as afterwards wee perceiued: for whether he was put in fright of vs, not knowing at first what we were, whether friends or foes, or of sudden ioy when he vnderstand we were his olde consorts and countreymen, hee became idle-headed, and for eight dayes space neither night nor day tooke any naturall rest, and so at length died for lacke of sleepe. [Marginal note: A miraculous effect of extreme feare or extreme ioy.] Here two of our men, whereof the one was diseased with the skuruie, and the other had bene nine moneths sicke of the fluxe, in short time while they were on the Iland, recouered their perfect health. We found in this place great store of very holesome and excellent good greene figs, orenges, and lemons very faire, abundance of goates and hogs, and great plentie of partriges, Guiniecocks, and other wilde foules. [Marginal note: The description of the commodities of the ile of santa Helena.] Our mariners somewhat discontented being now watered and hauing some prouision of fish, contrary to the will of the capitaine, would straight home. The capitaine because he was desirous to goe for Phernambuc in Brasil, granted their request. And about the 12 of Aprill 1593. we departed from S. Helena, and directed our course for the place aforesayd. The next day our capitaine calling vpon the sailers to finish a foresaile which they had in hand, some of them answered that vnlesse they might goe directly home, they would lay their hands to nothing; whereupon he was constrained to folow their humour. And from thence-foorth we directed our course for our countrey, which we kept vntill we came 8 degrees to the Northward of the Equinoctiall, betweene which 8 degrees and the line, we spent some sixe weekes, with many calme and contrary winds at North, and sometimes to the Eastward, and sometimes to the Westward: which losse of time and expense of our victuals, whereof we had very smal store, made vs doubt to keepe our course and some of our men growing into a mutinie threatned to breake vp other mens chests, to the ouerthrow of our victuals and all our selues, for euery man had his share of his victuals before in his owne custody, that they might be sure what to trust to, and husband it more thriftily. [Sidenote: The gulfe of Paria, or Bocca del Dragone passed.] Our captaine seeking to preuent this mischiefe, being aduertised by one of our companie which had bene at the Ile of Trinidada in M. Chidleis voyage, that there we should be sure to haue refreshing, hereupon directed his course to that Iland, and not knowing the currents, we were put past it in the night into the gulfe of Paria in the beginning of Iune, wherein we were 8 dayes, finding the current continually setting in, [Sidenote: A good note.] and oftentimes we were in 3 fadomes water, and could find no going out vntil the current had put vs ouer to the Westernside vnder the maine land, where we found no current at all, and more deep water; and so keeping by the shore, the wind off the shore euery night did helpe vs out to the Northward. [Sidenote: The Ile of Mona.] Being cleare, within foure or fiue days after we fell with the Ile of Mona where we ankered and rode some eighteene dayes. In which time the Indians of Mona gaue vs some refreshing. And in the meane space there arriued a French ship of Cane in which was capitaine one Monsieur de Barbaterre, of whom wee bought some two buts of wine and bread, and other victuals. Then wee watered and fitted our shippe, and stopped a great leake which broke on vs as we were beating out of the gulfe of Paria. And hauing thus made ready our ship to goe to Sea, we determined to goe directly for Newfound-land. But before we departed, there arose a storme the winde being Northerly, which put vs from an anker and forced vs the Southward of Santo Domingo. [Sidenote: The Ile of Sauona enuironed with flats.] This night we were in danger of shipwracke vpon an Iland called Sauona, which is enuironed with flats lying 4 or 5 miles off; yet it pleased God to cleare vs of them, [Sidenote: Cape de Tiberon.] and so we directed our course Westward along the Iland of Santo Domingo, and doubled Cape Tiberon, and passed through the old channell betweene S. Domingo and Cuba for the cape of Florida: And here we met againe with the French ship of Caen, whose Captaine could spare vs no more victuals, as he said, but only hides which he had taken by traffike vpon those Ilands, wherewith we were content and gaue him for them to his good satisfaction. After this, passing the Cape of Florida, and cleere of the channell of Bahama, we directed our course for the banke of Newfound-land. Thus running to the height of 36 degrees, and as farre to the East as the Ile of Bermuda the 17 of September finding the winds there very variable, contrarie to our expectation and all mens writings, we lay there a day or two the winde being northerly, and increasing continually more and more, it grewe to be a storme and a great frete of wind: which continued with vs some 24 houres, with such extremetie, as it caried not onely our sayles away being furled, but also made much water in our shipppe, so that wee had six foote water in hold, and hauing freed our ship thereof with baling, the winde shifted to the Northwest and became dullerd: but presently vpon it the extremetie of the storme was such that with the labouring of our ship we lost our foremaste, and our ship grewe as full of water as before. The storme once ceased, and the winde contrary to goe our course, we fell to consultation which might be our best way to saue our liues. Our victuals now being vtterly spent, and hauing eaten hides 6 or 7 daies, we thought it best to beare back againe for Dominica, and the Islands adioyning, knowing that there we might haue some reliefe, whereupon we turned backe for the said Islands. But before we could get thither the winde scanted vpon vs, which did greatly endanger vs for lacke of fresh water and victuals; so that we were constrained to beare vp to the Westward to certaine other Ilandes called the Neublas or cloudie Ilands, towards the Ile of S. Iuan de porto Rico, where at our arriuall we found land-crabs and fresh water, and tortoyses, which come most on lande about the full of the moone. Here hauing refreshed our selues some 17 or 18 dayes, and hauing gotten some small store of victuals into our ship, we resolued to returne againe for Mona: vpon which our determination fiue of our men left vs, remaining still on the Iles of Neublas for all perswasions that we could vse to the contrary, which afterward came home in an English shippe. From these Iles we departed and arriued at Mona about the twentieth of Nouember 1593, and there comming to an anker toward two or three of the clocke in the morning, the Captaine, and Edmund Barker his Lieutenant with some few others went on land to the houses of the olde Indian and his three sonnes, thinking to haue gotten some foode, our victuals being all spent, and we not able to proceede any further vntill we had obteyned some new supply. We spent two or three daies in seeking prouision to cary aboord to relieue the whole companie. And comming downe to go aboord, the winde then being northerly and the sea somewhat growne, they could not come on shore with the boate, which was a thing of small succour and not able to rowe in any rough sea, whereupon we stayed vntill the next morning, thinking to haue had lesse winde and safer passage. But in the night about twelue of the clocke our ship did driue away with fiue men and a boy onely in it, our carpenter secretly cut their owne cable, leauing nineteene of vs on land without boate or any thing, to our great discomfort. In the middest of these miseries reposing our trust in the goodnesse of God, which many times before had succoured vs in our greatest extremities, we contented our selues with our poore estate, and sought meanes to preserue our liues. And because one place was not able to sustaine vs, we tooke our leaues one of another, diuiding our selues into seuerall companies. The greatest reliefe that we sixe which were with the Captaine could finde for the space of nine and twentie dayes was the stalkes of purselaine boyled in water, and now and then a pompion, which we found in the garden of the olde Indian, who vpon this our second arriual with his three sonnes stole from vs, and kept himselfe continually aloft in the mountaines. After the ende of nine and twentie dayes we espied a French shippe, which afterwards we vnderstood to be of Diepe, called the Luisa, whose Captaine was one Monsieur Felix, vnto whom wee made a fire, at sight whereof he tooke in his topsayles, bare in with the land, and shewed vs his flagge, whereby we iudged him French: so comming along to the Westerne ende of the Island there he ankered, we making downe with all speede vnto him. At this time the Indian and his three sonnes came downe to our Captaine Master Iames Lancaster and went along with him to the shippe. This night he went aboord the French man who gaue him good entertainement, and the next day fetched eleuen more of vs aboord entreating vs all very courteously. This day came another French shippe of the same towne of Diepe which remayned there vntil night expecting our other seuen mens comming downe: who, albeit we caused certaine pieces of ordinance to be shot off to call them, yet came not downe. Whereupon we departed thence being deuided sixe into one ship, and sixe into another, and leauing this Iland departed for the Northside of Saint Domingo, where we remained vntill April following 1594, and spent some two moneths in traffike with the inhabitants by permission for hides and other marchandises of the Countrey. In this meane while there came a shippe of New-hauen to the place where we were, whereby we had intelligence of our seuen men which wee left behinde vs at the Isle of Mona: which was, that two of them brake their neckes with ventring to take foules vpon the cliffes, other three were slaine by the Spaniards, which came from Saint Domingo, vpon knowledge giuen by our men which went away in the Edward, the other two this man of New-hauen had with him in his shippe, which escaped the Spaniards bloodie hands. From this place Captaine Lancaster and his Lieutenant Master Edmund Barker, shipped themselues in another shippe of Diepe, the Captaine whereof was one Iohn La Noe, which was readie first to come away, and leauing the rest of their companie in other ships, where they were well intreated, to come after him, on Sunday the seuenth of Aprill 1594 they set homewarde, and disbocking through the Caijcos from thence arriued safely in Diepe within two and fortie dayes after, on the 19 of May, where after two dayes we had stayed to refresh our selues, and giuen humble thankes vnto God, and vnto our friendly neighbours, we tooke passage for Rie and landed there on Friday the 24 of May 1594, hauing spent in this voyage three yeeres, sixe weekes and two dayes, which the Portugales performe in halfe the time, chiefely because wee lost our fit time and season to set foorth in the beginning of our voyage.

We vnderstood in the East Indies by certaine Portugeles which we tooke, that they haue lately discouered the coast of China, to the latitude of nine and fiftie degrees, finding the sea still open to the Northward: giuing great hope of the Northeast or Northwest passage. Witnesse Master Iames Lancaster.

* * * * *

Certaine remembrances of an intended voyage to Brasill, and the Riuer of Plate, by the Edward Cotton, a ship of 260 Tunnes of Master Edward Cotton
of Southampton, which perished through extreme negligence neare Rio Grande in Guinie, the 17 of July 1583.

Articles of Couenants agreed vpon betweene Edward Cotton Esquier, owner of the good ship called the Edward Cotton of Southampton, and of all the marchandizes in her laden, of the one part, and William Huddie gentleman, Captaine of the said ship, Iohn Hooper his Lieutenant, Iohn Foster Master, Hugh Smith Pilot for the whole voyage, and William Cheesman marchant, on the other part.

1 To obserue and keepe the dayly order of Common prayer aboord the ships, and the companie to be called thereunto, at the least once in the day, to be pronounced openly.

2 Item, that they be ready with the first faire winde, to set saile and sailes in the voyage, and not to put into any port or harbour, but being forcibly constrained by weather, or other apparent and vrgent cause.

3 Item, that they take in, at or about the Isles of Cape Verde, to the quantitie of 25 or 30 tuns of salt, to be imployed among other the owners marchandize, at Santos, and S. Vincent, to his onely behoofe, and the rest

of the salt, so much as shall be needed for victuall, and for sauing of the hides to be kept aboord, and the same salt to be prouided either at the fishermens hands neere the said Isles for trucke of commodities, or els to be taken in at the aforesayd Isles, at discretion of the aboue-named.

4 Item, vpon the due performance of this voiage, the owner bindeth himselfe by this deede, to yeeld vnto any such of the companie, as shall refuse their shares before they depart from the coast of England, 20 markes a single share, for the dutie of the whole voiage, making not aboue 75. shares single in the whole.

5 Item, the company according as they be appointed by the officers of the said ship aboue named, shall at all times be most ready to doe their painfull indeuor, not onely aboord, but in all labours at the land, according to the direction giuen by the aboue named officers, vpon paine of forfeiture of their shares and wages, the same to be diuided amongst the company.

6 Item, that the shares be taken at their returne out of al the traine oile, and hides of the seales, and of all other commodities gotten by their handie labour, and of the salt that shall be vended and other commodities, at, or neere the coast of Brasil, to allow after 9 li. the tunne freight, whereof one third to goe to the company.

7 Item, that if any man shall practise by any deuise or deuises whatsoeuer, to alter the voiage from the true purpose and intent of the owner, viz. to make their first port at Santos, and Saint Vincent, and there to revictuall and traffike, and from thence to the riuer of Plate to make their voyage by the traine, and hide of the seales, with such other commodities as are there to be had, according as the owner, with diuers that haue gouernment in the said ship, are bound to her highnesse by their deedes obligatorie in great summes, that all such practisers, vpon due proofe made, shall lose their whole intertainement due by shares or otherwise for this sayde voyage to be adiuged by the Captaine, his Lieutenant, the Master, Pilot, and marchant, or three of them at least, whereof the Captaine to be one.

8 Item, that the pinnesse be ready at al times to serue the marchants turne vpon his demand, to take in wares and commodities, and to cary and recary to and from the shore, when, and as oft as neede shall be, and to giue due attendance at the marchant and marchants direction during the whole voyage.

9 Item, that no head or chiefe officer being set downe for such an officer vnder the hand of the owner, at the going to sea of the said shippe, shall or may be displaced from his said place or office, without great cause, and his misdemeanor to be adiudged by the Captaine, and his Lieutenant, the

Master, the Pilot, and the marchant, or by the consent of three of them at least.

10 Item, that vpon the returne of the shippe to the coast of England, the Maister and Pilot put not into any port or harbour, to the Westward of Southampton, but forced by weather, or such like vrgent cause.

William Huddie.
Iohn Hooper.
Hugh Smith.
John Foster.
William Cheesman.

* * * * *

A direction as well for the Captaine, and other my friends of the shippe, as especially for William Cheesman Marchant, for the voyage to the riuer of Plate.

[Sidenote: The Ile of S. Sebastian.] At your comming to the Isle of Saint Sebastian, vpon the coast of Brasill, you shall according to your discretions, make sale of such commodities, as you may thinke will be thereabout well vented, and likewise to buy commodities without making longer stay there then your victuals be prouiding, but rather to bespeake commodities against your returne from the riuer of Plate, especially of Amber, Sugar, Greene ginger, Cotton wooll, and some quantitie of the peppers of the countrey there. Also for Parats and Munkies, and the beast called Serrabosa. Also you shall barrell vp of the beefe called Petune, two or three barrels, and to lose no good opportunitie, to gather of the Indian figges, and the graines of them to preserue drie, in such quantitie as conueniently may be done: and touching the making of the traine, and preseruing of the hides, I leaue it wholly to the order and the discretion of the chiefe of the companie. Also that in any road where the ship shall ride vpon the coast of America, triall be made with the dragges, for the pearle Oisters, and the same being taken, to be opened and searched for pearle in the presence of the Captaine, his Lieutenant, the Master, the Pilot, and marchant, or three of them, whereof the Captaine or his Lieutenant to be one, and to remaine in the custodie of the Captaine and marchant, vnder two lockes, either of them to haue a key to his owne locke, and that a true inuentorie be deliuered also to the Master and Pilot of the said pearle or other iewels of price gotten in the said voiage, to the intent that no partie be defrauded of his due, and that no conccalment be made of any such thing vpon forfeiture, the partie to lose his share and dutie for the voyage that shall so conceale and not reueale it vnto the officers aboue named. Also to doe your best indeuour to try for the best Ore of golde, siluer, or other rich mettals whatsoeuer. Forget not also to bring the kernels and seeds of strange plants with you, the Palmito with his fruit inclosed in him. Serue God, keepe good watch, and stand alwayes vpon your garde.

Edward Cotton.

These things being thus ordered, and the ship of the burden of 260 tunnes, with 83 men of all sortes furnished, and fully appointed for the voyage, began to set saile from Hurst Castle vpon Friday the 20 of May, Anno 1583, and the 17 day of Iuly ensuing fell with the coast of Guinie, to take in fresh water, where, through meere dissolute negligence, she perished vpon a sand, with the most part of the men in her, as appeareth by the confession of one that escaped, the substance and tenor whereof is this.

* * * * *

The confession of William Bends Masters Mate in the Edward Cotton, the 21 of October, Ann. 1584.

He sayth, that the 17 day of Iuly, Anno 1583. hauing some lacke of fresh water, they put roome vpon the coast of Guinie, where they were set vpon a sand about 8 leagues from the shore, and this Examinate, with 29 more, got into the pinnesse, who arriued in an Island, being desolate of people, and fiue miles in compasse, where they rested 18 dayes through force of weather, hauing nought to eate but grasse. [Sidenote: Rio Grande.] The rest of the company the ship being splitted in two and in quarters, got them into one of the after quarters, and by the helpe of raftes came also a shore into another Island neere to Rio Grande, where they all died as he supposeth.

The other 30 in the pinnesse, at the end of 18 dayes, departed that Island, and came to Saint Domingo, where comming on shore, they were taken of the Moores, and stripped naked. And they buried one Coxe [Marginal note: One Coxe an old English man buried aliue by the Moores of Rio Grande in Guinea.] an olde man aliue, notwithstanding his pitifull lamentation and skrikings: the rest hauing Rice and water allowed them, liued there a certaine time. This Examinate was at last sold to a Portugall, with whom he dwelt the space of a quarter of a yere, and in the end, a Portugall Carauel comming, thither, his master laded the same with Negroes, and he obtained leaue of his master to goe in the same Carauell, and by that meanes arriued at Lisbone, and from thence came into England the 17 of October, 1584, leauing behinde him of his companie aliue, Richard Hacker, Iohn Baker, Iohn Mathew, and a boy, with two others which were gone beyond Saint Domingo: all which, as he saith, were so sicke and diseased, that he iudged them to be long before this time dead.

* * * * *

The Letters patents or priuiledges granted by her Maiestie to certaine Noble men and Marchants of London, for a trade to Barbarie, in the yeere 1585.

Elizabeth by the grace of God Queene of England, France, and Ireland, defender of the faith, &c. to the Treasurer & Barons of our Eschequer, and to al Maiors, shirifs, constables, customers, collectors of our customes and subsidies, controllers, searchers, and keepers of our hauens and creekes, ports and passages, within this our realme of England and the dominions of the same and to al our officers, ministers and subiects, and to all other whosoeuer to whom it shall or may appertaine, and to euery of them greeting. Whereas it is made euidently and apparently knowen vnto vs, that of late yeeres our right trustie and right welbeloued councellors, Ambrose Erle of Warwike, and Robert Erle of Leicester, and also our louing and naturall subiects, Thomas Starkie of our citie of London Alderman, Ierard Gore the elder, and all his sonnes, Thomas Gore the elder, Arthur Atie gentleman, Alexander Auenon, Richard Staper, William Iennings, Arthur Dawbeney, William Sherington, Thomas Bramlie, Anthony Garrard, Robert How, Henry Colthirst, Edward Holmden, Iohn Swinnerton, Robert Walkaden, Simon Lawrence, Nicholas Stile, Oliuer Stile, William Bond, Henrie Farrington, Iohn Tedcastle, Walter Williams, William Brune, Iohn Suzan, Iohn Newton, Thomas Owen, Roger Afield, Robert Washborne, Reinold Guy, Thomas Hitchcocke, George Lydiat, Iohn Cartwright, Henry Paiton, Iohn Boldroe, Robert Bowyer, Anthonie Dassell, Augustine Lane, Robert Lion, and Thomas Dod, all of London, Marchants now trading into the Countrey of Barbary, in the parts of Africa, vnder the gouernement of Muly Hammet Sheriffe, Emperor of Morocco, and king of Fesse and Sus, haue sustained great and grieuous losses, and are like to sustaine greater if it should not be preuented: In tender consideration whereof, and for that diuers Marchandize of the same Countries are very necessary and conuenient for the vse and defence of this our Realme of England, and for diuers other causes vs specially mouing, minding the reliefe and benefit of our said subiects, and the quiet trafique and good gouernment to be had, and vsed among them in their said trade, of our speciall grace, certaine knowledge, and meere motion haue giuen and granted, and by those presents for vs, our heires and successors, doe giue and grant vnto the saide Earles of Warwike and Leicester, Thomas Starkie, Ierard Gore the elder, Arthur Atie gentleman, Alexander Auenon, Richard Staper, William Iennings, Arthur Dawbenie, William Sherrington, Thomas Bramlie, Anthonie Gerrard, Robert Howe, Henry Colthirst, Edward Holmden, Iohn Swinnerton, Robert Walkaden, Simon Lawrence, Nicholas Stile, Oliuer Stile, William Bond, Henry Farrington, Iohn Tedcastle, Walter Williams, William Brune, Iohn Suzan, Iohn Newton, Thomas Owen, Roger Afild, Robert Washborne, Rainold Guie, Thomas Hitchcocke, George Lidiate, Iohn Cartwright, Henry Payton, Iohn Baldroe, Robert Bowyer, Anthony

Dassell, Augustine Lane, Robert Lion, and Thomas Dod, that they and euery of them by themselues or by their factors or seruants, and none others, shall and may, for, and during the space of 12. yeeres, haue and enioy the whole freedome and libertie in the saide trafique or trade, vnto or from the said countrey of Barbary, or to or from any part thereof, for the buying and selling of all maner of wares and marchandizes whatsoeuer, that now or accustomably heretofore haue bene brought or transported, from, or to the said country of Barbary, or from or to any of the cities, townes, places, ports, roades, hauens, harbors, or creeks of the said country of Barbary, any law, statute, graunt, matter, customes or priuileges, to the contrary in any wise notwithstanding.

And for the better establishing, ordering and gouerning of the said Erles of Warwike and Leicester, Thomas Starkie, &c. abouesaid, their factors, seruants and assignes in the trade aforesaid, we for vs, our heires and successors, doe by these presents giue and graunt full licence to the saide Thomas Starke, Ierard Gore the elder, and the rest aforesaide, and euery of them from time to time, during the said terme of twelue yeeres, at their pleasures to assemble and meete together in any place or places conuenient within our citie of London, or elsewhere, to consult of, and for the said trade, and with the consent of the said Erie of Leicester, to make and establish good and necessary orders and ordinances for and touching the same, and al such orders and ordinances so made, to put in vse and execute, and them or any of them with the consent of the said Erle of Leicester, to alter, change and make voyde, and if need be, to make new, at any time during the saide terme, they or the most part of them then liuing and trading, shall finde conuenient.

Prouided alwayes, that the ordinances or any of them bee not contrary or repugnant to the lawes, statutes or customes of this our Realme of England. And to the intent that they onely to whom the said libertie of trafique is graunted by these our Letters patents, and none other our Subiects whatsoeuer, without their special consent and licence before had, should during the said terme haue trade or trafique for any maner of Marchandizes, to, or from the said countrey of Barbary, or to, or from any Citie, town, place, port, harbor or creeke within the said countrey of Barbary, to, or out of our said Realmes and dominions, wee doe by these presents straightly charge, commaund, and prohibite all and euery our Subiects whatsoeuer, other then only the said Erles of Warwike and Leicester, Thomas Starkie, and the rest abouesaid, and euery of them by themselues, or by their Factors or seruants during the saide terme, to trade or trafique, for or with any marchandize, to, or from the saide Countrey of Barbary, or to, or from any the dominions of the same, as they tender our fauour, and will auoyde our high displeasure, and vpon paine of imprisonment of his and their bodies, at our will and pleasure, and of forfeiting all the marchandizes, or the full value thereof, wherewith they or any of them during the saide terme, shall trade or trafique to or from the said countrey of Barbary, or to, or from the dominions of the same, contrary to this our priuilege and prohibition, vnlesse it be by and with the expresse licence, consent, and agreement of the saide Erles of Warwike and Leicester, Thomas Starkie, Ierard Gore the elder, and all his sonnes, Thomas Gore the elder, Arthur Atie Gentleman, Alexander Auenon, Richard Straper, William Iennings, Arthur Dawbnie, William Sherington, Thomas Bramlie, Anthonie Gerrard, Robert Howe, Henry Colthirst, Edward Holmden, Iohn Swinnerton, Robert Walkaden, Simon Lawrence, Nicholas Stile, Oliuer Stile, William Bond, Henry Farington, Iohn Tedcastle, Walter Williams, William Brune, Iohn Suzan, Iohn Newton, Thomas Owen, Roger Afield, Robert Washborne, Rainold Guy, Thomas Hitchcock, George Lidiate, &c. or by, and and with the expresse licence and consent of the more part of them then liuing and trading, first had and obtained, so alwayes, that the sayd Earle of Leicester be one, if hee bee liuing.

And we further for vs, our heires and successors of our speciall grace, meere motion and certaine knowledge, do graunt to the said Erles of Warwike and Leicester, Thomas Starkie, and the rest abouesaid, and to euery of them, that nothing shall be done, to be of force or validitie touching the said trade or trafique, or the exercise thereof, without or against the consent of the saide Erles, Thomas Starkie, (and the others before named) during the time of these our Letters patents for 12. yeeres as aforesaid.

And for that the said Erles, Thomas Starkie, &c. and euery of them aforesaid should not be preuented or interrupted in this their said trade, we do by these presents for vs, our heires and successours, straightly prohibite and forbid all maner of person or persons, as well strangers of what nation or countrey soeuer, as our owne Subiects, other then onely the said Erles, Thomas Starkie, &c. and euery of them as aforesaid, that they nor any of them from hencefoorth during the said terme of 12. yeeres, do or shall bring, or cause to be brought into this our Realme of England, or to any the dominions thereof, any maner of marchandizes whatsoeuer growing, or being made within the said Countrey of Barbary, or within any the dominions thereof, vnlesse it be by and with the license of the more part of them then liuing, first had and obtained, so alwayes that the sayd Erle of Leicester (if hee be liuing) be one, vnder the paine that euery one that shall offend or doe against this our present prohibition here last aboue mentioned in these presents, shall forfeite and lose all and singular the said marchandizes to be landed in any our realmes and dominions, contrary to the tenor and true meaning of this our prohibition in that behalfe prouided:

the one moitie of all and euery which said forfaitures whatsoeuer mentioned or specified in these our present Letters patents, shalbe to vs, our heires and successors: And the other moity of al and euery the said forfaitures, we doe by these presents of our certaine knowledge and meere motion clearely and wholy for vs, our heires and successors giue and graunt vnto the said Erles, Thomas Starkie, &c. And these our Letters patents, vpon the onely sight thereof, without any further warrant, shal bee sufficient authoritie to our Treasurer of England for the time being, to our Barons of the Exchequer, and to all other our officers that shall haue to deale in this behalfe, to make full allowance vnto the said Erles, Thomas Starkie, &c. their deputies or assignes of the one moitie of all and singular the goods, marchandizes and things whatsoever mentioned in these our present Letters patents, to be forfaited at any time or times during the said terme of twelue yeres: which said allowance we doe straightly charge and commaund from time to time to be made to the sayd Erles, Thomas Starkie, &c. and to euery of them accordingly, without any maner of delay or deniall or any of our officers whatsoever, as they tender our fauour and the furtherance of our good pleasure. And wee doe straightly charge and commaund, and by these presents prohibite all and singular Customers and Collectors of our customes and subsidies, and comptrollers, of the same, of and within our Citie and port of London, and all other portes, creekes, and places within this our Realme of England, and euery of them, that they ne any of them take or perceiue, or cause, or suffer to be taken, receiued, or perceiued for vs and in our name, or to our vse, or to the vses of our heires or successors of any person or persons, any sum or summes of money, or other things whatsoeuer during the said terme of 12. yeeres, for, and in the name and liew or place of any custome, subsidy and other thing or duties to vs, our heires or successors due or to be due for the customes and subsidies of any marchandizes whatsoeuer growing, being made or comming out of the said countrey of Barbary, or out of the dominions thereof, nor make, cause, nor suffer to be made any entrie into our or their books of customs and subsidies, nor make any agreement for the subsidies and customs, of, and for any the said marchants, sauing onely with, and in the name of the said Erles, Thomas Starkie, &c. or the most part of them, as they and euery of them will answers at their vttermost perils to the contrary. And for the better and more sure obseruation of this our graunt, wee will, and grant for vs, our heires and successors by these presents, that the Treasurer and barons of our Exchequer for the time being, by force of this our graunt or enrolment thereof in the said court at al and euery time and times during the said terme of 12 yeeres, at and vpon request made vnto them by the said Erles, Thomas Starkie, &c. or by the atturneis, factors, deputies or assignes of them, or the most part of them then liuing and trading, shall and may make and direct vnder the seale of the said Exchequer, one or more sufficient writ or writs, close or patents, vnto euery or any of our said customers, collectors or controllers of our heires and successors in all and euery, or to any port or ports, creeke, hauens, or other places within this our realme of England, as the Erles, Thomas Starkie, &c. or any the atturneis, factors, deputies or assignes of them or the most part of them then liuing and trading, shall at any time require, commaunding and straightly charging them and euery of them, that they nor any of them at any time or times during the said term of 12. yeeres, make any entrie of any wares or marchandizes whatsoeuer, growing, being made or comming out or from the said countrey of Barbary, or the dominions thereof, nor receiue or take any custome, subsidie or other entrie, or make any agreement for the same, other then with or in the name of the said Erles, Thomas Starkie, &c, the factor or factors, deputies or assignes of them or the most part of them then liuing and trading, according to this our graunt, and the true meaning thereof, and according to our saide will and pleasure before in these presents declared. In witnesse whereof we haue caused these our Letters to be made patents. Witnesse our selfe at Westminster the 5. day of Iuly in the 27. yeere of our reigne.

* * * * *

The Ambassage of Master Henry Roberts, one of the sworne Esquires of her
  Maiesties person, from her highnesse to Mully Hamet Emperour of Morocco
  and the King of Fesse and Sus, in the yeere 1585: who remained there as Liger for the space of 3. yeeres. Written briefly by himselfe.

Vpon an incorporation granted to the Company of Barbary Marchants resident in London, I Henry Roberts one of her Maiesties sworne Esquires of her person, was appointed her highnesse messenger, and Agent vnto the aforesaid Mully Hamet Emperor of Marocco, king of Fesse, and Sus. And after I had receiued my Commission, instructions, and her Maiesties letters, I departed from London the 14. of August in the yeere 1585. in a tall ship called the Ascension, in the company of the Minion and Hopewell, and we all arriued in safetie at Azafi a port of Barbary, the 14. of September next following. The Alcaide of the towne (being the kings officer there, and as it were Maior of the place) recalled mee with all humanitie and honour, according to the custome of the Countrey, lodging me in the chiefest house of the towne, from whence I dispatched a messenger (which in their language they call a Trottero) to aduertise the Emperour of my arriuall: who immediately gaue order, and sent certaine souldiers for my guard and conduct, and horses for my selfe, and mules for mine owne and my companies carriages. Thus being accompanied with M. Richard Euans, Edward Salcot, and other English Marchants resident there in the

Countrey, with my traine of Moores and carriages, I came at length to the riuer of Tensist, which is within foure miles of Marocco: and there by the water side I pitched my tents vnder the Oliue trees: where I met with all the English Marchants by themselues, and the French and Flemish, and diuers other Christians, which attended my comming. And after we had dined, and spent out the heat of the day, about foure of the clocke in the afternoone we all set forward toward the Citie of Marocco, where we arriued the said day, being the 14. of September, and I was lodged by the Emperours appointment in a faire house in the Iudaria or Iurie, which is the place where the Iewes haue their abode, and is the fairest place, and quietest lodging in all the Citie.

After I had reposed my selfe 3 dayes, I had accesse to the kings presence, delinered my message and her Maiesties letters, and was receiued with all humanitie, and had fauourable audience from time to time for three yeeres: during which space I abode there in his Court, as her Maiesties Agent and Ligier: and whensoeuer I had occasion of businesse, I was admitted either to his Maiestie himselfe, or to his vice Roy, whose name was Alcayde Breme Saphiana, a very wise and discreet person, and the chiefest about his Maiestie. The particulers of my seruice, for diuers good and reasonable causes, I forbeare here to put downe in writing.

After leaue obtained, and an honourable reward bestowed by the Emperour vpon me, I departed from his Court at Marocco the 18. of August 1588. toward a garden of his, which is called Shersbonare, where he promised mee I should stay but one day for his letters: howbeit, vpon some occasion I was stayed vntil the 14. of September at the kings charges, with 40. or 50. shot attending vpon me for my guard and safetie.

From thence at length I was conducted with all things necessary to the port of Santa Cruz, being six dayes iourney from Marocco, and the place where our shippes do commonly take in their lading, where I arriued the 21. of the same moneth. In this port I stayed 43. dayes, and at length the second of Nouember I embarqued my selfe, and one Marshok Reiz a Captaine and a Gentleman, which the Emperour sent with mee vpon an Ambassage to her Maiestie: and after much torment and foule weather at Sea, yet New-yeres day I came on land at S. Iues in Cornwall, from whence passing by land both together vp towards London, we were met without the Citie with the chiefest marchants of the Barbary Company, well mounted all on horsebacke, to the number of 40. or 50. horse, and so the Ambassadour and myselfe being both in Coche, entred the citie by torchlight, on Sunday at night the 12. of Ianuary 1589.

* * * * *

Este es vn traslado bien y fielmente sacado da vna carta real del Rey Muley Hamet de Fes y Emperador de Marruecos, cuyo tenor es este, que Segue.

Con el nombre de Dios piadoso y misericordioso, &c. El sieruo de Dios soberano, el conquistador per su causa, el successor ensalçado por Dios, Emperador de los Moros, hijo del Emperador de los Moros, Iariffe, Haceni, el que perpetue su honora, y ensalçe su estado. Se pone este nuestro real mandado en manos de los criados de neustras altas puertas los mercadores Yngleses; para que por el sepan todos los que la presente vieren, come nuestro alto Conseio les anpara con el fauor de Dios de todo aquello, que les enpeciere y dannare en qualquiera manera, que fueren offendidos, y en qualquiera viaie, que fueren, ninguno les captinarà en estos nuestros reynos, y puertos, y lugares, que a nos pertenescen: y que les cubre el anporo de nuestro podor de qualquiera fatiga; y ningun los impida commano de enemistad, ni se darà causa, de que se agrauien en qualquiera manera con el fauor de Dios y de sua comparo. Y mandamos à los Alcaydes de los nuestros puertos y fortalezas, y à los que en estos nuestros reynos tienen cargo, y à toda la gente commun, que no les alleguen en ninguna manera, con orden, de que sean offendidos en ninguna manera; y esto serà necessariamente: Que es escrita en los medios dias de Rabel, segundo anno de nueue çientos, y nouenta y seys.

Concorda el dia d'esta cara con veynte dias de Março del anno de mil y quiniento y ochenta y siete, lo qual yo Abdel Rahman el Catan, interprete per su Magestad saquè, y Romançe de verbo ad verbum, como en el se contiene, y en Fee dello firmo de my nombre, fecho vt supra.

Abdel Rahman el Catan.

The same in English.

This is a copy well and truely translated of an edict of Muley Hamet king of Fez and Emperour of Marocco, whose tenor is as followeth: To wit, that no Englishmen should be molested or made slaues in any part of his Dominions, obtained by the aforesaid M. Henry Roberts.

In the name of the pitifull and the mercifull God, &c. The seruant of the supreme God, the conqueror in his cause, the successor aduanced by God, the Emperour of the Moores, the sonne of the Emperour of the Moores, the Iariffe, the Haçeny, whose honour God long increase and aduance his estate. This our princely commandement is deliuered into the hands of the English marchants, which remaine in the protection of our stately palaces: to the ende that all men which shall see this present writing, may vnderstand that our princely counsaile wil defend them by the fauor of God, from any thing that may impeach or hurt them in what sort soeuer they shalbe wronged: and that, which way soeuer they shall trauaile, no man shall take them captiues in these our kingdomes, ports, and places which belong vnto vs, which also may protect and defend them by our authoritie from any molestation whatsoeuer: and that no man shall hinder them by laying violent hand vpon them, and shall not giue occasion that they may be grieued in any sort by the fauour and assistance of God. And we charge and command our officers of our hauens and fortresses, and all such as beare any authority in these our dominions, and likewise all the common people, that in no wise they do molest them, in such sort that they be no way offended or wronged. And this our commandement shall remaine inuiolable, being registred in the middest of the moneth of Rabel in the yeere 996.

The date of this letter agreeth with the 20. of March 1587. which I Abdel Rahman el Catan, interpretour for his Maiestie, haue translated and turned out of the Arabian into Spanish word for word as is conteined therein: and in witnesse thereof haue subscribed my name as aforesaid.

Abdel Rahman el Catan.

* * * * *

En nombre de Dios el piadoso piadador.

Oracion de Dios sobre nuestro Sennor y Propheta Mahumet, y los allegados à el.

[Sidenote: A letter of Mully Hamet to the Earle of Leicester.] El sieruo de Dios, y muy guerrero, y ensalsado por la graçia de Dios, Myra Momanyn, hijo de Myra Momanyn, nieto de Myra Momanyn, el Iarif, el Hazeny, que Dios sustenga sus reynos, y enhalse sus mandados, para el Sennor muy affamado y muy illustre, muy estimado, el Conde de Leycester, despues de dar las loores deuidas à Dios, y las oraçiones, y saludes deuidas à le propheta Mahumet. Seruirà esta por os hazer saber que llegò a qui à nuestra real Corte vuestra carta, y entendimos lo que en ella se contiene. Y vuestro Ambaxador, que aqui esti en nuestra corte me dio à entender la causa de la tardança de los rehenes hasta agora: el qual descuento reçebimos, y nos damos por satisfechos. Y quanta à lo que à nos escriueys por causa de Iuan Herman, y lo mesmo que nos ha dicho el Ambaxador sobre el, antes que llegâsse vuestra carta por la quexa del ambaxador, que se auia quexado del, ya auiamos mandado prender lo, y assi que da aora preso, y quedera, hasta que se le haga la iusticia que mas se le ha de hazer. Y con tanto nuestro Sennor os tenga en su guardia. Hecha en nuestra corte real en Marruecos, que Dios sostenga, et 28. dias del mes de Remodan anno 996.

The same in English.

In the Name of the mercifull and pitifull God.

The blessing of God light vpon our Lord and prophet Mahumet, and those that are obedient vnto him.

The seruant of God both mightie in warre and mightily exalted by the grace of God Myra Momanyn, the son of Myra Momanyn, the Iarif, the Hazeni, whose kingdoms God maintaine and aduance his authoritie: Vnto the right famous, right noble, and right highly esteemed Erle of Leicester, after due praises giuen vnto God, and due blessings and salutations rendered vnto the prophet Mahumet. These are to giue you to vnderstand, that your letters arriued here in our royal Court, and we wel perceiue the contents thereof. And your Ambassador which remaineth here in our Court told me the cause of the slownesse of the gages or pledges vntil this time: which reckoning we accept of, and holde our selues as satisfied. And as touching the matter wherof you write vnto vs concerning Iohn Herman, and the selfe same complaint which your Ambassador hath made of him, before the comming of your letter, we had already commaunded him to be taken vpon the complaint which your Ambassadour had made of him, whereupon he still remaineth in hold, and shall so continue vntil further iustice be done vpon him according to his desert. And so our Lord keepe you in his safeguard. Written at our royall court in Marocco, which God maintaine, the 28. day of the moneth Remodan, Anno 996. [Marginal note: Which is with vs 1587.]

* * * * *

The Queenes Maiesties letters to the Emperour of Marocco.

[Sidenote: The Queenes letters to the Emperour.] Muy alto, y muy poderoso
Sennor,

Auiendo entendido de parte de nuestro Agente la mucha aficion, y volontad, que nos teneys, y quanta honta, y fauor le hazeys por amor nuestro, para dar nos tanto mayor testimonio de vuestra amistad, hemos recebido de lo vno y de le otro muy grande contento, y satisfacion; y assy no podemos dexar de agradesceroslo, como mereceys. Vuestras cartas hemos tambien recibido, y con ellas holgadonos infinitamente, por venir de parte de vn Principe, à quien tenemos tanta obligacion. Nuestro Agente nos ha escripto sobre ciertas cosas, que desseays ser os embiadas de aqui: Y, aunque queriamos poder os en ello puntualmente conplazer, como pidiz, ha succedido, que las guerras, en que stamos al presente occupadas, no nos lo consienten del todo: Hemos però mandado que se os satisfaga en parte, y conforme à lo que por agora la necessitad nos permite, como mas particularmente os lo declarará nuestro Agente: esperando, que lo reciberreys en buena parte y conforme al animo, con que os lo concedemos. Y porque nos ha sido referido, que aueys prometido de proceder contra vn

Iuan Herman vassallo nuestro, (el qual nos ha grauemente offendido) de la manera, que os lo demandaremos, auemos dado orden à nuestro dicho Agente de deziros mas parcularmente lo que desseamos ser hecho a cerca deste negocio, rogando os, que lo mandeys assi complir: y que seays seruido de fauorescer siempre al dicho Agente, y tener lo en buen credito, como hasta agora aueys hecho, sin permiter, que nadie os haga mudar de parecer a cerca de las calumnias, que le podran leuantar, ny dudar, que no complamos muy por entero todo, lo que de nuestra parte os prometiere. Nuestro Sennor guarde vostra muy alta y muy poderosa persona: Hecha en nuestra Corte Real de Grenewich a 20. de Iulio 1587.

The same in English.

Right high and mightie Prince, Hauing vnderstood from our Agent the great affection and good wil which you beare vs, and how great honour and fauor you shew him for our sake, to the end to giue vs more ample testimonie of your friendship, we haue receiued very great contentment and satisfaction, as wel of the one as of the other: and withall we could not omit to magnifie you, according to your desert. We haue also receiued your letters, and do not a litle reioyce thereof, because they come from a prince vnto whom we are so much beholden. Or Agent hath written vnto vs concerning certaine things which you desire to bee sent vnto you from hence. And albeit we wish that we could particularly satisfie you, as you desire, yet it is fallen out, that the warres, wherein at this present we be busied wil not suffer vs fully to doe the same: neuerthelesse, wee haue commaunded to satisfie you in part, and according as the present necessitie doeth permit vs, as our Agent will declare vnto you more particularly, hoping you will receiue it in good part, and according to the good will wherewith wee graunt the same. [Sidenote: Iohn Herman an English rebel.] And because it hath bene signified vnto vs that you haue promised to proceed in iustice against one Iohn Herman our subiect, which hath grieuously offended vs, in such sort as wee haue sent word vnto you, wee haue giuen order to our said Agent, to informe you more particularly in that which we desire to be done in this busines, praying you also to command the same to be put in execution: and that it would please you always to fauour our said Agent and to hold him in good credite, as you haue done hitherto, not suffering your selfe to be changed in your opinion, for all the false reports which they may raise against him, nor to doubt that wee will not accomplish at large all that he shall promise you on our behalfe. Our Lord keepe and preserue your right high and mightie person. Written in our royall Court at Greenwich the 20. of Iuly 1587.

* * * * *

A Patent granted to certaine Marchants of Exeter, and others of the West parts, and of London, for a trade to the Riuer of Senega and Gambia in Guinea, 1588.

Elizabeth by the grace of God Queene of England, France and Ireland, defender of the faith, &c. To our Treasurer and Admirral of England, our Treasurer and Barons of our Exchequer, and all and euery our Officers, ministers and subiects whatsoeuer, greeting. Whereas our welbeloued subiects William Brayley, Gilbert Smith, Nicolas Spicer, and Iohn Doricot of our City of Exeter marchants, Iohn Yong of Coliton in our county of Deuon marchant, Richard Doderige of Barnstable in our saide County of Deuon Marchant, Anthonie Dassell, and Nicolas Turner of our Citie of London Marchants, haue bene perswaded and earnestly moued by certaine Portugals resident within our Dominions, to vndertake and set forward a voyage to certaine places on the coast of Guinea; Videlicit, from the Northermost part of the Riuer commonly called by the name of the Riuer of Senega, and from and within that Riuer all along that coast vnto the Southermost part of another Riuer commonly called by the name of Gambra, and within that Riuer: [Sidenote: A former voyage to Gambra.] which, as we are informed they haue already once performed accordingly: And for that we are credibly giuen to vnderstand that the further prosecuting of the same voyage, and the due and orderly establishing of an orderly trafique and trade of marchandize into those Countries, wil not only in time be very beneficial to these our Realmes and dominions, but also be a great succour and reliefe vnto the present distressed estate of those Portugals, who by our princely fauour liue and continue here vnder our protection: And considering that the aduenturing and enterprising of a newe trade cannot be a matter of small charge and hazard to the aduenturers in the beginning: we haue therefore thought it conuenient, that our said louing subiects William Brayley, Gilbert Smith, Nicholas Spicer, Iohn Doricot, Iohn Young, Richard Doderige, Anthonie Dassell, and Nicholas Turner, for the better incouragement to proceede in their saide aduenture and trade in the said Countreis, shal haue the sole vse and exercise thereof for a certaine time. In consideration whereof, and for other waightie reasons and considerations, vs specially moouing, of our speciall grace, certaine knowledge and meere motion, we haue giuen and graunted, and by these presents for vs, our heires and successors doe giue and graunt vnto the said William Brayley, Gilbert Smith, Nicholas Spicer, Iohn Doricot, Iohn Young, Richard Doderide, Anthony Dassell and Nicholas Turner, and to euery of them, and to such other our Subiects as they or the most part of them shall thinke conuenient to receiue into their Company and society, to be the traders with them into the said Contreis, that they and euery of them by themselues or by their seruants or Factors and none others, shall and may for and during the full space and terme of tenne yeeres next ensuing the date of these presents, haue and enioy the free and whole trafique, trade and feat of marchandise, to and from the said Northermost part of the said Riuer, commonly called by the name of the Riuer of Senega: and from and within that riuer all along the coast of Guinea, vnto the Southermost part of the said Riuer, commonly called by the name of the Riuer of Gambra, and within that Riuer also. And that they the said William Brayley, Gilbert Smith, Nicholas Spicer, Iohn Doricot, Iohn Yong, Richard Doderige, Anthony Dassel and Nicholas Turner, and euery of them, by themselues or by their seruants or Factors, and such as they or the most part of them shall receiue into their Company and societie, to be traders with them into the sayd Countreis (as is aforesaid) and none others, shall and may, for, and during the said space and terme of 10. yeres, haue and enioy the sole and whole trafique or trade of marchandize into and from the said places afore limitted and described, for the buying and selling, bartering and changing of and with any goods, wares, and marchandizes whatsoeuer, to be vented had or found, at or within any the cities, townes, or places situated or being in the countries, partes and coastes of Guinea before limitted, any law, statute, or graunt, matter, custome or priuileges to the contrary in any wise notwithstanding. And for the better ordering, establishing, and gouerning of the said societie and Company in the said trade and trafique of marchandizes, and the quiet, orderly, and lawfull exercise of the same, We for vs, our heires, and successors, do by these presents giue and graunt full license and authority vnto the said William Brayley, Gilbert Smith, Nicholas Spicer, Iohn Doricot, Iohn Yong, Richard Doderige, Anthonie Dassell, and Nicholas Turner, and to such others as they shall receiue into their saide societie and company to be traders into the said countreis, as is aforesaid, and to euery of them, that they or the most part of them shall and may at all conuenient times at their pleasures, assemble and meete together in any place or places conuenient, aswell within our citie of Exeter, as elsewhere within this our Realme of England, or other our dominions, during the said terme of ten yeere, to consult of, for, and concerning the saide trade and trafique of marchandize, and from time to time to make, ordaine, and stablish good, necessary, and reasonable orders, constitutions, and ordinances, for, and touching the same trade. And al such orders, constitutions, and ordinances so to be made, to put in vse and execute, and them, or any of them, to alter, change, and make voyd, and, if neede be, to make new, as at any time, during the said terme of ten yeeres, to them, or the most part of them then trading, as is aforesaide, shall be thought necessary and conuenient. Vnto all and euery which said orders, constitutions, and ordinances, they, and euery of them, and all other persons which shall hereafter be receiued into the saide societie and Company, shall submit themselues, and shall well and duely obserue, performe, and obey the same, so long as they shall stand in force, or else shall pay and incurre such forfeitures, paines, and penalties, for the breach thereof, and in such maner and forme, and to such vses and intents, as by the saide orders, constitutions, and ordinances shall be assessed, limitted and appointed. So alwayes, as the same orders, constitutions and ordinances be not repugnant or contrary to the lawes, statutes, and customes of this Realme of England, nor any penaltie to exceede the reasonable forme of other penalties, assessed by the Company of our Marchants, named Aduenturers. And to the intent that they onely, to whom the said power and libertie of trafique and trade of marchandize is graunted by these our letters patent aforesaid, and none others whatsoeuer, without their speciall consent and license before had, shall, during the said terme of ten yeeres, vse, or haue trade or trafique, with or for any maner of goods or marchandizes, to and from the saide coastes or parts of Guinea afore limited: Wee doe by these presents, by our royall and supreme authoritie, straightly charge and commaund, that no person or persons whatsoeuer, by themselues, or by their factors, or seruants, during the said terme of 10. yeres, shall in any wise trade or trafique, for or with any goods or marchandizes, to or from the said coasts and parts of Guinea afore limited, other then the said William Brayley, Gilbert Smith, Nicholas Spicer, Iohn Doricot, Iohn Yong, Richard Doderige, Anthony Dassell, and Nicholas Turner, and such as from time to time, they, or the most part of them, shall receiue into their societie and company, to be traders with them, as is aforesaid, as they tender our fauour, and will auoyde our high displeasure, and vpon paine of imprisonment of his or their bodies, at our will and pleasure, and to lose and forfeit the ship or shippes, and all the goods, wares, and marchandizes, wherewith they, or any of them, shal, during the said terme of 10. yeres, trade, or trafique to or from the said Countries, or any part thereof, according to the limitation aboue mentioned, contrary to our expresse prohibition and restraint, in that behalfe. And further, we do by these presents giue and graunt full power and authoritie to the said William Braily, Gilbert Smith, Nicholas Spicer, Iohn Doricot, Iohn Yong, Richard Doderige, Anthony Dassell, and Nicholas Turner, and to such other persons, as they shal receiue into their society and company, to be traders with them, as is aforesaid, and the most part of them, for the time being: that they, and euery of them, by themselues, their factors, deputies, or assignes, shall and may, from time to time, during the said terme of 10. yeres, attach, arrest, take, and sease all, and all maner of ship, and ships, goods, wares, and marchandizes whatsoeuer, which shall be brought from, or caried to the said coasts and parts of Guinea afore limited, contrary to our will and pleasure, and the true meaning of the same, declared and expressed in these our letters patents. Of all and euery which said forfaitures whatsoeuer, the one third part shall be vnto vs, our heires, and successors, and another thirde part thereof we giue and graunt by these presents, for and towards the reliefe of the saide Portugals continuing here vnder our protection, as is aforesaid. And the other third part of al the same forfaitures, we do by these presents, of our certaine knowledge and meere motion, for vs, our heires and successors, giue and grant cleerely and wholy vnto the said William Brayley, Gilbert Smith, Nicholas Spicer, Iohn Doricot, Iohn Yong, Richard Doderige, Anthony Dassel, and Nicholas Turner, and such other persons, as they shall receiue into their societie, and company, as is aforesaid. And these our letters patents, or the inrolment or exemplification of the same, without any further or other warrant, shall from time to time, during the said tenne yeeres, be a sufficient warrant and authoritie to our Treasurer of England, for the time being, and to the barons of our Exchequer, and to all other our officers and ministers whatsoeuer, to whom it shall or may appertaine, to allow, deliuer, and pay one thirde part of all the said forfeitures, to the vse of the said Portugals, and one other thirde part of the same forfeitures, to the saide William Brayley, Gilbert Smith, Nicholas Spicer, Iohn Doricot, Iohn Yong, Richard Doderige, Anthony Dassell, and Nicholas Turner, and such other persons, as they shall receiue into their societie and Company, to be traders with them, as aforesaide, to their owne proper vse and behoofe: which said allowances and paiments thereof, our will and pleasure is, and we do straightly charge and commaund, to bee from time to time duely made and performed accordingly, without any delay or denial of any our officers aforesaid, or any other our officers or ministers whatsoeuer. And we do straightly charge and command, and by these presents probibite all and singular our customers, collectors, and farmers of our Customes and subsidies, and controllers of the same, of and within our ports of the citie of London, and the Citie of Exeter, and all other ports, creekes, and places, within this our Realme of England, and euery of them, and all other our officers and ministers whatsoeuer, which haue or shall haue any dealing or intermedling, touching our said Customes and subsidies, that they, ne any of them by themselues, their clearks, deputies, or substitutes, or any of them take or receiue, or in any wise cause or suffer to be taken or receiued for vs, or in our name, or to our vse, or for, or in the names or to the vses of our heires or successors, or any person, or persons, any summe or summes of money, or other things whatsoeuer, during the saide terme of ten yeeres, for, or in the name, lieu, or place of any Custome, subsidie, or other thing or duetie, to vs, our heires, or successors, due, or to be due, for the Customes or subsidies of any such goods, wares, or marchandizes, to be transported, caried, or brought to or from the priuileged places, before in these presents mentioned, or any of them: nor make, nor cause to be made any entry into, or of the bookes of subsidies or customes, nor make any agreement for the Customes or subsidies, of, or for any goods, wares or merchandizes, to bee sent to, or returned from any the priuleged places, before in these presents mentioned, sauing onely with, and in the name, and by the consent of the saide William Brayley, Gilbert Smith, Nicholas Spicer, Iohn Doricot, Iohn Yong, Richard Doderige, Antonie Dassel, and Nicholas Turner, or of some of them, or of such as they or the most part of them shall receiue into their societie and Company, as aforesaid. Prouided alwaies, that if at any time hereafter, we our selues, by our writing signed with our proper hand, or any sixe or more of our priuie Counsell, for the time being, shall by our direction, and by writing signed and subscribed with their hands, signifie and notifie to the said William Brayley, Gilbert Smith, Nicholas Spicer, Iohn Doricot, Iohn Yong, Richard Doderige, Anthony Dassell, and Nicholas Turner, or to any of them, or to any other, whom they or the most part of them shal receiue into their Companie and society, as is aforesaid, or otherwise to our officers in our ports of Exeter, or Plimouth, by them to be notified to such as shall haue interest in this speciall priuilege, that our will and pleasure is, that the said trade and trafique shal cease, and be no longer continued into the saide coastes and partes of Guinea before limited: then immediatly from and after the ende of sixe moneths next insuing, after such signification and notification so to be giuen to any of the said Company and societie, as is aforesaid, or otherwise to our Officers in our ports of Exeter or Plimouth, by them to be notified to such as shall haue interest in this speciall priuilege, these our present letters Patents, and our graunt therein contained shall be vtterly voyde, and of none effect, ne validitie in the lawe, to all intents and purposes: any thing before mentioned to the contrary in any wise notwithstanding. Witnesse our selfe at Westminster, the thirde day of May, in the thirtieth yere of our Reign 1588.

* * * * *

A voyage to Benin beyond the Countrey of Guinea, set foorth by Master Bird and Master Newton Marchants of London, with a shippe called the Richard of Arundell, and a Pinesse; Written by Iames Welsh, who was chiefe Master of the said voyage, begunne in the yeere 1588.

Vpon the twelft of October wee wayed our ankers at Ratcliffe and went to Blackwall. And the next day sayling from thence, by reason of contrary winde and weather, wee made it the 25. of October before wee were able to reach Plimouth, and there we stayed (to our great expense of victuals) for lacke of winde and weather vnto the 14. of December.

On Saturday the said 14. of December we put from thence, and about midnight were thwart of the Lizart.

[Sidenote: Rio del oro is in 22. degrees and 47. min.] Thursday the second of Ianuary wee had sight of the land neere Rio del oro, God be thanked, and there had 22. degrees of latitude, and 47. minutes.

[Sidenote: Cauo de las Barbas.] The thirde of Ianuary wee had sight of Cauo de las Barbas, and it bare Southeast fiue leagues off.

[Sidenote: Crosiers.] The 4. we had sight of the Crosiers in the morning.

[Sidenote: Cauo Verde in 14. degr. 43. m.] Tuesday the 7. day we had sight of Cauo verde, and I find this place to be in latitude 14. degrees, and 43. minutes, being 4. leagues from the shoare.

[Sidenote: Cauo de Monte.] Friday the 17. Cauo de Monte bare off vs North Northeast, we sounded and had 50. fathom blacke oase, and at 2. of the clocke it bare North Northwest 8. leagues off. [Sidenote: Cauo Mensurado.] And Cauo Mensurado bare of vs East and by South, and wee went Northeast with the maine: here the current setteth to the East Southeast alongst the shoare, and at midnight wee sounded and had 26. fathome blacke oase.

The 18. in the morning we were thwart of a land, much like Cauo verde, and it is as I iudge 9. leagues from Cauo Mensurado; it is a hill sadlebacked, and there are 4. or 5. one after another: and 7. leagues to the Southward of that, we saw a row of hils sadlebacked also, and from Cauo Mensurado are many mountaines.

[Sidenote: Rio de Sestos. Cauo dos Baixos.] The 19. we were thwart Rio de Sestos, and the 20. Cauo dos Baixos was North and by West 4. leagues off the shoare, [Sidenote: Tabanoo.] and at afternoone there came a boate frome the shoare with 3. Negroes, from a place (as they say) called Tabanoo. And towards euening we were thwart of an Island, and a great many of small Islands or rockes to the Southward, and the currant came out of the Souther-boord: we sounded and had 35. fathomes.

[Sidenote: A French ship at Ratire. Crua.] The 21. wee had a flat hill that bare North Northeast off vs, and wee were from the shoare 4. leagues, and at 2. a clocke in the afternoone we spake with a Frenchman riding neere a place called Ratire, and another place hard by called Crua. [Sidenote: A current to the Southeastward.] This Frenchman caried a letter from vs to M. Newton: wee layd it on hull while wee were writing of our letter; and the current set vs to the Southward a good pase alongst the shore South Southeast.

The 25. we were in the bight of the Bay that is to the Westward of Capo de Tres puntas: the currant did set East Northeast.

The 28. we lay sixe glasses a hull tarying for the pinesse.

[Sidenote: Caou de tres puntas.] The last of Ianuary the middle part of Cape de tres puntas was thwart of vs three leagues at seuen of the clocke in the morning: and at eight the pinnesse came to an anker: and wee prooued that the current setteth to the Eastward: and at sixe at night the Vttermost lande bare East and by South 5. leagues, and we went Southwest, and Southwest and by South.

Saturday the first of February 1588. we were thwart of a Round foreland, which I take to be the Eastermost part of Capo de tres puntas: and within the saide Round foreland was a great bay with an Island in the said bay.

[Sidenote: The Castle of Mina.] The second of February wee were thwart of the Castle of Mina, and when the thirde glasse of our Looke-out was spent, we spied vnder our Larbord-quarter one of their Boates with certaine Negroes, and one Portugale in the Boate, wee haue had him to come aboord, but he would not. [Sidenote: Two white watch-houses.] And ouer the castle upon the hie rockes we did see as it might be two watch-houses, and they did shew very white: and we went eastnortheast.

[Sidenote: Monte Redondo.] The 4 in the morning we were thwart a great high hill, and vp into the lande were more high ragged hilles, and those I reckoned to be but little short of Monte Redondo. Then I reckoned that we were 20 leagues Southeastward from the Mina, and at 11 of the clocke I sawe two hilles within the land, these hils I take to be 7 leagues from the first hils. And to sea-ward of these hilles is a bay, and at the east end of the bay another hill, and from the hils the landes lie verie low. We went Eastnortheast, and East and by North 22 leagues, and then East along the shore.

[Sidenote: Villa longa.] The 6 we were short of Villa longa, and there we met with a Portugall Carauell.

The 7 a faire temperate day, and all this day we road before Villa longa.

The 8 at noone we set saile from Villa longa, and ten leagues from thence we ankered againe and stayed all that night in ten fadom water.

[Sidenote: Rio de Lagos.] The ninth we set saile, and all alongst the shore were very thicke woodes, and in the afternoone we were thwart a riuer, and to the Eastward of the riuer a litle way off was a great high bush-tree as though it had no leaues, and at night we ankered with faire and temperate weather.

The 10 we set sayle and went East, and East and by South 14 leagues along the shoare, which was so full of thicke woods, that in my iudgement a man should haue much to doe to passe through them, and towards night we ankered in 7 fadome with faire weather.

[Sidenote: Very shallow water.] The 11 we sayled East and by South, and three leagues from the shore we had but 5 fadome water, and all the wood vpon the land was as euen as if it had beene cut with a paire of gardeners sheeres, and in running of two leagues we descerned a high tuft of trees vpon the brow of a land, which shewed like a Porpose head, and when wee came at it, it was but part of the lande, and a league further we saw a headland very low and full of trees, and a great way from the land we had very shallow water, then we lay South into the sea, because of the sands for to get into the deepe water, and when we found it deepe, we ankered in fiue fadom thwart the riuer of Iaya, in the riuers mouth.

The 12. in the morning we road still in the riuers mouth. This day we sent the pinnesse and the boat on land with the marchants, but they came not againe vntil the next morning. The shallowest part of this riuer is toward the West, where there is but 4 fadom and a halfe, and it is very broad. [Sidenote: Rio de Iaya.] The next morning came the boate aboord, and they also said it was Rio de Iaya. Here the currant setteth Westward, and the Eastermost land is higher then the Westermost Thursday the 13 we set saile, and lay South Southeast along the shore, where the trees are wonderfull euen, and the East shore is higher then the West shore, and when wee had sayled 18 leagues we had sight of a great riuer, then we ankered in three fadom and a halfe, and the currant went Westward. [Sidenote: Rio Benin.] This riuer is the riuer of Benin, and two leagues from the maine it is very shallowe.

[Sidenote: A currant Westward.] The 15 we sent the boat and pinesse into the riuer with the marchants, and after that we set saile, because we road in shallow water, and went Southsoutheast, and the starboard tacke aboord vntill we came to fiue fadom water, where we road with the currant to the Westward: then came our boat out of the harbour and went aboord the pinnesse. The West part of the land was high browed much like the head of a Gurnard, and the Eastermost land was lower, and had on it three tufts of trees like stackes of wheate or corne, and the next day in the morning we sawe but two of those trees, by reason that we went more to the Eastward. And here we road still from the 14 of Februarie vntill the 14 of Aprill, with the winde at Southwest.

The 16 of Februarie we rode still in fiue fadom, and the currant ranne still to the Westward, the winde at Southwest, and the boat and pinnesse came to vs againe out of the riuer, and told vs that there was but ten foote water vpon the barre. All that night was drowsie, and yet reasonable temperate.

The 17 a close day, the winde at Southwest. Our marchants wayed their goods and put them aboord the pinnesse to goe into the riuer, and there came a great currant out of the riuer and set to the Westward.

The 18 the marchants went with the boat and pinnesse into the riuer with their commodities. This day was close and drowsie, with thunder, raine, and lightning.

The 24 a close morning and temperate, and in the afternoone the boat came to vs out of the riuer with our marchants.

Twesday the 4 of March, a close soultry hot morning, the currant went to the Westward, and much troubled water came out of the riuer.

[Sidenote: Sicknesse among our men.] The 16 our pinnesse came a boord and
Anthonie Ingram in her, and she brought in her 94 bags of pepper, and 28 Elephants teeth, and the Master of her and all his company were sicke. This was a temperate day and the winde at Southwest.

The 17. 18. and 19 were faire temperate weather and the winde at Southwest. This day the pinnesse went into the riuer againe, and carried the Purser and the Surgion.

The 25 of the said moneth 1589 we sent the boate into the riuer.

[Sidenote: The death of the Captaine. Pepper and Elephants Teeth.] The 30 our pinnesse came from Benin, and brought sorowfull newes, that Thomas Hemstead was dead and our Captaine also, and she brought with her 159 Cerons or sackes of pepper and Elephants teeth.

[Sidenote: A good note.] Note that in all the time of our abiding here, in the mouth of the riuer of Benin, and in all the coast hereabout it is faire temperate weather, when the winde is at Southwest. And when the winde is at Northeast and Northerly, then it raineth, with lightning and thunder, and is very intemperate weather.

The 13 of Aprill 1589 we set saile homewards in the name of Iesus. In the morning we sayled with the winde at Southwest, and lay West and by North, but it prooued calme all that night, and the currant Southeast.

The 14 the riuer of Benin was Northeast 7 leagues from the shore, and there was little winde and towards night calme.

The 17 a faire temperate day the winde variable, and we had of latitude foure degrees and 20 minutes.

The 25 a faire temperate day the winde variable, and here we had three degrees and 29 minuts of latitude.

[Sidenote: A deceiptfll currant.] The 8 of May we had sight of the shore, which was part of Cauo de Monte, but we did not thinke we had beene so farre, but it came so to passe by reason of the currant. In this place M. Towrson was in like maner deceiued with the currant.

The 9 we had sight of Cauo de monte.

The 17 a darke drowsie day, this was the first night that I tooke the North starre.

The 26 a temperate day with litle winde, and we were in 12 degrees and 13 minutes of latitude.

The 30 we met a great sea out of the Northwest.

The 6 of Iune we found it as temperate as if we had beene in England, and yet we were within the height of the sunne, for it was declined 23 degrees, and 26 minuts to the Northward, and we had 15 degrees of latitude.

The 8 faire and temperate as in England, here we met with a counter sea, out of the Southborde.

The 15 a faire temperate day, the winde variable, here we had 18 degrees and fiftie nine minutes;

[Sidenote: Rockweed or Saragasso all along the sea.] The 12 of Iuly in 30 degrees of latitude we met with great store of rockweed, which did stick together like clusters of grapes, and this continued with vs vntill the 17 of the said moneth, and then we saw no more, at which 17 day we were in two and thirtie degrees sixe and fortie minutes of latitude.

The 25 at sixe of the clocke in the morning, we had sight of the Ile of Pike, it bare North and by East from vs, we being 15 leagues off.

The 27 we spake with the poste of London and she told vs good newes of England.

The nine and twentieth we had sight of the Island of Cueruo, and the 30 we saw the Island of Flores.

The 27 of August in 41 degrees of latitude we saw 9 saile of Britons, and three of them followed vs vntill noone, and then gaue vs ouer.

The 30 we had sight of Cape Finisterre.

The eight of September at night wee put into Plimouth sound, and road in Causon Bay all night.

The 9 we put into Catwater and there stayed vntill the 28 of September, by reason of want of men and sicknesse.

The nine and twentieth we set sayle from Plimouth, and arriued at London the second of October 1589.

The commodities that we caried in this voyage were cloth both linnen and woollen, yron worke of sundry sorts, Manillios or bracelets of copper, glasse beades, and corrall.

The commodities that we brought home were pepper and Elephants teeth, oyle of palme, cloth made of Cotton wool very curiously wouen, and cloth made of the barke of palme trees. Their monie is pretie white shels, for golde and siluer we saw none. [Sidenote: Inamia, a kind of bread in Benin.] They haue also great store of cotton growing: their bread is a kind of roots, they call it Inamia, and when it is well sodden I would leaue our bread to eat of it, it is pleasant in eating, and light of digestion, the roote thereof is as bigge as a mans arme. Our men vpon fish-dayes had rather eate the rootes with oyle and vineger, then to eate good stockfish. [Sidenote: Wine of palm trees.] There are great store of palme trees, out of which they gather great store of wine, which wine is white and very pleasant, and we should buy two gallons of it for 20 shels. They haue good store of sope, and it smelleth like beaten violets. Also many pretie fine mats and baskets that they make, and spoones of Elephants teeth very curiously wrought with diuers proportions of foules and beasts made vpon them. There is vpon the coast wonderfull great lightning and thunder, in so much as I neuer hard the like in no Countrey, for it would make the decke or hatches tremble vnder our feete, and before we were well acquainted with it, we were fearefull, but God be thanked we had no harme. The people are very gentle and louing, and they goe naked both men and women vntill they be married, and then they goe couered from the middle downe to the knees. [Sidenote: Abundance of honey.] They would bring our men earthen pottes of the quantitie of two gallons, full of hony and hony combes for 100 shelles. They would also bring great store of Oranges and Plantans which is a fruit that groweth upon a tree, and is like vnto a Cucumber but very pleasant in eating. It hath pleased God of his mercefull goodnesse to give me the knowledge how to preserue fresh water with little cost, [Marginal note: This preseruatiue is wrought by casting into an hogshead of water an handful of bay-salt, as the author told me.] which did serue vs sixe moneths at the sea, and when we came into Plimmouth it was much wondered at, of the principal men of the towne, who said that there was not sweeter water in any spring in Plimmouth. Thus doth God prouide for his creatures, vnto whom be praise now and for euermore, Amen.

* * * * *

The voiage set forth by M. Iohn Newton, and M. Iohn Bird marchants of London to the kingdome and Citie of Benin in Africa, with a ship called the Richard of Arundell, and a pinnesse, in the yere 1588. briefly set downe in this letter following, written by the chiefe Factor in the voyage to the foresaid Marchants at the time of the ships first arriual at Plimouth.

Worshipful Sirs, the discourse of our whole proceeding in this voyage wil aske more time and a person in better health then I am at this present, so that I trust you will pardon me, till my comming vp to you: in the meane time let this suffice. Whereas we departed in the moneth of December from the coast of England with your good ship the Richard of Arundell and the pinnesse, we held on our direct course towards our appointed port, and the 14 day of Februarie following we arriued in the hauen of Benin, where we found not water enough to carry the ship ouer the barre, so that we left her without in the road, and with the pinnesse and ship boat, into which we had put the chiefest of our marchandise, [Sidenote: Goto in Benin.] we went vp the riuer to a place called Goto, where we arriued the 20 of February, the foresaid Goto being the neerest place that we could come to by water, to go for Benin. [Sidenote: The great citie of Benin.] From thence we presently sent Negroes to the king, to certifie him of our arriuall, and of the cause of our comming thither: who returned to vs againe the 22 day with a noble man in their company to bring vs vp to the Citie, and with 200 Negroes to carrie our commodities: hereupon the 23 day we deliuered our marchandize to the Kings Factor, and the 25 day we came to the Citie of Benin, where we were well intertained: The sixe and twenty day we went to the Court to haue spoken with the king, which (by reason of a solemne feast then kept amongst them) we could not doe: but yet we spake with his Veadore, or chiefe man, that hath the dealing with the Christians: and we conferred with him concerning our trading, who answered vs, that we should have all thing to our desire, both in pepper and Elephants teeth.

The first of March, we were admitted to the kings presence, and he made vs the like courteous answere for our traffike: the next day we went againe to the Court, where the foresaid Veadore shewed vs one basket of greene pepper, and another of dry in the stalkes: wee desired to haue it plucked from the stalks and made cleane, who answered, that it would aske time, but yet it should be done: and that against another yeere it should be in better readines, and the reason why we found it so vnprepared was, because in this kings time no Christians had euer resorted thither, to lade pepper. The next day there were sent vs 12 baskets, and so a litle euery day vntill the 9 of March at which time we had made vpon 64 serons of pepper, and 28 Elephants teeth. In this time of our being at Benin (our natures at this first time not so well acquainted with that climate) we fell all of vs into the disease of the feuer, whereupon the Captaine sent me downe with those goods which we alreadie had receiued, to the rest of our men at Goto: where being arriued, I found all the men of our pinnesse sicke also, and by reason of their weaknes not able to conuey the pinnesse and goods downe to the place where our ship road: but by good hap within two houres after my comming to Goto, the boate came vp from the ship, to see how all things stood with vs, so that I put the goods into the boat, and went downe towards the ship: but by that time I was come aboord, many of our men died: namely, Master Benson, the Cooper, the Carpenter, and 3 or 4 more, and my selfe was also in such a weake state that I was not able to returne againe to Benin. Whereupon I sent vp Samuel Dunne, and the Chirurgian with him to our men, that were about to let them blood, if it were thought needfull: who at their comming to Benin, found the Captaine and your sonne William Bird dead, and Thomas Hempsteede very weake, who also died within two dayes after their comming thither. This sorrowfull accident caused them with such pepper and teeth, as they could then find, speedily to returne to the ship, as by the Cargason will appeare: at their comming away the Veadore tolde them, that if they could or would stay any longer time, he would vse all possible expedition to bring in more commodities: but the common sicknesse so increased and continued amongst vs all, that by the time our men which remained were come aboord, we had so many sicke and dead of our companie, that we looked all for the same happe, and so thought to loose both our ship, life, countrey and all. Very hardly and with much adoe could we get vp our ankers, but yet at last by the mercie of God hauing gotten them vp, but leauing our pinnesse behind vs, we got to sea, and set saile, which was vpon the 13 of Aprill. After which by little and little our men beganne to gather vp their crums and to recouer some better strength: and so sailing betwixt the Ilands of Cape Verde, and the maine we came to the Islands of the Azores vpon the 25 of Iuly, where our men beganne a fresh to grow ill, and divers died, among whom Samuel Dun was one, and as many as remained liuing were in a hard case: but in the midst of our distresse, it fell so well out, by Gods good prouidence, that we met with your ship the Barke Burre, on this side the North cape, which did not only keepe vs good companie, but also sent vs sixe fresh men aboord, without whose helpe, we should surely haue tasted of many inconueniences. But by this good meanes we are now at the last arriued in Plimouth, this 9 day of September: and for want of better health at this time, I referre the further knowledge of more particularities till my comming to London. Yours to commaund Antony Ingram.

* * * * *

The second voyage to Benin, set foorth by Master Iohn Newton, and Master
  Iohn Bird Marchants of London in the yeere 1590 with a ship called the Richard of Arundell of the burthen of one hundreth tunnes, and a small pinnesse, in which voyage Master Iames Welsh was chiefe Maister.

The third of September 1590 we set saile from Ratclife, and the 18 of the said moneth we came into Plimouth sound, and the two and twentieth we put to sea againe, and at midnight we were off the Lisart, and so passed on our voyage vntill the 14 of October, on which day we had sight of Forteuentura one of the Canarie Islands, which appeared very ragged as we sailed by it.

The 16 of October, in the latitude of 24 degrees and nine minutes we met with a great hollow sea, the like whereof I neuer saw on this coast, and this day there came to the ships side a monstrous great fish (I thinke it was a Gobarto) which put vp his head to the steepe tubs where the cooke was in shifting the victuals, whom I thought the fish would haue caried away.

The 21 in this latitude of 18 degrees we met with a countersea out of the North boord, and the last voyage in this very place we had the countersea out of the South, being very calme weather as now it is also.

[Sidenote: A token of a Northerly winde.] The 24 we had sight of Cauo Verde, and the 25 we met with a great hollow sea out of the North, which is a common signe that the winde will be Northerly, and so it prooued.

The 15 of Nouember we met with three currants out of the West and Northwest, one after another, with an houres time betweene each currant. This was in the latitude of 6 degrees and 42 minutes.

[Sidenote: Great currants.] The 18 day we met with two other great currants out of the Southwest, and the 20 we saw another current out of the Northeast, and the 24 we had a great current out of the Southsouthwest, and at 6 of the clocke towards night we had 3 currents more.

The 27 we thought that we had gone at the least 2 leagues and a halfe euery watch, and it fell out that we sailed but one league euery watch for the space of 24 houres, by meanes of a great billow and current that came still out of the South.

The 5 of December in setting the watch we cast about and lay East Northeast, and Northeast, and here in 5 degrees and a halfe our pinnesse lost vs wilfully.

The 7 at the going downe of the Sunne we saw a great blacke spot in the Sunne, and the 8. day both at rising and setting we saw the like, which spot to our seeming was about the bignesse of a shilling, being in 5 degrees of latitude, and still there came a great billow of the southerboord.

The 14 we sounded and had 15 fadom water and grosse red sand, and 2 leagues from the shore the currant set Southeast along the shore with a billow still out of the southerboord.

[Sidenote: Two rocks.] The 15 we were thwart a rocke somewhat like the Mewstone in England, it was 2 leagues from vs, here we sounded and had 27 fadom, but the rocke is not aboue a mile from the shore, and a mile farther we saw another rocke and betweene them both broken ground; here we sounded and had but 20 fadome and blacke sand, and we might see plaine that the rockes went not along the shore, but from the land to the seaward, and about 5 leagues to the Southwards we sawe a great bay, here we had 4 degrees and 27 minuts.

[Sidenote: A French ship of Hunfleur.] The 16 we met with a French ship of Hunfleur, who robbed our pinnesse, we sent a letter by him, and this night we saw another spot in the sunne at his going downe. And towards euening we were thwart of a riuer, and right ouer the riuer was a high tuft of trees.

[Sidenote: Cauo del las Palmas.] The 17 we ankered in the riuers mouth, and then we found the land to be Cauo de las Palmas, and betweene vs and the cape was a big ledge of rockes, one league and a halfe into the sea, and they bare to the West of the Cape, we saw also an Island off the point of the foreland, thus it waxed night that we could perceiue no more of the lande, but onely that it trended in like a bay, where there runneth a streame as if it were in the riuer of Thames, and this was the change day of the Moone.

The 19 a faire temperate day, and the wind South, we went East, and the lande a sterne of vs West, and it shewed low by the water side like Islands, this was the East of Cauo de las Palmas, and it trended in with a great sound, and we went East all night, and in the morning wee were but 3 or 4 leagues from the shore.

The 20 we were thwart of a riuer railed Rio de los Barbos.

The 21 we went along the shore East, and 3 or 4 leagues to the West of Cauo de tres puntas, I find the bay to be set deeper then it is by 4 leagues, and at 4 of the clocke the land begun to shewe high, and the first part of it full of Palme trees.

The 24 still going by the shore, the land was very low and full of trees by the water side, and at 12 of the clocke we ankered thwart of the riuer called, Rio de Boilas. Here we sent our boate a shore with the marchants, but they durst not put into the riuer because of a great billow that continually brake at the entrance vpon the barre.

The 28 we sailed alongst the shore, and ankered at night in seuen fadom because a great current would haue put vs backe, which came from the East Southeast from Papuas.

[Sidenote: Arda.] The 29 at noone we were thwart of Arda, and there we tooke a Carauel but the men were fled on land, then we went aboord her, but she had nothing in her but only a litle oyle of Palme trees, and a few roots. The next morning, our Captaine and marchants went to meete Portugals, that came in a boate to speake with vs, where they communed about the buying of the Carauell of our men againe, and the Portugals promised that we should haue for the Carauell, certaine bullocks and Elephants teeth, and they gaue vs one tooth and one bullocke presently, and sayd they would bring vs the rest the next day.

[Sidenote: Ianuarie.] The first of Ianuarie our Captaine went on land to speake with the Portugales, but when he saw they did dissemble, he came aboord againe, and presently we vnrigged the Carauell, and set her on fire before the towne. Then we set saile and went along the coast, where we saw a Date tree, the like whereof is not in all that coast vpon the water side, also we fell on ground a litle in one place: [Sidenote: Villa longa.] Thus we went to Villa longa, and there ankered.

[Sidenote: Rio de Lagoa.] The third we were as far shot as Rio de Lagoa, where our marchants went a shore and vpon the barre they found 3 fadom flat, but they went not in because it was late. There is also to the Eastward of this riuer a Date tree higher than all the rest of the other trees thereabout. Thus we went along the coast, and euery night ankered, and al the shore as we went was full of trees and thicke woods.

[Sidenote: The riuer Iaya.] The 6 day in the morning it was very foggy, so that we could not see the land, and at three of the clocke in the afternoone it cleared vp, and then we found our selues thwart of the riuer of Iaya, and when we found the shallow water, we bare into the sea South, as we did the voyage before, and came to an ancre in fiue fadom water. [Sidenote: The riuer Benin.] The next day we set saile againe, and towards noone we were thwart of the riuer of Benin in foure fadom water.

The 10 day our Captaine went on land with the shallop at 2 a clocke in the afternoone. All this weeke it was very foggy euery day vntill ten a clocke, and all this time hitherto hath beene as temperate as our summer in England. This day we went into the road and ankered, and the west point of the road bare East northeast off vs, wee riding in foure fadome water.

[Sidenote: Goto.] The 21 a faire temperate day, this day M. Hassald went to the towne of Goto, to heare newes of the Captaine.

The 23 came the Carauell, and Samuell in her, and she brought 63 Elephants teeth, and three bullocks.

The 28 a faire temperate day, and towards night there fell much raine, lightning, and thunder, this day our boate came aboord from Goto.

The 24 of Februarie, we tooke in 298 Cerons or sackes of pepper, and 4 Elephants teeth, and the winde was at Southeast. And the 26 we put the rest of our goods into the Carauell, and M. Hassald went with her to Goto.

The 5 of March the Carauel came againe and brought 21 Cerons of pepper, and 4 Elephants teeth.

The 9 of Aprill our Carauell came aboord with water for our prouision for the sea, and this day also we lost our shallope.

The 17 a drowsie rainie day, and in the afternoone we saw 3 great spoutes of raine, two on our larbord side, and one right with the ships head, but God be thanked, they came not at vs, and this day we tooke in the last of our water for the sea, and the 26 we victualed our Carauell to go with vs to the sea.

The 27 we set saile to goe homewarde with the winde at Southwest, and at two a clocke in the afternoone, the riuer of Benin was Northeast 8 leagues from vs.

The 3 of May we had such a terrible gust with raine, lightning and thunder, that it tore and split our fore saile, and also the Carauels foresayle and maine-sayle, with the wind at Southeast.

The 12 a faire temperate day, much like our sommer mornings in England, being but one degree and a halfe from the line, but at midnight we had a cruell gust of raine; and the wind at northeast.

The 24 we were South from Cauo de las Palmas 37 leagues.

The first of Iuly we had sight of the Iland of Braua, and it bare East 7 leagues off, and this Island is one of the Islands of Cauo Verde.

The 13 of August we spake with the Queenes ships, the Lord Thomas Howard being Admirall, and sir Richard Greeneuill Viceadmirall. They kept vs in their company vntill the 15 day night, themselues lying a hull, in waight for purchase 30 leagues to the Southwest of the Island of Flores.

[Sidenote: We departed in company of a prise.] The 15 we had leaue to depart with a fly-boat laden with sugar that came from Sant Thome, which was taken by the Queenes ships, whereof my Lord Admirall gaue me great charge, not to leaue her vntill she were harbored in England.

The three and twentieth the Northeast part of the Island of Coruo bare of vs East and by South sixe leagues off.

The 17 of September we met with a ship of Plimouth that came out of the West Indies, but she could tell vs no newes. The next day we had sight of another sayle, this day also one of our company named M. Wood died.

The 23 we spake with the Dragon of my Lord of Cumberland, whereof Master
Iuie was Maister.

The second of October we met with a ship of New-castle which came from Newfoundland, and out of her we had 300 couple of Newland fish.

The 6 we had sight of Sillie, and with raine and winde we were forced to put into S. Maries sound, where we staied all night, and 4 dayes after.

The 11 we set saile againe, and comming out had three fadom vpon the barre at a high water, then we lay out Southeast, through Crow-sand, and shortly after we had sight of the lands end, and at ten of the clocke we were thwart of the Lysart.

The 13 we were put into Dartmouth, and there we stayd vntill the 12 of December. From thence we put out with the winde at West, and the 18 of December, God be praised, we ankered at Limehouse in the Thames, where we discharged 589 sacks of Pepper, 150 Elephants teeth, and 32 barrels of oile of Palme trees.

The commodities that we caried out this second voyage were Broad cloth, Kersies, Bayes, Linnen cloth, Yron vnwrought, Bracelets of Copper, Corall, Hawks belles, Horsetails, Hats, and such like.

This voyage was more comfortable vnto vs then the first, because we had good store of fresh water, and that very sweet: for as yet we haue very good water in the shippe which we brought out of the riuer of Benin the first day of Aprill 1591. and it is at this day (being the 7 of Iune 1592.) to be seene aboord the ship as cleare and as sweet as any fountaine can yeeld.

In this voyage we sailed 350 leagues within halfe a degree of the equinoctiall line, and there we found it more temperate than where we rode. [Marginal note: It is more temperate vnder the equinoctiall, then on the coast of Guinie and Benin.] And vnder the line we did kill great store of small Dolphines, and many other good fishes, and so did we all the way, which was a very great refreshing vnto vs, and the fish neuer forsooke vs vntil we were to the Northwards of the Ilands of Azores, and then we could see no more fish, but God be thanked wee met with good company of our countrey ships which were great comfort vnto vs, being fiue moneths before at Sea without any companie. By me Iames Welsh master of the Richard of Arundell, in both these voyages to the riuer of Benin.

* * * * *

An Aduertisement sent to Philip the second king of Spaine from Angola by one Baltazar Almeida de Sousa, touching the state of the forsayd countrey, written the 21 of May. 1591.

The 26 of Iuly I certified your maiestie by Iohn Frere de Bendanha your maiesties pay-master and commissioner, with the gouernour Paulo Dias, which is lately deceased, of all things that happened the 28 of December in the yere last past 1590. Now I thought it conuenient to aduertise your maiestie what hath fallen out since that time, which is as foloweth. The gouernour Luis Serrano encamped himselfe eight leagues from Cabasa, where the Negro king dwelleth with 350 Portugal souldiers: and afterward being there encamped, it hapned that the King of Matamba sent a strong and mightie army, and in warlike maner, with strange inuentions for the sayd purpose. [Sidenote: 114 Portugals slaine in Angola.] So the king of Angola gaue this other king battell, and the gouernour sent 114 souldiers Portugals to helpe the said king of Angola: in which battell it was the will of God that our army was ouerthrown and all slaine, as well our Portugals as the Moores which tooke part with them. So with this ouerthrow it happened that this realme the second time hath rebelled against your maiestie. Herevpon the Governour assembling the rest of his Portugal souldiers, to the number of 250 altogether, went to Amasanguano, which is now his place of abode. Moreouer, besides the manifold losses which haue befallen the Portugals in this realme, your maiestie hath sustained other great misfortunes in your lands and goods. And because I cannot personally come to certifie your maiestie thereof, I thought it good to write some part of the same whereby your maiestie may vnderstand the estate of this countrey. This realme for the most part thereof hath twise benne wonne, and twise lost for want of good gouernment For here haue bene many gouernours which haue pretended to do iustice, but haue pitifully neglected the same, and practised the cleane contrary.

[Sidenote: The only way to reduce a rebellous kingdom vnto obedience.] And this I know to be most true. But the onely way to recouer this realme, and to augment your maiesties lands, goods and treasure, must be by sending some noble and mighty man to rule here, which must bring authoritie from your maiestie, and by taking streight order that euery captaine which doeth conquere here may bee rewarded according to his deserts. Likewise your maiestie must send hither 2000 good souldiers, with munition and sufficient store of prouision for them. And by this means your highnesse shall know what yeerely reuenue Angola will yeeld vnto your coffers, and what profit will grow thereof. Otherwise your maiestie shall reape but litle benefit here. If with my presence I may doe your maiestie any seruice in giuing information of the state of this realme, as one which haue had experience thereof, and haue seene the order of it, vpon the vnderstanding of your maiesties pleasure herein, I will do my best endeuour. [Sidenote: An vsuall trick of lewd gouernours.] And the cause whereof I haue not done this heretofore hath bene, by reason that the Gouernors of this realme would suffer none of the captaines which haue conquered this countrey to informe your maiestie of that which is needfull for your seruice, and the augmenting of this conquest. Our lord preserue your catholique person with increase of many kingdomes, and the augmentation of youre crowne. Written, in the conquest of the realme of

Angola the 21 of May 1591. Your majesties most loiall subiect, Baltazar Almeida de Souza.

* * * * *

Confimatio treugarum inter Regem Angliæ Eduardum quartum, et Ioannem secundum Regem Portugalliæ, datarum in oppido montis Maioris 8 Februarij, et apud Westmonasterium 12 Septembris, 1482, anno regni 22 Regis Eduardi quarti, lingua Lusitanica ex opere sequenti excerpta.

Libro das obras de Garcia de Resende, que tracta da vida è feitos del Rey dom Ioham secundo.

Embaixada que el Ray mandou à el Rey d'Inglaterra, cap.33

Eda qui de Monte Mor mandou el Rey por embaixadores à el rey dom Duarte de Inglaterra Ruy de Sousa pessoa principal è de muyto bon saber é credito, de que el Rey muyto confiaua, é ho doutor Ioam d'Eluas, é Fernam de Pina por secretario. E foram por mar muy honradamente com muy boa companhia: hos quaes foram en nome del Rey confirmar as ligas antiquas com Inglaterra, que polla condisan dellas ho nouo Rey de hum reyno é do outro era obrigado à mandar confirmar: é tambien pera mostrarem ho titolo que el rey tinha no senhorio de Guinee, pera que depois de visto el rey d'Inglaterra defendesse em todos seus reynos, que ninguen armasse nem podesse mandar à Guinee: é assi mandasse desfazer buna armada, que pera las faziam, per mandado do Duque de Medina Sidonia, hum Ioam Tintam é hum Guilherme Fabiam Ingreses. Com ha qual embaixada el rey d'Inglaterra mostrou receber grande contentamento, é foy delle com muyta honra recebida, é em tudo fez inteiramente ho que pellos embaixadores lhe foy requerido. De que elles trouxeran autenticas [Marginal note: These writings are in the tower.] escrituras das diligencias que con pubricos pregones fizeram: é assi as prouisones das aprauasones que eran necessarias: é com tudo muyto ben acabado, é ha vontade del rey se vieram.

The Ambassage which king Iohn the second, king of Portugall, sent to Edward the fourth king of England, which in part was to stay one Iohn Tintam, and one William Fabian English men, from proceeding in a voyage which they were preparing fot Guinea, 1481, taken out of the booke of the workes of Garcias de Resende, which intreateth of the life and acts of Don Iohn the second, king of Portugall. Chap. 33.

And afterwards the king sent as Ambassadours from the towne of Monte maior to king Edward the fourth of England, Ruy de Sousa, a principall person, and a man of great wisedome and estimation, and in whom the king reposed great trust, with doctor Iohn d'Eluas, and Ferdinand de Pina, as secretarie. And they made their voyage by sea very honourably, being very well accompanied. [Sidenote: The first cause of this ambassage.] These men were sent on the behalfe of their king, to confirme the ancient leagues England, wherein it was conditioned that the new king of the one and of the other kingdome, should be bound to send to confirme the olde leagues. [Sidenote: The second cause.] And likewise they had order to shew and make him acquainted with the title which the king held in the segneury of Ginnee, to the intent that after the king of England had seene the same, he should giue charge thorow all his kingdomes, that no man should arme or set foorth ships to Ginnee: [Sidenote: The third cause.] and also to request him, that it would please him to giue commandement to dissolue a certaine fleet, which one Iohn Tintam and one William Fabian, English men, were making, by commandement of the duke of Medina Sidonia, to goe to the aforesayd parts of Ginnee. With which ambassage the king of England seemed to be very well pleased, and they were receiued of him with very great honour, and he condescended vnto all that the ambassadours required of him, at whose hands they receiued authenticall writings of the diligence which they had performed, with publication thereof by the heralds: and also prouisoes of those confirmations which were necessary. And hauing dispatched all things well, and with the kings good will, they returned home into their countrey.

* * * * *

A relation sent by Melchior Petoney to Nigil de Moura at Lisbon, from the Iland and Castle of Arguin, standing a little to the southward of Cape Blanco, in the Northerly latitude of 19 degrees, concerning the rich and secret trade from the inland of Africa thither: Anno 1591.

[Sidenote: Commodities fit for Arguin.] As concerning the trade to this Castle and Iland of Arguin, your worship is to vnderstand, that if it would please the kings maiesty to send hither two or three carauels once in a yeere with Flanders and Spanish commodities, as Bracelets of glasse, Kniues, Belles, Linnen-cloth, Looking-glasses, with other kindes of small wares, his hignesse might do great good here. For 50 leagues vp into the land the Moores haue many exceedingly rich golde mines; insomuch that they bring downe their golde to this Castle to traffique with vs: and for a small trifle they will give vs a great wedge of gold. And because here is no trade, the sayd Moores cary their golde to Fez being 250 leagues distant from hence, and there doe exchange the same for the forsayd kindes of commodities. By this meanes also his maiesty might stop that passage, and keepe the king of Fez from so huge a mass of golde. [Sidenote: Scarlet and fine Purple cloth greatly accepted.] Scarlet-clothes, and fine Purples are greatly accepted of in these parts. It is a most fertile country within the land, and yeeldeth great store of Wheat, flesh of all kindes, and abundance of fruits. [Sidenote: A good harbor before the Castle of Arguin.] Therefore if it were possible, you should do well to deale with his maiesty, either himselfe to send a couple of carauels, or to giue your worship leaue to traffique here: for here is a very good harbour where ships may ride at ancre hard by the Castle. The countrey where all the golde-mines are is called The kingdome of Darha. [Marginal note: Concerning this kingdome reade Leo Africanus a little after the beginning of his 6 booke.] In this kingdome are great store of cities and townes; and in euery city and towne a Captaine with certaine souldiers; which Captaines are lords and owners of the sayd townes. One city there is called Couton, another Xanigeton, as also the cities of Tubguer, Azegue, Amader, Quaherque, and the towne of Faroo. The which townes and cities are very great and fairely built, being inhabited by rich Moores, and abounding with all kinde of cattell, Barley and Dates. And here is such plenty of golde found vpon the sands by the riuers side, that the sayd Moores usually cary the same Northward to Marocco, and Southward to the city of Tombuto in the land of Negros, which city standeth about 300 leagues from the kingdome of Darha; and this kingdome is but 60 leagues from this Iland and Castle of Arguin. Wherefore I beseech your worship to put his maiesty in remembrance hereof; for the sayd cities and townes are but ten dayes iourney from hence. I heartily wish that his maiesty would send two or three marchants to see the state of the Countrey, who might trauell to the aforesayd cities, to understand of their rich trade. For any man may go safe and come safe from those places. And thus without troubling of your worship any further, I humbly take my leaue. From the Iland and Castle of Arguin the 20 of Ianuary 1591.

Your worships seruant

Melchior Petoney.

* * * * *

The voyage of Richard Rainolds and Thomas Dassel to the riuers of Senega and Gambra adioining vpon Guinea, 1591 with a discourse of the treasons of certaine of Don Antonio his seruants and followers.

By vertue of her Maiesties most gracious charter giuen in the yeere 1588, and in the thirtieth yeere of her Highnesse reigne, certaine English marchants are granted to trade, in and from the riuer of Senega to and in the riuer of Gambra, on the Westerne coast of Africa. The chiefest places of traffique on that coast betweene these riuers, are these:

[Sidenote: The names of the chiefe places of traffike between Senega and Gambra.] 1 Senega riuer: The commodities be hides, gumme, elephants teeth, a few graines, ostrich feathers, amber-griece, and some golde.

2 Beseguiache, a towne by Capo Verde * [sic—KTH] leagues from Senega riuer: The commodities be small hides, and a few teeth.

3 Refisca Vieio, a towne 4 leagues from Beseguiache: The commodities be small hides, and a few teeth now and then.

4 Palmerin, a towne 2 leagues from Refisca: The commodities be small hides, and a few elephants teeth now and then.

5 Porto d'Ally, a towne 5 leagues from Palmerin: The commodities be small hides, teeth, amber-griece, and a little golde: and many Portugals are there.

6 Candimal, a towne halfe a league from Porto d'Ally: The commodities be small hides, and a few teeth now and then.

7 Palmerin, a towne 3 leagues from Candimal: The commodities be small hides, and a few teeth now and then.

8 Ioala, a towne 6 leagues from Palmerin: The commodities be hides, waxe, elephants teeth, rice, and some golde: and many Spaniards and Portugals are there.

9 Gambra riuer: The commodities are rice, waxe, hides, elephants teeth, and golde.

The Frenchmen of Diepe and New-hauen haue traded thither aboue thirty yeres: and commonly with four or five ships a yere, whereof two small barks go into the riuer of Senega. The other were wont (vntill within these four yeres, that our ships came thither) to ride with their ships in the road of Porto d'Ally and so sent their small shaloups of six or eight tunnes to some of these places on the Sea coast before repeated. Where in all places generally they were well beloued and as courteously entertained of the Negros, as if they had been naturally borne in the country. And very often the Negros come into France and returne againe, which is a further increasing of mutuall loue and amity. Since our comming to that coast the Frenchmen ride with their shippes at Refisca Vieio and suffered vs to ancre with our shippes at Porto d'Ally. The Frenchmen neuer vse to go into the riuer of Gambra: which is a riuer of secret trade and riches concealed by the Portugals. For long since one Frenchman entered the riuer with a small barke which was betrayed, surprised and taken by two gallies of the Portugals.

In our second voyage and second yeere there were by vile treacherous meanes of the Portugals and the king of the Negros consent in Porto d'Ally and Ioala about forty Englishmen cruelly slaine and captiued, and most or all of their goods confiscated: whereof there returned onely two, which were marchants. And also by procurement of Pedro Gonsalues, one of Don Antonio the kings seruants, Thomas Dassel and others had bene betrayed, if it had not pleased Almighty God to reueale the same, whereby it was preuented.

From the South side of Senega riuer on the Sea coast vnto about Palmerin is all one kingdome of Negros. The kings name is Melick Zamba, who dwelleth two dayes iourney within the land from Refisca.

The 12 of Nouember 1591, I Richard Rainolds and Thomas Dassel factors in a ship called the Nightingale of London 125 tunnes, and a pinnesse called the Messenger of 40 tonnes arriued neere vnto Capo Verde at a little Iland called The Iland of liberty. At this Iland we set vp a small pinnesse, with which we cary our marchandise on land when wee traffique. And in the meane time Thomas Dassel went with the great pinnesse to traffike with Spaniards or Portugals in Porto d'Ally or Ioala. Ouer against the sayd Iland on the maine is an habitation of the Negros called Besegueache. The alcaide or gouernor thereof with a great traine came aboord in their canoas to receiue the kings dueties for ankerage and permitting the quiet setting vp of our pinnesse: who liked passing well that no Portugall came in the shippe, saying, we should be better thought of by the king and people, if we neuer did bring Portugall, but come of our selues as the Frenchmen euer did and doe. And to purchase the more loue, I Richard Rainolds gaue him and all his company courteous entertainment. Also vpon his intreaty, hauing sufficient pledge aboord, I and others went on land with him. At this instant there was great warre betweene this alcaide and another gouernor of the next prouince. Neuerthelesse vpon our arriuall truce was taken for a space; and I with our company conducted among both enemies to the gouernors house in Besegueache, and were gently and friendly feasted after their maner, and with some presents returned safe aboord againe. The next day the alcaide came aboord againe, to wil me to send some yron and other commodities in the boat to traffike with the Negros, and also requested me that I would go to Refisca with the ship; which I did. And one thing I noted, that a number of Negros attended the alcaides landing in warlike maner with bowes and poisoned arrowes, darts poisoned, and swords, (because that the enemies by reason of the truce taken were there also to view the ship) who for the most part approched to him kneeling downe and kissed the backe of his hand.

The 17 of Nouember we weyed anker; and by reason no French ship was yet come, I went to the road of Refisca: where I sent for the alcaides interpreters, who came thither aboord, and receiued of me the kings duties for to haue free traffike with the Negros, with whom dayly I exchanged my yron and other wares for hides and some elephants teeth, finding the people very friendly and tractable. And the next day after our arriuall I went vp into the land about three miles to the towne of Refisca, where I was friendly vsed and well entertained of the alcaide, and especially of a yoong nobleman called Conde Amar Pattay, who presented me with an oxe for my company, goats and some yoong kids, assuring me that the king would be glad to heare of the arriuall of a Christians ship, whom they called Blancos, that is, white men: especially of an English ship. And so dayly the yong Conde came with a small company of horsemen to the sea side, feasting me very kindly and courteously. And the fift of December he with his traine came aboord to see the ship; which to them seemed woonderfull, as people that seldome had seene the like: who tolde me that his messenger from the king was returned; and the king reioyed much to heare that English men were come with a ship to trade in his ports; and being the first Englishman that euer came with a ship, I was the better welcome; promising that I or any Englishman hereafter should be wel intreated and find good dealing at their hands. And further the Conde on the kings behalfe and his owne, earnestly requested, that before my departure off the coast I would returne againe to his road to conferre with him for the better continuance and confirming of amity betweene them and Englishmen: which I agreed vnto. And so shewing him and his company the best friendship and courtesie I could, he went on shore, and should haue had the honor of our ordinance but that he desired the contrary, being amazed at the sight of the ship and noise of the gunnes, which they did greatly admire.

The 13 of December at night we weighed anker, and arriued the 14 day at the road of Porto d'Ally, which is another kingdome: the king thereof is called Amar Meleck, and sonne to Meleck Zamba the other king, and dwelleth a dayes iourney and an halfe from Porto d'Ally. When we had ankered, the kings kinsmen being gouernors, with all the officers of that towne came aboord to receiue all duties for the ship and licence to traffike due to the king; who there generally seemed to be very glad that no Portugall was come in our ship out of England; saying it was the kings pleasure we should bring none hereafter; for that the king did esteeme them as people of no truth; and complained of one Francisco de Costa seruant to Don Antonio, how he had often and the last yere also abused and deluded their king Amar Meleck in promising to bring him certaine things out of England, which he neuer performed, and deemed that to be the cause of his staying behinde this voyage, and that neither Spaniard nor Portugall could abide vs, but reported very badly and gaue out hard speeches tending to the defamation and great dishonour of England: [Sidenote: The monstrous lies of a Portugall.] and also affirmed that at the arriuall of an English ship called The Command, of Richard Kelley of Dartmouth, one Pedro Gonsalues a Portugall that came in the sayd ship from Don Antonio reported vnto them, that we were fled out of England and come away vpon intent to rob and do great spoile vpon this coast to the Negros and Portugals, and that Thomas Dassel had murdered Francisco de Acosta since our comming from England, who was comming to their king in our ship with great presents from Don Antonio, and desired that at our arriuall stay might be made of our goods and our selues in secret maner; which they denied, not giuing credit to his report, hauing bene often abused by such friuolous and slanderous speeches by that nation; telling me their king was sory for the former murder and captiuity of our nation, and would neuer yeeld to the like, hauing the Portugals and Spaniards in generall hatred euer since, and conceiueth much better of our countrey, and vs, then these our enemies report of. [Sidenote: Port Dally the chief place of trade.] For which I yeelded them hearty thanks, assuring them they should finde great difference betweene the loyalty of the one and disloyalty of the other; and so payed their dueties: and for that it was the chiefe place of trade, I shewed them how I was resolued to goe to their king with certaine presents which we had brought out of England; which we determined for the more honor and credit of our countrey, and augmenting of their better affection toward vs.

All this while Thomas Dassel was with our great pinnesse at the towne of Ioala, being in the kingdome of king Iocoel Lamiockeric, traffiking with the Spaniards and Portugals there. And the forenamed Pedro Gonsalues, which came out of England, was there also with other English marchants about the busines of Rich. Kelley; and as it should seeme, for that he could not obtaine his mischieuous pretended purpose against Thomas Dassel and others at the towne of Porto d'Ally, where I Richard Rainolds remained, he attempted with consent of other Portugals which were made priuy to his intent to betray the sayd Thomas Dassel at this towne, and had with bribes seduced the chiefe commanders and Negros to effect his wicked and most villanous practise: which as God would, was reuealed to the sayd Thomas Dassel by Rich. Cape an Englishman and seruant to the forenamed Rich. Kelley: to whom this sayd Pedro Gonsalues had disclosed his secret treachery, willing him with all expedition to stand vpon his guard. [The Cherubin of Lime at Ioala.] Whereupon Thomas Dassel went aboard a small English barke called The Cherubin of Lime, and there one Iohn Payua a Portugall and seruant of Don Antonio declared, that if he and one Garcia a Portugall of the sayd towne would haue consented with Pedro Gonsalues, the sayd Thomas Dassel had bene betrayed long before. And vpon this warning Thomas Dassel the next day hauing gotten three Portugals aboord, aduised for our better securities to send two on land, and detained one with him called Villa noua, telling them that if the next day by eight of the clocke, they would bring Pedro Gonsalues aboard to him, he would release the sayd Villa noua, which they did not. And Thomas Dassel hauing intelligence that certaine Negros and Portugals were ridden post ouerland to Porto d'Ally with intent to haue Richard Rainolds and his company stayd on land, being doubtfull what friendship soeuer the vnconstant Negros professed (by reason they be often wauering being ouercome with drinking wine) how they would deale, to preuent the dangerous wiles that might be effected in the road by Portugals, and for better strength, the 24 of December he came with his pinnesse and Portugall to ride in the road of Porto d'Ally, where our great shippe the Nightingall was: who was no sooner arriued but he had newes also from the shore from Iohn Baily Anthony Dassels seruant, who was there with our goods detained by the Portugals means, that aboue 20 Portugals and Spaniards were come from Ioala by land, and Pedro Gonsalues in their company, to take order for the releasing of Villa noua. So hauing had conference two or three dayes with the Commanders, the Negros, some Spaniards, and some Portugals, in the end by due examination of the matter the Negros seeing how vilely Pedro Gonsalues had delt, he being in their power, sayd he should suffer death or be tortured, for an example to others. But we in recompense of his cruelty pitied him and shewed mercy, desiring the Negros to intreat him well though vndeserued: and therevpon the Commanders brought him aboord the pinnesse to Thomas Dassel to do with him what he would: where at his comming from the shore, for lauish speeches which he used of Princes, he was well buffetted by a Spaniard, and might haue bene slaine, if for our sakes he had not bene rescued.

[Sidenote: Note.] While I went on shore with Villa noua, the sayd Pedro Gonsalues confessed vnto Thomas Dassel that he did enquire of some Negros and Portugals if he might not stay him and his goods in the land, and that he did nothing but by commission from his king by his letters which he receiued from London in Dartmouth after we were departed from London, for that we presumed to come to Guinea to traffike without a seruant of his: and further, that he had power or procuration from Francisco de Costa the Portugall that stayed behinde in England to detaine the goods of Anthony Dassel in Guinea.

By consent of M. Francis Tucker, Iohn Browbeare, and the rest of the factours of Richard Kelley, with whom this Pedro Gonsalues came, for auoiding further mischiefe that might be practised, we agreed that the sayd Pedro Gonsalues should stay aboord our shippe, and not goe any more on land vntill they departed. So the ninth of Ianuary he was deliuered aboord to goe for England in the same ship wherein he came: who was all the time of his abode in our shippe both courteously and friendly vsed at my hands, much against the mariners willes, who could not abide such a wicked creature and caitiue, that is nourished and relieued in our countrey, and yet by villanous meanes sought the destruction of vs all.

The Spaniards and Portugals though they be dissemblers and not to be trusted, when they perceiued how king Amar Melicks Negros befriended and fauored vs, and that it would be preiudiciall to their trade for diuers respects, if we should any way be iniuried, renounced the sayd practises, detesting the author, and protested to defend vs in such cases with all faithfulnesse: desiring we would, as the king of Negros had commanded vs, neuer bring Portugal with vs more: vsing this phrase in disdaine of such as came out of England, let your Portugals be barres of yron: for in trueth in regard of the rich trade maintained by Frenchmen and by vs of late, they esteeme more of one barre of yron then of twenty Portugals which we should bring out of England: who at their comming thither very subtilly disaduantage vs, and doe great hurt to euery party.

At the beginning of these broiles the king Amar Melick had sent his chiefe secretary and three horses for me Richard Rainolds: but I denied to goe by reason of the hurley burley, though I might haue had Negros of account for pledges aboord: yet we sent the presents vnto the king; who so soone as he vnderstood the cause why I came not to him, being sory and offended thereat, commanded presently by proclamation, that no iniury should be offered vs in his dominions by his owne people, or suffered to be done by Spaniards or Portugals. And if the Negros ioyning to his kingdome should confederate with the Spaniards and Portugals to molest or trouble vs; that his subiects the Negros should be ready to ayde, succor and defend vs. In which people appeared more confident loue and good will toward vs, then euer we shall finde either of Spaniards or Portugals, though we should relieue them of the greatest misery that can be imagined.

In the riuer of Senega no Spaniard or Portugall vse to trade: and onely one Portugall called Ganigoga dwelleth farre within the riuer, who was maried to a kings daughter.

[Sidenote: Note this trade.] In the townes of Porto d'Ally and Ioala, being townes of chiefest trade, and in the townes of Canton and Cassan in the riuer of Gambra are many Spaniards and Portugals resident by permission of the Negros; who haue rich trades there along the coast, especially to San Domingo and Rio grande, not far distant from Gambra riuer; whither they transport the yron which they buy of Frenchmen and vs, and exchange it for Negros; which be caried continually to the West Indies in such ships as came from Spaine. [Sidenote: A rich trade for golde in Rio grande.] Also by the gouernors order and Renters of Castel de Mina and other places, where golde is, vpon the coast of Guinea, they haue a place limited how farre they must go to trade within the riuer of Gambra; and further they may not go vpon paine of confiscation of their goods, and losse of life: for that the Renters themselues send at certaine times their owne barkes within the riuer to such places, where as they haue great store of golde. And in all these places hereabouts, where we vse to trade, they haue no Fort, Castle, or place of strength, but onely trading by the Negros safeconduct and permission. And the most part of the Spaniards and Portugals that be resident in these places be banished men or fugitiues, for committing most hainous crimes and incestuous acts, their life and conuersation being agreeable; and they are of the basest behauiour that we haue euer seene of these nations in any other countrey.

* * * * *

A briefe relation concerning the estate of the cities and prouinces of Tombuto and Gago written in Marocco the first of August 1594, and sent to
M. Anthony Dassel marchant of London.

My hearty commendations premised: your letter of late I receiued, and found that you would haue me discouer vnto you the estate and quality of the countreyes of Tombuto and Gago. And that you may not thinke me to slumber in this action, wherein you would be truely and perfectly resolued, you shall vnderstand, that not ten dayes past here came a Cahaia of the Andoluzes home from Gago, and another principall Moore, whom the king sent thither at the first with Alcaide Hamode, and they brought with them thirty mules laden with gold. I saw the same come into the Alcasaua with mine owne eies: and these men themselues came not poore, but with such wealth, that they came away without the kings commandement; and for that cause the king will pay them no wages for the time they haue beene there. On the other side they dare not aske the king for any wages. And when Alcaide Hamode saw that the Cahaia of the Andoluzes would not stay in Gago with him, he thought good to send these thirty mules laden with golde by him, with letters of commendations, by which the king smelled their riches that they brought with them: and this was the cause of the kings displeasure towards them. So now there remaineth in Gago Alcaide Hamode, and Alcaide Iawdara, and Alcaide Bucthare. And here are in a readinesse to depart in the end of next September Alcaide Monsor, Ben Abdrahaman Allies, Monsor Rico with fiue thousand men, most of the fettilase, that is to say, of fier match, and muskets. [Sidenote: Commodities for Gago.] There is gone good store of reds and yellowes: and this yere here was want of the same commodity; but I trust the next yere wil be no want. But in fine the king doth prosper wel in those parts, and here are many pledges come hither, and namely three of the kings sonnes of Gago and the Iustice; I saw them come in with the treasure. Now when Alcaide Monsor commeth to Gago, the which will be in Ianuary next, then returneth hither Alcaide Hamode with all the treasure, and Alcaide Monsor is to keepe Gago vntill the king take further order. And thus much for Gago. Thus not hauing any other thing to write at this present, I commend you to the mercifull tuition of the almighty.

From Marocco the first of August 1594.

Your assured friend Laurence Madoc.

* * * * *

Another briefe relation concerning the late conquest and exceeding great riches of the cities and prouinces Tombuth and Gogo, written from Morocco the 30 August 1594, to M. Anthony Dassel marchant of London aforesayd.

Louing friend M. Dassel, two of your letters I haue receiued, one by the shippe called The Amity, the other by the Concord: the chiefest matter therein was to be satisfied of the king of Morocco his proceedings in Guinea. Therefore these are to let you vnderstand that there went with Alcaide Hamode for those parts seuenteene hundred men: who passing ouer the sands, for want of water perished one third part of them: [Sidenote: Tombuto taken.] and at their comming to the city of Tombuto, the Negros made some resistence: but to small purpose, for that they had no defence but with their asagaies or iauelings poisoned. [Sidenote: Gago taken.] So they tooke it, and proceeded to the city of Gago, where the Negros were in numbers infinite, and meant to stand to the vttermost for their countrey: but the Moores slew them so fest, that they were fain to yeeld, and do pay tribute by the yere. The rent of Tombuto is 60 quintals of golde by the yeere: the goodnesse whereof you know. What rent Gago will yeeld, you shall know at the Spring, for then Alcaide Hamode commeth home. The rent of Tombuto is come by the cafelow or carouan, which is, as aboue mentioned, 60 quintals. The report is, that Mahomed bringeth with him such an infinite treasure as I neuer heard of: it doth appeare that they haue more golde then any other parte of the world beside. The Alcaide winneth all the countrey where he goeth without fighting and is going downe towards the sea coast. The king of Marocco is like to be the greatest prince in the world for money, if he keepe this countrey. But I make account assoone as the king of Spaine hath quietnesse in Christendome, he wil thrust him out: for that the kings force is not great as yet; but he meaneth to be stronger. There is a campe ready to go now with a viceroy: the speech is with 3000 men: but I thinke they will be hardly 2000; for by report, 3000 men are enough to conquer all the countrey: for they haue no defence of importance against an enemy. I thinke Hamode will be returned home in Ianuary or thereabout: for he stayeth but for the comming of the viceroy. Mulley Balasen the kings sonne of Marocco was slaine in Guinea by his own men, and they were presently killed, because they should tell no tales. And thus leauing to trouble you, I commit you to God, who prosper you in all your proceedings. From Marocco the first of August 1594.

Yours to command for euer Laurence Madoc.

Of these two rich cities and kingdomes of Tombuto and Gago Leo Africanus writeth at large in the beginning of his seuenth booke of the description of Africa, which worthy worke is to be annexed vnto the end of this second volume.

* * * * *

A briefe extract of a patent granted to M. Thomas Gregory of Tanton, and others, for traffique betweene the riuer of Nonnia and the riuers of Madrabumba and Sierra Leona on the coast of Guinea, in the yeere 1592.

In May the 34 yeere of our gracious soueraigne Queene Elizabeth, a patent of speciall licence was granted to Thomas Gregory of Tanton in the county of Somerset, and to Thomas Pope, and certaine other marchants to traffique into Guinea from the Northermost part of the riuer of Nonnia to the Southermost parts of the riuers of Madrabumba and Sierra Leona, and to other parts as well to the Southeast as to the Northwest, for a certaine number of leagues therein specified which amount to an hundred or thereabout. Which patent was granted for the terme of ten yeeres: as appeareth at large in the sayd patent recorded in the Rolles in her Majesties Chancery.

* * * * *

The maner of the taking of two Spanish ships laden with quicksiluer and the Popes bulles, bound for the West Indies, by M. Thomas White in the Amity of London, 1592.

The 26 of Iuly 1592, in my returning out of Barbary in the ship called the Amity of London, being in the height of 36 degrees or thereabout, at foure of the clocke in the morning we had sight of two shippes, being distant from vs about three or foure leagues: by seuen of the clocke we fetched them vp, and were within gunshot: whose boldnesse, hauing the king of Spaines armes displayed, did make vs judge them rather ships of warre then laden with marchandise. And as it appeared by their owne speeches, they made full account to haue taken vs: it being a question among them, whether it were best to cary vs to S. Lucar, or to Lisbon. We waued ech other a maine. They hauing placed themselues in warlike order one a cables length before another, we began the fight. In the which we continued, so fast as we were able to charge and discharge, the space of fiue houres, being neuer a cables length distant either of vs from other. In which time we receiued diuers shot both in the hull of our ship, masts, and sailes, to the number of 32 great, besides 500 musket shot and harquebuzes a crocke at the least, which we tolde after the fight. And because we perceiued them to be stout, we thought good to boord the Biscaine, which was on head the other: where lying aboord about an houre, and plying our ordinance and small shot; in the end we stowed all his men. Now the other in the flieboat, thinking we had entred our men in their fellow, bare roome with vs, meaning to haue layed vs aboord, and so to haue intrapped vs betwixt them both: which we perceiuing, fitted our ordinance so for him, as we quitted our selues of him, and he boorded his fellow: by which meanes they both fell from vs. Then presently we kept our loofe, hoised our top-sailes, and weathered them, and came hard aboord the flieboat with our ordinance prepared, and gaue her our whole broad side, with the which we slew diuers of their men; so as we might see the blood run out at the scupper holes. After that we cast about, and new charged all our ordinance, and came vpon them againe, willing them to yeeld, or els we would sinke them: whereupon the one would haue yeelded, which was betweene winde and water; but the other called him traitor. Vnto whom we made answere, that if he would not yeeld presently also, we would sinke him first. [Sidenote: Marke this othe.] And thereupon he understanding our determination, presently put out a white flag, and yeelded, and yet refused to strike their own sailes, for that they were sworne neuer to strike to any Englishman. We then commanded their captaines and masters to come aboord vs; which they did. And after examination and stowing them, we sent certaine of our owne men aboord them, and strook their sailes, and manned their ships: finding in them both 126 persons liuing, and 8 dead, besides those which they themselues had cast ouerboord. So it pleased God to giue vs the victory being but 42 men and a boy, whereof 2 were killed and 3 wounded: for the which good successe we giue God the only praise. These two rich prizes laden with 1400 cheste of quicksiluer with the armes of Castile and Leon fastened vpon them, and with a great quantity of bulles or indulgences, and gilded Missals or Seruice books, with an hundred tonnes of excellent wines, we brought shortly after into the riuer of Thames vp to Blacke-wall.

By the taking of this quicksiluer, about 1400 chests, the king of Spaine loseth for euery quintall of the same a quintall of siluer that should haue beene deliuered him by the masters of the mines there, which amounteth to 600000 pounds.

More by taking of his bulles, to wit, two millions and 72 thousand for liuing and dead persons for the prouinces of Noua Hispania, Iucatan, Guatimala, the Honduras, and the Phillippinas, taxed at two reals the piece. And more for eighteene thousand bulles taxed at foure reals, amounteth all to 107700 pounds. Summa totalis 707700 li.

More there were taken ten fardels of gilt missals and breuiaries sent for the kings account.

So the hindrance that the king receiueth by the losse of his bulles and quicksiluer amounteth as is abouesaid: besides the sacking of his wines, about 100 tunnes, whereby his fleet is disappointed of a great part of their prouision.

* * * * *

A true report of the honourable seruice at Sea perfourmed by Sir Iohn Burrough Knight, Lieutenant generall of the fleet prepared by the honour. Sir Walter Ralegh Knight, Lord warden of the Stanneries of Cornwall and Deuon. Wherein chiefly the Santa Clara of Biscay, a ship of 600 tunnes was taken, and the two East Indian caraks, the Santa Cruz and the Madre de Dios were forced, the one burnt, and the other taken and brought into Dartmouth the seuenth of September, 1592.

Sir Walter Ralegh vpon commission receiued from her Maiesty for an expedition to be made to the West Indies, slacked not his vttermost diligence to make full prouision of all things necessary, as both in his choise of good ships, and sufficient men to performe the action euidently appeared. For his shippes which were in numbre 14 or 15, those two of her Maiesties, the Garland and the Foresight were the chiefest; the rest either his owne or his good friends or aduenturers of London. For the gentlemen his consorts and officers, to giue them their right, they were so well qualited in courage, experience, and discretion, as the greatest prince might repute himselfe happy to be serued with their like. The honor of Lieutenant generall was imposed vpon sir Iohn Burrough, a gentleman, for his manifold good and heroicall parts, thought euery way worthy of that commandement: with whom after sir W. R. returned was ioyned in commission sir Martin Frobisher, who for his speciall skill and knowledge in marine causes had formerly caried imploiments of like or greater place. The rest such as heretofore had giuen to the world sufficient proofe of their valour in diuers seruices of the like nature. With these ships thus manned sir Walter Ralegh departed towards the West countrey, there to store himselfe with such further necessaries as the state of his voyage did needfully require: where the Westerly windes blowing for a long time contrary to his course, bound and constrained him to keepe harborough so many weekes, that the fittest season for his purpose was gone, the mindes of his people much altered, his victuals consumed: and withall, her Maiesty vnderstanding how crosly all this sorted, began to call the proceeding of this preparation into question: insomuch that, whereas the sixt of May was first come before sir Walter could put to sea, the very next day sir Martin Frobisher in a pinnesse of my lord Admirals called The Disdaine, met him, and brought to him from her Maiesty letters of reuocation, with commandement to relinquish (for his owne part) the intended attempt, and to leaue the charge and conduct of all things in the hands of sir Iohn Burrough and sir Martin Frobisher, But sir Walter finding his honor so farre engaged in the vndertaking of this voyage, as without proceeding he saw no remedy either to salue his reputation, or to content those his friends which had put in aduentures of great summes with him; and making construction of the Queenes letters in such sort as if her commandement had bene propounded in indifferent termes, either to aduance forward or to retire, at his owne discretion; would in no case yeeld to leaue his fleet now vnder saile. Wherefore continuing his course into the sea, he met within a day or two, with certaine sailes lately come from Spaine: among which was a ship appertaining to Monsieur Gourdon gouernor of Caleis, and found aboord her one M. Neuel Dauies an Englishman, who hauing endured a long and miserable captiuity for the space of twelue yeeres, partly in the inquisition in Spaine, was now by good fortune escaped, and vpon returne to his countrey. This man, among other things, reported for certaine, that there was little hope of any good this yeere to be done in the West India; considering that the king of Spaine had sent expresse order to all the Ports both of the Ilands and of Terra firma, that no ship should stirre that yeere, nor any treasure be layed aboord for Spaine. But neither this vnpleasant relation nor ought els could stay his proceedings, vntill a tempest of strange and vncouth violence arising vpon Thursday the 11 of May, when he was athwart the Cape Finister, had so scattered the greater part of the fleet, and sunke his boats and pinnesses, that as the rest were driuen and seuered, some this way and some that, sir Walter himselfe being in the Garland of her Maiesty was in danger to be swallowed vp of the Sea. Whereupon sir W. Ralegh finding that the season of the yere was too farre gone to proceed with the enterprise which he had vpon Panama, hauing bene held on the English coast from February till May, and thereby spent three moneths victuals; and considering withall, that to lie vpon the Spanish coast or at the Ilands to attend the returne of the East or West Indian fleets was rather a worke of patience then ought els: he gaue directions to sir Iohn Burgh and sir M. Frobisher to diuide the fleet in two parts; sir M. with the Garland, cap. George Gifford, cap. Henry Thin, cap. Grenuile and others to lie off the South cape, thereby to amaze the Spanish fleet, and to holde them on their owne coast; while sir I. Burgh, capt. Robert Crosse, capt. Tomson, and others should attend at the Ilands for the caraks or any other Spanish ships comming from Mexico or other parts of the West Indies. Which direction tooke effect accordingly; for the king of Spaines Admirall receiuing intelligence that the English fleet was come on the coast, attended to defend the South parts of Spaine, and to keepe himselfe as nere sir Mart. Frobisher as he could, to impeach him in all things which he might vndertake; and thereby neglected the safeconduct of the caraks, with whom it fared as hereafter shall appeare. Before the fleet seuered themselues they mette with a great Biscain on the Spanish coast called Santa Clara a ship of 600 tunnes.

The noise of the artillery on both sides being heard, immediatly they drew to their fleet; where after a reasonable hot fight, the ship was entred and mastered, which they found freighted with all sorts of small yron-worke, as horse shoes, nailes, plough-shares, yron barres, spikes, boults, locks, gimbols, and such like, valued by vs at 6000 or 7000 li. but woorth to them treble the value. This Biscain was sailing towards S. Lucar, there to take in some further prouision for the West India. This ship being first roomaged, and after sent for England, our fleet coasted along towards the Southcape of S. Vincent, and by the way about the Rocke neere Lisbon, sir Iohn Burrough in the Robucke spying a saile a farre off, gaue her present chase; which being a flieboat and of good saile, drew him farre Southwards before he could fetch her; but at last she came vnder his lee and strooke saile. The master of which flieboat comming aboord him, confessed that the king indeed had prepared a great fleet in S. Lucar and Cadiz, and (as the report in Spaine was currant) for the West Indies. But indeed the Spanish king had prouided this fleet vpon this counsell. He receiued intelligence, that sir Walter Ralegh was to put out strong for the West India: to impeach him, and to ranconter his force he appointed this fleet; although looking for the arriuall of his East Indian caraks, he first ordained those ships to waft them from the Açores. But perswading himselfe, that if the fleet of sir Walter Ralegh did go for the West India, then the Ilands should haue none to infest them but some small men of warre, which the caraks of themselues would be well able to match; his order was to Don Alonso de Baçan brother to the Marques of Santa Cruz, and Generall of his armada, to pursue sir Walters fleet, and to confront him, what course soeuer he held. [Sidenote: Sir Iohn Burrough in great danger of the Spanish fleet.] And that this was true, our men in short time by proofe vnderstood: for sir Iohn Burrough, not long after the taking of his last prize the flieboat, as he sailed backe againe towards the rest of his company, discouered the Spanish fleet to sea-ward of him: which hauing likewise espied him betwixt them and the shore, made full account to bring him safe into Spanish harbour; and therefore spred themselues in such sort before him, that indeed his danger was very great: for both the liberty of the sea was brought into a narrow straight, and the shore being enemy could giue him no comfort of reliefe: so that trusting to Gods helpe onely and his good saile, he thrust out from among them in spight of all their force, and to the notable illusion of all their cunning, which they shewed to the vttermost, in laying the way for his apprehension. [Sidenote: The Ile of S. Michael.] But now sir Iohn Burrough hauing happily escaped their clouches, finding the coast guarded by this fleet, and knowing it was but folly to expect a meeting there with sir Martin Frobisher (who vnderstanding of this armada aswell as himselfe, would be sure not to come that way) beganne to shape his course to the Açores according to sir W. Raleghs direction, and came in sight of S. Michael, running so neere by Villa Franca, that he might easily discerne the shippes lying there at anker. [Sidenote: Diuers small ships taken.] Diuers small carauels both here and betweene S. Georges and the Pike in his course towards Flores he intercepted; of which no great intelligence for his affaires could be vnderstood. [Sidenote: Santa Cruz a village in the Ile of Flores.] Arriuing before Flores vpon Thursday the 21 of Iune, towards euening, accompanied onely with captaine Caufield and the Master of his shippe, the rest not being yet arriued, he made towards the shore with his boat, finding all the people of Santa Cruz, a village of that Iland, in armes, fearing their landing, and ready marshalled to defend their towne from spoile. Sir Iohn contrariwise made signes of amity vnto them by aduancing a white flagge, a common token of peace, which was answered againe of them with the like: whereupon ensued entercourses of good friendship; and pledges were taken on both sides, the captaine of the towne for them, and captaine Caufield for our: so that whatsoeuer our men wanted, which that place could supply either in fresh water, victuals, or the like, was very willingly granted by the inhabitants; and good leaue had they to refresh themselues on shore as much and as oft as they would without restraint. [Sidenote: Newes of the East Indian caraks.] At this Santa Cruz sir Iohn Burrough was informed, that indeed there was among them no expectation of any fleet to come from the west, but from the East, that no longer since then three dayes before his arriuall a carak was passed by for Lisbon, and that there were foure carafes more behinde, of one consort. Sir Iohn being very glad of this newes, stayed no longer on shore, but presently imbarqued himselfe, hauing onely in company a small barke of threescore tunnes belonging to one M. Hopkins of Bristoll. In the meane while that these things thus passed at Flores, part of the rest of the English fleet, which sir Iohn Burrough had left vpon the coast of Spaine, drew also towards the Açores: and whereas he quickly at sea had discouered one of the caraks, the same euening he might descry two or three of the Earle of Cumberlands ships (whereof one M. Norton was captaine) which hauing in like sort kenned the carak, pursued her by that course which they saw her to runne towards the Ilands. But on no side was there any way made by reason of a great calme which yeelded no breath to spread a saile. Insomuch that fitly to discouer her what she was, of what burthen, force, and countenance sir Iohn Burrough tooke his boat, and rowed the space of three miles, to make her exactly: and being returned, he consulted with the better sort of the company then present, vpon the boording her in the morning. [Sidenote: A carak called The Santa Cruz set on fire.] But a very mighty storme arising in the night, the extremity thereof forced them all to wey ankers, yet their care was such in wrestling with the weather not to lose the carak, that in the morning the tempest being qualified, and our men bearing againe with the shore, they might perceiue the carak very neere the land, and the Portugals confusedly carrying on shore such things as they could any maner of way conuey out of her; and seeing the haste our men made to come vpon them, forsook her; but first, that nothing might be left commodious to our men, set fire to that which they could not cary with them, intending by that meanes wholly to consume her; that neither glory of victory nor benefit of shippe might remaine to ours. And least the approch and industry of the English should bring meanes to extinguish the flame, thereby to preserue the residue of that which the fire had not destroyed; being foure hundred of them in number and well armed, they entrenched themselues on land so neere to the carak, that she being by their forces protected, and our men kept aloofe off, the fire might continue to the consumption of the whole. This being noted by sir Iohn Burrough he soone prouided a present remedy for this mischiefe. [Sidenote: An hundred of our men land.] For landing one hundred of his men, whereof many did swim and wade more then brest high to shore, and easily scattering those that presented themselues to guard the coast, he no sooner drew toward their new trenches, but they fled immediatly, leauing as much as the fire had spared to be the reward of our mens paines. Here was taken among others one Vincent Fonseca a Portugall, Purser of the carak, with two others, one an Almaine and the second a Low-dutchman, canoniers: who refusing to make any voluntary report of those things, which were demanded of them, had the torture threatened, the feare whereof at the last wrested from them this intelligence, that within fifteene dayes three other greater caraks then that lately fired would arriue at the same Iland: and that being fiue caraks in the fleet at their departure from Goa, to wit, the Buen Iesus admirall, the Madre de Dios, the S. Bernardo, the S. Christophoro, and the S. Cruz, (whose fortune you haue already heard) they had receiued speciall commandement from the king not to touch in any case at the Iland of S. Helena, where the Portugall caraks in their returne from the East India were alwayes till now woont to arriue to refresh themselues with water and victuals. And the kings reason was; because of the English men of warre, who (as he was informed) lay there in wait to intercept them. [Sidenote: Angola a new watering place for caraks.] If therefore their necessity of water should driue them to seeke supply any where, he appointed them Angola in the maine of Africa, with order there to stay onely the taking in of water to auoid the inconuenience of infections where vnto that hot latitude is dangerously subiect. The last rendeuous for them all was the Iland of Flores, where the king assured them not to misse of his armada thither sent of purpose for their wafting to Lisbon. Vpon this information sir Iohn drew to counsel, meeting there Captaine Norton, captain Dountain, captain Abraham Cocke, captaines of three ships of the Earle of Cumberland, M. Tomson of Harwich cap. of the Dainty of sir Iohn Haukins, one of sir W. Raleghs fleet, and M. Christopher Newport cap. of the Golden dragon newly returned from the West India, and others. These being assembled, he communicated with them what he had vnderstood of the foresaid examinates, and what great presumptions of trueth their relation did cary: wishing that forasmuch as God and good fortune had brought them together in so good a season, they would shew the vttermost of their indeuors to bring these Easterlings vnder the lee of the English obedience. Hereupon a present accord on all sides followed not to part company or leaue of those seas till time should present cause to put their consultations in execution. The next day her Maiesties good ship the Foresight commanded by sir Rob. Crosse came in to the rest: and he likewise informed of the matter was soone drawen into this seruice. Thus sir Iohn with al these ships departing thence 6 or 7 leagues to the West of Flores, they spread themselues abroad from the North to the South, ech ship two leagues at the least distant from another. By which order of extension they were able to discouer the space of two whole degrees at sea. In this sort they lay from the 29 of Iune to the third of August, what time cap. Thomson in the Dainty had first sight of the huge carak called the Madre de Dios, one of the greatest receit, belonging to the crowne of Portugall. The Dainty being of excellent saile got the start of the rest of our fleet, and begun the conflict somewhat to her cost, with the slaughter and hurt of diuers of her men. Within a while after, sir Iohn Burrough in the Robucke of sir W. Raleghs, was at hand to second her, who saluted her with shot of great ordinance, and continued the fight within musket shot assisted by cap. Tomson and cap. Newport till sir R. Crosse viceadmirall of the fleet came vp being to leeward, at whose arriuall sir I. Burgh demanded of him what was best to be done, who answered, that if the carak were not boorded she would recouer the shore and fire herselfe as the other had done. Whereupon sir I. Burgh concluded to entangle her; and sir R. Crosse promised also to fasten himselfe to her together at the instant; which was performed: but after a while sir Iohn Burgh receiuing a shot with a canon perier vnder water and ready to sinke, desired sir R. C. to fall off, that he might also cleere himselfe, and saue his ship from sinking, which with difficulty he did: for both the Roebucke and the Foresight were so intangled, as with much adoe could they cleere themselues.

[Sidenote: The Madre de Dios taken.] The same euening sir R. Crosse finding the carak then sure and drawing neere the Iland perswaded his company to boord her againe, or els there was no hope to recouer her: who after many excuses and feares, were by him incouraged, and so fell athwart her foreships all alone; and so hindered her sailing that the rest had time to come vp to his succour, and to recouer the carak yer she recouered the land: and so toward the euening after he had fought with her alone three houres single, my lord of Cumberlands two ships came vp, and with very little losse entred with sir R. Crosse, who had in that time broken their courages, and made the assault easie for the rest.

The generall hauing disarmed the Portugals, and stowed them for better security on all sides, first had presented to his eyes the true proportion of the vast body of this carak, which did then and may still iustly prouoke the admiration of all men not formerly acquainted with such a sight. But albeit this first apparance of the hugenesse thereof yeelded sights enough to entertaine our mens eyes: yet the pitifull obiect of so many bodies slaine and dismembred could not but draw ech mans eye to see, and heart to lament, and hands to helpe those miserable people, whose limnes were so torne with the violence of shot, and paine made grieuous with the multitude of woundes. No man could almost steppe but vpon a dead carkase or a bloody floore, but specially about the helme, where very many of them fell suddenly from stirring to dying. For the greatnesse of the stirrage requiring the labour of twelue or fourteene men at once, and some of our shippes beating her in at the sterne with their ordinance often times with one shot slew foure or fiue labouring on either side of the helme; whose roomes being still furnished with fresh supplies, and our artillery still playing vpon them with continuall volleys, it could not be but that much bloud should be shed in that place. [Sidenote: Exceeding humanity shewed to the enemy.] Whereupon our Generall moued with singular commiseration of their misery, sent them his owne chyrurgions, denying them no possible helpe or reliefe that he or any of his company could affoord them. Among the rest of those, whose state this chance had made very deplorable, was Don Fernando de Mendoça Grand captaine and Commander of this Carake: who indeed was descended of the house of Mendoça in Spaine; but being married into Portugall, liued there as one of that nation; a gentleman well stricken in yeeres, well spoken, of comely personage, of good stature, but of hard fortune. In his seuerall seruices against the Moores he was twise taken prisoner, and both times ransomed by the king. In a former voyage of returne from the East India he was driuen vpon the Baxos or sands of Iuda nere the coast of Cephala, being then also captaine of a caracke which was there lost, and himselfe, though escaping the sea-danger, yet fell into the hands of infidels on land; who kept him vnder long and grieuous seruitude. Once more the king carying a louing respect to the man, and desirous to better his condition, was content to let him try his fortune in this Easterly nauigation, and committed vnto him the conduct of this caracke, wherein he went from Lisbon Generall of the whole fleet, and in that degree had returned, if the Vice-rey of Goa embarked for Portugall in the Bon Iesus had not, by reason of his late office, bene preferred. Sir Iohn intending not to adde too much affliction to the afflicted, moued with pity and compassion of humane misery, in the end resolued freely to dismisse this captaine and the most part of his followers, to their owne countrey, and for the same purpose bestowed them in certaine vessels furnished with all kindes of necessary prouision. This businesse thus dispatched, good leasure had he to take such view of the goods as conueniency might affoord. And hauing very prudently (to cut off the vnprofitable spoile and pillage whereunto he saw the minds of many inclined) seised vpon the whole to her Maiesties vse, after a short and slender romaging and searching of such things as first came to hand, he perceiued that the wealth would arise nothing disanswerable to expectation; but that the variety and grandure of all rich commodities would be more then sufficient to content both the aduenturers desire and the souldiers trauell. And here I cannot but enter into the consideration and acknowledgement of Gods great fauor towards our nation, who by putting this purchase into our hands hath manifestly discouered those secret trades and Indian riches, which hitherto lay strangely hidden, and cunningly concealed from vs; whereof there was among some few of vs some small and vnperfect glimse onely, which now is turned into the broad light of full and perfect knowledge. Whereby it should seeme that the will of God for our good is (if our weaknesse could apprehend it) to haue vs communicate with them in those East Indian treasures, and by the erection of a lawfull traffike to better our meanes to aduance true religion and his holy seruice. The caracke being in burden by the estimation of the wise and experienced no lesse then 1600 tunnes had full 900 of those stowed with the grosse bulke of marchandise, the rest of the tunnage being allowed, partly to the ordinance which were 32 pieces of brasse of all sorts, partly to the passengers and the victuals, which could not be any small quantity, considering the number of the persons betwixt 600 and 700, and the length of the nauigation. To giue you a taste (as it were) of the commodities, it shall suffice to deliuer you a generall particularity of them, according to the catalogue taken at Leadenhall the 15 of September 1592. [Sidenote: A briefe catalogue of the sundry rich commodities of the Madre de Dios.] Where vpon good view it was found, that the principall wares after the iewels (which were no doubt of great value, though they neuer came to light) consisted of spices, drugges, silks, calicos, quilts, carpets and colours, &c. The spices were pepper, cloues, maces, nutmegs, cinamom, greene ginger: the drugs were beniamin, frankincense, galingale, mirabolans, aloes zocotrina, camphire: the silks, damasks, taffatas, sarcenets, altobassos, that is, counterfeit cloth of gold, vnwrought China silke, sleaued silke, white twisted silke, curled cypresse. The calicos were book-calicos, calico-launes, broad white calicos, fine starched calicos, course white calicos, browne broad calicos, browne course calicos. There were also canopies, and course diaper-towels, quilts of course sarcenet and of calico, carpets like those of Turky; whereunto are to be added the pearle, muske, ciuet, and amber-griece. The rest of the wares were many in number, but lesse in value; as elephants teeth, porcellan vessels of China, coco-nuts, hides, eben-wood as blacke as iet, bedsteads of the same, cloth of the rindes of trees very strange for the matter, and artificiall in workemanship. All which piles of commodities being by men of approued iudgement rated but in reasonable sort amounted to no lesse then 150000 li. sterling, which being diuided among the aduenturers (whereof her Maiesty was the chiefe) was sufficient to yeeld contentment to all parties. [Sidenote: The capacity and dimensions of the Madre de Dios.] The cargazon being taken out, and the goods fraighted in tenne of our ships sent for London, to the end that the bignesse, heigth, length, bredth, and other dimensions of so huge a vessell might by the exact rules of Geometricall obseruations be truly taken, both for present knowledge, and deriuation also of the same vnto posterity, one M. Robert Adams, a man in his faculty of excellent skill, omitted nothing in the description, which either his arte could demonstrate, or any mans iudgement thinke woorthy the memory. After an exquisite suruey of the whole frame he found the length from the beak-head to the sterne (whereupon was erected a lanterne) to containe 165 foote. The breadth in the second close decke whereof she had three, this being the place where there was most extension of bredth, was 46 feet and ten inches. She drew in water 31 foot at her departure from Cochin in India, but not aboue 26 at her arriual in Dartmouth, being lightened in her voyage by diuers meanes some 5 foote. She caried in height 7 seuerall stories, one maine Orlop, three close decks, one fore-castle, and a spar-decke of two floores a piece. The length of the keele was 100 foote, of the maine-mast 121 foot, and the circuite about at the partners 10 foote 7 inches, the maine-yard was 106 foote long. By which perfect commensuration of the parts appeareth the hugenesse of the whole, farre beyond the mould of the biggest shipping vsed among vs either for warre or receit.

Don Alonso de Baçan hauing a great Fleet and suffering these two caraks, the Santa Cruz to be burnt, and the Madre de Dios to be taken, was disgraced by his prince for this negligence.

* * * * *

The firing and sinking of the stout and warrelike Carack called Las Cinque Llaguas, or, The fiue Wounds, by three tall Ships set foorth at the charges of the right honorable the Erle of Cumberland and his friends: Written by the discreet and valiant captaine M. Nicholas Downton.

In the latter ende of the yeere 1593. the right honourable Erle of Cumberland, at his owne charges and his friends, prepared 3 ships, all at equall rate, and either of them had like quantitie of victuals, and like numbers of men, there being embarked in all 3 ships 420 men of al sorts. [Marginal note: Besides these three ships there was a pinnas called the Violet, or the Why not I.] The Roial Exchange went as Admirall, wherein

M. George Caue was captaine. The May-flower Viceadmirall vnder the conduct of William Anthonie: and the Sampson, the charge whereof it pleased his honour to commit vnto me Nicholas Dounton. Our directions were sent vs to Plimmouth, and we were to open them at sea.

The sixt of Aprill 1594 we set sayle in the sound of Plimmouth, directing our course toward the coast of Spaine.

The 24 of the sayd moneth at the Admirals direction wee diuided our selues East and West from ech other, being then in the heigth of 43 degrees, with commaundement at night to come together againe.

The 27 day in the morning we descried the May-flower and the litle Pinnasse with a Prise that they had taken, being of Viana in Portugall, and bound for Angola in Africa. This Barke was of 28 tunnes, hauing some 17 persons in the same. [Sidenote: Commodities fit for Angola.] There were in her some 12 Buts of Galicia wine, whereof we tooke into euery shippe a like part, with some Ruske in chests and barrels, with 5 buts of blew course cloth, and certaine course linnen-cloth for Negros shirts, which goods were diuided among our fleet.

The 4 of May we had sight of our Pinnasse, and the Admirals Shallop which had taken three Portugall Carauels, whereof they had sent two away and kept the third.

The second of Iune we had sight of S. Michael. The third day in the morning we sent our small pinnasse, which was of some 24 tunnes, with the small Carauell which we had taken at the Burlings to range the road of all the Ilands, to see if they could get any thing in the same: appointing them to meet vs W. S. W. 12 leagues from Faiall. Their going from vs was to no purpose. They missed comming to vs when we appointed, as also we missed them, when we had great cause to haue vsed them.

The 13 of Iune we met with a mightie Carack of the East. Indies, called Las cinque Llagas, or The fiue wounds. The May-flower was in fight with her before night. I, in the Sampson, fetched her vp in the euening, and as I commanded to giue her the broad side, as we terme it, while I stood very heedefully prying to discouer her strength: and where I might giue counsel to boord her in the night when the Admirall came vp to vs, and as I remember at the very first shot she discharged at vs, I was shot in a litle aboue the belly, whereby I was made vnseruiceable for a good while after, without touching any other for that night. Yet by meanes of an honest truehearted man which I had with me, one captaine Grant, nothing was neglected: vntill midnight when the Admirall came vp, the May-flower, and the Sampson neuer left by turnes to ply her with their great ordinance; but then captaine Caue wished vs to stay till morning, at what time each one of vs should giue her three bouts with our great ordinance, and so clap her aboord: but indeed it was long lingered in the morning vntil 10 of the clocke before wee attempted to boord her. The Admirall laid her a boord in the mid ship: the May-flower comming vp in the quarter, as it should seeme, to lie at the sterne of the Admirall on the larboord-side. The captaine of the sayd May-flower was slaine at the first comming vp: whereby the ship fell to the sterne of the out-licar of the Carack, which (being a piece of timber) so wounded her foresaile, that they sayd they could come no more to fight, I am sure they did not, but kept aloofe from vs. The Sampson went aboord on the bow, but hauing not rome enough, our quarter lay on the Exchanges bow, and our bowe on the Caracks bowe. The Exchange also at the first comming had her captaine M. Caue shot into both the legs, the one whereof he neuer recouered, so he for that present was not able to doe his office, and in his absence he had not any that would vndertake to lead out his company to enter vpon the enemie. My friend captaine Grant did lead my men on the Caracks side, which being not manfully backed by the Exchanges men, his forces being smal, made the enemie bolder than he would haue bene, whereby I had six men presently slaine and many more hurt, which made them that remained vnhurt to returne aboord, and would neuer more giue the assault. I say not but some of the Exchanges men did very well, and many more (no doubt) would haue done the like, if there had bene any principall man to haue put them forward, and to haue brought all the company to the fight, and not to haue run into corners themselues. But I must needs say, that their ship was as well prouided for defence, as any that I haue seene. And the Portugals peraduenture encouraged by our slacke working, plaied the men and had Barricados made, where they might stand without any danger of our shot. They plied vs also very much with fire, so that most of our men were burnt in some place or other: and while our men were putting out of the fire, they would euer be plying them with small shot or darts. This vnusuall casting of fire did much dismay many of our men and made them draw backe as they did. When we had not men to enter, we plied our great ordinance much at them as high vp as they might be mounted, for otherwise we did them little harme, and by shooting a piece out of our forecastle being close by her, we fired a mat on her beak head, which more and more kindled, and ran from thence to the mat on the bow-sprit, and from the mat vp to the wood of the bow-sprit, and thence to the top saile yard, which fire made the Portugals abaft in the ship to stagger, and to make shew of parle. But they that had the charge before encouraged them, making shew, that it might easily be put out, and that it was nothing. Whereupon againe they stood stifly to their defence. Anone the fire grew so strong, that I saw it beyond all helpe, although she had bene already yeelded to vs. Then we desired to be off from her, but had little hope to obtaine our desire; neuerthelesse we plied water very much to keep our ship well. Indeed I made little other reckoning for the ship, my selfe, and diuers hurt men, then to haue ended there with the Carak, but most of our people might haue saved themselues in boats. And when my care was most, by Gods prouidence onely, by the burning asunder of our spritsaile-yard with ropes and saile, and the ropes about the spritsaile-yarde of the Carack, whereby we were fast intangled, we fell apart, with burning of some of our sailes which we had then on boord. The Exchange also being farther from the fire, afterward was more easily cleared, and fell off from abaft And as soone as God had put vs out of danger, the fire got into the fore-castle, where, I think, was store of Beniamin, and such other like combustible matter, for it flamed and ran ouer all the Carack at an instant in a maner. The Portugals lept ouer-boord in great numbers. Then sent I captaine Grant with the boat, with leaue to vse his owne discretion in sauing of them. So he brought me aboord two gentlemen, the one an old man called Nuno Velio Pereira, which (as appeareth by the 4 chapter in the first booke of the woorthy history of Huighen de Linschoten) was gouernour of Moçambique and Cefala, in the yeere 1582. and since that time had bene likewise a gouernour in a place of importance in the East Indies. And the shippe wherein he was comming home was cast away a little to the East of the Cape of Buona Speranza, and from thence be traueiled ouer-land to Moçambique, and came as a passenger in this Carack. The other was called Bras Carrero, and was captaine of a Carack which was cast away neere Moçambique, and came likewise in this ship for a passenger. Also three men of the inferior sort we saued in our boat, onely these two we clothed and brought into England. The rest which were taken vp by the other ship boats, we set all on shore in the Ile of Flores, except some two or three Negros, whereof one was borne in Moçambique, and another in the East Indies. This fight was open off the Sound between Faial and Pico 6 leagues to the Southward. The people which we saued told vs that the cause why they would not yeeld, was, because this Carack was for the king, and that she had all the goods belonging to the king in the countrey for that yeere in her, and that the captaine of her was in fauor with the king, and at his returne into the Indies should haue bene Viceroy there. And withall this ship was nothing at all pestered neither within boord nor without, and was more like a ship of warre then otherwise: moreouer she had the ordinance of a Carak that was cast away at Moçambique, and the company of her, together with the company of another Carack that was cast away a little to the Eastwards of the Cape of Buona Speranza. Yet through sicknesse which they caught at Angola, where they watered, they say, they had not now aboue 150 white men, but Negros a great many. They likewise affirmed that they had three noblemen and three ladies in her, but we found them to differ in most of their talke. All this day and all the night she burned, but the next morning her poulder which was lowest being 60 barrels blew her abroad, so that most of the ship did swim in parts aboue the water. Some of them say, that she was bigger then the Madre de Dios, and some, that she was lesse: but she was much vndermastered, and vndersailed, yet she went well for a ship that was so foule. The shot which wee made at her in great Ordinance before we layde her aboord might be at seuen bouts which we had, and sixe or 7 shot at a bout, one with another, some 49 shot: the time we lay aboord might be two houres. The shot which we discharged aboord the Carack might be some twentie Sacars. And thus much may suffice concerning our daungerous conflict with that vnfortunate Carack.

The last of Iune after long traversing of the seas we had sight of another mightie Carack which diuerse of our company at the first tooke to be the great S. Philip the Admiral of Spaine, but the next day being the first of Iuly fetching her vp we perceiued her indeede to be a Carack, which after some few shot bestowed vpon her we summoned to yeeld; but they standing stoutly to their defence vtterly refused the same. Wherefore seeing no good could be done without boording her I consulted what course we should take in the boording. But by reason that wee which were the chiefe captaines were partly slaine and partly wounded in the former conflict, and because of the murmuring of some disordered and cowardly companions, our valiant and resolute determinations were crossed: and to conclude a long discourse in few words, the Carack escaped our hands. After this attending about Coruo and Flores for some West Indian purchase, and being disappointed of our expectation, and victuals growing short, we returned for England, where I arriued at Portesmouth the 28 of August.

* * * * *

The casting away of the Tobie neere Cape Espartel corruptly called Cape Sprat, without the Straight of Gibraltar on the coast of Barbarie. 1593.

The Tobie of London a ship of 250 tunnes manned with fiftie men, the owner whereof was the worshipful M. Richard Staper, being bound for Liuorno, Zante and Patras in Morea, being laden with marchandize to the value of 11 or 12 thousand pounds sterling, set sayle from Black-wall the 16 day of August 1593, and we went thence to Portesmouth where we tooke in great quantine of wheate, and set sayle foorth of Stokes bay in the Isle of Wight, the 6. day of October, the winde being faire: and the 16 of the same moneth we were in the heigth of Cape S. Vincent, where on the next morning we descried a sayle which lay in try right a head off vs, to which we gaue chase with very much winde, the sayle being a Spaniard, which wee found in fine so good of sayle that we were faine to leaue her and giue her ouer. Two dayes after this we had sight of mount Chiego, which is the first high-land which we descrie on the Spanish coast at the entrance of the

Straight of Gibraltar, where we had very foule weather and the winde scant two dayes together. Here we lay off to the sea. The Master, whose name was George Goodley, being a young man, and one which neuer tooke charge before for those parts, was very proud of that charge which he was litle able to discharge, neither would take any counsel of any of his company, but did as he thought best himselfe, and in the end of the two dayes of foule weather cast about, and the winde being faire, bare in with the straights mouth. The 19 day at night he thinking that he was farther off the land than he was, bare sayle all that night, and an houre and an halfe before day had ranne our shippe ypon the ground on the coast of Barbarie without the straight foure leagues to the South of Cape Espartel. Whereupon being all not a litle astonied, the Master said vnto vs, I pray you forgiue me; for this is my fault and no mans else. The company asked him whether they should cut off the main mast: no said the Master, we will hoyse out our boate. But one of our men comming speedily vp, said, Sirs, the ship is full of water, well sayd the Master, then cut the mayne-mast ouer boord: which thing we did with all speede. But the afterpart suddenly split a sunder in such sort that no man was able to stand vpon it, but all fled vpon the foremast vp into the shrouds thereof; and hung there for a time: but seeing nothing but present death approch (being so suddenly taken that we could not make a raft which we had determined) we committed our selues vnto the Lord and beganne with dolefull tune and heauy hearts to sing the 12 Psalme. Helpe Lord for good and godly men &c. Howbeit before we had finished foure verses the waues of the sea had stopped the breathes of most of our men. For the foremast with the weight of our men and the force of the sea fell downe into the water, and vpon the fall thereof there were 38 drowned, and onely 12 by Gods prouidence partly by swimming and other meanes of chests gote on shoare, which was about a quarter of a mile from the wracke of the ship. The master called George Goodley, and William Palmer his mate, both perished. M. Cæsar also being captaine and owner was likewise drowned: none of the officers were saued but the carpenter.

We twelue which the Lord had deliuered from extreme danger of the Sea, at our comming ashore fell in a maner into as great distresse. At our first comming on shore we all fell downe on our knees, praying the Lord most humbly for his merciful goodnesse. Our prayers being done, we consulted together what course to take, seeing we were fallen into a desert place, and we traueled all that day vntill night, sometimes one way and sometimes another, and could finde no kinde of inhabitants; onely we saw where wilde beasts had bene, and places where there had bene houses, which after we perceiued to haue bene burnt by the Portugals. So at night falling into certaine groues of oliue trees, we climed vp and sate in them to auoid the danger of lions and other wilde beasts, whereof we saw many the next morning. The next day we trauelled vntill three of the clocke in the afternoone without any food but water and wilde date roots: then going ouer a mountaine, we had sight of Cape Espartel; whereby we knew somewhat better which way to trauell, and then we went forward vntill we came to an hedgerow made with great long canes; we spied and looked ouer it, and beheld a number of men aswell horsemen as footmen, to the number of some fiue thousand in skirmish together with small shot and other weapons. And after consultation what we were best to do, we concluded to yeeld our selues vnto them, being destitute of all meanes of resistance. So rising vp we marched toward them, who espying vs, foorthwith some hundred of them with their iauelings in their hands came running towards vs as though they would haue run vs thorow: howbeit they onely strooke vs flatling with their weapons, and said that we were Spaniards: and we tolde them that we were Englishmen: which they would not beleeue yet. By and by the conflict being ended, and night approching, the captaine of the Moores, a man of some 56 yeres olde, came himselfe vnto vs, and by his interpreter which spake Italian, asked what we were and from whence we came. One Thomas Henmer of our company which could speake Italian, declared vnto him that we were marchants, and how by great misfortune our ship, marchandise, and the greatest part of our company were pitifully cast away vpon their coast. But he void of all humainity and all manhood, for all this, caused his men to strip vs out of our apparel euen to our shirts to see what money and iewels we had about vs: which when they had found to the value of some 200 pounds in golde and pearles they gaue vs some of our apparel againe, and bread and water onely to comfort vs. The next morning they carried vs downe to the shore where our shippe was cast away, which was some sixteene miles from that place. In which iourney they vsed vs like their slaues, making vs (being extreame weake,) to carry their stuffe, and offering to beat vs if we went not so fast as they. We asked them why they vsed vs so, and they replied, that we were their captiues: we said we were their friends, and that there was neuer Englishman captiue to the king of Marocco. So we came downe to the ship, and lay there with them seuen dayes, while they had gotten all the goods they could, and then they parted it amongst them. After the end of these seuen dayes the captaine appointed twenty of his men wel armed, to bring vs vp into the countrey: and the first night we came to the side of a riuer called Alarach, where we lay on the grasse all that night: so the next day we went ouer the riuer in a frigate of nine oares on a side, the riuer being in that place aboue a quarter of a mile broad: and that day we went to a towne of thirty houses, called Totteon: there we lay foure dayes hauing nothing to feed on but bread and water: and then we went to a towne called Cassuri, and there we were deliuered by those twenty souldiers vnto the Alcaide, which examined vs what we were: and we tolde him. He gaue vs a good answere, and sent vs to the Iewes house, where we lay seuen dayes. In the meane while that we lay here, there were brought thither twenty Spaniards and twenty Frenchmen, which Spaniards were taken in a conflict on land, but the Frenchmen were by foule weather cast on land within the Straights about Cape de Gate, and so made captiues. Thus at the seuen dayes end we twelue Englishmen, the twelue French, and the twenty Spaniards were all conducted toward Marocco with nine hundred souldiers horsemen and fotmen, and in two dayes iourney we came to the riuer of Fez, where we lodged all night, being prouided of tents. The next day we went to a towne called Salle, and lay without the towne in tents. From thence we trauelled almost an hundred miles without finding any towne, but euery night we came to fresh water, which was partly running water and sometime raine water. So we came at last within three miles of the city of Marocco, where we pitched our tents: and there we mette with a carrier which did trauel in the countrey for the English marchants: and by him we sent word vnto them of our estate; and they returned the next day vnto vs a Moore, which brought vs victuals, being at that instant very feeble and hungry: and withall sent vs a letter with pen, inke, and paper, willing vs to write vnto them what ship it was that was cast away, and how many and what men there were aliue. For said they we would knowe with speed, for to morow is the kings court: and therefore we would know, for that you should come into the citie like captiues. But for all that we were carried in as captiues and with ropes about our neckes as well English as the French and Spaniards. And so we were carried before the king: and when we came before him he did commit vs all to ward, where wee lay 15 dayes in close prison: and in the end we were cleared by the English Marchants to their great charges; for our deliuerance cost them 700 ounces, euery ounce in that country contayning two shillings. And when we came out of prison we went to the Alfandica, where we continued eight weekes with the English marchants. At the end of which time being well apparelled by the bountie of our marchants we were conueyed downe by the space of eight dayes iourney to S. Cruz, where the English ships road: where we tooke shipping about the 20 of March, two in the Anne Francis of London, and fiue more of vs fiue dayes after in the Expedition of London, and two more in a Flemish flie-boat, and one in the Mary Edward also of London, other two of our number died in the countrey of the bloodie-fluxe: the one at our first imprisonment at Marocco, whose name was George Hancock, and the other at S. Cruz, whose name was Robert Swancon, whose death was hastened by eating of rootes and other vnnatural things to slake their raging hunger in our trauaile, and by our hard and cold lodging in the open fields without tents. Thus of fiftie persons through the rashnesse of an vnskilfull Master ten onely suruiued of vs, and after a thousand miseries returned home poore, sicke, and feeble into our countrey.

Richard Iohnson.
William Williams Carpenter.
Iohn Durham.
Abraham Rouse.
Iohn Matthewes.
Thomas Henmore.
Iohn Siluester.
Thomas Whiting.
William Church.
Iohn Fox.

* * * * *

The letters of the Queenes most excellent Maiestie sent by one Laurence Aldersey vnto the Emperour of Aethiopia, 1597.

Inuictissimo potentissimoque Abassenorum regi, magnoque vtriusque Aethiopiæ imperatori &c.

Elizabetha Dei gratia Angliæ, Franciæ, et Hiberniæ regina, fidei defensor &c. summo ac potentissimo Æthiopiæ imperatori salutem. Quod ab omnibus qui vbiuis terrarum ac gentium sunt regibus principibusque præstari par et æquum est, vt quanquàm maximo locorum interuallo dissiti, et moribus ac legibus discrepantes, communem tamen generis humani societatem tueri et conseruare, mutuáque vt occasio ferret, charitatis et beneuolentiæ officia velint exercere: in eo nos de vestra fide atque humanitate spem certissimam concipientes huic subito nostro Laurentio Alderseio in regnum vestrum proficiscenti, hasce literas nostras, quibus et nostra erga vos beneuolentia testata sit, et illum hinc profectum esse constet, potissimùm vobis indicandus dedimus. Qui cùm orbis terrarum perscrutandi cognoscendique studio permotus, multis antehàc regionibus peragratis, iam tandem in eas regiones, quæ vestræ ditionis sunt, longum, periculosumque iter instituat: cùm ipse existimauit, tum nos etiam sumus in eadem opinione, ad incolumitatem suam, atque etiam ad gratiam apud vos, plurimum illi prafuturum, si diplomate nostro munitus, beneuolenentiæ nostræ et profectionis hinc suæ testimonium ad vos deferret. Nam cum summus ille mundi conditor rectorque præpotens Deus, regibus principibusque qui suam vicem gerunt, orbem terrarum, suis cuique finibus pro rata portione designatis, regendum atque administrandum dederit; eoque munere ius quoddam inter eos fraternæ necessitudinis, æternumque foedus ab illis colendum sanxerit: non erit (vt arbitramur) ingratum vobis, cùm beneuolentiæ nostræ significationem, tàm immensa maris ac terrarum spatia transgressam, ab vltima Britannia ad vos in Aetheiopiam perferri intellexeritis. Nobisque rursùs erit incundum, cùm subditorum nostrorum prædicatione, ab ipsis Nili fontibus, et ab ijs regionibus quæ solis cursum definiunt, fama vestri nominis ad nos recurret. Erit igitur humanitatis vestræ huic subdito nostro eam largiri gratiam, vt in ditionem vestram sub præsidio ac tutela vestri nominis intrare, ibique saluus et incolumis manere possit: quod ipsum etiam ab aliis principibus, per quorum regiones illi transeundum erit magnoperè petimus, nobisque ipsis illud honoris causa tributum existimabimus: néque tamèn maiorem hac in re gratiam postulamus, quàm vicissim omnium principum subditis, omniumque gentium hominibus ad nos commeantibus liberrimè concedimus. Datum Londini quinto die Nouembris: anno regni nostri tricesimo nono: annoque Dom. 1597.

The same in English.

To the most inuincible and puissant king of the Abassens, the mightie Emperour of Aethiopia the higher and the lower.

Elizabeth by the grace of God Queene of England, France and Ireland, defender of the faith, &c. To the most high and mightie Emperour of Aethiopia greeting. Whereas it is a matter requisite and well beseeming all kings and princes of what lands or nations soeuer, be they neuer so much disseuered in place or differing in customes and lawes, to maintaine and preserue the common societie of mankinde, and, as occassion shall be offered, to performe mutuall duties of charitie and beneuolence: we for that cause concerning most undoubted hope of your princely fidelity and courtesie, haue giuen vnto this our subiect Laurence Aldersey intending to trauell into your dominions, these our letters to be deliuered without faile vnto your Highnesse, to the end they may be a testimony of our good will towards you and of our saide subiect his departure from England. Who, after his trauels in many forren countreys, being as yet enflamed with a desire more throughly to surueigh and contemplate the world, and now at length to vndertake a long and daungerous iourney into your territories and regions: both the sayd Laurence thought, and our selues also deemed, that it would very much auaile him, as well for his owne safetie as for the attayning of your fauour, if, being protected with our broad seale, hee might transport vnto your Highnesse a testimony of our louing affection and of his departure from hence. For sithence almightie God the highest creatour and gouernour of the world hath allotted vnto kings and princes his vicegerents [sic—KTH] ouer the face of the whole earth, their designed portions and limits to be ruled and administred by them; and by this his gift hath established among them a certaine law of brotherly kindnesse, and an eternall league by them to be obserued: it will not (we hope) seeme vnpleasant vnto your highnesse, when you shall haue intelligence of our louing letters sent so huge a distance ouer sea and land, euen from the farthest realme of England vnto you in Aethiopia. On the other side our selues shall take great solace and delight, when as by the relation of our owne subiects, the renowme of your name shall be brought vnto vs from the fountains of Nilus, and from those regions which are situate vnder the Southerne Tropike. May it please you therefore of your princely clemencie to vouchsafe so much fauour on this our subiect, that he may, vnder the safeguard and protection of your name, enter into your highnesse dominions, and there remaine safe and free from danger. Which fauour and courtesie wee doe likewise most earnestly request at the hands of other princes, through whose Seigniories our said subject is to passe; and we shall esteeme it as done vnto our selfe and for our honours sake.

Neither do we require any greater fauour in this behalfe, then we are vpon the like occasion most ready to graunt unto the subiects of all princes and the people of all Nations, trauelling into our dominions. Given at London the fift day of Nouember, in the thirtie and ninth yeere of our reigne: and in the yeare of our Lord 1597.

APPENDIX

THE OMISSIONS OF CALES VOYAGE.

[Footnote: The Editor takes this opportunity of making grateful acknowledgements to the Marquis of Stafford, for his permission to print this Tract from his curious Manuscript; and to the Reverend H. J. Todd, for furnishing him with the accurate transcript from which it is printed.]

The first and greatest occasion let slip in our Voyage was, that we did not possess ourselues of the fleete that was bound for the Indies, the lading whereof would not onelie haue paid all charges of the iorneie, but haue enabled vs a great while to wage warre with Spaine, with the meanes of Spaine. To which I aunswere, that if either I had ben followed the first morning of our comminge before the harbor when I bare with it, or if we had entred the same Sundaie in the afternoone when we were vnder saile, and within cannon shot of the enemies fleete, or after the men of warre were taken and burnt, the nexte daie if anie shipping had gone vp as I vrged by mine owne speech sent by Sir Anthonie Ashlie, who being secretaire at wars was to record euerie mans seruice or omission; if anie of these had ben don, then I saie had that fleete ben easilie possessed. For the first morning they had neither their men aboard, as it was since confessed by our prisoners, nor were provided of any counsel what to doe. In the afternoone the same daie we had found the men of warre and the Marchaunts fleet altogether in one bodie, and engaged them both at once, so as at the same time we had defeated the one, we had possessed the other. And the next daie presentlie vpon the fight and victorie against the Kings shipps, we had found them all so amazed and confounded as they would haue thought of nothing but of sauing themselues, and we had taken the ships, the riches in them, and the fleet of gallies, without striking a blow; as both our prisoners and captaines out of the gallies haue assured vs. But the first morninge when I boare with the harbor, almost all the fleet came to an ancker by the point Saint Sebastian a league wide of me, and gaue the enemie leasure to send men and all necessaries aboard. When I was gon in, I could neither get my companion to waigh his anckor, nor most of those that were waied to goe in with me. And the next daie I had much a do to make our ships fight at all. And when God had giuen vs victorie, my perswasions nor protestations could make them that were sea-commaunders go or send vp to possess the fleet of the Indies, whiles we assailed the towne, so as the enemie had almost 48. howers to burne his owne shipps.

The second imputation that maie be laid to vs, was, that we did abandon Cales, when we were possesst of it, whereas the holding of it would haue ben a naile not in the foote of this great monarch but in his side, and haue serued for a diversion of all the wars in these parts. To which I aunswere, that some of our sea-commaunders, and especiallie my colleague, did not onelie oppose themselues to that designe, (whose oppositions mine instructions made an absolute barre,) but when we came to see how the forces that should be left there might be victualed till succours came, the victualls were for the most part hidden and embeazled, and euery ship began at that instant to feare their wants, and to talke of goeing home; soe as I should neither haue had one ship to staie at Cales, nor victualls for the garrison for 2. moneths. And therefore I was forced to leaue Cales, and did not choose to abandon it.

The third obiection we haue to aunswere is, whie we did not lie for the carricks and Indian ships, seing we were on the coast the verie time that is thought fittest for their intercepting and vsual of their retourne. In which I must first cite the testimonie of all our commanders by land and sea, that when we had in our retourne from Cales doubled the Cape St. Vincent comonlie called the South Cape, I vrged our going to th' Islands of Ozores, founding my selfe vpon these reasons: first, that it was more certaine to attend them at the land-fall where theie must needs touch, then to seeke them in the wide sea; and next, that the aduises sent out of Spaine and Portingall since our being of myght meete them at the Islands, and make them divert from coming thither. Besides, the Spaniards after theie saw vs engaged at Cales would neuer suspect or dreame of our goeing to the Islands. And when this counsell was reiected, and we come in the sight of Lisbon, I there againe pressed the lieing for them with a selected fleet, and offered vpon that condition to send home the land-forces, and all such ships as want of victualls, leaks sickness, or anie thing els had made vnfit to staie out at sea. But first the L. Admirall and Sr. Wa[l]ter Rawligh did directlie by attestation vnder their hands contradict the first proposition that I made, that some ships should attend that seruice. And when we came to the hypothesis, which were fitt and their captaines content to staie out in all the fleet, except the Low Countrie Squadron, there could be found but two, my L. Thom. Howard and my selfe; so as by the whole counsell at wars, it was resolued that as well my offer and opinion, as euerie mans els amongst vs, should be kept vnder his hand, for our particuler discharges, and I be barred of staieing, except my L. Admirall would assent to leaue some 8. or 10. of the Marchaunts ships besides 2. of the Queenes: which he refused to doe: and soe our dessigne brake of.

The last omission maie seeme to be in this, that since all our seruice consisted in taking or distroyinge the Spanish shipping and sea prouisions, that we did not looke into all his chiefe ports, and do him in that kind as much hurt as we might haue done. To which I aunswere, that first my end in going to Cales was not onlie because it was a principall port and the likeliest to be held by vs, by cause of the seat and naturall strength of it; but also for that it was the farthest good porte south-ward; so as beginning with it we might, if some greater seruice did not diuert vs, goe to all the good ports betwixt that and the northmost ports of Biskaie: which was a better waie then to haue begonne or giuen the enemie an alarum in the middest of his Countrie, or the neerest ports to vs; for so our attempts would haue ben more difficile, and our retreats at last from those farthest ports less safe; considering the wants, infections, and other inconveniences that for the most parte doe accompanie the retraicts of our fleet and armies in long iourneies. But after we had ended at Cales, it was by all our seamen thought a capitall offence to name the goeing ouer the Barre at St. Lucars. Betwixt St Lucars and Lisbone there is no good porte. From Lisbone I was barred by name, if it had bene free for vs to haue gone. Yet our seamen are made of the same stuffe, Sr. Francis D: and his companie was, when theie lost the occasion of his taking Lisbone, for feare of passing by the castle of St. Iulian's. From Lisbone to the Groine there is no port to hold the Kings or anie other great shipping. To the Groin with cart-ropes I drew them: for both I vowed and protested against their refusall, and parted companie with them when they offered to hold another course. But when we came to the mouth of the harbor, and sent in some of our small vessells, we saw there was nothing there, nor yet at Furroll; for into that port also we made our discouveries to looke.

After which discouverie we held our last counsell. And then I vrged our goeing to St. Audica, the passage St. Sebastian, and all other good ports all along the coast. But mine associat did altogether refuse to goe farther alonge the coaste, complaininge of wants, and obiecting our being embayed, and I know not what. In which opinion Sir Walter Rawlighe strengthened him; and theie were both desirous to take vpon them the honnor of breaking that dessigne. And of landing at the Groyne, or attempting the towne, theie would not heare by anie meanes. And presentlie euery man cried to set saile homewards. Since which time theie haue made such haste, as I, tarieing behind to bring along with me the St. Andrew taken at Cales and the flie boate that carries our artillarie haue lost them all, sauing Monsieur Oauerworme and his squadron, and some few small shipps.

[These "Omissions" were not included in the early editions, but appeared in Woodfall's edition of 1812].

INDICES.

Where the same Document a given in Latin and English, the reference is to the English Version.

Milton Keynes UK
Ingram Content Group UK Ltd.
UKHW030622061024
449204UK00004B/402